Economy, Polity, and Society
British Intellectual History 1750–1950

GW00496516

Economy, Polity, and Society and its companion volume *History, Religion, and Culture* aim to bring together new essays by many of the leading intellectual historians of the period while at the same time serving as a tribute to the work of Donald Winch and John Burrow. The essays in *Economy, Polity, and Society* begin by addressing aspects of the eighteenth-century attempt, particularly in the work of Adam Smith, to come to grips with the nature of 'commercial society' and its distinctive notions of the self, of political liberty, and of economic progress; they then explore the adaptations of and responses to the Enlightenment legacy in the work of such early nineteenth-century figures as Jeremy Bentham, Tom Paine, Maria Edgeworth, and Richard Whately; and finally, in discussions which range up to the middle of the twentieth century, they explore particularly telling examples of the conflict between economic thinking and moral values.

STEFAN COLLINI is Reader in Intellectual History and English Literature in the University of Cambridge. He was formerly Reader in Intellectual History at the University of Sussex, and is the author of several publications in intellectual history, including *That Noble Science of Politics* (with Donald Winch and John Burrow) (1983), *Matthew Arnold* (1994), and *English Pasts* (1999).

RICHARD WHATMORE is Lecturer in Intellectual History in the School of English and American Studies, University of Sussex. A former Choate Fellow at Harvard University, he is the author of *Republicanism and the French Revolution: An Intellectual History of Jean Baptiste Say's Political Economy* (2000).

BRIAN YOUNG is Lecturer in Intellectual History in the School of English and American Studies, University of Sussex. He was British Academy Postdoctoral Fellow at Jesus College, Oxford, and is the author of *Religion and Enlightenment in Eighteenth-Century England* (1998).

Economy, Polity, and Society

British Intellectual History 1750–1950

edited by

Stefan Collini

Richard Whatmore

Brian Young

CAMBRIDGE
UNIVERSITY PRESS

PUBLISHED BY THE PRESS SYNDICATE OF THE UNIVERSITY OF CAMBRIDGE
The Pitt Building, Trumpington Street, Cambridge CB2 IRP, United Kingdom

CAMBRIDGE UNIVERSITY PRESS
The Edinburgh Building, Cambridge CB2 2RU, UK http://www.cup.cam.ac.uk
40 West 20th Street, New York, NY 10011–4211, USA http://www.cup.org
10 Stamford Road, Oakleigh, Melbourne 3166, Australia
Ruiz de Alarcón 13, 28014 Madrid, Spain

First published 2000

Printed in the United Kingdom at the University Press, Cambridge

Typeface Plantin 10/12 pt   *System* QuarkXPress™   [SE]

A catalogue record for this book is available from the British Library

Library of Congress Cataloguing in Publication data

Economy, Polity, and Society: British Intellectual History 1750–1950 /
edited by Stefan Collini, Richard Whatmore, Brian Young.
    p. cm.
Includes index.
ISBN 0 521 63018 5 (hbk.) – ISBN 0 521 63978 6 (pbk.)
    1. Great Britain – Intellectual life – 18th century.   2. Great Britain –
Intellectual life – 19th century.   3. Great Britain – Intellectual life – 20th
century.   4. Great Britain – Politics and government.   5. Great Britain –
Economic conditions.   1. Collini, Stefan, 1947–   11. Whatmore, Richard.
III. Young, Brian.
DA533.E37 2000
941 21–dc21   99-042116

ISBN 0 521 63018 5 hardback
ISBN 0 521 63978 6 paperback

Contents

Preface   *page* vii

General introduction   I
STEFAN COLLINI

Presentation of *Economy, Polity, and Society*   22

Part I

1   Sociability and self-love in the theatre of moral sentiments:
    Mandeville to Adam Smith   31
    E. J. HUNDERT

2   'That noble disquiet': meanings of liberty in the discourse
    of the North   48
    DARIO CASTIGLIONE

3   Language, sociability, and history: some reflections on the
    foundations of Adam Smith's science of man   70
    NICHOLAS PHILLIPSON

4   Adam Smith and tradition: the *Wealth of Nations* before
    Malthus   85
    RICHARD F. TEICHGRAEBER III

Part II

5   Economy and polity in Bentham's science of legislation   107
    DAVID LIEBERMAN

6   'A gigantic manliness': Paine's republicanism in the 1790s   135
    RICHARD WHATMORE

7   Irish culture and Scottish enlightenment: Maria
    Edgeworth's histories of the future   158
    MARILYN BUTLER

8 Improving Ireland: Richard Whately, theology, and political
   economy   181
   NORMAN VANCE

Part III

9 Political and domestic economy in Victorian social thought:
   Ruskin and Xenophon   205
   JANE GARNETT

10 State and market in British university history   224
   SHELDON ROTHBLATT

11 Mr Gradgrind and Jerusalem   243
   DONALD WINCH

   List of contributors   267
   Acknowledgements   269
   Index   270

Preface

Although this book has been planned and written to be read and used in its own right, *Economy, Polity, and Society* and its companion volume, *History, Religion, and Culture*, form a two-book set whose scope is signalled by their common sub-title, *British Intellectual History 1750–1950*. The primary aim of the publication of these two volumes is to bring together the work of many of the leading scholars in what has become a flourishing field in the last couple of decades. But their appearance is also intended to be a way of paying tribute to the impact on that field of the work of two individuals in particular, John Burrow and Donald Winch. Winch and Burrow were for many years the animating spirits of a small group who, at the time, all taught at the University of Sussex, a group which has, in consequence, sometimes been referred to as 'the Sussex School' (a label whose appropriateness is discussed in the 'General Introduction'). In the year 2000 both men reach the retiring-age of sixty-five, and although they will both, we may hope, long continue to be active and prominent in the practice of intellectual history, a collection of their friends and admirers did not want to let this joint landmark pass unrecognised. A pleasing consequence of this originating purpose is that all the contributors to these two volumes have some connection – personal, intellectual, or institutional – with Intellectual History at Sussex and/or with Burrow and Winch as individuals, whether as students, colleagues, or friends. A colloquium was held at Sussex in September 1998 at which draft versions of all the essays were presented and discussed, and at which there was considerable collective brooding on how best to revise and integrate the essays for publication. Throughout, Donald Winch and John Burrow have been kind enough to indulge their friends in their folly, affecting a certain superficial embarrassment (presumably as a mask for their actual deep embarrassment), but nonetheless agreeing both to be participants in the colloquium and contributors to these volumes. It is characteristic of them that they should prefer to contribute to a collaborative enterprise in this way, adding their voices to a set of continuing conversations rather than simply receiving tributes from others, and in this spirit no special indulgence has been granted them as contributors by the implacable and stony-faced (but perhaps not altogether stony-hearted) editors.

This originating purpose also dictates the arrangement of the introductory material. The 'General introduction', which discusses the field of intellectual history as a whole, and Burrow's and Winch's contributions to it in particular, is reproduced in both volumes; it is then followed by a 'Presentation' specific to each particular volume, which briefly attempts to introduce the subject-matter covered by the essays and to draw out some of their relations and common themes. Readers impatient to engage with the substantive historical material should, therefore, skip the 'General Introduction' and proceed directly to the 'Presentation of *Economy, Polity, and Society*'.

General introduction

I

It may be that there is no longer any need to justify the term 'intellectual history' or the practice for which it stands. If this is so – experience can, alas, still occasionally cause one to wonder – then it is a very recent development indeed, at least in Britain. Only two or three decades ago, the label routinely encountered more than its share of misunderstanding, some of it rather wilful, especially perhaps on the part of some political and social historians. There was, to begin with, the allegation that intellectual history was largely the history of things that never really *mattered*. The long dominance of the historical profession by political historians tended to breed a kind of philistinism, an unspoken belief that power and its exercise was what 'mattered' (a term which invited but rarely received any close scrutiny). The legacy of this prejudice is still discernible in the tendency in some quarters to require ideas to have 'influenced' the political elite before they can be deemed worthy of historical attention, as though there were some reason why the history of art or of science, of philosophy or of literature, were somehow of less interest and significance than the histories of policies and parliaments. In the course of the 1960s and 1970s, the mirror-image of this philistinism became even more common, particularly in the form of the claim that ideas of any degree of systematic expression or formal sophistication did not merit detailed historical scrutiny because they were, by definition, only held by a small educated minority. The fact is, of course, that much which legitimately interests us in history was the work of minorities (not always of the same type, be it noted), and it remains true, to repeat an adaptation of a famous line of E. P. Thompson's that I have used elsewhere, that it is not only the poor and inarticulate who may stand in need of being rescued from the enormous condescension of posterity.

A further, related misconception has been the charge, which still has some currency, that intellectual history is inherently 'idealist', where that term is used pejoratively to signify the belief (or, more often, assumption) that ideas develop by a logic of their own, without reference to other human activities or to what is loosely called their 'social context'. There was possibly some truth to this as a criticism of some of the work written a couple of generations ago, particularly that originating in the history of philosophy, but it is simply false as a description of what intellectual history must be like. The intellectual historian is someone who happens to find the reflective and expressive life of the past to be of interest: it is the vulgarest kind of reductivism or ideology-spotting to presume that this betrays an unspoken belief in the superiority of one form of human activity, still less an underlying commitment to a monocausal view of history.

In some quarters, the very term 'intellectual history' itself generated unease, with the result that 'the history of ideas' has sometimes been preferred as an alternative label. However, the danger here is that the emphasis on the 'history of *ideas*' may precisely suggest that we are dealing with autonomous abstractions which, in their self-propelled journeyings through time, happened only contingently and temporarily to find anchorage in particular human minds, a suggestion encouraged by the long German tradition of *Geistesgeschichte* or *Ideengeschichte* which, revealing its Hegelian ancestry, looked to the history of philosophy to provide the pattern of human history as a whole. By contrast, the term 'intellectual history' signals more clearly that the focus is on an aspect of human activity and is in this respect no different from 'economic history', 'political history', and so forth.

One final, more local, form of resistance took the form of the suggestion – only partly facetious, one fears – that there is no need for intellectual history in the case of Britain since it, at least in the modern period, has been a society with no worthwhile or significant ideas, or, in another version, one where ideas are of no consequence, or, marginally less crass, one where the preferred idiom is that of the practical or the implicit (as though these, too, were not susceptible of historical analysis). In each of these claims, not only is the premise deeply disputable but the logic is, anyway, plainly faulty, as though one were to conclude that there could be no economic history of sub-Saharan Africa or no constitutional history of post-war Italy.

Given this still-recent history of prejudice and misunderstanding, one of the striking features of the essays in these volumes is their lack of defensiveness: they are written as contributions to an area of scholarship which is already rich and complex, and their tone does not suggest any felt need to justify the larger enterprise. And it is indeed the case that the last couple of decades have seen an impressive efflorescence of work in intellectual history understood in the broad terms sketched here. Where previously the 'history of ideas' was often, especially in the modern period, a pursuit cultivated by philosophers, political theorists, literary critics, social scientists, and others pursuing the 'pre-history' of their own disciplines, recent work in 'intellectual history' is much more likely to be done by those with a trained and cultivated interest in a particular period of the past, seeking to apply the same standards of historical evidence and judgement to the intellectual life of that period as their colleagues have traditionally displayed towards its political, social, and economic life. Instead of works which cut a 'vertical' (and often teleological) slice through the past with titles like 'The History of Sociology from Montesquieu to Weber', 'The Growth of Economic Theory from Smith to Friedman', 'The Making of Modern Historiography from Gibbon to Braudel', and so on, the tendency of recent work has been towards excavating a more 'horizontal' site, exploring the idioms and preoccupations of a past period as they manifest themselves in thought and discussion about various issues that cannot readily be assigned to current academic pigeon-holes. In other words, rather than constructing a 'history of ideas', where the emphasis is on the logical structure of certain arguments that are seen as only contingently and almost irrelevantly located in the past, the informing aspiration has been to write an 'intellectual history', which tries to recover the thought of the past in its complexity and, in a sense which is neither self-contradictory nor trivial, as far as possible in its own terms.

However, although I have been suggesting that intellectual history is now becoming an established and, on the whole, accepted sub-discipline even in Britain, it would be a disagreeable consequence of the hyper-professionalism of modern academic life were this to result in the formation of a new disciplinary trade-union, with all the characteristics of parochialism and exclusiveness, together with the attendant demarcation disputes, that threaten to characterise such bodies in their militant phase. It is surely a sign of cultural health rather than of corporate weakness that several of the contributors to these volumes would not wish to be constantly or exclusively classified as 'intellectual historians', and indeed that their institutional affiliations span several academic departments, including English, History, Politics, Law, and Religious Studies.

It will, I trust, be obvious that the brief characterisation of intellectual history offered in the preceding paragraphs is open to dispute and has in fact been vigorously disputed in recent years. The work of Michel Foucault and his followers has encouraged a rather different form of engagement with the 'discourses' dominant in past societies – one which often displaces purposive historical agents from the scene altogether – and more recently still, styles of work deriving from literary theory and cultural studies have attempted to shift attention yet further away from the meaning-laden utterances of those who can be identified as members of some kind of 'elite'. Meanwhile, detailed historical work on a broad range of aspects of the intellectual life of the past continues to be carried on in a variety of less noisy or self-advertising modes. The result of these developments has been an inevitable and largely healthy pluralism of approaches: now that the legitimacy of the activity itself no longer needs to be argued for, intellectual historians can be allowed the same luxuries of disagreement and rivalry as have long been enjoyed by the more established branches of the historian's trade. And precisely because this plurality of approaches *is* now coming into being, it may be appropriate to switch the focus of attention from these general considerations to examine at slightly greater length the specific contributions to this field made by John Burrow and Donald Winch.

II

Insofar as the activity of intellectual history *has* received institutional embodiment and cultural recognition as an academic discipline or sub-discipline in Britain in the last generation or so, it has been particularly identified with the University of Sussex. Sussex was the first British university to offer a degree programme in the subject and to establish posts explicitly defined as being in the field of 'Intellectual History'. In the course of the 1970s and 1980s, some observers, claiming to find certain shared characteristics in the work published by some of those responsible for this programme, began to refer to 'the Sussex School'. This label can, at best, only ever have served as a piece of academic shorthand or argot, while at worst it was a culpable form of exaggeration or reification. No such 'school' exists or ever existed if that term be taken to imply common adherence to an explicit and exclusive methodological programme. It would be more accurate to say that the comparatively flexible and inter-disciplinary structure of Sussex in those decades provided a congenial berth for a group of like-minded scholars whose interests typically tended to fall across or between the domains of the better-established academic disciplines. (I shall return to a consideration of the nature of this 'like-mindedness' in section III below.) In any event, what most certainly *is* beyond dispute is the fact that Donald Winch and John Burrow were for many years the leading figures in this group at Sussex.

Since this is not the place to attempt to recap the entire career of either Burrow or Winch, I shall merely touch on some of the more significant stages in their respective formations as intellectual historians. It is, of course, sobering for the historian above all to be brought to realise just how hard it is to reconstitute, let alone account for, the intellectual trajectories even of one's close friends, a difficulty compounded as much as eased by the risks of relying overmuch on one's own rather randomly accumulated personal archive. And anyway, perhaps writings that are in the public domain are merely the by-product or end-result of some primal process of self-fashioning – indirect records of some now unde-tectable early shifts in the tectonic plates of temperament and disposition. Perhaps the ministrations of any number of careers advisers were otiose from the moment in which the young John Burrow stumbled on Figgis's *Gerson to Grotius* in his school library and was enthralled rather than baffled; perhaps all that has followed was already prefigured in the scene in which the teenage Burrow, crouched on the floor next to the family wireless, took notes, no doubt of a daunting illegibility even then, from a series of talks on 'Freedom and its Betrayal' by a speaker he had up till that point never heard of called Isaiah Berlin. And why it was that, at almost exactly the same time, the young Donald Winch was to be found rather self-consciously reading Plato's *Republic* while on holiday by the shores of the Baltic, or why it was that, though a student of economics, he chose to attend, for two years running, Michael Oakeshott's lectures on the history of political thought – these may be matters which defy further explanation, though in each case the temptations of teleology are strong (and have here not been altogether resisted).

Academically, both men were shaped in the 1950s. For John Burrow, an undergraduate at Christ's College from 1954 to 1957, the initial schol-arly context was provided by the Cambridge History Tripos, and more especially its options in the history of political thought where he was par-ticularly stimulated by the teaching of Duncan Forbes. At an early stage, Burrow had found the dominant genres of political and economic history less than wholly congenial, and after graduating he embarked, under the benign but necessarily somewhat distant supervision of Kitson Clark, on an ambitious Ph.D. on Victorian theories of social evolution, which was submitted in 1961. More broadly, his mentor at this time in the ways of the world, no less than in the duties and opportunities of being a historian, was J. H. Plumb, an academic talent-spotter and trainer with an unmatchably successful record. A research fellowship at Christ's was followed by a college lectureship at Downing, but by the time the revised version of his thesis appeared as a book in 1966, Burrow had moved to a lectureship at the recently founded University of East Anglia.

Evolution and Society: A Study in Victorian Social Theory was an extraor-dinarily assured debut. The book decisively challenged the assumption that the source of mid-Victorian ideas of social evolution was to be found in the application of Darwin's biological theories, and instead traced the attempts of figures such as Spencer, Maine, and Tylor to address questions of cultural variety within the framework of a (sometimes profoundly troubled) belief in progress. As a result, the book immediately established itself as a pioneering contribution to the history of anthropology as well as a provocative exploration of a central aspect of Victorian culture. That the argument of *Evolution and Society* certainly did not reflect any lack of appreciation on Burrow's part of the intellectual change that Darwin *had* wrought was demonstrated by his introduction to the Penguin *Origin of Species* in 1968, while his familiarity with European, and especially German, sources in the Romantic period was evident in his substantial introduction to his new translation of Wilhelm von Humboldt's *The Limits of State Action*, published in 1969.

In Donald Winch's intellectual formation, the LSE and the discipline of Economics occupied something of the same place that Cambridge and History did for John Burrow. An undergraduate between 1953 and 1956, Winch opted to specialise in international economics under the tutelage of James Meade, but he was already revealing himself as being at least as interested in Popper's teaching on scientific method or, as mentioned earlier, Oakeshott's on the history of political thought. Moving to Princeton for graduate study, he fell under the influence of Jacob Viner, of whom he later wrote a perceptive and affectionate memoir, and began to specialise in the history of economic thought. On returning to Britain after a year's teaching at Berkeley, a post at Edinburgh was followed in 1963 by a lectureship at Sussex, which soon led to rapid promotion, and he became Reader and then, in 1969, Professor of the History of Economics.

His first book, *Classical Political Economy and Colonies*, published in 1965, already displayed what were to become trademark qualities: the substance combined a quiet mastery of the technicalities of the history of economic theory with a sure grasp of the historical embeddedness of such ideas, while the manner exhibited a seemingly unforced alliance between clarity and argumentative vigour. The book compelled the historians of government policy in the period to learn their economic letters, while at the same time infiltrating some awkward complexities into the standard chronicles of 'the rise of political economy'. A certain distance from his initial disciplinary formation was already manifest in his declared intention to 'steer clear of the history of economic analysis for its own sake in order to remain close to the issues as seen by the participants' (*Classical Political Economy and Colonies*, p. 3). In other ways, too, Winch was already contesting that canonical account of early political economy which confined itself to the Holy Trinity of Smith the Father, Ricardo the Son, and Mill the Holy Ghost, one fruit of his historical attentiveness to less fashionable figures being the substantial editorial labour of his edition of James Mill's *Selected Economic Writings* which was published in 1966.

Both men, therefore, began by initially pursuing a somewhat under-favoured branch of a powerful discipline (respectively History and Economics) and then progressively reacting against the coerciveness and complacency of representatives of mainstream traditions of those disciplines. Both had encountered the constraints of orthodox 'discipline' history as written by present practitioners of a given discipline, especially the 'pre-history of anthropology' in Burrow's case and the 'pre-history of economics' in Winch's. By the late 1960s, partly as a result of this experience, their respective scholarly interests were, quite independently of each other, moving closer together under the broad rubric of the history of social thought or of the social sciences. From his arrival at Sussex, Donald Winch had been closely involved in teaching a 'contextual' course, compulsory for all final-year students in the School of Social Sciences, called 'Concepts, methods, and values in the social sciences' (always known, not always affectionately, as CMV). In the mid-1960s he was instrumental in adding an option in 'The historical development of the social sciences' to the existing course which had previously been confined to philosophical and methodological issues. In those expansionary days, it was possible to think of making appointments to match such academic initiatives, and it was Winch, in his role as (a notably young) Dean of the School of Social Sciences, who first invited John Burrow, by then Reader in History at East Anglia, to Sussex, initially to lecture for the new course, and eventually to take up a post teaching it. (The first exchange of letters – 'Dear Mr Burrow'/'Dear Mr Winch' – has, in retrospect, something of an *84 Charing Cross Road* feel about it.) As a result, in 1969 Burrow was appointed to a post principally responsible for teaching the historical part of CMV; a few years later he transferred to the School of English and American Studies.

The University of Sussex had been founded in 1961 with the deliberate aim of 're-drawing the map of learning', and institutional expression had been given to this ideal by not establishing conventional academic departments, but instead grouping scholars with related interests into schools of study, usually with an area basis such as the School of European Studies or the School of English and American Studies. Within and across these schools, 'majors' were taught in particular subjects, while students had also to spend approximately half their time on school 'contextual' courses (such as CMV). 'Subject groups' were responsible for these majors and these were the nearest Sussex came in those days to having orthodox departments. Both the ethos and the structure of Sussex in the late 1960s and early 1970s were favourable to innovation, and it was this supportive setting that permitted the establishment initially of an MA and then, in 1969, of a undergraduate 'major' in Intellectual History, the first such degree programme to be set up at a British university. These early initiatives were undertaken by members of staff who had initially been appointed to more traditionally defined posts, such as Peter Burke in History and Michael Moran in Philosophy; crucial support was provided by James Shiel from Classical Studies and the then recently retired Helmut Pappé. A new lectureship in Intellectual History, the first to be formally designated as such, was established in 1972 and initially held by Larry Siedentop, and then, from 1974, by Stefan Collini (to whom I shall, for the sake of narrative propriety, sometimes have to refer, as here, in the third person).

The years during which these institutional arrangements were being established and consolidated – roughly the late 1960s to the mid-1970s – also saw shifts, or perhaps just modulations, in the intellectual interests of both Donald Winch and John Burrow. Winch's interest in the interaction between economic expertise and political exigency was for some time principally focused on the twentieth century, and his *Economics and Policy: A Historical Study* (1969) broke what was then new ground in its exploration of the ways in which Keynesian arguments came to penetrate the policy-making establishments of both Britain and the United States. In terms of both chronology and of sources, the book's range was impressive, moving from Alfred Marshall's attempts to accommodate the challenge of 'the social problem' within the absorbent framework of his *Principles of Economics* in the 1890s to the measures undertaken by the Kennedy–Johnson administrations of the 1960s. The interest in the role of economic advisers was sustained, and supported by a daunting display of expertise in the official and archival sources, in a study of the Economic Advisory Council of the 1930s, which was jointly written with Susan Howson and published in 1976. But, as already indicated, his earliest work had been on the foundations of political economy in the late eighteenth and early nineteenth centuries, an area of research which he never entirely deserted, as evidenced by his substantial introduction to the Penguin edition of books IV and V of Mill's *Principles of Political Economy* in 1970 and his Everyman edition of Ricardo's *Principles of Political Economy and Taxation* in 1973. Moreover, by the mid-1970s, Winch had begun to read widely in recent work by early-modern intellectual historians on the roles played by the languages of 'civic humanism' and 'natural jurisprudence' in the development of political thought during that period, and he brought the fruits of this reading to bear on the interpretation of the most canonical of all figures in the history of economic thought in his *Adam Smith's Politics: An Essay in Historiographic Revision*, which was published in 1978. This characteristically combative book sought to rescue Smith from the retrospective teleologies of the historians of economics, and to restore him to his eighteenth-century context, principally but by no means exclusively his Scottish context. This relatively short, tightly argued book was to have considerable impact both within and beyond the confines of the history of political economy, not least through its firm insistence on the distinction between the goal of recovering the historicity of a past writer and that of using the name of that writer to legitimate a variety of political or academic enterprises in the present.

During these same years, the focus of John Burrow's scholarly work also underwent some change, essentially away from its initial concentration on the history of social and political thought towards a broader engagement with Victorian culture and historiography. His essay for J. H. Plumb's *Festschrift*, published in 1974, '"The Village Community" and the Uses of History in Late-Nineteenth-Century England', signalled an early step in this direction by focusing on the historical writings of figures such as Maine, Freeman, and Maitland. At the same time, partly through the structure of teaching at Sussex (especially after his move into the School of English and American Studies), Burrow was drawn more deeply into the relations between history and literature in nineteenth-century Britain; some incidental fruits of this experience may be found in his contributions to *The Victorians*, edited by Laurence Lerner, a volume in the 'Context of English Literature' series which appeared in 1978. This phase of Burrow's work culminated triumphantly in *A Liberal Descent: Victorian Historians and the English Past*, which was published in 1981 and was joint winner of the Wolfson Prize for History for that year. The book's principal sections discuss the vast, sprawling narrative histories of Macaulay, Stubbs, Freeman, and Froude and the intellectual and historiographical traditions within which they worked, but this flat inventory signally fails to do justice to the book's widely ramifying explorations of Victorian cultural sensibility. There is now abundant evidence of how its account of the nineteenth-century Whig tradition of historical writing has left its mark on scholarship across a wide range of topics, some far removed from the confines of the history of historiography. Yet for many readers, the book's distinctiveness and charm lie in the ways in which the writing allows a cultivated sensibility to direct, inform, and give appropriately modulated expression to its historical analysis, simultaneously catching and doing justice to the idiosyncrasy of his chosen historians while placing them within intellectual and literary traditions which are characterised with great richness and subtlety.

In the early 1980s, Collini, Winch, and Burrow collaborated in writing *That Noble Science of Politics: A Study in Nineteenth-Century Intellectual*

History, whose publication in 1983 marked, both practically and symboli-
cally, the high point of their collaborative endeavour. Perhaps the least
awkward way to provide some characterisation of the book here is to
quote from the preface which was specially written (in 1996) for the
Japanese translation.

> In the nature of things, a book that sets out to challenge or repudiate accepted dis-
> ciplinary boundaries is likely to run the risk of baffling some of its readers. As one
> reviewer sympathetically put it: 'This is going to be a perplexing book for many.
> Librarians will wonder how to classify it. Specialists in politics and economics will
> be embarrassed at its demonstration of how what they thought sewn up can be
> unstitched. Tutors will wonder what passages their pupils can be trusted not to
> misunderstand.' As the Prologue to the book was intended to make clear, some of
> the intellectual energy that fuelled its writing came from our shared negative reac-
> tion to certain prevailing disciplinary dispensations. Most obviously, we repudi-
> ated those forms of 'the history of the social sciences' which consisted in finding
> 'precursors' and 'founding fathers' for contemporary social scientific specialisms
> from among past writers the specificity and integrity of whose concerns thereby
> came in for some very rough treatment indeed . . . We also repudiated the coer-
> civeness of the priorities encouraged by 'the history of political theory', an enter-
> prise which has enjoyed such a strong institutional position in the
> Anglo-American scholarly world that political, economic, and social historians all
> too easily take it to *be* intellectual history. And, more obviously, we took our dis-
> tance from those kinds of approaches which are united in little else than in assum-
> ing that intellectual activity is best understood as a reflection or by-product of
> some allegedly more fundamental social or economic process . . . Without wishing
> to set up a new meta-discipline or to propose a panacea for wider cultural ail-
> ments, we continue to regard intellectual history of the kind exhibited in this book
> as a flexible and responsible approach to the intellectual life of the past. In certain
> respects, intellectual history pursued in this manner may itself be regarded as
> having a kind of 'anti-specialist' identity, both because it cannot be equated with
> the history of one subject-matter or discipline and because it cannot be reduced to
> one methodology or vocabulary.

Although there has been no further attempt at direct collaboration, it is
clear from the prefaces and acknowledgements in their subsequent works
(to cite only evidence that is in the public domain) that the ties of friendship and intellectual exchange between the three authors remain close.
However, the partly parallel and partly divergent trajectories followed by
Winch and Burrow since that period must also be noted here.

John Burrow's stylish 'Past Masters' volume on Gibbon was published
in 1985, and in the same year he gave the Carlyle Lectures at Oxford,
which were then published in 1988 under the title *Whigs and Liberals:
Continuity and Change in English Political Thought*. This slim volume testified, as its preface acknowledged, to Burrow's 'long-standing interest in
the impact of historicist ways of thinking on European, and above all

British, culture in the post-Romantic period' (*Whigs and Liberals*, p. viii).
It set some of the familiar ideas of nineteenth-century liberalism in a new
perspective by tracing continuities and discontinuities with that broadly
Whig tradition of political thinking whose richness and longevity have
only become fully apparent with the scholarship of the last generation,
and the book gracefully sketched some of the ways in which conceptions
of variety or diversity were seen as essential to social and individual
energy and vitality. The attempt to establish some perspectival balance in
understanding the ceaseless gavotte of continuity and change is, of
course, the stock-in-trade of all historians, but it is in a deeper sense at the
heart of Burrow's scholarly sensibility and informs his recurring preoccupation with the mutations of intellectual traditions. As he put it in his
speech accepting an honorary degree at the University of Bologna in
1988: 'Our relations to the past, or to what we conceive it to be, are, it
seems to me, full of ambiguity and fascination; at once indispensable and
civilising and also, as perhaps all worthwhile relations are, perilous. We
may derive from them both confidence and complacency, nourishment of
identity and the bigotry of exclusiveness.'

Winch's contributions to *That Noble Science* signalled what were to be
his principal preoccupations during the ensuing decade: on the one hand,
the question of the fate of Smith's ambitious programme in the hands of
various putative successors, and, on the other, what was to prove a long
engagement with the work and reputation of Robert Malthus. The former
issued in a stream of essays in the 1980s and early 1990s – essays often
couched in revisionist terms in an attempt to counter the later appropriation of some eighteenth- or nineteenth-century figure. His carefully
crafted 'Past Masters' volume on Malthus in 1987 was the chief expression of the latter concern, but Winch was also closely involved in enabling
the Royal Economic Society edition of *An Essay on the Principle of
Population* finally to see the light of day, and this was later followed by his
own edition in the Cambridge Texts in the History of Political Thought
series in 1992. The invitation to deliver the Carlyle Lectures at Oxford for
1995 provided the opportunity to present the outlines of the synthesis of
many years of work in these related areas, the full version of which was to
be published in 1996 as *Riches and Poverty: An Intellectual History of
Political Economy in Britain, 1750–1834*.

Even in what has thus far been an exceptionally productive writing life,
Riches and Poverty stands out as a remarkable achievement. The book provides a learned, thickly textured account of the ways in which arguments
over economic matters (in the broadest sense of the term) in this crucial
period were bound up with and expressive of wider political and social
identities. Its command of the purely *theoretical* complexities of classical

political economy is evident yet never foregrounded: instead, the main strands of the period's attempts to grapple analytically with a new range of issues about wealth and poverty are threaded into a thickly peopled narrative tapestry, and the book is studded with intellectual vignettes that are as impressive for their concision as for their scholarship, whether it be in discussing the differences between Smith and Ferguson on the appropriateness of taking a 'philosophic' view of the rebellion of the American colonies, or in discriminating shades of unfairness in the treatment of Malthus by the leading 'Lake poets'. The book may only now be starting to make its presence felt, but it will in time surely do what all outstanding works of historical scholarship do, namely, to make it harder, or at the very least less excusable, to write the kind of shoddy, simplistic accounts of 'classical political economy' or 'the 1790s' that are regularly to be found in treatments of this period written by economists and literary scholars as well as by some historians.

As their new essays in these two volumes suggest, the stream of outstanding publications by these two authors shows no signs of drying up: at the time of writing, John Burrow is just on the point of completing a large study of European intellectual history between 1848 and 1914, while Donald Winch is organising a major British Academy project on the peculiarities of British economic experience since the Industrial Revolution. However, the last decade or so has seen some significant changes in the institutional bases from which the activities chronicled here have been carried on, changes which may make 'the Sussex School' less appropriate than ever as a collective label. In 1986 Stefan Collini left Sussex to take up a post in the Faculty of English in Cambridge, a move reflecting and encouraging a shift in his interests away from the early focus on the history of social and political thought to a concern with literary and cultural criticism, as well as a move from the nineteenth to the twentieth century. In 1995 John Burrow became the first holder of the newly established Chair of European Thought at Oxford, resuming an engagement with nineteenth-century European thinkers and writers that had been largely in the background of his intellectual activities since the late 1960s, though it had never been wholly absent. The personnel of the group at Sussex changed in other ways, too. Following Collini's departure, Anna Bryson held a lectureship there from 1986 to 1992 and Richard Whatmore and Brian Young have been lecturers in Intellectual History since 1993. Martin van Gelderen succeeded John Burrow as Professor of Intellectual History in 1995, and the appointment of Blair Worden to a Chair of History in the following year further strengthened Sussex's standing in the early-modern period. Structural reorganisation within the university led in 1997 to proposals for the establishment of the

Centre for Literary and Intellectual History, an arrangement which would give institutional expression to the close collaborative links already existing with colleagues such as Norman Vance in English, and Donald Winch formally moved into this Centre in 1998. In institutional terms, there have, therefore, been both dispersals and continuities, and at this point it is proper to leave others to take up the story, or stories, in other ways in the future.

III

The term 'the Sussex School' has, as I have already emphasised, never been more than a piece of academic shorthand, but insofar as any reality lay behind the label, it would have to be found in a series of works published from the late 1970s onwards. These in no sense constituted a coordinated programme, but they perhaps evinced certain common qualities of approach and manner, and they all focused on a series of interconnecting themes and figures in British intellectual history from roughly the mid-eighteenth to the mid-twentieth centuries. The principal titles, in chronological order, were probably the following:

> *Adam Smith's Politics: An Essay in Historiographic Revision* (1978);
> *Liberalism and Sociology: L. T. Hobhouse and Political Argument in Britain 1880–1914* (1979);
> *A Liberal Descent: Victorian Historians and the English Past* (1981);
> *That Noble Science of Politics: An Essay in Nineteenth-Century Intellectual History* (1983);
> *Whigs and Liberals: Change and Continuity in English Political Thought* (1988);
> *Public Moralists: Political Thought and Intellectual Life in Britain 1850–1930* (1991);
> *Riches and Poverty: An Intellectual History of Political Economy in Britain 1750–1834* (1996).

All three authors also published volumes in the Oxford 'Past Masters' series at much the same time: John Burrow's *Gibbon* (1985), Donald Winch's *Malthus* (1987), and Stefan Collini's *Arnold* (1988). It was no doubt characteristic that these three books should have dealt with figures normally seen as the intellectual property of three very different modern disciplines – respectively, History, Economics, and English. Over these two decades, these books were, of course, accompanied by numerous articles, essays, and reviews, some of which occasionally took a more polemical or critical stance towards works by other scholars in the field. The perception of a characteristic 'Sussex' style may also have been encouraged by the fact that a number of younger scholars who had been graduate students there began to publish work in a not dissimilar vein, including two of the contributors to these volumes, Julia Stapleton and Dario Castiglione (as well as Philip Ironside who would have been a contributor but for ill health). Notable publications from this generation include Stapleton's *Englishness and the Study of Politics: The Social and Political Thought of Ernest Barker* (1994) and Ironside's *The Social and Political Thought of Bertrand Russell: The Development of an Aristocratic Liberalism* (1996).

The work of the scholars who have been regarded as at the heart of this group has thus taken the form of substantive books and essays rather than programmatic manifestos, and its characteristics can therefore not easily be encapsulated in a few sentences. But it would be reasonable to say that the informing spirit of much of this work has been the attempt to recover past ideas and re-situate them in their intellectual contexts in ways which resist the anachronistic or otherwise tendentious and selective pressures exerted by contemporary academic and political polemic. Work in this vein has also attempted to be alert to questions of style and register, to the nuances of individual voice as well as the animating presence of intellectual traditions, and to recognise the different levels of abstraction and practical engagement involved in work in different genres. The aim has been to offer a more thickly textured sense of the interplay between, say, literary, historiographical, and economic ideas in the cultural life of Britain since the Enlightenment, as well as much subtler characterisations of the relations between such ideas and the broader social and political developments of this period.

Intellectual history in this vein has, as already observed, eschewed adherence to any of the methodological programmes or tight conceptual schemes which have from time to time been elaborated and defended in general terms – the sociology of knowledge, the history of unit ideas, the mapping of *mentalités*, the study of political languages, the critique of ideologies, the recovery of authors' intentions, the archaeology of epistemes, the deconstruction of texts, and so on. The intellectual practice of both Winch and Burrow has, of course, displayed closer affinities to some of these approaches than to others, notably to those expounded in the methodological essays of John Pocock and Quentin Skinner (leaders of what, with equal imprecision and a fine disregard for geography, has sometimes been dubbed 'the Cambridge School'). But a characteristic of the work of Burrow, Winch, and their associates has been a certain deliberate eclecticism and a preference for letting substantive scholarship speak for itself (a preference which is not to be confused with the theoretical stance of 'empiricism', properly so called), and such collective distinctiveness as this work has displayed has been more a matter of tone and level of treatment, of common preoccupations and similar dispositions, than of adherence to the precepts of any one interpretive scheme. Moreover, this work has not for the most part been directly addressed to those working in the highly contentious (and only partly historical) sub-field of 'the history of political thought', and insofar as it *has* dealt with past political debate it has, especially in recent years, certainly not con-centrated on relations between past political theorising and contempo-rary moral and political philosophy, as so much of the work in that field continues to do. As their titles indicate, the essays in these two volumes range fairly widely over aspects of cultural and intellectual life in Britain during this period, as a result of which the history of political theory as such receives only glancing or incidental treatment.

In their occasional public ruminations on their practice, both Burrow and Winch have explored the value and limitations of the metaphor of 'eavesdropping on the conversations of the past' as a way of gesturing towards the intellectual historian's characteristic role, both immediately adding the rider that what is overheard has also to be (to use another meta-phor) 'translated' for the benefit of the contemporary reader. Other, similar metaphors could no doubt capture other aspects of the constant journey-ing between strangeness and familiarity which is the historian's task, but at the heart of this practice has been an underlying respect for the brute fact that the thoughts and feelings of the historical agents being studied are *theirs* not ours, and that a certain empathy and interpretive charity are essential if the activity of historical understanding is to involve anything more than merely confirming one's appearance in a mirror. (This, inciden-tally, is one reason why the historian who is seeking understanding rather than simply collecting information need never be afraid of the glib charge of antiquarianism; the past can have no capacity to surprise us if we merely visit it to provide material for *our* debates and preoccupations.) In practical terms, this rules out an excessive high-handedness in our dealings with the dead; as Winch has put it in discussing ways of 'achieving historical under-standing': 'I would confess . . . to following a fairly simple rule of thumb in such matters: past authors should be treated as one would wish one's own writings and beliefs to be treated, should the positions, by some amazing twist of fate, be reversed' (*Riches and Poverty*, p. 30). The contrast with what is suggested by the revealing metaphor of 'interrogating texts' is striking: interrogators know in advance the kinds of thing they are expecting to learn, often subjecting their victims to some pretty ungentle kinds of pres-sure until the process yields the desired information.

Ultimately, the most appropriate as well as most effective way to indi-cate some of the distinctive characteristics of the work of Winch and Burrow would be through an extended analysis of their *practice*, and this, of its nature, cannot be undertaken in the brief compass available here. Instead, a couple of more or less arbitrarily chosen passages from their work must do duty for a fuller critical account. In the case of *A Liberal Descent*, almost any sentence taken at random could be used to illustrate how a layered richness of understanding seeks and finds expression in a prose that is sinuous and complex, yet entirely free from inert, clogging abstractions. Thus, from the discussion of Macaulay:

The *History* is much more than the vindication of a party; it is an attempt to insinuate a view of politics, pragmatic, reverent, essentially Burkean, informed by a high, even tumid, sense of the worth of public life, yet fully conscious of its interrelations with the wider progress of society; it embodies what Hallam had merely asserted, a sense of the privileged possession by Englishmen of their history, as well as of the epic dignity of government by discussion (*A Liberal Descent*, p. 93).

No-one, not even the most inveterate Jamesian, could be tempted to describe this prose style as 'spare'. And yet there is a curious form of economy of expression here, a compacting into one sentence of elements which, taken alone, could too easily become blandly propositional and, hence, exaggerated. Even the wilful disregard for the usual proprieties in the use of the semi-colon plays, I am sorry to have to acknowledge, its part. As in the treatment of each of the major historians he discusses, the sense of intimacy with Macaulay here is intense, but it is the opposite of mimetic: it 'places' Macaulay's characteristic themes, and such placing always depends upon the kind of distance engendered by reflection and comparison. The voice in this passage, as in the book as a whole, is knowledgeable, but not insinuatingly knowing; it embodies both sympathy and understanding, without in the least threatening to patronise or to recruit.

Or, for a different range of effects, one may turn to the book's discussion of Freeman's deliberate use of an archaising, 'native' style in his *Norman Conquest*:

Like Pre-Raphaelite painting and the earnestness of Victorian Gothic, Freeman's restricted diction and syntactical austerity represent an attempt, conducted with revivalist zeal, to use archaism as a means of cleansing and renewal; as usual, the achieved effect is an almost fetidly intense, gamey Victorianism. Freeman's diction was of course not only restricted but necessarily in some measure deliberately archaic; there are times, though their preferred periods were different, when one is reminded of Rossetti's searching of old Romances for 'stunning words', though Rossetti's eclectic sensationalism was actually the reverse of Freeman's austerity: Strawberry Hill Gothick to Gilbert Scott's pedantry (*A Liberal Descent*, pp. 211–12).

Comparison and allusion rank high among Burrow's preferred literary instruments: his broad range of cultural reference yields unlooked-for similarities which simultaneously help isolate distinctiveness. His own vocabulary can be high, in more than one sense, but the manner is conversational rather than pedagogic, and in this passage the calculated off-handedness of the final clause has an aphoristic crispness, the effectiveness of which would be dissipated and perhaps even rendered doubtful in any more laboured exposition of the point. More than many historical figures, Freeman may now seem to invite mockery and even derision, and it is not the least of the achievements of the section of the book from which this passage comes that it resists this invitation, restoring intelligibility to his cultural enthusiasms and endowing his quirkiness with energy and purpose without ever merely sending him up or putting him down.

Turning to *Riches and Poverty*, one faces a different kind of difficulty in excerpting, since Winch's austerer style tends to produce its effects by means of a kind of sustained command. The following passage is simply one of dozens which display the book's incisive grasp of the choreography of intellectual alliance and antagonism as it introduces a discussion of the relations between the ideas of Smith, Burke, Paine, and Price at the end of the eighteenth century. Having remarked that Burke 'suggested the possibility of an inversion of the more familiar sequence expounded by Hume, Smith, and other Scottish historians of civil society, whereby commerce brings an improvement in manners and the arts and sciences in its train', Winch proceeds in characteristic fashion to allow historical complexity to erode the simplicities of later stereotypes:

Paine's extrapolation of the more widely accepted sequence into the future, however, and the welcome given to Smith's system of natural liberty by other contemporary opponents of Burke, has proved as useful to students of turn-of-the-century radicalism as it has to students of what later was seen as Burke's conservatism. In Paine's case, it has allowed him to be characterised as a spokesman for an upwardly mobile society of self-interested economic individualists, as the radical embodiment of all those 'bourgeois' qualities that Smith, alongside and in harmony with Locke, is supposed to represent [a footnote hauls a selection of eminent miscreants into the dock at this point]. As in the case of Burke, some of the resulting characterisations have had an homogenising effect on the diverse qualities of radicalism in this period. Including Price alongside Paine in this comparative exercise acts as a reminder that supporters of revolution did not always speak with the same voice when diagnosing the economic conditions most likely to consort with republican institutions. Price did not fully share Paine's 'Smithian' confidence in the progressive potential contained in the spread of commerce and manufacturing. Nor, as we shall see, did Smith share Paine's belief in the capacity or necessity for commerce to civilise by revolutionising government (*Riches and Poverty*, p. 131).

The passage is in some ways a promissory note, one made good by the rest of the chapter from the opening paragraphs of which it is taken. It is, typically, argumentative, and it is revisionist in the way complex, freshly seen history is always revisionist, in refusing the mind any easy resting-place in familiar modern categories. The chapter is entitled 'Contested Affinities', a phrase which is almost emblematic of the way Donald Winch writes intellectual history, with its constant attempt to do justice both to family resemblances and to family quarrels. The very structure of the prose vetoes any slack assimilation of what were subtly different positions, yet a clarity of outline survives through all attention to idiosyncrasy.

Or, for an example of how a seasoning of irony can contribute to, rather than detract from, fair-mindedness, consider his account of Arnold Toynbee's 'extraordinary lament' about the development of political economy earlier in the nineteenth century:

he regarded the failure to emancipate political economy from the influence of Ricardo's ruthless abstractions as a significant tragedy . . . As in the case of Keynes's equivalent regrets that the rigidities of Ricardian orthodoxy had vanquished Malthusian insights, the underlying belief in the importance of economic theory, whether as source of hope or betrayal, now seems almost as remarkable as the criticism. How could the mild-mannered Ricardo's theorems and parliamentary speeches be seen as so malevolent, let alone as so influential? . . . Yet Toynbee's horrified fascination with Ricardo and his own interest in political economy were not of the kind epitomised by George Eliot's character, Tom Tulliver, who was said to be fond of birds – that is, of throwing stones at them. Toynbee was earnestly seeking an accommodation between history and political economy, though his early death prevented the union from coming to fruition (*Riches and Poverty*, pp. 416–17).

By this point in the book, the reader will know how authoritative and deeply grounded are Winch's judgements about the extent of the exaggeration present in one generation's view of another; only someone so profoundly familiar with the intricacies of classical political economy *and* so well versed in the extensive literature about its alleged impact on policy could have earned the right to raise this question about Toynbee's reaction without seeming merely glib. The prose secretes a strong sense of proportion, as much by the balance of the sentences as by the quiet contrasts between 'tragedy' and 'regrets', between 'mild-mannered' and 'malevolent', and so on. Yet Toynbee's position is neither mocked nor dismissed; indeed, being placed alongside Keynes's 'equivalent regrets' almost confers an additional dignity on it. And as the passage from which this extract is taken continues, the conventional caricature of Toynbee, like the still more conventional caricature of Ricardo with which it is too easily contrasted, comes to seem exactly that.

Other passages from both authors could, of course, be cited to illustrate other traits, but there is just one general feature of the work of both Winch and Burrow which may merit separate mention here, particularly since it can lead to a misperception or undervaluing of that work in certain quarters. Neither of them has felt obliged to introduce every observation and to preface every claim with extensive lists of works by other scholars upon which they are building or against which they are reacting. Such slightly ritualised roll-calls of (not always entirely relevant) recent books and articles sometimes seem to be taken, particularly in the United States, as an indication, perhaps even a guarantee, of a work's scholarly seriousness. By contrast, although there is no lack of familiarity with the work of other scholars in the writings of Burrow and Winch – indeed, there is considerable evidence of their implicit engagement with it – both have opted for lightly carried learning in place of academic name-dropping. As Winch characteristically puts it at the end of the 'Prologue' to *Riches and Poverty*:

> Like any safety-conscious traveller to places that are new to me, I have read the work of the many *ciceroni* who have explored the territory before me. My footnotes record my debts to these sources and occasionally my opinions of those I have found less reliable as guides. As the term 'secondary sources' implies, however, none of them can ever be a satisfactory substitute for the real thing. For this reason, they will not be mentioned in the text from this point onwards (*Riches and Poverty*, p. 31).

IV

As indicated in the Preface earlier, these two volumes bring together the work of many of the leading scholars currently engaged in the field of modern British intellectual history. Needless to say, they write in their own distinctive styles, and their inclusion here should not be taken as an endorsement, and still less as any kind of imitation, of those features of the work of Burrow and Winch discussed in this introduction. Moreover, in assembling these essays, our aim has not been to try to produce a comprehensive 'intellectual history of modern Britain'; rather, each volume is devoted to a cluster of closely related themes. The contributions in *Economy, Polity, and Society* are primarily focused on the various ways in which 'economic thought' is inextricably embedded in a wider range of social and political debates, while those in *History, Religion, and Culture* particularly address the relations between historiography, religion, and conceptions of natural and social change. (The contents of each volume are summarised more fully in their respective 'Presentations'.)

In both volumes, the arrangement of essays is primarily thematic, while at the same time a rough chronological sequence from the mid-eighteenth to the mid-twentieth century is maintained. It has to be acknowledged that the second half of our stated period is dealt with somewhat less intensively than the first, and that, in particular, the years between 1900 and 1950 receive rather short shrift, apart from the essays by Winch and Stapleton (the unfortunate withdrawal of one contributor and the disabling illness of another reduced the planned coverage here). Something should also be said about the geographical or cultural limits of the terrain. Cultures are not discrete, sealed entities; ideas have scant respect for merely political boundaries, individuals belong to more than one 'culture', and the life of the mind is inherently cosmopolitan. Nonetheless, there is a certain pragmatic logic in confining attention to the intellectual life carried on within a given national culture, a unit often defined in primarily linguistic terms. Of course, a generation or two ago, these volumes might have been unselfconsciously sub-titled essays in *English* intellectual history, but both scholarly, and political developments have drawn attention to the problematic nature of that traditional label. In addition, passing references to links with the American colonies in the eighteenth century or with the problems of empire in the nineteenth are more easily accommodated under the wider term, and what one might call 'the Scotticisation of English culture' is an important theme of the first half of the nineteenth century in particular. For all these reasons, the use of the term 'British' in our sub-title can serve as no more than an approximate marker, a signal that these essays do not make the intellectual life of other societies such as France or Germany their primary focus, but equally that they do not confine themselves, rigidly and artificially, to the intellectual life of England in the strict, territorial sense.

It should also be clear that there are large areas of the intellectual history of the period in question which are, designedly, not covered in these volumes. There is, for example, little directly on the history of philosophy; similarly, although both Boyd Hilton's and John Burrow's essays touch on scientific topics, there is no sustained engagement with the history of scientific thought in this period; Brian Young's essay apart, there is little direct discussion of imperial themes, and so on for many other topics one might mention. These exclusions are intended to have no polemical significance; they are an incidental result of inviting contributions from scholars with a particular range of overlapping interests. Still less is popular culture made the focus of attention here; the essays overwhelmingly focus on ideas which attained a certain level of elaborated expression as part of the educated culture of their day. Again, this is not the outcome of some principled hierarchisation of subject-matters; the only 'principle' it could be said to instantiate is that one must study, and be allowed to study, what one finds interesting. But perhaps that is not, after all, an entirely unimportant principle. Jacob Burckhardt spoke of historiography as the record of what one age finds of interest in another. Not the least of the achievements of Donald Winch and John Burrow has been that they have helped us to find the intellectual life of Britain in this period so interesting.

Presentation of *Economy, Polity, and Society*

This volume opens with four essays which address aspects of the eighteenth-century attempt to come to grips with the nature of 'commercial society'; hardly surprisingly, Adam Smith occupies a prominent place in all four accounts. E. J. Hundert explores some of the ways in which a distinctively modern conception of the self emerged from perplexity about agency in the new social forms of eighteenth-century society. The commercial metropolis appeared to open up extensive possibilities for hypocrisy and role-playing, and it was Bernard Mandeville who first gave systematic expression to the new understanding of the relationship between motives and acts by concentrating on the dynamics of self-regard. In the Mandevillian scheme, individual character threatens to become nothing more than an artefact crafted by a role-player responding to the theatricality of the public nature of modern society. Eighteenth-century moralists were thereafter compelled to wrestle with the dangerous possibility that virtue was reducible to efficient dissembling, and that the self was no more than an internalised set of anticipations of the judgements likely to be made by others. Hundert concludes with a discussion of Smith, who sought to show that, unlike the social actor of Mandevillian provenance who merely seeks applause, the man of genuine self-command could be governed not by the desire for praise but by the standard of praiseworthiness itself.

Dario Castiglione's essay addresses the challenge posed to political thought by the new form of commercial society, and especially the rethinking of the distinctive nature of 'modern' (as opposed to 'ancient') liberty it provoked. He argues that the leading thinkers of the Scottish Enlightenment developed a systematic understanding of the nature and conditions of liberty in modern societies, an understanding which cannot be reduced to the familiar antinomies between 'positive' and 'negative', 'republican' and 'jurisprudential', and so on. Drawing on Montesquieu's account of liberty as the product of security, the Scots argued, against both Hobbesian voluntarists and those nostalgic for the city-states of antiquity, that political liberty needed to be seen as resulting from, first, the growth in the regularity of government and law, and, second, from a concomitant separation of and reciprocal check between the established powers in society. This allowed Hume to counter the traditional Whig claims about the glories of England's constitutional liberties with an account which emphasised the ways in which the growth of prosperity contributed indirectly to curbs on royal and noble power alike. This line of analysis thus represented liberty as dependent upon contingent historical circumstances, and it was Smith who, especially in his *Lectures on Jurisprudence*, provided the fullest account of this history. But even those Scottish moralists most sympathetic to ancient republicanism, such as Millar and, above all, Ferguson, adopted features of this analysis, allowing such traditionally 'civic humanist' values as independence, character, and participation to be re-defined as essential elements in the operation of 'liberty and security'. Castiglione concludes that this perception of the 'intrinsic fragilities of the liberty of the moderns' represented an underlying unity in what he dubs 'the discourse of the North'.

Nicholas Phillipson focuses directly on Smith himself, and considers the somewhat neglected intellectual foundations of Smith's understanding of historical development, an understanding which issued in the celebrated 'stadial' theory of evolution from 'nomadic' to 'commercial' societies. Phillipson traces the roots of Smith's philosophy of man to the confrontation between Hutcheson's teaching on 'moral sense' and Hume's more sceptical emphasis on the role of custom and the association of ideas. Smith's early writings explored the general contention that the progress of society had been dependent upon the invention of the general categories of language, and here Phillipson proposes that the key inspiration lay with Condillac's work on the relation between language and the development of the human mind. This concern with language underlay Smith's mature moral theory: even the notion of the 'impartial spectator', which Smith identified as the chief source of virtue in commercial society, can be regarded as a fiction generated within language and presupposing the extended categories of 'propriety' and so on which the human understanding had evolved. Phillipson concludes by pointing to the part played by the rhetorical and persuasive functions of language more generally in Smith's later moral thinking.

Richard Teichgraeber's essay considers some of the peculiarities of the development of Smith's reputation in Britain between the first publication of *The Wealth of Nations* in 1776 and the appearance of the first edition of Malthus's *Essay on Population* in 1798. The larger issues in play here concern the ways in which an intellectual tradition is established and certain works then come to be regarded as founding or 'canonical' texts in that tradition. From some time early in the nineteenth century, it became conventional to regard Smith as the founder of the discipline of political economy, but, as Teichgraeber emphasises, recent scholarship on Smith, not least that of Donald Winch himself, has drawn attention to the *dis*continuities between his own ambition to develop the 'science of the legislator' and his later reputation as an 'economist'. Teichgraeber, therefore, focuses on the different contexts of the initial reception of Smith's work, notably as part of the intellectual response to the French Revolution, where Smith's name was frequently invoked to support the claim that the implementing of liberal economic policies need not entail radical political upheaval. Teichgraeber also situates the early reputation of *The Wealth of Nations* within the great expansion of print culture in the closing decades of the eighteenth century, noting the gulf which separated this large and elaborately turned (and expensive) work from the great mass of the products of the new world of commercial publishing.

   The four essays in part II are all concerned with what may be seen as some of the consequences of the new thinking identified in part I, tracing different aspects of the relation between 'polity' and 'society' on the one hand and various understandings of the relatively new notion of 'economy' on the other. All four essays address these issues by focusing principally on the work of a single major figure. David Lieberman draws upon recent work in the history of late eighteenth- and early nineteenth-century political thought, much of it undertaken by other contributors to these two volumes, to re-assess the long-standing view of Bentham's legal and political thinking as being implicitly based on a generalisation of the model of 'economic man'. Lieberman challenges this view at several levels. First, he argues that in Bentham's 'science of legislation' maxims derived from the 'art' of political economy play a relatively minor part: Bentham accepted that a policy of laissez-faire was broadly conducive to material abundance, but he always accorded the state a far more interventionist role for all other purposes. Second, Lieberman shows that far from modelling social behaviour in general on economic conduct, Bentham recognised economic motivation as governing only a limited aspect of social life: important in so far as it was amenable to the operation of the mechanisms of incentive and deterrence, but far from co-extensive with the whole field of human action which was the proper concern of the legislator and jurist. And third, Lieberman argues that this misleading emphasis upon Bentham's 'economic psychology' has tended to distract attention from other, more consequential, sets of assumptions operative across his work, most notably those concerning the function of public opinion. Bentham treated the extensive and uncensored diffusion of 'information' as essential to the operation of a democratic polity; as Lieberman concludes, 'Hitherto we have been so devoted to finding behind Bentham's legislative theory a nation of shopkeepers, that we have neglected his commitments to a nation of newspaper readers.'

Questions about the relation between the political and economic sources of motivation in a commercial age are also at the heart of Richard Whatmore's discussion of Thomas Paine, a figure who has proved difficult to classify within the familiar categories of Anglo-American political thought of the period. Whatmore brings out how Paine's republicanism assumes a more identifiable character when it is re-situated in the context of eighteenth-century French thinking, especially that of Condorcet, but including the economic ideas of the Physiocrats and their successors. Paine was exercised by the question of how a republic, hitherto largely thought of as a form of government appropriate only to small states, could, in the era of the American and French revolutions, be adapted to larger political units. He particularly insisted on the need for a greater equality of material conditions in a commercial society if the energies of the citizens were to be harnessed to patriotic purposes. The 'manliness' of a republican state based on a generalised condition of moderate wealth was, Paine believed, what would enable it in the end to defeat those states still under the sway of the enervating power of monarchy and aristocracy. In these respects Paine directly challenged the convictions long cherished in Britain about the superior resilience and virtue of the 'mixed constitution' established in the seventeenth century.

Connections with the wider European, especially French, intellectual world also figure in Marilyn Butler's essay, though the principal affiliation here is with the legacy of the kind of eighteenth-century Scottish thinking discussed in part I. Butler focuses on the writings, fictional and non-fictional, of the Anglo-Irish novelist Maria Edgeworth from the 1790s and 1800s, the years around the Union. She establishes the close intellectual, and in some cases personal, links between the Edgeworth family circle and the enlightened world of late eighteenth-century Scotland, especially that of Dugald Stewart and his pupils, and she explores some of the resemblances between Edgeworth's writings on education and those of Adam Smith, especially their common emphasis on the cultivation of individual judgement in the child. More broadly, Butler situates Edgeworth's writings within contemporary debates about the cultural characteristics of the four countries of the British Isles, indicating how her depiction of Irish identity attempted to resist contemporary stereotypes, not least by drawing on a longer and more learned cultural inheritance. The final section of the essay documents the very close connections between the issues discussed in the early numbers of the *Edinburgh Review* and Edgeworth's novels and tales of the 1800s. In time, however, this association was to contribute to the eclipse of Edgeworth's reputation, as the charge of 'irreligion', to which her and her father's writings, especially on education, had long been vulnerable, now came to assume a more telling force in the heightened sectarian conflict of the 1820s and 1830s.

The problem of the economic and social development of Ireland is also the focus of the essay by Norman Vance, who, in passing, urges historians, including intellectual historians, to consider both religious issues and Irish affairs as central to the thought of the period. Vance explores the several dimensions of Richard Whately's career as churchman and economist, emphasising his commitment to the established church and his underlying belief in the role of religion in upholding the social order. Whately was also a stern supporter of the deterrent effect of the New Poor Law in both England and Ireland, even to the point of opposing outdoor relief during the Great Famine. But he insisted that political economy was a moral science which was compatible with spiritual as well as material welfare (this insistence underlay his vigorous denunciation of Mandeville's paradox about the relation between private vice and public benefit discussed in Hundert's essay). His endowment of a Chair in Political Economy at Trinity College, Dublin was one practical expression of his conviction that the study of the new subject was of the utmost importance in Ireland as in England, and Vance's portrait attempts to correct the imbalance in our understanding of Whately which is the legacy of a largely hostile historiographical tradition.

The three essays in part III explore broader aspects of the relation, especially sometimes the conflict, between economic thinking and more general cultural and moral values across a period which stretches from the early nineteenth century through, in the case of Winch's essay, to the middle of the twentieth century and even beyond. Jane Garnett looks at a point of intersection between the Victorian engagement with the culture of ancient Greece and the contemporaneous criticisms of the nature and scope of political economy. Starting from the root meaning of *oikonomia* as 'household management' and from the nineteenth-century fascination with Xenophon's treatise on that subject, Garnett explores the ways in which thinking about the reality of the household as a socio-economic unit, and especially about the implicit gendering of the 'labour' it involved, presented a challenge to the categories of a discipline premised on the ostensibly free choices of a calculating (and implicitly male) economic agent. The Victorian figure who particularly exploited the critical potential of this confrontation was John Ruskin (who is discussed from a different point of view in John Drury's essay in the companion volume, *History, Religion, and Culture*). Ruskin was drawn to the model of the household, as Garnett brings out, 'precisely because in the household it was by definition not possible to abstract economic from social relationships', yet few of his educated contemporaries took Ruskin seriously as a critic of the science. In contrast to the more organic tradition of Catholic social thought in Europe, other mid- and late Victorian attacks on political economy tended to result in the recalcitrant aspects of social behaviour being hived off as the subject-matter of other enquiries (for example, sociology or social work) rather than provoking a fundamental re-assessment of the categories of political economy itself.

It is often assumed that it was through the institutions of 'culture', especially as supported by the state, that the workings of economic forces in the nineteenth century (and after) were most effectively checked and resisted. Sheldon Rothblatt's essay re-examines the conventional assumption of the operation of a binary opposition between 'state' and 'market' in the development of universities in Britain. Rothblatt emphasises the variousness of the forces shaping universities in England and, a quite different model, in Scotland, and he brings out how many of the fundamental changes were what might be called 'demand-led' rather than being policy initiatives from above. Equally, he argues, the 'state' should not be seen as a monolithic and unchanging entity, but an assembly of different agencies the nature and scope of whose activities expanded dramatically from the early Victorian period. He contrasts the socially exclusive, academically conservative, Anglican colleges of Oxford and Cambridge in the first half of the century with the Scottish universities which had a much wider social recruitment, a more diverse and, in several respects, more 'applied' curriculum, and even less emphasis on the qualification of a degree as such. Rothblatt emphasises the ways in which the kind of educational market that the Scottish university offered was well suited to the social conditions of its parent society. He also explores the founding of a university in London on the 'Scottish' model, a piece of private enterprise which the state then took on a responsibility for regulating (Rothblatt's essay, like several others in these two volumes, incidentally illustrates what might be called the 'Scotticisation' of English intellectual life in the first half of the nineteenth century). The increased supervisory role of the state over the 'private' institutions of Oxford and Cambridge (itself sometimes a response to 'market demand') also accompanied the long drawn-out, uneven process through which they ceased to be defined in confessional terms. Rothblatt's analysis, then, resists any monocausal explanations: the demands of a growing bureaucracy, both domestic and imperial, the forces driving intellectual specialisation, the tendency towards 'established unbelief', and the social ambitions of genteel middle-class families were all among the sources shaping the character of the newly multiplied and much expanded universities in the second half of the century.

In the final essay, Donald Winch examines some of the successive re-workings of the idea of an essential fault-line in British culture from the early nineteenth century onwards, a division variously described as being between the tradition of Utilitarian and economic reasoning on one side and its Romantic and radical critics on the other, or, in Arnold Toynbee's famously succinct formula, between 'economists and human beings'. Winch brings out how the figure of Mr Gradgrind, from Dickens's *Hard Times*, came to function as an emblem of the supposed alliance between hard-headed Utilitarians and hard-hearted political economists as apologists for the new industrial order, and he briefly hints at some of the ways in which this homogenised and misdescribed the political and social views of the historical figures lumped together in this stereotype. Moving on from the nineteenth-century origins of this cliché, Winch discusses the way this interpretation was re-animated and given contemporary force in the writings of such influential intellectual figures in the twentieth century as F. R. Leavis, Raymond Williams, and E. P. Thompson. While attentive to the needs that this account of British culture served in their writings, he also points to its essential tendentiousness as intellectual history. At the root of this critical tradition Winch finds the unspoken assumption that those who saw themselves as committed to building a 'new Jerusalem' were entitled to condemn all those who attempted to analyse the actual operation of economic forces in an industrial society as merely colluding with its exploitative practices. In his conclusion, Winch implicitly calls, and not for the first time, for both a more accurate and sympathetic interpretation of the past and a more realistic and responsible politics in the present.

Part I

1 Sociability and self-love in the theatre of moral sentiments: Mandeville to Adam Smith

E. J. Hundert

I

When the anthropologist Marcel Mauss was invited to give the 1938 Huxley Memorial Lecture, he chose for his subject 'A Category of the Human Mind: the Notion of Person; the Notion of Self'.[1] Mauss thought that his contemporaries falsely believed that the idea of the self captured an innate human property, and that, due to this error, they subscribed to a socially divisive cult of the individual. He proposed that the conception of ourselves as unique is largely a historical artefact. Not only do other peoples hold very different notions of the self, but each conception is intimately connected to the specific ethical community to which persons belong. Mauss referred to ethnographic materials from North America, Australia and archaic Greece to show that in cultures where personhood is defined by kinship, descent and status, responsibility flows directly from family or clan membership, and neither love nor one's conscience alone serve as justifications for action. Only with the emergence of a more abstract conception of a person, seen as the locus of general rights and duties, could individuals understand themselves as endowed with a conscience and inner life. It is this notion of the person as the possessor of a moral consciousness, as the source of autonomous motivation and something capable of self-development, that is the foundation of our own self-understanding.

We, Mauss's current readers, are sceptical about there being any single narrative that could account for self-conceptions of the human subject, and we are more attentive than his contemporaries were to the impersonal nature of the forces that shape the individual's consciousness. Unlike Mauss, we have good reason to think of human capacities as biologically rooted, emerging at developmentally critical moments in

I would like to thank Mark Glouberman and Mark Phillips for their helpful criticisms.
[1] Marcel Mauss, 'A Category of the Human Mind: the Notion of Person; the Notion of Self', trans. W. D. Halls, in Michael Crithers *et al.*, *The Category of the Person. Anthropology, Philosophy, History* (Cambridge, 1985), pp. 1–25.

neurophysiological history. A conception of the self necessarily rests upon these processes, which function within histories so diverse that the indigenous psychology of other or earlier societies may be nearly inaccessible to us. Nevertheless, any plausible account of modern self-awareness must acknowledge Mauss's claim that an individualist mode of self-understanding has become distinctive of contemporary Western European cultures and their extensions in the Americas. These cultures are characterised on the one hand by role distance – the assumption that persons are in principle able to adopt or abandon roles with some freedom – and on the other by autonomy – the assumption of a capacity and responsibility to decide between actions and plans of life.

Mauss argued that the assumptions upon which modern self-understanding rests acquired much of their distinctive character during the eighteenth century. In this essay, I want to explore this insight by examining how a dominant conception of the person emerged from perplexity about moral agency in commercial society. I shall argue that through a century-long controversy ignited by the work of Bernard Mandeville about the effects of commerce on individual autonomy in commercial society, the stage-actor came to be taken as a representative individual within an altered public sphere – one in which theatrical practices shaped the language of morals, helping to form a distinctive and problematic conception of the modern moral subject.

The central concerns of eighteenth-century moral discourse – sociability and self-love – emerged from a shift in moral psychology first begun within a theological context: the sceptical doctrines associated with the Huguenot Pierre Bayle, and the Augustinian rigorism of La Rochefoucauld and late seventeenth-century French Jansenist divines, particularly Pierre Nicole.[2] Both groups anatomised forms of moral behaviour with the aim of demonstrating that a person's apparent practice of Christian virtue in no way provided an observer of these acts with knowledge about underlying motives. Since apparently virtuous acts were rewarded by public approbation, it was in the obvious interest of the vicious to mime the conventional signs of Christian piety. The majority of men acted according to socially prescribed conventions of propriety not because of their moral content, but in the expectation that such behaviour would win approval. Moreover, given that virtue could reasonably be understood as one of the masks available to fallen men in their pursuit of selfish interests, the difference between virtue and vice would have

---

[2] On this tradition, see Nannerl Keohane, *Philosophy and the State in France* (Princeton, 1980), pp. 283–311, and Dale Van Kley, 'Pierre Nicole, Jansenism and the Morality of Enlightened Self-Interest', in Alan C. Kors and Paul Korshin, eds., *Anticipations of the Enlightenment* (Philadelphia, 1987), pp. 69–85.

nothing to do with behaviour. Instead, the distinction between an act which stemmed from selfish desire and one whose source was Christian charity would, of necessity, be visible only to God as He inspected each human heart.

From these arguments two unsettling consequences followed. First, it was assumed that the great majority merely feigned Christian commitments while being, in reality, driven by self-love. Yet the fact that their behaviour was in principle indistinguishable from that of true Christians challenged the conventional assumption that believers who feared hell and yearned for salvation were more powerfully motivated toward virtuous action than were pagans, Jews, or atheists. Bayle drew the obvious conclusion: anyone, atheist or believer, could make a good subject, since civil conduct required no more than outward conformity to standards of propriety enforced by social pressure and underwritten by law. Civic rectitude required no spiritually enriched conscience.[3] Second, Pierre Nicole argued, just as the selfish wants of individuals could be harnessed to politically beneficial ends, so too could competing economic interests be made to obey similar constraints. Social utility and communal benefit could be understood as unintended consequences of historically domesticated forms of self-aggrandisement. The seemingly anarchic tendencies of the scramble for wealth, for example, revealed themselves at a deeper level to be structured social regularities attending the common pursuit of material gratification. Accordingly, expressions of self-regard could best be understood, not simply as examples of the propensity of Adam's heirs to sin but, again paradoxically, as features of the practices by virtue of which egoism had been locally disciplined.[4]

Mandeville's *Fable of the Bees* (1723 and 1728) transposed this mode of moral argument into a secular instrument of social understanding.[5] The

---

[3] See the contemporary English translation of Pierre Bayle's *Pensées divers sur le comète* [1683], *Miscellaneous Reflections on the Comet* (1708), pp. 212–25.

[4] See particularly, Pierre Nicole, 'Of Grandeur', and 'Of Christian Civility', in *Moral Essays, Contain'd in several TREATISES on many important duties* (1696), pp. 83–128 and 137–49. See too the Huguenot Jacques Abbadie, *The Art of Knowing Oneself: Or, An Inquiry into the Sources of Morality* (Oxford, 1695), pp. 126–87, and Jacques Esprit, *Discourses on the Deceitfulness of Human Virtues* (London, 1706), preface and pp. 37–8.

[5] All references placed parenthetically in the text refer to the volume and page number in the edition of F. B. Kaye, *The FABLE of the BEES: or, Private Vices, Public Benefits. By Bernard Mandeville. With a Commentary Critical, Historical, and Explanatory by F. B. Kaye*, 2 vols. (Oxford, 1924). For Mandeville's relationship to the theory of the passions in seventeenth-century Augustinian moral reflection, see Arthur O. Lovejoy, *Reflections on Human Nature* (Baltimore, 1961), lectures III–V and Laurence Dickey, 'Pride, Hypocrisy and Civility in Mandeville's Social and Historical Theory', *Critical Review*, 4, 3 (Summer, 1990), pp. 387–431. For a comprehensive account of Mandeville's eighteenth-century identity, see E. J. Hundert, *The Enlightenment's 'Fable': Bernard Mandeville and the Discovery of Society* (Cambridge, 1994).

book's notorious maxim, 'Private Vices, Publick Benefits', encapsulated Mandeville's thesis that contemporary society is an aggregation of persons driven by passions for gain and approbation – passions which necessarily bind individuals together neither by shared civic commitments nor by moral rectitude but by the fetters of envy, competition, and exploitation. Only passions can move one to act, he argued, and the object of any passion can be nothing other than one's own perceived interest or pleasure. Mandeville, re-shaping his French ideological inheritance, gave prominence to the role of the demands of the social environment in governing the passions of all social actors into expressive conjunctions of judgement and feeling whose local embodiments could only be realised within the established conventions of sociability within a given public sphere.

In the societies that Mandeville focused upon, persons were not merely driven by the universal appetites for authority and esteem: in the metropolitan centres of European commerce, outward displays of wealth were widely accepted as a direct index of social power. 'People, where they are not known,' he observed,

are generally honour'd according to their Clothes and other Accoutrements they have about them; from the riches of them we judge of their Wealth, and by their ordering of them we guess at their Understanding. It is this which encourages every Body . . . to wear Clothes above his rank, especially in large and populous cities where obscure men may hourly meet with fifty strangers to one acquaintance, and consequently have the pleasure of being esteemed by a vast majority, not as what they are, but what they appear to be (I: pp. 127–8).

Mandeville consolidated a revolution in the understanding of the relationship between motives and acts by viewing commerce and sociability as reciprocal features of the dynamics of self-regard. He sought to comprehend the consequences of the behaviour of persons for whom opportunities for consumption and display encouraged forms of self-presentation that were the vehicles through which they established their social identities.

Mandeville argued that if moral judgements were in fact nothing other than expressions of feeling (passion), then the operative traditions of Christian moral psychology could not be enlisted to explain the status and workings of human desire. These judgements had to be set in a different problem-space from the one typically assumed by Mandeville's contemporaries. He placed the expression of supposedly moral sentiments in the context of responses to opportunities for the satisfaction of self-interest. Social action could be conceived in terms of an individual's search for pleasure and the success with which he managed to satisfy his desires. Since these desires had self-regard as their foundation, and since, crucially, this self-regard depended upon public approbation, Mandeville could explain why persons so often spoke and acted in ways which appeared moral: in so doing they would garner public rewards. He further argued that both speech and action are most usefully understood instrumentally. Behaviour in public was a species of performance designed to win approval; in the final analysis public behaviour consisted in a series of performances whose success depended upon no genuine moral standard, but on how well a social actor could satisfy his desires within the given regime of rewards and punishments.

Mandeville, then, effectively redescribed the scene of moral activity. Contrary to what was typically believed, the civil arena was not populated by rationally endowed, undivided consciousnesses enquiring into those choices which directly affected their own souls and the good of their community. The moral agent anatomised in *The Fable* was, in effect, an intersubjectively defined, socially situated participant in a communal drama: a person driven by passions who of necessity competes in a public market for marks of esteem. This individual's desires alone form the premises of his practical reasoning, while the material and symbolic rewards of the social order to which he belongs become constituent features of his own identity. In this world, personality is discontinuous with Christian moral commitment, social standing and identity are distributed through the mechanisms of the market, and character is nothing more than an artefact crafted by role-players within theatrical forms of social exchange.

The initially French inflection given to the Augustinian language of morals served Mandeville's critical purpose of exposing the irreducible gap between natural impulse and virtuous action without abandoning the rigorous moral rhetoric shared by many of his critics. By speaking in their language, he could satirically pose as an advocate of the most severe ethical standards, and then, from an elevated rhetorical position, insist that 'it is impossible that . . . mere Fallen Man . . . could be sociable . . . without Hypocrisy' (I: pp. 348–9). This mock-Augustinian stance further enabled Mandeville to situate the distance between motive and act within a theatrical perspective. He placed in a commercial context the ancient insight that actions on the stage and in society each have as part of their content the possibility of being both performed and understood as features of a role, and then he showed how the meaning of these performances can never be transparent – an actor's explicit professions notwithstanding – since roles are filled by persons who must, as a condition of success, perform them in certain socially specified ways. Not only do public acts invite, but they also always demand interpretation by members of the audience, who by their responses alone certify an agent's success or failure. As in John Gay's *The Beggar's Opera* (1728), to which

Mandeville compared his own unmasking efforts (II: p. 6), actors may play the roles of criminals, who themselves play roles as 'gentlemen', 'merchants' and 'ladies' before an audience meant to read its own values into these impostures.

II

The ancient, originally Stoic figure of the *theatrum mundi*, the world seen as a stage, had been employed for centuries to expose the artificial boundaries placed upon acceptable public behaviour. The theatrical metaphor was a rhetorical device employed to unmask worldly ambition and pretence. For Jacques, in Shakespeare's *As You Like It*, the reminder that 'all the world's a stage' served the traditional function of recalling to individuals the fact that they were subject to the scrutiny of a higher power into whose care their souls were entrusted. Within the conceptual ambit of the theatre persons could be viewed as puppets in a drama of which they remained unaware – unwitting actors who inhabited roles which had an illusory, because merely mundane, significance. For Shakespeare, the metaphor of the world as a stage served as an instrument of social intelligibility in the restricted though important sense of reasserting the central Christian doctrine of the spiritual role-nakedness of all persons.

Mandeville's purposes in emphasising the theatricality of public life differed significantly. Theatricality serves him as a conceptual instrument for the examination of modern consciousness, not merely as a convenient metaphor for human relations derived from the language of the playhouse. He employed theatricality to emphasise the distance between genuine knowledge and mere appearance in the minds of social actors themselves more than to expose the vanity of human aspirations from a celestial perspective. Mandeville argued that an environment had arisen in which features of one's identity previously thought to be essential and enduring had become mere markers distinguishing practices of display and role distance that could be altered or discarded when they came into conflict with contemporary forms of economic opportunity.

By the early eighteenth century the *theatrum mundi* had emerged as an enabling device with which Epicurean radicals like Mandeville could analyse the gulf between the detached observer of the world and the mass of men who remained imaginatively ensnared by the world's public rituals. 'The Wise Man', in John Digby's 1712 rendition of Epicurus, 'shall reap more Benefit, and take more Satisfaction in the public Shews, than other Men. He there observes the different Characters of the Spectators; he can discover by their looks the effect of the Passions that moves 'em, and amidst the Confusion that reigns in these places . . . he has the Pleasure to find himself the only person undisturb'd'.[6] Mandeville adopted this perspective, aggressively so. He conceived of the false beliefs of his contemporaries as distorting ideological residues generated by commercial society's tacit conventions. The wise man becomes a student of this society by virtue of his ability to stand aloof from those public spectacles through which these myths are enacted. 'To me', Mandeville said,

it is a great Pleasure, when I look on the Affairs of human Life, to behold . . . what various and often strangely opposite Forms the hope of Gain and thoughts of Lucre shape Men, according to the different Employments they are of, and Stations they are in. How gay and merry does every Face appear at a well-ordered Ball . . . [but we must] . . . examine these People . . . as to their Inside and the different Motives they act from' (I: pp. 349–50).

A prominent line of eighteenth-century moral argument regarding the theatricality of public life derived from the conventions of the London stage. Both the procedures and objectives of this theatre were effectively articulated into aesthetic principles by the critic John Dennis.[7] Dennis argued that the theatre should be understood as at once entertaining and moving, yet essentially harmless and even possessing the potential for moral instruction. Because the passions evoked in the theatre are inspired under conditions in which the audience remains aware of its self-imposed distance from the dramatic action, even the arousal of painful feelings could be controlled and so rendered pleasurable. This view depended upon a strict conceptual distinction between the passions derived from Descartes, who understood passions as physiological humours prone to excitement, either from external sources or from will and cognition, both of which could be controlled by reason. Thus even the evocation of sadness in the playhouse was capable of producing pleasure in the spectator, so Descartes argued in *The Passions of the Soul* (1649). For 'when passions are only caused by the stage adventures which we see represented in the theatre, or by other similar means which, not being able to harm us in any way, [they] seem pleasurably to excite our soul in affecting it'.[8]

Writers on aesthetics and students of the stage could, then, accept a modern mechanist account of the relationship of the passions to the actions of the human body associated with Harvey (whose discoveries helped to place the heart as the site of the passions) as well as with

---

[6] John Digby, *Epicurus's Morals* (1712), p. 52.

[7] John Dennis, *The Advancement and Reformation of Poetry*, in *The Critical Works of John Dennis*, ed. Edward Niles Hooker, 2 vols. (Baltimore, 1939–45), vol. I.

[8] René Descartes, *Philosophical Works*, trans. E. S. Haldane and G. R. T. Ross, 2 vols. (Cambridge, 1911), I, p. 373. See too Dennis, *The Advancement and Reformation of Poetry*, p. 364. For the conceptual dilemmas attendant to this view, see Anthony Levi, *French Moralists. The Theory of the Passions, 1585–1649* (Oxford, 1964), pp. 238–99, and Susan James, *Passion and Action* (Oxford, 1997), pp. 85–123.

Descartes, while at the same time retaining a classical understanding of theatrical engagement, an understanding which stressed the power of consciousness to discipline feelings. Just as contemporary guides to manners took the passions to be 'Nature's never-failing Rhetoric', contemporary artists and critics concentrated on the representation of the passions as the crucial element in the portrayal of character.[9] A true 'painting of the passions' was taken to be the highest praise one could bestow on any attempt to depict the vicissitudes of human nature. The dramatic artist's business was to know the best way of representing each passion so as to make the audience respond appropriately. An intricate set of rules, laid out in theatrical guidebooks and treatises which together formed the first systematic body of writing on the theory and practice of acting in the West, provided for artists and their audiences the affective conventions through which the passions could be portrayed.[10] So popular was the London stage that Hume was moved to quip that the public was more excited by the prospect of a great actor's performance 'than when our prime minister is to defend himself from a motion for his removal for impeachement'.[11] Here, in Europe's most commercially successful form of public entertainment,[12] the focus was on theatre as performance rather than drama conceived as literature, with plays primarily regarded as vehicles for the actor's virtuosity. Indeed, the details of facial aspect, gesture and tone of voice, which Garrick, the greatest actor of his day, put forward as the essential elements of his *Essay on Acting* (1744), had already begun to be catalogued in the *Thesaurus Dramaticus* (1724), a guide to the 'poetical beauties' of the English stage, published shortly after Mandeville's *Fable*.

The abbé Du Bos's seminal work on aesthetics, *Critical Reflections on Poetry and Painting* (1719), became the authoritative statement of aesthetic principles associated with the stage during the first half of the eighteenth century.[13] For Du Bos, each passion has its particular natural

---

[9] Brewster Rogerson, 'The Art of Painting the Passions', *Journal of the History of Ideas*, 14, 1 (1953), pp. 68–94. See too, Lawrence Lipking, *The Ordering of the Arts in Eighteenth-Century England* (Princeton, 1970), pp. 38–65.

[10] See Marvin Carlson, *Theories of the Theatre* (Ithaca, 1984), pp. 112–40; Joseph R. Roach, *The Player's Passion: Studies in the Science of Acting* (Newark, Del., 1988), pp. 58–115, and William Worthen, *The Idea of the Actor: Drama and the Ethics of Performance* (Princeton, 1984), ch. 2.

[11] David Hume, 'Of Eloquence', *Essays Moral, Political and Literary* (Oxford, 1963), p. 100.

[12] John Brewer, *The Pleasures of the Imagination. English Culture in the Eighteenth Century* (New York, 1997), pp. 357–83.

[13] J.-B. Du Bos, *Réflexions critiques sur la poesie et sur peinture*, 3 vols. (Paris, 1719; second revised edition, 1732); English translation, 1748. On Du Bos's importance, see D. G. Charleton, 'J.-B. Du Bos and Eighteenth-Century Sensibility', *Studies in Voltaire and the Eighteenth Century*, 266 (1990), pp. 151–62.

expression, tone and gesture, which 'rise, as it were mechanically within us'.[14] The principal merit of the drama, he argues, consists in the imitation of just those objects which excite our passions. It is the specific business of the actor to revive these passions within himself in order more effectively to convey their natural signs to the audience. Spectators are moved in the theatre when 'artificial' (as opposed to naturally occurring) passions are aroused; and in providing the best representation of the 'symptoms and nature' of the passions, drama serves as a vehicle of moral instruction and emotional refinement. The inherently distancing conditions of the theatre, however, ensure that the spectator's pleasure 'is never attended with those disagreeable consequences, which [would] arise from the serious emotions caused by the [dramatic] object itself'.[15] Like Dennis, and in a manner similar to Shaftesbury in the *Characteristics* (1711), Du Bos claimed that an enlightened 'public' can properly assess the value of a spectacle because its sentiments are refined by education and experience to form a kind of sixth sense, *le sentiment*.[16] Audiences are thus enabled to form disinterested judgements, particularly about those powerfully moving expressions of emotion which could not effectively be conveyed in words.[17] 'The spectator therefore preserves his understanding, notwithstanding the liveliest emotion. He receives the impression of the passions, but without . . . falling into extravagances.'[18] The view expressed here is virtually identical to Addison's in *The Spectator*, where he claims that a modern public, a 'Fraternity of Spectators', is composed of 'every one that considers the World as a Theatre, and desires to form a right Judgement of those who are actors in it'.[19] These 'impartial spectators', Addison added, are able to 'consider all the different pursuits and Employments of Men, and . . . will [be able to] find [that] half [of] the[ir] Actions tend to nothing else but Disguise and Imposture; and [realise that] all that is done which proceeds not from a Man's very self is the Action of a Player'.[20] The polite, theatrical presentation of self demanded in the everyday life of the modern civic realm stood in constant but not disabling tension with the requirements of morality.

III

Mandeville agreed that an individual's character could best be understood as a distinct amalgam of discrete passions. But one must always bear in mind that he was a physiological materialist who denied that the passions were subject purely to rational control, either on the stage or in

---

[14] Du Bos, *Réflexions*, III, p. 179; see too, I, p. 10.   [15] *Ibid.*, p. 24.   [16] *Ibid.*, II, p. xxii.
[17] *Ibid.*, p. xxi.   [18] *Ibid.*, III, pp. xiii and xvi.
[19] *The Spectator*, ed. Donald F. Bond, 5 vols. (Oxford, 1965), no. 274.   [20] *Ibid.*, no. 370.

the street. Indeed, one of Mandeville's primary purposes was to expose this view as an example of the 'Practical Part of Dissimulation' (II: p. 77) and hypocrisy which the doctrines of politeness of Addison and Shaftesbury were meant to conceal.[21] Mandeville insists that members of the *beau monde* in commercial societies could never adhere to the codes of polite intercourse promoted by Addison, Steele, Shaftesbury, and Du Bos while at the same time remaining morally independent and cognitively undeluded agents. These persons are required to adopt highly stylised public personae as they regularly confront virtual strangers whose approbation they seek, especially in the widening public spaces whose rituals had become the subjects of popular art and in strictly commercial settings like the London Exchange, where material interest alone formed a social bond, promoting civilised intercourse amongst persons with otherwise incommensurable habits and beliefs.[22]

Mandeville was quick to notice (II: p. 39) that members of the enlarged public at London's theatres themselves provided a microcosm of a novel social universe, in which people who had recently risen from obscurity by successful speculation could pretend to elevated status.[23] When Mandeville's adversary William Law attacked the moral impropriety of the stage, he observed that the patrons at London's theatres were convinced of their right to judge a play as it was being performed,[24] a point famously made again by Samuel Johnson in mid-century,[25] and typified by Boswell, for whom the theatre was the exemplary site for the practised

[21] See, especially, Lawrence Klein, *Shaftesbury and the Culture of Politeness: Moral Discourse and Cultural Politics in Early Eighteenth-Century England* (Cambridge, 1994).

[22] Voltaire, *Lettres philosophiques*, Letter 6. See *Fable*, I, p. 343, where Mandeville claims that traders would have no more civility 'than Bulls', had not interest brought them together.

[23] John Dennis, *A Large Account of the Taste in Poetry* (London, 1702), in *The Critical Works of John Dennis*, I, p. 293. See too, for example, the comments about the social composition of London audiences by Henri de Valbourg Misson, *Mémoires et observations faites par un voyage en Angleterre* (The Hague, 1698), pp. 63–4; Harry W. Pedicord, 'The Changing Audience', in Robert D. Hume, ed., *The London Theatrical World, 1660–1800* (Carbondale, Ill., 1980), pp. 239–46; Leo Hughes, *The Drama's Patrons. A Study of the Eighteenth-Century London Audience* (Austin, Tex., 1971), pp. 97ff.

[24] William Law, *The Absolute Unlawfulness of Stage-Entertainment Fully Demonstrated* (1726), p. 9.

[25] In a prologue of 1747, spoken by Garrick when he began his career as manager of Drury Lane, Johnson wrote:

> Ah! let not Censure term our Fate our choice
> The Stage, but echoes back the publick Voice.
> The Drama's Laws the Drama's Patrons give
> For we that live to please, must please to live.

Quoted in James J. Lynch, *Box Pit and Gallery: Stage and Society in Johnson's London* (Berkeley, 1953), p. 204. For the audience as a participant in theatrical performances, see Dane Farnsworth Smith and M.L. Lawhon, *Plays About the Theatre in England, 1737–1800* (Albuquerque, 1953).

display of the states of feeling of 'a gentlemen in disguise'.[26] In *On the Profession of a Player* (1770), Boswell argued that the role-playing that he found so liberating had been refined into an art through the cultivation by professional actors of the capacity for 'double feeling'. When Boswell went to a packed Drury Lane Theatre to see Garrick play Lear, followed by a rendering of George Coleman's popular comedy *Polly Honneycomb*, he testified how, for both actor and spectator, performance had come to be understood as a discontinuous series of heightened moments of affective engagement, directed to spectators prepared by their emotional expectations and theatrical habits to respond in a similar fashion. 'I kept myself at a distance from all acquaintances', Boswell reports, 'and got . . . into a proper frame. Mr Garrick gave the most satisfaction . . . I was fully moved, and shed an abundance of tears. [Then at] the farce . . . I laughed a good deal.'[27]

Encounters in the theatre offered a model for the rehearsal of public expression, where members of the audience could conceptually remove themselves from their companions, and then, in imaginative isolation, experience those states of feeling whose appropriately performed outward signs were evidence of a distinguished sensibility. Shortly before Boswell saw Garrick, the narrator of *Tom Jones* commented upon the virtual homology between acting practices and social perception when he departed from the telling of his hero's story to reflect on the colonisation of public discourse by theatrical metaphors. The 'comparison between the world and the stage', Henry Fielding wrote,

has been carried so far and become so general that some . . . words proper to the theatre and which were at first metaphorically applied to the world are now indiscriminately and literally spoken of both: thus stage and scene are by common use grown as familiar to us, when we speak of life in general, as when we confine ourselves to dramatic performances; and when we mention transactions behind the curtain, St James's is more likely to occur to our thoughts than Drury-Lane.[28]

Mandeville, who was Fielding's primary critical target, adhered to the ancient view of a necessarily hostile relationship between theatricality and moral intimacy, and held that individuals would become divided personalities as the social pressures of civil society required them to adopt the strategic poses of actors in public life. But he denied that public histrionics were necessarily destructive of the modern political body and its social fabric, on the grounds that a genuine sense of duty could hardly be

---

[26] Leo Damrosch, *Fictions of Reality in the Age of Hume and Johnson* (Madison, 1989), pp. 73–9.
[27] James Boswell, *Boswell's London Journal*, ed. Frederick Pottle (New Haven, 1950), p. 27. For other examples of this type of response, see Hughes, *The Drama's Patrons*, pp. 136–7.
[28] Henry Fielding, *Tom Jones* VI, 1.

expected of persons whose professions of intent were always mediated by increasingly artful masks of propriety. Instead, Mandeville celebrated theatrical relations as inherent attributes of political and economic life in advanced societies. The management of appearances lay at the heart of the self-governance of egoists, notably members of the monied and educated classes, who 'conform to all Ceremonies that are fashionable', and who 'make a Shew outwardly of what is not felt within, and counterfeit what is not real'.[29] Mandeville's view was that the envy and emulative propensities characteristic of commercial societies had become the propulsive features of civil life. In nations shaped by commerce, men regarded themselves as consuming and displaying animals, creatures whose enlarged appetites are governed by the need for esteem within an expanding world of marketable goods.

Mandeville's understanding of social action as theatrical rests on the assumption that commercial societies are distinguished by the encouragement given their members to conduct their lives with studied self-misrepresentation. The modern reign of fashion was at once an instrument of and spur to such deceptive practices, depending as it did upon an explosion of mobile wealth and its associated ideology of manners. Social actors, most especially those recently propelled into the higher orbits of society, were seen repeatedly to conceal their intentions, because the exposure of self-regarding purposes would make their achievement impossible. From this perspective, hypocrisy emerged in Mandeville's vision as a defining feature of human conduct in advanced societies, especially in the commercial metropolis, where opportunities for personation were virtually endless.

The awareness of others as beholders complicit in accepting the necessity of representing themselves as their fellows wish to see them engendered in eighteenth-century moral argument a shared perspective on the sources of conduct. In the language that Addison and Shaftesbury did so much to fashion, persons of refinement were both actors and spectators in relation to their own lives, lives that could be reduced to itineraries shaped by the techniques of politeness for the private monitoring of one's public persona. This language expressed the legitimation anxieties of a disenchanted audience seeking to normalise the relations of persons conscious of the gulf between inherited moral standards and contemporary requirements for social success. This is one reason why philosophers like Hume, who employed the same language, often expressed perplexity about identity and moral agency, and so strenuously devoted their intel-

---

[29] Bernard Mandeville, *An Enquiry into the Origins of Honour, and the Usefulness of Christianity in War* [1732] (reprinted London, 1971), pp. 162 and 189.

lectual energies to discover those features of a self possessing undistorted moral sentiments.[30] Mandeville's *Fable* articulated the assumptive background against which this language developed, as Hume acknowledged when he named Mandeville as one of 'the late philosophers in England, who have begun to put the science of man on a new footing'.[31]

Mandeville's significant ideological accomplishment in this regard consisted in providing an argument about the centrality of the passions that effectively set the terms in which the eighteenth-century language of sociability addressed the problem of moral autonomy by considering the prospect that the modern self had acquired the opinions of others as part of its content. After encountering *The Fable*, intellectuals of the next two generations were obliged to confront the claim that reason's essential practical role consists in answering those questions which the passions provide the only motives for asking. If reason's purpose is to prescribe means for the achievement of the ends set by the passions, and if this same reason judges those means only in terms of their instrumental power, then, as Mandeville insisted, any plausible account of morals would have to be undertaken within the context of a hierarchy of desires. An epistemology of sense impressions and ideas, founded upon a notion of an internal theatre of sensations and wedded to a psychology of analytically distinct passions, shaped in the eighteenth century a conception of personality moulded solely through interaction with the objects it encounters. Within this conceptual space, in which the person is conceived of as a strictly arranged ensemble of dispositions and sentiments and the social actor understood as motivated by his schedule of preferences, actions may plausibly be considered in terms of the divided personality's need to establish an 'outward appearance' for the approval of others, while simultaneously attempting to satisfy its hidden impulses. When Hume asserted that 'reason is, and ought only to be the slave of the passions and can never pretend to any other office than to serve and obey them',[32] he distilled this precept into a philosophical principle, and drew from it an account of the development of morals founded upon the intersubjective, histrionic relationships Mandeville had located at the heart of commercial sociability. 'In general', Hume wrote,

the minds of men are mirrors to one another . . . not only because they reflect each other's emotions, but also because those rays of passions, sentiments and opinions may often be reverberated . . . Thus the pleasure which a rich man receives from

---

[30] See especially David Hume, *A Treatise of Human Nature*, ed. L. A. Selby-Bigge (Oxford, 1955), I.iv.7, where Hume gives his famous account of personal identity as nothing but a heap of perceptions. At the same time, at *Treatise* I.i.5, Hume continues to speak of 'self, or that individual person', of whose actions and sentiments each of us is intimately conscious.   [31] *Ibid.*, p. xvii.   [32] *Ibid.*, III.iii.3.

his possessions being thrown upon the beholder, causes a pleasure and esteem; which sentiments again, being perceived and sympathized with, encrease the pleasure of the possessor; and being once more reflected, become a new foundation for pleasure and esteem in the beholder . . . But the possessor has also a secondary satisfaction in riches arising from the love of esteem he acquires by them, and this . . . secondary satisfaction of vanity becomes one of the principal recommendations of riches, and is the chief reason we either desire them for ourselves or esteem them in others.[33]

Beginning his enquiry from the spectator's point of view, and presuming along with Mandeville that the individual's judgements are governed by the compound of his passions, Hume not only views the self as a kind of theatre, 'where several perceptions successively make their appearance, pass, re-pass, glide away',[34] but also argues that the individual's limited sympathies for the welfare of others can both be furthered and fully explained in terms of an essentially self-interested beholder's responses to the postures and demands of his fellows. Hume saw in the theatre and its audience the model of contemporary European culture, an arena where individuals are obliged to interact with others in order to secure public approbation, and in which they may advance their private ambitions only by respecting the rules of civility.[35]

For Adam Smith, similarly, social life of necessity resembles a masquerade,[36] despite the discreditable ends for which social actors ply their talents.[37] For the approbation and disapprobation of oneself which we call conscience is a mirror of feeling – a social product that is an effect of each of us judging others as a spectator while finding others as spectators judging us. We then come to judge our own conduct. In opposition to the 'indulgent and partial spectator' of Mandeville's 'licentious system',[38] Smith argued that 'we examine it as we imagine an impartial spectator would',[39] as an agent who is, 'by definition someone who is not acting'.[40] Smith sought to show that unlike the social actor of Mandevillian provenance who merely seeks applause, the man of genuine self-command could be governed not by the desire for praise but by the standard of praiseworthiness itself. Yet most men, the ambitious or deferential in Smith's account, are moved, although to different outcomes, by the universal desire to dominate the scene where 'the abstract idea of a perfect

[33] *Ibid.*, II.ii.5.   [34] *Ibid.*, I.iv.6.
[35] David Hume, *Enquiry Concerning the Principles of Morals*, ed. L. A. Selby-Bigge (Oxford, 1975), V.ii.180.
[36] Adam Smith, *The Theory of Moral Sentiments*, ed. D. D. Raphael and A. L. Macfie (Oxford, 1976), VII.2.4.10. Hereafter, *TMS*.
[37] Adam Smith, *An Inquiry into the Nature and Causes of the Wealth of Nations*, ed. R. H. Campbell and A. S. Skinner (Oxford, 1976), p. 124.   [38] *TMS*, VII.2.4.
[39] *Ibid.*, III.4.6.
[40] T. D. Campbell, *Adam Smith's Science of Morals* (London, 1971), p. 102.

and happy state' is being staged.[41] This is the theatre where one's naturally formed moral capacities meet the temptations of fortune. Here persons meet not for common action directed by common ends, but to expose themselves to 'the public admiration', either by playing or by competing for roles; and in this public space admiration is bestowed only to the extent that one's role allows for visibility: 'To be observed, to be attended to, to be taken notice of with sympathy, complacency and approbation.'[42] Men require mirrors, for without society, a man 'could no more think of his own character . . . than of the beauty or deformity of his own face', and the only mirror in which he can view his character 'is placed in the countenance and behaviour of those he lives with'.[43] Smith argued that if

[w]e begin . . . to examine our own passions and conduct, and to consider how these must appear to [others] . . . [w]e suppose ourselves the spectators to our own behaviour, and endeavor to imagine what effect it would, in this light, produce upon us. This is the only looking-glass by which we can, in some measure, with the eyes of other people, scrutinize the propriety of our own conduct.[44]

With their Scots colleague Adam Ferguson, who worried that moderns in polite societies 'rate our fellow-citizens by the *figure* they are able to make' and thereby 'lose every sense of distinction arising from merit',[45] Hume and Smith concurred that the abiding problem posed by commercial sociability was to show how individuals could be thought of as moral if they were irreducibly prideful and vain, and that the dynamics of commerce depended upon the encouragement of these disturbing natural propensities. They confronted the possibility that, as Smith put it, 'society may subsist among different men, as among different merchants, from a sense of its utility, without any mutual love or affection; and though no man in it should owe any obligation, or be bound in gratitude to any

[41] *TMS*, I.3.2.3. It is worth noting that Smith devoted much greater attention to self-command in the final 1790 edition of the *TMS*, showing how this attribute was becoming more powerfully threatened as commercial society enlarged.   [42] *Ibid.*, I.3.2.1 and 4.
[43] *Ibid.*, III.1.3.
[44] *Ibid.*, III.1.5. Compare, Anthony Ashley Cooper, third Earl of Shaftesbury, *Characteristics of Men, Manners, Opinions, Times, etc.*, ed. John M. Robertson, 2 vols. (London, 1900), I, p. 257, where the mind is referred to as 'a spectator or auditor of other minds'. See, too, Jonah Barish, *The Anti-Theatrical Prejudice* (Berkeley, 1981), pp. 243–55, and Joseph J. Spengler, 'Smith Versus Hobbes: Economy Versus Polity', in F. R. Glahe, ed., *Adam Smith and The Wealth of Nations* (Boulder, Colo., 1978), p. 43, who points out that the 'invisible hand' was compared by Fontenelle in *Pluralité des mondes* (1686), a work Smith knew, to 'that of an Engineer who, hidden in the pit of a French Theatre, operated "the Machines of the Theatre" in motion on the stage'. For the role of the theatre in Smith's larger project, see Charles Griswold, Jr, *Adam Smith and the Virtues of Enlightenment* (Cambridge, 1998), ch. 1.
[45] Adam Ferguson, *An Essay on the History of Civil Society* (1767), ed. Duncan Forbes (Edinburgh, 1966), p. 352.

other, it may still be upheld by a mercenary exchange of good offices, according to agreed valuation'.[46] They confronted, in other words, the possibility that in commercial societies, where social standing and public identity depended so intensely upon the opinion of others, one's moral autonomy always threatened to be compromised, since practical reason had few defences where beliefs were decisively shaped by economic contingency. As Hume conceded, the Mandevillian figure, 'a sensible knave', after taking the measure of the way in which human affairs are conducted, has grounds to think 'that an act of iniquity or infidelity will make a considerable addition to his fortune without causing any breach in the social union'.[47] And Smith, as Nicholas Phillipson points out elsewhere in this volume, while seeking to defeat Mandeville's challenge, grew increasingly sensitive to the frailty of the judgements of 'the man of self-command' when confronted with the praise and blame of the self-interested actors with whom he must live. A few 'wise men' belonging to a 'select . . . small party' may resist the approbation of 'the great mob of mankind', Smith wrote in the final, 1790, edition of *The Theory of Moral Sentiments*; but most persons seeking their fortune in society 'too frequently abandon the path of virtue', since the applause they naturally seek is so rarely offered for virtues made unfashionable in the world of commercial exchange.[48]

The founders of the new political economy, for whom Mandeville's *Fable* posed the major obstacle in their attempt to articulate the moral legitimacy of commercial society,[49] were thus faced with the argument that character itself was in essence a social artefact rather than the expression of moral virtue, a construct existing in an intersubjective space circumscribed by the demands of others and within which a person's public identity was of necessity devised. Once this challenge was addressed in the idiom of the passions which *The Fable* elevated into a dominant vocabulary amongst post-Protestant (or post-Augustinian) intellectuals, persons could be understood, not as individuals who establish their authenticity by responding to an inner voice, but as players pressured by circumstance and goaded by opportunity to perform so as to elicit that public approbation demanded by their dominant passions. Kant, who praised Mandeville as one of the philosophers who discovered the principles governing the 'constitution of society',[50] drew the appropriate conclusion from these premises when lecturing to his students for the last time. 'The more civilised men become', he observed, 'the more

---

[46] *TMS*, II.2.3.2.   [47] Hume, *Enquiry*, XI. ii. 232.   [48] *TMS*, I.3.3.
[49] Donald Winch, *Riches and Poverty. An Intellectual History of Political Economy in Britain, 1750–1834* (Cambridge, 1996), pp. 57–90.
[50] Immanuel Kant, *The Critique of Practical Reason*, trans. T. K. Abbott (London, 1909), Part 1, Book 1, ch. 1, 'Of the Principles of Pure Practical Reason', p. 129.

they become actors. They want to put on a show and fabricate an illusion of their own persons.'[51] The language of an efflorescent London stage, and of naturalistic theories of acting first crafted in Britain, ideally suited the purposes of intellectuals intent on comprehending what they understood to be a culturally transformed society, one in which personation was required for public identity. And until the eighteenth-century vocabulary of the passions was succeeded by a new, Romantic language of the emotions – a language in which the self could be conceived as existing apart from its enacted relationships, and persons could understand themselves as moved by integrated patterns of feeling which shape a unique identity – the theatrical plasticity of the self that helped to shape eighteenth-century reflections on commercial modernity would retain its central place on the horizon of social understanding.

[51] Immanuel Kant, *Anthropology from a Pragmatic Point of View*, trans. Mary J. Gregor (The Hague, 1974), pp. 14–15. Translation amended.

2 'That noble disquiet': meanings of liberty in the discourse of the North

Dario Castiglione

I

In spite of recurrent criticism, Isaiah Berlin's famous distinction between two concepts of liberty maintains its grip on the imagination of Anglo-American political historians and philosophers.[1] Perhaps it does indeed capture a genuine difference between 'two . . . families of conception of political freedom abroad in our civilisation'.[2] Yet there is more to liberty than meets the conceptual eye.

Berlin admitted that negative and positive liberty 'start at no great logical distance from each other', though they address two slightly different questions: 'who is master?' and 'over what am I master?' When taken together, answers to these questions give content to any perception of what it means to be free. In more recent phases of European history, however, the negative and positive conceptions were progressively subject to 'fission' by means of a separation of 'higher' and 'lower' conceptions of the self which resulted in positive liberty becoming identified with something different: with authority and with the moral conditions for liberty itself.[3] Hence the recurrent temptation to those writers whom Berlin takes to be metaphysically and holistically inclined to sacrifice the 'real' for the 'ideal' self.[4]

Scottish intellectual history during the eighteenth century possesses various advantages in any attempt to locate the moment when Berlin's

I am grateful for comments on an earlier draft by the editors, the participants at the Sussex colloquium, Luisa Pesante, and Marco Geuna. My greatest debt is owed to Donald Winch for his help in preparing the final version.

[1] I. Berlin, 'Two Concepts of Liberty', in *Four Essays on Liberty* (Oxford, 1969).
[2] C. Taylor, 'What's Wrong with Negative Liberty', in A. Ryan, ed., *The Idea of Freedom* (Oxford, 1979), p. 175.
[3] See Berlin's introduction to *Four Essays*, pp. xliii–xlv. The importance of this 'fission', or *historical* watershed, has often been overlooked by those who have taken issue with Berlin's distinction on *conceptual* grounds.
[4] Notice Berlin's use of the following statement by Constant as his epigraph to the introduction to *Four Essays*: 'L'on immole à l'être abstrait les êtres réels: et l'on offre au peuple en masse l'holocauste du peuple en détail.'

two questions began to separate – or, as will be contended here, they do
not entirely do so. The period has been identified as one such moment,
with recent political historiography being divided over whether a jurisprudential or a republican paradigm can best capture the intellectual
context of the Scottish science of society and politics, with the former
emphasising negative, and the latter positive understandings of liberty.[5]
Less controversially, there is widespread recognition that the Scots were
not united on this issue for reasons connected with their divergent understandings of the import of commercial society. What better place, then, to
survey the bifurcation of negative and positive conceptions of liberty?

The Scottish context is made more relevant by the influence that the
Scots are believed to have exercised on the work of Benjamin Constant,
whose distinction between the liberty of the ancients and moderns was
the model for Berlin's own.[6] The title of this essay, 'That noble disquiet'
(cette noble inquiétude), is borrowed from the speech in which Constant
made that distinction. It may come as a surprise that Constant referred to
political liberty as one of the foundations without which 'it would be a
folly like that of a man who, because he only lives on the first floor, does
not care if the house itself is built on sand'.[7] Stephen Holmes has maintained that the concluding remarks of the speech delivered in 1819 were
superimposed on an earlier text, conceived in the aftermath of the Terror,
and therefore more sanguine in its praise of individual liberty to the
exclusion of political involvement. But he has also argued that, though
largely motivated by changes in political circumstances, the superimposi-
tion does not make the discourse incoherent.[8] In the modernised form of
representative government, the exercise of political liberty remained
indispensable as an instrumental guarantee for the more individualistic

[5] For an interpretation of the Scottish contribution to the modern idea of liberty along
jurisprudential lines, cf. above all D. Forbes, 'Sceptical Whiggism, Commerce, and
Liberty', in A. S. Skinner and T. Wilson, eds., *Essays on Adam Smith* (Oxford, 1976); and
K. Haakonssen, *Natural Law and Moral Philosophy. From Grotius to the Scottish
Enlightenment* (Cambridge, 1981). David Wootton suggests that John Pocock's discussion
of the civic humanist tradition is mainly based on a positive interpretation of liberty:
'Introduction: The Republican Tradition: From Commonwealth to Common Sense', in
D. Wootton, ed., *Republicanism, Liberty, and Commercial Society, 1649–1776* (Stanford,
1994), pp. 17–18. For an insightful synthesis of the history of the seventeenth- and eighteenth-century division of positive and negative conceptions, cf. M. M. Goldsmith,
'Liberty, Virtue and the Rule of Law, 1689–1770', in Wootton, ed., *Republicanism, Liberty*,
pp. 197–232.
[6] For a discussion of both Constant's distinction and the way in which it has superficially
been assimilated to Berlin's positive and negative, see S. Holmes, *Benjamin Constant and
the Making of Modern Liberalism* (New Haven, 1984). He also remarks on the 'surprise'
(p. 39) that some of Constant's remarks on political liberty may cause.
[7] B. Constant, *The Liberty of the Ancients Compared with that of the Moderns* in *Political
Writings*, ed. B. Fontana (Cambridge, 1988), p. 326.
[8] Holmes, *Benjamin Constant*, chs. 1 and 2 *passim*.

liberty of the moderns.[9] Constant's case goes beyond this, however, by maintaining that human beings are not motivated by their own happiness alone (*le bonheur*). There is something that spurs them to higher things, and this noble disquiet is self-development (*perfectionnement*), a form of intellectual and moral progress. In a passage of an unpublished paper on 'perfectibilité' Constant sketched the march of the human mind (*l'esprit humain*) towards the achievement of individual liberty. It described this as both the secret spring and the actualisation of the manifold material and moral progress taking place in those countries where liberty was given the opportunity to thrive.[10] But political liberty provided the setting in which individual liberty can be nourished. It did so by engaging citizens in the care of their own interests, by enlarging their spirit and ennobling their thinking, and by making them intellectually equal. All this made 'political liberty the most powerful, the most effective means of self-development'.[11]

Faced with such warmth in defence of political liberty in the modern context, Constant's position clearly cannot be described reductively as a purely instrumental vindication. Political liberty is 'the most effective *means* of self-development' because it is an important *form of expression* of a fundamental human drive (*cette noble inquiétude*) towards self-improvement.[12] The dual character of this participatory conception of freedom is implicitly acknowledged by Berlin when he remarks that, contrary to what he has been *held to believe*, he is in no doubt that positive liberty and democratic self-government are 'valid universal goals' and 'needs'.[13] The reason why Berlin and Constant have been held to favour negative or modern liberty respectively is that the thrust of their arguments was to remind people of the fundamental meaning of liberty *at the time* they were writing.

The admission that historical contingencies drive our judgement of different conceptions of liberty has not been accorded sufficient attention by those opposed to Berlin's simple distinction, which has often been criticised for being insufficiently inclusive or wrong. Recognition of the historicity of the attribution of value suggests a third kind of criticism. If the value historically attached to liberty is independent of any purely conceptual understanding, the clarification we obtain from conceptual distinc-

---

[9] On the 'modernisation' of political liberty in Constant, see L. Jaume, *L'Individu effacé. Ou le paradoxe du libéralisme français* (Paris, 1997), pp. 82–6. On instrumental conceptions of republican liberty, cf. Q. Skinner, *Liberty Before Liberalism* (Cambridge, 1998), and P. Pettit, *Republicanism. A Theory of Freedom and Government* (Oxford, 1997), chs. 1 and 2.

[10] B. Constant, 'Fragments d'un essai sur la perfectibilité de l'espèce humaine', in *Ecrits littéraires*, ed. P. Delbouille, 3 vols. (Tübingen, 1800–13), III, 1, p. 441.

[11] Constant, *The Liberty of the Ancients*, p. 327.   [12] Emphasis supplied.

[13] Berlin, *Four Essays*, pp. xlvi–xlvii.

tions may be at the expense of the complexities of historical debate. These need to be recognised for what they are: complexities. Scottish authors often made use of a linguistic expression that neatly conveys the point: they spoke of 'systems of liberty', by which they meant something more than the simple idea (concept or idealisation) of liberty itself. 'System' stands for the way in which liberty becomes institutionalised in political life and thereby made part of people's ideas, opinions, and everyday experience. Returning, then, to my title, 'that noble disquiet' is not meant to suggest that this is the conceptual kernel of the Scottish idea of liberty; rather that, in constructing their various systems of liberty, the Scots, like other eighteenth-century authors, had to grapple with the whole experience underlying the modern demand for liberty.

II

My title can also be read in a different light, revealing its paronomastic intention.[14] This shifts the argument from the conceptual to the historiographic context. The success of recent scholarship in challenging proleptic and ideological versions of the history of political thought from the seventeenth century onwards has created its own historiographic problems for those interested in the Scottish Enlightenment. Having re-established the historical traditions that were the actual intellectual diet of Scottish authors, the task of interpreting the rich Scottish vein to be found in later British political thinking becomes more problematic. *That Noble Science of Politics* was partly conceived as a contribution to this problem. The review of nineteenth-century thinking on 'things political' in that book begins with those who were most directly under the influence of what Walter Bagehot called the 'system of Edinburgh', 'the general, diversified, omnipresent information of the North' which, by virtue of its 'speculative' and 'dubious' nature, tended 'to cultivate habits of independent thought and original discussion'.[15] John Burrow and Donald Winch have separately explored the complexities of the Scottish inheritance in several of their works, aiming to establish a balance between attention to the vocabulary and idioms in which the Scots formulated their own theories, and sensibility to the way in which these theories later reverberated in increasingly diversified intellectual contexts, serving different purposes in the process.

The idea of liberty at the core of the emerging liberal discourse seems to require a similar sensitivity towards linguistic embeddedness and the

---

[14] The object of the paronomastic reference is, of course, S. Collini, J. W. Burrow, and D. Winch, *That Noble Science of Politics: A Study in Nineteenth-Century Intellectual History* (Cambridge, 1983). [15] *Ibid.*, p. 23.

processes of transformation. The resonance of these Scottish ideas of liberty rests partly on their capacity to articulate a complex relationship between experience and its conceptualisation, partly on their encapsulation of a repertoire of understandings through which it is possible to make sense of phenomena that exceed the narrow confines of historical contingency.

But there is another historiographic point involved in the reconstruction of the system(s) of liberty of the North. There is a plurality of visions among the Scots which goes back to the Act of Union and to the different perceptions of whether, and if so what kind of, liberty was lost at that historic moment. As we have learnt from recent scholarship, the controlling intellectual contexts of Scottish moral and political writings were the only partly overlapping languages of civic humanism and natural jurisprudence. Separate explorations of these contexts have done much to illuminate the way in which the Scottish moralists contributed, from a distinctive position, to cosmopolitan debates on commerce and liberty, government, justice, and the science of legislators, as well as to the more parochial disputes of British politics.

From a more strictly *political* perspective, the Scottish moralists represented, as John Pocock has maintained, the abandonment of the 'search for liberty in self-sufficiency in favour of one for liberty in increasing sociability and exchange'. Scottish theories gave to the 'mobilization of commerce and politeness in support of Whiggism and the union . . . a state of imaginative completeness', though they did so without ceasing to be aware of the dangers of civilisation.[16] From a slightly different perspective, the Scottish literati's appreciation of the effects of commerce on liberty also gained from the *scientific* or detached outlook of natural jurisprudence – filtered through Montesquieu's historical lesson – which added to the 'completeness' of their systematic vision and kept their assessment of the 'dangers' of civilisation and modern liberty within a 'realistic' framework. This is what gives, in Duncan Forbes's influential formulation, the 'scientific' (or in some cases 'sceptical') gloss to Scottish Whiggism.[17]

Nonetheless, keeping the argumentative resources of the two languages separate in their formulation but convergent in their intentions may not be sufficient to present a more unified picture of Scottish responses: first, because authors like Hume and Smith, thanks to the originality of their theories, succeeded in blending the underlying preoccupations of the two languages, keeping them under strict philosophical control – something

---

[16] J. G. A. Pocock, 'The Varieties of Whiggism from Restoration to Reform', in *Virtue, Commerce and History* (Cambridge, 1985), p. 253.
[17] See Forbes, 'Sceptical Whiggism', *passim*.

which other authors were less able to achieve; second, because the sensibility of the Scots to a kind of dual audience they had partially internalised does not overcome the opposition between an emerging justiciary meaning of liberty and a classical republican understanding of it.

A fault-line identified by ancient and modern understandings of liberty suggests a divided legacy: one stream of the Scottish Enlightenment going underground, only to re-emerge in the greatly transformed guise of discourses on social, as opposed to political, freedom, while the other joined forces with a more individualistic and utilitarian vision that would appear to triumph during the nineteenth century. This implies two distinct 'systems' of the North, offering two different perspectives on Berlin's bifurcation. However, if one takes the 'discourse' – a term of art, here preferred to 'system' – of the North in the broader educational sense meant by Bagehot, there may be scope for a more unified legacy. This may be a more compelling interpretation if an analysis of Scottish debate reveals that the fault-line between ancient and modern, or positive and negative, conceptions has been overdrawn.

III

There is no doubt, as Forbes and others have amply illustrated, that a fundamental insight of Hume and the Scottish moralists at large was to develop the critique of the classical republican idea of liberty, already outlined by Hobbes, Montesquieu, and the natural lawyers, into a more precise characterisation of liberty as security of the individual under the rule of law in modern commercial societies.[18] This characterisation implied a double operation. On the one hand, it involved identifying the political and legal conditions under which individuals could feel secure in their rights and properties, and over their own lives. These conditions mainly consisted in *regularity* of the law and the operations of government. Such regularity was seen as the end-product of the progress of civilisation, the ability to grasp the idea of a general rule being considered a late development in the history of man and presupposing a sophisticated level of understanding.[19]

On the other hand, the association of liberty and security with regular government and the rule of law put into question the assumption for so long made by republican authors that political liberty consisted in that double chain that linked the freedom of the citizens to that of the state: citizens' freedom to order their own affairs clearly depending on the

---

[18] D. Forbes, *Hume's Philosophical Politics* (Cambridge, 1979), p. 102; cf. also C. J. Berry, *Social Theory of the Scottish Enlightenment* (Edinburgh, 1997), pp. 128–9.
[19] Forbes, *Hume*, p. 102.

freedom of the state from external domination, and on their living under a free (i.e. republican) form of government.[20] Obviously, the latter link was controversial, and the one most resisted by those authors who emphasised the dependence of liberty on regularity and predictability.

But the justiciary and non-republican character of this emerging idea of liberty needs qualification. Hobbes had offered a powerful argument against the republican idea by suggesting that whenever the law demands obedience citizens are not at liberty, a fact that was true of all political regimes.[21] This argument carried philosophical implications that the Scots did not find agreeable to their own views of justice and political society. The treatment of law and liberty as opposites was unacceptable. As Hutcheson remarked, following here an established line of thinking in natural jurisprudence, 'natural liberty' only implies freedom from 'human power', not from laws and obligations.[22] The same applies to civil liberty: 'we should never look upon laws as subversive of liberty; but that its sole enemy is the capricious humours and will or command of men in power'.[23] Laws protect against the abuse of force. By willingly relying on them citizens do not cease to be free. The 'strictest polity', with the most 'exact regulations of manners, and a constant discipline', can still harbour great freedom in its midst.[24]

Hutcheson's rejection of the Hobbesian view of law did not jeopardise the possibility of a non-republican reading of liberty. This rested on equating natural and civil law, both of which acted as a framework for freedom of action, regardless of the constitutional setting in which the state of civil liberty first arose. As Hutcheson noted, Greeks and Romans 'had another precise meaning to the *populus liber*, denoting by that term only *Democracies*' or some form of popular rule.[25] The 'modern plans of law' were less concerned with the education and discipline of the citizens, leaving them freer to act according to their natural liberty.[26] In this respect, the liberty of the moderns and that of the ancients differed not only in form, but also in extent, since more was left to the judgement of private individuals.

There was, however, another problem in the Hobbesian lesson on liberty that was not entirely solved by Hutcheson's version of it. This was the reconciliation of the idea of natural liberty – which justified freedom of action by appeal to natural self-sufficiency and the no-harm principle –

[20] For a classical statement see Machiavelli, *Discorsi sopra la prima deca di Tito Livio* (Milan, 1984).

[21] T. Hobbes, *Leviathan*, ed. R. Tuck (Cambridge, 1996), pp. 145–9, especially p. 149.

[22] F. Hutcheson, *A Short Introduction to Moral Philosophy* [1747] (Hildesheim, Olms reprint, 1969), p. 139.   [23] *Ibid.*, p. 307.

[24] F. Hutcheson, *System of Moral Philosophy* [1755], 2 vols. (Hildesheim, Olms reprint, 1969), II, p. 282.   [25] *Ibid.*, I, p. 282.   [26] *Ibid.*, II, p. 294.

with the role played by sociability in the Scots' own view of the progress of civil society. Hutcheson himself considered the necessity of social life to be derived from the law of nature, both because he viewed sociability as an inherent quality of the human species and because human survival and happiness greatly depended on it. It followed that particular attention needed to be paid to the cultivation of the social virtues as a condition of liberty.[27] But his understanding of sociability was mainly teleological, while other Scots, taking their cue from Montesquieu, were more interested in the way in which the historicity of social relationships transformed the moral and political environment.

As Richard Sher has recently argued, Montesquieu, in book 18 of *De l'esprit des lois*, offered a particular version of a more primitive form of liberty, associating this with savage and barbarian societies, where people enjoy 'great liberty' because their nomadic style of life makes them less willing to accept the authority and interference of leaders.[28] Primitive liberty in this sense bears some relation to natural liberty as understood by the natural lawyers, since in both cases liberty depends on personal independence (full autonomy from others) and absence of governance. But in the state of primitive liberty this absence is the product of the inability of savages and barbarians to endure authority. It is neither required by their mode of subsistence, nor were they capable of understanding its utility. These points were taken up by Adam Ferguson, who considered savages to be incapable of accepting the imposition of either tasks or superiors; they were seduced by a kind of life 'where no rules of behaviour are prescribed, but the simple dictates of the heart'.[29]

In his *Lectures on Jurisprudence*, Smith further developed the theme. In describing the early origins of government he suggested that hunter societies have 'no regular government', mainly because they are small-scale societies, comprising only a limited number of independent families with no significant property. Justice is administered by *ad hoc* agreements and compromises, occasionally involving the ostracism of those members who have committed specific crimes and whose behaviour threatens the peace of the community.[30] This way of living together, according to

---

[27] *Ibid.*, I, pp. 287–92.

[28] R. B. Sher, 'From Troglodytes to Americans: Montesquieu and the Scottish Enlightenment on Liberty, Virtue, and Commerce', in Wootton, *Republicanism, Liberty*, p. 375; and Montesquieu, *De l'esprit des lois*, in *Œuvres complètes*, ed. A. Masson, 3 vols. (Paris, 1950–55), 18, xv, vol. I, p. 310.

[29] A. Ferguson, *An Essay on the History of Civil Society*, ed. D. Forbes (Edinburgh, 1966), p. 96; and *Principles of Moral and Political Science* [1792], 2 vols. (Hildesheim, reprint, 1975), II, pp. 460–1. Cf. also J. Millar, *The Origin of the Distinction of Ranks* (Edinburgh, 1806), pp. 240–1.

[30] A. Smith, *Lectures on Jurisprudence*, ed. R. Meek, D. Raphael, and P. Stein (Oxford, 1978) [hereafter, *LJ*], pp. 404, 207.

Smith, amounted more or less to living 'according to the laws of nature', and therefore to a state of 'natural liberty'.[31] The proper beginnings of government, or so Smith maintained, can only be seen in societies of shepherds, where political authority became 'absolutely necessary' once property had been established.[32] Although Smith suggested that during this second stage of development the early forms of government must have been fundamentally democratic, he considered this to be unpropitious soil for liberty. The uncouth liberty of hunters was progressively eroded by the 'great opportunity of authority and influence' that the community now had over individuals, ostracism from a settled society leaving them in a more perilous condition. Economic differentiations in societies in which there was property but no luxury led to a more direct form of dependence of the poor upon the rich, with political and civil dominion reflecting the natural forms of superiority. Chieftains in such societies were like 'petty princes', making this stage similar to what occurred later under feudal power.[33]

For Smith, then, liberty in its proper civil sense was the historical product of two parallel developments that took place during the succeeding two stages of society, characterised by the diffusion of agriculture first, and trade and manufacturing later. The two processes consisted of the creation of more regular systems of justice and governance, something that had already begun in the society of shepherds with the establishment of property; and in the erosion of the system of personal dependence associated with commerce.[34] The early progress of liberty was concomitant with the establishment of republican governments in those ancient nations where physical and historical conditions made it possible for them both to cultivate the land and to make progress in a number of branches of trade and manufacture.[35] The liberty thereby created, as Hume wryly reminded 'passionate admirers of the ancients', was civil and political, though not 'domestic'.[36]

Smith's conjectural account of the early establishment of liberty suggests that he, like Hume, did not consider regularity and security as properties exclusive to modern societies. In contrast with the shepherd and feudal stages of society, which oscillated between impatience with authority and servile types of dependence, the ancients had succeeded in creating liberty in the form of regularity. It should come as no surprise,

[31] *LJ*, p. 404.   [32] *Ibid.*, pp. 208, 404.   [33] *Ibid.*, pp. 405, 202, 211.
[34] On how equality is conducive to civil liberty cf. also D. Hume, *Essays: Moral, Political and Literary*, ed. E. Miller (Indianapolis, 1987), p. 401.   [35] *LJ*, pp. 408–9.
[36] Hume, *Essays*, p. 383; cf. also Millar, *Origin*, p. 282. The target here is the position advanced by Andrew Fletcher at the turn of the century, which, though not supportive of slavery in itself, advocated family servitude to combat diffuse social dependence. See A. Fletcher, *Political Works*, ed. J. Robertson (Cambridge, 1997), pp. 56–81.

therefore, that Ferguson and Millar, who were more sensitive to the allures of ancient liberty, also embraced the idea of liberty as security and regularity. Ferguson did so repeatedly in *An Essay on the History of Civil Society*, though, as we shall see, he often qualified it by reference to the need for political vigilance.[37] But in both the *Principles of Moral and Political Science* and in a more polemical piece of writing against Price on the American crisis, Ferguson took a more decided view of the importance of liberty as security by concluding that 'the Liberty of every class and order is not proportioned to the power they enjoy, but to the security they have for the preservation of their rights'.[38] In Millar's case we have the testimony of John Craig that he valued 'personal freedom' above its political and civil aspects.[39] This would seem to be confirmed by his lectures on government, and is also consistent with the political positions of his early writings before the events following 1776 and during the 1790s changed the political scene for good.[40]

So the Scottish moralists agreed that the liberty that did not depend on security and regularity was that of savages and barbarians; it was not the ancient liberty of the classical civilisation of Greece and Rome. The traditional association between the liberty of the citizens, in the limited sense of security in their own rights, and the republican form of government partly rested on a rejection of the unsettling effects that the will and prerogatives of the monarch had upon the operations of the law and the political constitution. Republics were a government of laws and not men because they were successful in checking what Hutcheson and others described as the 'rapacious' and 'capricious' forms that the will of those in power could take. Ancient monarchies, on the other hand, had no such inbuilt defences against tyranny.[41] Before the diffusion of the civilising effects of commerce and manufacturing the best that could be said of monarchs, as Hume remarked of the reign of Elizabeth, was that they exercised a measure of self-denial in '[entering] into every part of the administration; [so] that the instances of a high exerted prerogative were not so frequent'.[42] This self-restraint, however, was not enough to make

---

[37] Ferguson, *Essay*, pp. 156, 261, and 263.
[38] Ferguson, *Principles*, II, pp. 461 and 465; and *Remarks on a Pamphlet lately published by Dr Price* (London, 1776), pp. 4–13; cf. Sher, 'From Troglodytes', pp. 399–401; and Berry, *Social Theory*, p. 108.
[39] J. Craig, 'Account of the Life and Writings of John Millar', prefixed to Millar, *Origin*, p. cxi.
[40] On the lectures on government, see Haakonssen, *Natural Law*, pp. 164–5. For a discussion of two phases in Millar's thought, see M. Ignatieff, 'John Millar and Individualism', in I. Hont and M. Ignatieff, eds., *Wealth and Virtue* (Cambridge, 1983), pp. 329–32; see also Millar, *Origin*, book VI, section iv.   [41] Hutcheson, *System*, II, p. 282.
[42] D. Hume, *The History of England*, 6 vols. (Indianapolis, 1983), VI, p. 430; cf. Forbes, *Hume*, p. 160.

monarchies conducive to liberty, which was therefore justly regarded as the prerogative of republics.[43]

The trouble with ancient liberty, as Smith put it, was that it was lost.[44] The inevitable corruption of both 'defensive' and 'conquering' republics was the reason for the loss. Smith gave a fairly traditional account of the decadence and dissolution of the ancient republics, whose fall he explained as the result of 'improvements in mechanic arts, commerce, and the arts of war'.[45] The long series of changes that led from imperial Rome to the introduction of the feudal system consisted in undoing the conditions of broad social and political equality that, in the passage from shepherd to agrarian and commercial societies, had first made it possible to keep the arbitrary power of rulers in check. With the advent of feudal government 'the democraticall part of the constitution was now altogether abolished', allowing kings and barons to take full control of public affairs.[46] Throughout the process, the dependence of the poor on the rich had increased: 'in those disorderly times, every great landlord was a sort of petty prince. His tenants were his subjects. He was their judge, and in some respects their legislator in peace, and their leader in war.'[47] Similar accounts of feudal subordination, where the nobles 'held the people in servitude', 'because they [the people] entirely depended upon him [the baron] for subsistence', were offered in more sketchy form by Ferguson and Millar.[48] The reason for this increased subordination lay in what Smith saw as a universal maxim, namely that a proximate power is more oppressive than a distant one. The maxim applied both to shepherd societies and to the government of allodial and feudal lords, but an earlier formulation can be found in Hume's comparison between civil and domestic subordination:

As much as submission to a petty prince, whose dominions extend not beyond a single city, is more grievous than obedience to a great monarch; so much is domestic slavery more cruel and oppressive than any civil subjection whatsoever. The more the master is removed from us in place and rank, the greater liberty we enjoy; the less are our actions inspected and controlled; and the fainter that cruel comparison becomes between our own subjection, and the freedom, and even dominion of another.[49]

Besides being an explanation for the burdensome power of petty princes, the psychological components of Hume's argument offered one of the

---

[43] Cf. Hume, *Essays*, pp. 115–17 on the lack of security in early monarchical forms of government; and pp. 124–5 on republican superiority over monarchies.   [44] *LJ*, pp. 410–11.
[45] *Ibid.*, p. 413.   [46] *Ibid.*, pp. 258, 418.
[47] A. Smith, *An Inquiry into the Nature and Causes of the Wealth of Nations*, ed. R. Campbell and A. S. Skinner, 2 vols. (Oxford, 1976) [hereafter, *WN*], vol, p. 383.
[48] Ferguson, *Essay*, p. 131; and Millar, *Origin*, pp. 174–5 at 175.   [49] Hume, *Essays*, p. 383.

explanatory keys to the history of how liberty was regained. Smith was once again the author who provided the most sophisticated account of this part of the story. From a certain perspective, feudalism itself could be considered as a first step towards liberty: 'the introduction of feudal law, so far from extending, may be regarded as an attempt to moderate the authority of the great allodial lords'.[50] This argument followed Montesquieu on the ambiguous legacy of feudal laws 'which did infinite good and ill . . . which produced rule with an inclination to anarchy and anarchy with a tendency to order and harmony'.[51] As Millar put it towards the end of his reflections on the natural progress of government in rude societies, the partially positive influence of feudal law and government was due to the way in which they reflected a multiplicity of interests that in partly balancing one another became 'especially useful for the defence and security of the people'.[52] By bringing the allodial lords under a single structure of government, the feudal system introduced an elementary form of regulation and restraint upon their power. Henceforth baronial power found itself in a continuous struggle with the crown and the clergy, both of which favoured a partial emancipation of the people from their more immediate, and therefore more oppressive, masters.[53]

The paradoxical conclusion to which the Scottish moralists came in their analysis of the restoration of liberty was that this partly depended on an increase in the absolute power of centralised institutions, particularly those of the crown. While in ancient times monarchical power was always a threat to liberty, in the changed conditions of feudal and post-feudal society it assisted in the restoration of liberty in large polities. Yet it was still not enough to produce an entire system of liberty ensuring security in the possession of individual rights. For liberty to prevail, Smith maintained, it was necessary for the 'power of the nobles . . . [to have] been brought to ruin.'[54] This was the result of the 'silent and insensible' revolution associated with commerce which made the tenants independent and placed the power of the nobility on a level with that of the gentry, the burghers, or the commercial interest. In this fashion 'a regular government was established in the country as well as in the city, nobody having sufficient power to disturb its operations in the one any more than in the other'.[55] There were other, more direct, ways in which the more extensive commerce of the modern world had been instrumental in favouring

---

[50] *WN*, I, p. 417.
[51] Montesquieu, *Esprit*, 30, i, vol. II, p. 299. The translation is from *The Spirit of the Laws*, eds. A. M. Cohler, B. C. Miller, and H. S. Stone (Cambridge, 1989), p. 619.
[52] Millar, *Origin*, p. 212.
[53] *LJ*, pp. 454, 259, and 188; cf. also Montesquieu, *Esprit*, vol. I, pp. 180–1.   [54] *LJ*, p. 264.
[55] *WN*, I, pp. 418–21.

liberty via order and good government.[56] The creation of an extensive web of private interests, expectations, and habits imposed a salutary discipline on governments, the regularity of whose acts was therefore both the product and one of the preconditions for success in large and opulent societies.[57]

What precisely the Scots regarded as modern about modern liberty, and why it was superior to ancient versions, should now be apparent. The preconditions for ancient liberty were difficult to reproduce in the modern context. Equality, virtue, the capacity to endure hardship, military prowess, and the leisure to participate in public affairs, had all been undermined by commerce, with its far-reaching effects on the manners, life styles, and aspirations of the bulk of the population. Those same preconditions were further weakened by other changes in modern polities: the increase in the size and complexity of political communities as well as the disappearance of slavery. Commerce also proved more successful in imposing discipline on government because it did so more gently and effectively. It had levelled the social and political power of the nobility and imposed constraints on political power at large, making it less likely that, even when used absolutely, this could be done arbitrarily. Hume observed that during the last two hundred years there had been no prince in Europe whose actions could be regarded as tyrannical as those of many Roman emperors.[58]

This brings in a further difference between ancient and modern liberty. Monarchical power had been instrumental in the creation of liberty by mitigating the proximate and hence more oppressive domination of the nobility. It was also possible to maintain, as Hume insistently did, that in modern civilised conditions 'monarchies were a government of Laws, not of Men'. They had been 'found susceptible of order, method, and constancy, to a surprizing degree', with beneficial effect upon the security of property, on people's industriousness, and on the arts.[59] Consideration of forms of government had thus become largely irrelevant. Liberty was more dependent on the particular institutions and attitudes that guaranteed regularity of law and less on the underlying principles of government. Indeed, as Hume argued, the first principle of each and every form of government was one and the same: opinion.[60] In the new conditions of civilised government, popular rule was, if anything, less regular and

---

[56] *Ibid.*, I, p. 412.
[57] Cf. Donald Winch, *Adam Smith's Politics. An Essay in Historiographic Revision* (Cambridge, 1978), ch. 4.   [58] Hume, *Essays*, p. 94.
[59] *Ibid.* For a republican Whig statement of the effects of liberty, see J. Trenchard and T. Gordon, *Cato's Letters: or Essays on Liberty, Civil and Religious, and Important other Subjects*, ed. R. Hamowy, 2 vols. (Indianapolis, 1995), I, pp. 420–93.
[60] Hume, 'Of the First Principles of Government', in *Essays*.

orderly than under modern monarchies, which were largely based on the stabilising influence of the opinion of interest entertained by men of middle rank – those who were more likely to sustain liberty.

In reflecting on the science of politics Dugald Stewart implicitly brought the whole Scottish discourse on liberty as security to a unity.[61] Political economy, he argued, was concerned with the *tendency* of laws and government, while the theory of government dealt with their *origin*. He regarded these as separate issues, and considered the former to be superior to the latter, since it directly concerned the happiness of people. The consequence for political liberty was

> *not* that the share of political power vested in the people is of trifling moment, but that its importance to their happiness depends on the protection and support it provides for their civil rights. *Happiness* is, in truth, the only object of legislation which is of *intrinsic* value; and what is called *Political Liberty*, is only one of the means of obtaining this end.[62]

IV

So much for the Scottish contribution to the idea of liberty as security and regularity. In the British context this helped to undermine the prejudices of vulgar Whigs, who failed, as Duncan Forbes remarked, to see the difference between civil and political liberty and were unmoved by the progress of civilised monarchies.[63] Nonetheless, the Scots portrayed the difference between ancient and modern ideas as one of degree rather than kind. Their fundamental innovation was to explain what had taken the place of the politics of personal and constitutional virtue in making liberty secure. But the connection between the civil and political dimensions was not entirely lost. In the paragraph following the one just quoted, Stewart admitted that 'it is not less evident, that the only effectual and permanent bulwark against the encroachments of tyranny, is to be found in the political privileges which the Constitution secures to the governed'.[64] Even though he insisted that such privileges were to be looked at as *means* to ensure both civil liberty and people's happiness, the admission is of some consequence. It suggests that liberty as security can be understood in two distinct senses: one that makes it dependent on the regularity of politics and law, while the other emphasises the need for safeguards against the abuse and arbitrary exercise of power.

Montesquieu had approached 'political liberty' from both of these

---

[61] D. Stewart, *Lectures on Political Economy*, in *The Collected Works*, 11 vols. (Edinburgh, 1854–60), VIII, pp. 21–4. Stewart refers to a similar distinction in Hume's essay 'Of the Origin of Government'. Cf. also *LJ*, p. 401.   [62] Stewart, *Lectures*, p. 23.
[63] Forbes, *Hume*, pp. 142–50.   [64] Stewart, *Lectures*, p. 23.

perspectives, one being constitutional in his enlarged sense of the term, the other being treated more from the citizen's point of view. The latter consisted in the security the citizen has when enjoying his rights, where this largely depends on customs and those prohibitions and punishments which reveal the character of the ruler.[65] Security as safeguard is more evident in relation to the constitution, where it derives from the distribution and equipoise of the law-making powers. Political liberty in this case is a relational concept describing a state of relative domination between different groups in society.[66] Political liberty exists where power checks power.[67] Hence Montesquieu's insistence that the security of citizens depends on the separation and division of powers, creating a *gouvernement modéré*. Notice, however, that moderation had to be translated into an effective check on power. The separation of powers needed to be buttressed by the social differentiation of authority, with different functions being performed by particular social groups and by those occupying roles within institutions that represented real interests. This was a theory of mixed government operating as another instance of the politics of checks and balances. Montesquieu's other prescriptions aimed, on the one hand, to strengthen the executive to counter the increasing power of the legislative; and, on the other, to ensure that the legislative branch of government reflected the common good. This, he maintained, was possible by reworking the republican theory of government that gave legislative power to the people as a whole by introducing the principle of representation. The advantage of placing legislative power in the hands of the representatives was not so much to involve the people in the higher functions of government, but to ensure that affairs of state were deliberated upon by a more select assembly, reflecting, however, concrete interests.

Although Montesquieu used the English case as the main illustration for his discussion of the way in which moderate governments harbour political liberty, his misgivings on the sustainability of the experiment show that he considered it to be anomalous. The English experience contrasted with his emphasis on the role of the intermediate powers – which he still conceived in largely feudal terms – in moderating the action of government. Due to a number of circumstances and to the effect of the laws themselves on the manners and customs of the people, in Britain the function of moderation rested on an industrious middle class with strong commercial interests.[68] This had enhanced the power of the legislature, dangerously tilting the constitution towards a democratic form that was often on the brink of corruption.[69]

---

[65] *Esprit*, 12, ii, vol. I, p. 202.   [66] 'Fragments', in *ibid.*, vol. II, p. 471.   [67] *Ibid.*, 12, iv.
[68] *Ibid.*, 19, 27.   [69] *Ibid.*, 5, ix.

Hume famously agreed with this interpretation, which he described as 'nouvelle et frappante'.[70] Against Whiggish ideas of an ancient constitution, he insisted that a new constitutional settlement had emerged in 1688 from several swings of the ideological pendulum. It had contributed to a novel system of liberty that made Britain a modern commonwealth where prosperity and politeness could be found alongside liberty. Part of the novelty consisted in the mixture of the two ideological systems of liberty, one of which insisted on the strengthening of the power of the crown, while the other defended civil liberties. Although different in both details and historiographical interpretation, Hume's ideological reconstruction developed some of Montesquieu's ideas on constitutional liberty. This he took to have been established neither as a consequence of the granting of certain fundamental liberties nor as the result of popular control. It was the outcome of a more subtle, indeed fragile, mechanism of social and institutional balance that had been recently, but insensibly, achieved through the integration of different interests and powers within the fabric of the British mode of government. In describing this process Hume used the image of a tidal wave, which graphically conveyed a mixed image of something happening suddenly but at the same time imperceptibly.[71] The new balance was often achieved through paradoxical routes, like the discipline of self-restraint that patronage and 'corruption' had on the Commons by checking the interest of the whole by one of its parts.[72] Its persistence had made it possible for liberty to be taken to unexpected heights without yet jeopardising the security of citizens and that of the commonwealth.

From the accounts that Montesquieu and Hume gave of what made English liberty resilient, and how this quality largely depended on the liberty of the constitution, it is clear how much this was conceptualised in terms of the security that comes from safeguards. In constitutional terms, as Ferguson remarked in his *Principles*, these consisted in the 'separation' and 'mutual counterpoise' of all functions of government, so that no partial interests were allowed to 'prevail in the spirit and tendency of every law, or warp every judgement in the application of it'.[73] In broader social terms, it was not simply a matter of avoiding a 'dangerous accumulation of power', so that 'the great principles of order, resulting from the just authority of government and the privileges of the people, be admitted *in form*'. It was also a matter of an adjustment of the 'forces of the state . . . to give them effect'.[74]

This emphasis on the substantive features of the process by means of which moderate governments provided a safeguard for political liberty

---

[70] D. Hume, *The Letters of David Hume*, ed. J. Y. T. Greig, 2 vols. (Oxford, 1932), I, p. 34.
[71] Hume, *Essays*, p. 51.   [72] *Ibid.*, p. 45.   [73] Ferguson, *Principles*, II, p. 491.
[74] *Ibid.*, II, p. 492.

implicitly suggests that much depended on historical contingencies. In his *Lectures on Jurisprudence*, Adam Smith provided a historical synthesis. He listed a number of causes that at times fortuitously contributed to securing liberty both as safeguard and as regularity, so creating an entire system of political and civil liberty. The causes were broadly of two kinds. One set prevented full ascendancy of the crown, whose power had increasingly become absolute as a consequence of the weakening in the power of the barons; the other helped to establish a fully independent and regular administration of justice.[75] With regard to the first group of causes, the lack of a standing army, thought unnecessary because of the geographical conditions of the country, made the crown dependent on the Parliament for its revenue. This dependency increased in direct proportion both to the financial needs of the crown and the ascendancy of the Commons. The latter's authority was finally sanctioned by portraying themselves as representatives of the whole people, displacing the Lords as the main deliberative chamber, and entrenching their position by appeal to custom. It is probably in this sense that Smith maintained that 'the system of government now supposes a system of liberty as a foundation'.[76] With reference to the sovereign's dependence on Parliament for taxation and the way in which the presence of various interests and procedures had brought some rationality to the management of public revenue, he also stated that 'here is a happy mixture of all the different forms of government properly restrained and a perfect security to liberty and property'.[77]

But as this 'happy mixture' was taking shape so was a second group of transformations concerning the independence of judges, the limitation of judicial discretion, the establishment of courts, the selection of juries, the procedures for impeachment, and the implementation of *habeas corpus*. Although each of these transformations increased the liberty of subjects by relying on 'the great accuracy and precision of the law', they also ensured, as Ferguson said, that the liberty of the people was not simply established 'in form' but also 'given effect'.

V

The observation that in modern polities liberty as security is the result, on the one hand, of the growth in the regularity of government and law; and,

---

[75] *LJ*, pp. 420–6, 270–82.   [76] *Ibid.*, p. 271.
[77] *Ibid.*, pp. 421–2. See Winch, *Adam Smith*, pp. 95–7. Notice how Smith's insistence on the effectiveness of what one can only describe as 'informal' mechanisms of checks and balances contrasts both with formal readings of the theory of the separation of powers and with the kind of 'realism' advocated by someone like Fletcher, when he insisted that only by placing the sword in the hands of the people could one be sure to limit the power of rulers: *Political Works*, pp. 2–4.

on the other, of the often accidental separation and reciprocal check of established powers, may explain why both Hume and Smith regarded the latter as being the product of modern times.[78] It may also explain why the idea of liberty as security did not arouse controversy, despite the different political and ideological consequences drawn from it by Scottish moralists. The divergence between their views emerges more clearly when we move from the negative to more positive connotations of modern liberty. This does not entail a return to the conceptual distinction questioned at the beginning of this essay, but it does show how the negative elements so far associated with security led naturally into more positive considerations of what is required of rulers and ruled to maintain liberty.

It is often remarked, with some truth, that the insistence on liberty as security comes with an emphasis on the role of institutions and political machinery over that of character and virtue: government of laws versus government of men.[79] However, the important role played by social processes in determining the various elements of liberty as security shows that, although in different forms from those advocated in the strongly moralised language of virtue and social independence associated with civic humanism, there is an important sense in which character and interest formation are related to the stability, regularity, and limits of the machinery of law and government. This involves a conception of independence as a *necessary* condition of liberty. The preoccupation with these subjective elements was common to all Scottish writers of the period, despite differences in their judgements on the relative balance between causes for optimism and anxiety and the precise means of redressing the balance.

There was indeed cause for optimism in surveying modern liberty. Although in the previous sections I have emphasised the more 'negative' sense in which commercial society, according to the Scots, contributed to a more secure liberty, those same causes and effects can be looked at from the more 'positive' perspective of character formation. The effects of the diffusion of commerce and manufacture were comprehensive. They applied to the status, dispositions, interests, and manners of the people, all of which were relevant to their sense of security and their spirit of liberty. As we know from Donald Winch, Smith (and Millar after him) was particularly insistent on the way in which commercial transactions had separated economic dependence from natural or psychological deference.[80] Although the increased division of labour made people economically

---

[78] A. Smith, *Lectures on Rhetoric and Belles Lettres*, ed. J. C. Bryce (Oxford, 1979), p. 176; Hume, *Essays*, 'Independency of Parliament'; cf. also Winch, *Adam Smith*, p. 95.

[79] Cf. Forbes, *Hume*, pp. 224–30; and Winch, *Smith*, p. 177.

[80] Winch, *Adam Smith*, pp. 87–91.

reliant on the services of others, this was a generalised dependency, which by subordinating one person to many, but to no-one in particular, made them personally independent. Several consequences flowed from this. First, economic dependence ceased to carry with it the kind of natural subordination characteristic of domestic servitude or slavery. Second, there were profound psychological changes in the relationships between people: the sense of personal independence made the poor less subject to the influence of the rich, releasing them from more immediate surveillance and interference. Third, all this had profound consequences for social stratification and the political distribution of power.

It could also be argued that natural, psychological, and socio-political independence were supportive of industriousness and other social qualities that the Scots increasingly associated with the stabilising role of men of middling rank, whose sentiments and passions were harnessed by the more secure, rational, and predictable calculation of interests.[81] Moreover, commerce operated on the manners of people by encouraging sociability, communication, refinement, and gentleness.[82] Since manners were as much corrupted by the experience of absolute dominion as by utter subordination, this was true with regard to most social groups, from the industrious poor to people of high rank.[83] Ambition also took a gentler turn when it involved pursuit of commercial and private interests rather than power and domination.[84] Everything considered, the characters and new forms of independency fostered by commercial society compared favourably with the civic humanist sense of independence that came with property and possession of arms. The salutary effects on liberty made it possible to argue that the one-way causal relationship between liberty and commerce established by the republican and vulgar Whig literature could now be safely reversed.[85]

But this optimistic view was not free from anxieties. These took two main forms. There was anxiety about the effects that commercial independence could have on the stability of authority. As I have remarked above, the Scots considered their society to be a society of ranks where order was still the function of social hierarchy. This did not need to take the form of either natural subordination or superstitious belief. Modern civilisation had done away with both. Nevertheless, it still required a certain respect for authority.[86] Commercial society was partly subversive

[81] A. O. Hirschman, *The Passions and the Interests* (Princeton, 1977).
[82] Cf. Hume, 'Of Civil Liberty', in *Essays*; Millar, *Origin*, p. 233; and Smith *LJ*, p. 333; cf. Winch, *Adam Smith*, p. 79.   [83] Cf. note 36 above.
[84] Cf. Smith, *Theory of Moral Sentiments*, ed. D. D. Raphael and A. L. Macfie (Oxford, 1976), pp. 64–5.   [85] Cf. note 59 above.
[86] Hume, 'Of the First Principle of Government', in *Essays*; *LJ*, pp. 318 and 401.

of this, both from the bottom, by relaxing natural and psychological dependence, and from the top, by making property more mobile and volatile. Both aspects of this anxiety were reflected in Hume's preoccupations with the Wilkes episode and the threat he associated with public debt – cases where there had been a relaxation in the responsibility of ruled and rulers respectively. The public debt, in particular, as both Hume and Ferguson insisted, placed excessive power 'in the hands of a precipitant and ambitious administration', thereby altering the balance in the constitution.[87]

The second anxiety was that of indifference and civic privacy, which, as we saw at the beginning of this paper, became increasingly evident to Constant as the experience of the Terror loomed less large in the politics of post-Napoleonic France. Because of their more pronounced republican sympathies, this anxiety emerged with greater force in Ferguson's and Millar's writings. The diffusion of opulence and the increasing store set by personal security and independence carried the danger of growing indifference to the public good. Against this threat, Ferguson developed what Sher has called a rear-guard civic humanism.[88] The thrust of Ferguson's argument was that civic involvement is necessary to prevent indifference from breeding despotism. This instrumental construction of liberty as participation is entirely consistent with what we described above as the safeguard understanding of security.

But Ferguson also offered a more expressive understanding of participation in public affairs as a form (indeed, perhaps the only form) of education that could foster internalisation of public spirit.[89] He gave two different justifications for this. One emphasised the close link between liberty, equality, and justice. Personal happiness required that security should not be acquired at the expense of justice and equality. This had other important implications for recognition of merit and the allocation of public offices. Civic privacy depleted the human resources available to serve public ends, besides corrupting the criteria for evaluating contributions to public good.[90] The second justification pointed to the corrupting and self-defeating nature of the satisfactions that came from purely private pursuits.[91] The enfeebling influence of civic privacy had the further effect of preparing the ground for political slavery.[92] These were, of course, traditional civic humanist preoccupations. It is not by accident, for instance, that neither Hume nor Smith approved of Ferguson's *Essay*. But Ferguson's preoccupations grew out of the same analysis of modern

---

[87] Ferguson, *Essay*, p. 234.   [88] Sher, 'From Troglodytes', p. 398.
[89] Ferguson, *Institutes of Moral Philosophy* [1773] (New York and London: reprint, 1978), pp. 267–8.   [90] *Ibid.*, p. 293.   [91] Ferguson, *Essay*, p. 160.
[92] *Ibid.*, book VI, v: 'Of corruption, as it tends to political slavery'.

liberty. Indeed, Hume and Smith, though Smith in greater measure, were not immune from such preoccupations, as testified, for instance, by the providentialist gloss that Smith put upon his analysis of the role that the admiration for wealth and power has in the progress of society.[93] Similar expressive considerations underlie the complex position that Smith took on martial spirit and mental mutilation, on which he based his view of government's direct intervention in education as an important precondition of citizenship and therefore for the maintenance of liberty.[94]

The arguments mustered by Smith in support of a standing army under the control of officers with social roots in the community and under the indirect check of 'the martial spirit of the great body of the people', are interesting not only with reference to the issue of character-building, but also because they have great affinity with arguments often advanced in support of representation as the modern form of political liberty. As already mentioned with reference to Montesquieu, representation could be looked upon either as a way of giving a share in government to the people, or as a means for keeping them at sufficient distance to avoid the dangers of mass politics. Eighteenth-century authors were as suspicious of this as the ancients had been. The 'aphorisms' on which Hume reposed his cautious exercise in utopia were entirely consistent with this intuition: the 'lower sort of people' were good at judging things placed within the compass of their own experience and *influence*, but unfit to judge of greater matters or to select people for high office.[95] The whole structure of his 'perfect commonwealth' was meant to produce a natural progression of decision-making bodies, reflecting this maxim and a number of others subordinate to it. But the important element that political representation brings to the administration of the public good as well as to the organisation of its defence is that it expresses an idea of liberty as *influence* – a point evident to the ancients in their support for political participation and not entirely lost to the moderns. The development of the connection between influence and representation was indeed the main route through which a number of republican themes were now approached and adapted to large polities in modern conditions. This is evident from Smith's brief treatment of the issue in the *Wealth of Nations*, where he considered this as the way in which the interests of the colonies could be fully encompassed within the British constitution, bringing the latter to greater perfection.[96] More obviously, this also became one of the great themes of both American and French republicanism and of their impact on later political thinking.[97]

---

[93] Smith, *Theory of Moral Sentiments*, IV, i.   [94] Cf. Winch, *Adam Smith*, ch. 5, *passim*.
[95] Hume, 'Idea of a Perfect Commonwealth', in *Essays*.   [96] *WN*, II, p. 624.
[97] Cf. Richard Whatmore's contribution to this volume for a discussion of the importance of political representation in Paine's revival and transmission of republican themes.

Thrown out of the door of the politics of modern large and commercial societies, participation was re-admitted through the window of representation: a form of influence at a distance, which was therefore more moderate and more controllable than the direct presence of the masses.

In different ways, independence, character-building, and influence were therefore considered by the Scots to be important conditions for the preservation of liberty as security. In so far as this was conceived as resting on socio-political safeguards, it was almost impossible to separate security from its conditions. This is what gave the latter as much an instrumental as an expressive value. The perception of the intrinsic fragilities of the liberty of the moderns represented an underlying unity within the discourse of the North. Its enduring legacy can be found in a series of 'speculative' and 'dubious' arguments bearing meanings that may continue to have relevance to political thinking in our own time.

3 Language, sociability, and history: some reflections on the foundations of Adam Smith's science of man

Nicholas Phillipson

I

Adam Smith is often described as a member of 'the Scottish historical school' and as the author of a science of man that was framed and focused by a distinctive theory of history. But what sort of historian was he? Smith always thought of 'history' in conventional terms, as the study of political and military events, their causes and consequences. Like William Robertson, however, he believed that such an enterprise had philosophic potential. He thought that Tacitus had transformed the traditional scope of history by paying attention to 'the temper and internall disposition of the severall actors who had shaped events' and had shown that history was of value to 'a science no less usefull, to wit, the knowledge of the motives by which men act.'[1] But although history studied in this Tacitean fashion could yield up information about the minds of statesmen and generals and the secret causes of particular policies, Smith was more interested in a history which explained the hidden causes of civilisation's progress from its barbarous to its polished states in terms of changes in the means of subsistence and the distribution of property. It was a move which heralded the appearance of that celebrated stadial theory of history which Dugald Stewart, somewhat opaquely described as 'conjectural history' and which remains one of the intellectual glories of the Scottish Enlightenment.[2]

Historians of historiography are entitled to point out that Smith and fellow stadial theorists like Robertson, Kames, and Millar – Ferguson's

---

I am grateful to John Pocock for comments on an earlier draft of this essay.

[1] A. Smith, *Lectures on Rhetoric and Belles-Lettres*, ed. J. G. Bryce (Indianapolis, 1985), pp. 112–13. Cf. William Robertson's Collingwoodian observation that 'In order to complete the history of the human mind, and attain to a perfect knowledge of its nature and operations, we must contemplate man in all those various situations wherein he has been placed': *The Works of William Robertson D.D.*, 8 vols. (Oxford, 1825), VI, p. 259.

[2] D. Stewart, 'Account of the Life and Writings of Adam Smith LD.D', in *Adam Smith: Essays on Philosophical Subjects*, ed. W. P. D. Wightman, J. C. Bryce, and I. S. Ross (Oxford, 1980), p. 293.

theory took a somewhat different form – were strikingly cautious in exploiting the resources of this new approach to history, using it as a conceptual resource to refresh traditional agendas rather than as the foundation stone of a new, general history of civilisation. Robertson, for example, used his celebrated stadial accounts of the progress of feudal society in Europe and of savage society in America to throw light on a traditional Tacitean preoccupation with the *arcana imperii* and the mental worlds of the kings and *conquistadores* who had laid the political and imperial foundations of the modern world. Kames, Millar, and Smith himself used stadial history to reconstruct the conceptual foundations of the somewhat battered natural law tradition which had formed so important a part of Scottish academic moral philosophy teaching. The *grand projet* of a new history of civilisation built on stadial foundations lay beyond the reach of their – or indeed anyone else's – scholarship if not their imagination and intelligence.

Every Scot was sensitive to the Montesquieuian dimension of stadial history. After all, stadial analysis provided them with a powerful tool for studying what Montesquieu had called the *relations* between the laws and customs of past ages by demonstrating their functional value for peoples whose lives were circumscribed by the means of subsistence and the distribution of property that were to be found in given times and given places. At the same time, they found in stadial history a means of highlighting the problems that must occur when laws and customs and the political institutions which sustain them are at odds with changing attitudes to subsistence and property. And in this they, and above all Smith, found a context in which to situate the political problems of preserving liberty in an age in which the spirit of commerce was often at odds with laws and customs whose origins lay in the needs of a feudal age.

Many of these questions have attracted scholarly attention. What is often overlooked is the theory of human nature and the theory of sociability on which the stadial theory of history rested. Here Smith's thought was to be of critical importance to the new historiography. His theory of human nature was developed in lectures about language, rhetoric, taste, morals, and justice, given in Edinburgh and Glasgow between the late 1740s and 1763 and in the *Theory of Moral Sentiments* (1759), and it is significant that his thought on these subjects developed in parallel with his thinking about jurisprudence and history. His theory of human nature was 'experimental' in the Humean sense that it was based on the observation of human behaviour as it appeared in society, and it was designed to show how human beings acquire the cognitive skills they need to articulate and satisfy their needs in the course of common life. It was thus a theory of sociability which was derived from a natural history of the progress of the self-understanding of human beings who were faced with the problem of living sociably in societies whose mores were shaped by distinctive economies, constitutions, and cultures. His theory of human nature was thus a theory of sociability which was only intelligible when it was set in the context of a general theory of the progress of civilisation. It is with the origins and nature of this theory that this essay is concerned. As we shall see, it was a theory which placed great stress on the socialising function of speech and language.

Smith's thinking about sociability was deeply influenced by the philosophical education he received from Francis Hutcheson at Glasgow between 1737 and 1740 and by the education he gave himself at Oxford between 1740 and 1746. From Hutcheson, he received an introduction to a neo-Stoic system of moral philosophy which was intended to reactivate an idiom that was under pressure from the scepticism and Epicureanism of Hobbes and Mandeville. Hutcheson wanted to rebut two of Mandeville's charges: that men were naturally selfish, and that claims that they were capable of genuinely benevolent behaviour were the product of hypocrisy or self-deception. His rebuttal was based on two observations about human nature: that human beings are naturally attracted by what they believe to be virtuous behaviour and repelled by vice; and that they have a profound longing to be able to think of themselves as virtuous. Indeed Hutcheson's moral theory suggests that unless men and women are able to satisfy this latter need, they will be imperfectly socialised and unable to contribute to the public good. How, then, could they be assured that virtue and the benevolence which inspires it was genuine and uncontaminated by self-deception and hypocrisy? Hutcheson attempted to show, famously and controversially, that our capacity for virtue was controlled by an inner faculty, a moral sense, which formed part of the constitution of the mind, and ensured that benevolent actions would serve the public good and the good of humanity generally. He concluded that the task of the modern Stoic moralist was to advertise the existence of this inner sense, demonstrate its powers, and show citizens that it was prudent as well as virtuous to submit to its guidance. Because this moral sense formed part of the constitution of the mind, he was able to speak of man's capacity for virtue as 'natural', and because its cultivation simply meant submitting to the dictates of our own nature, he was able to claim that virtue was a skill which could be easily cultivated by those who were prepared to cultivate liberty and the public good.

From Hutcheson, Smith learned to think of the Stoic and Augustinian longing for virtue as a fundamental moral need which would have to be satisfied if men and women were to be truly sociable. He also realised that a society that was unable to satisfy its subjects' moral needs would be unable to maximise its productive capacity. Hutcheson also taught him that, in a cynical Mandevillian age, we would never be able to experience the joys of self-approval unless we could be sure that we were capable of genuinely virtuous conduct. Unfortunately, like many Scots, Smith did not believe in the existence of the moral sense. Instead, he was to construct a new theory of morality which showed how our capacity for virtue and the self-assurance which offered us those feelings of liberty and what the Stoics called *apathaeia,* were derived from what David Hume called the experience of common life and from the use of language.

After leaving Glasgow in 1740, Smith spent six years at Balliol College, Oxford as a Snell Exhibitioner. Although we know next to nothing about these Oxford years, it seems likely that he spent them distancing himself from the neo-Stoic culture of Hutcheson's Glasgow and preparing the ground for his own theory of human nature.[3] They were years spent in relative intellectual isolation in an environment which Smith did not find particularly congenial. Dugald Stewart thought that he must have spent much of his time reading the philosophy and literature of the ancient and modern world and particularly that of France, always with an eye on the study of human nature.[4] His taste for ancient and modern tragedy, above all his love of Racine; his reading of La Rochefoucauld and the *Moralistes*; his relish for the labyrinthine sentimental fiction of Marivaux and Richardson suggest that he was intrigued by moral and psychological complexity, by questions about the meaning of *amour de soi* and *amour propre* and by the dilemmas of those who found it difficult to satisfy their moral needs. It was a French moral landscape which suggested that the moral needs of modern citizens were more intricate and harder to satisfy than Hutcheson had realised.

I am also tempted to believe that contemporary rumours that Smith read Hume's *Treatise* at Oxford were true.[5] The *Treatise* had been published in 1739 and 1740 while Smith was still at Glasgow and its existence was well known to Hutcheson. However, he is unlikely to have recommended a text of which he greatly disapproved. But Smith must have known about Hume's activities; his close friend, James Oswald of Dunnikier, was a friend of Hume and an enthusiastic publicist and for this reason alone it seems biographically plausible to think of Smith as an early reader of the *Treatise*.[6] But whenever he read the *Treatise* – and for

---

[3] What is known of Smith's Oxford career is summarised in I. S. Ross's invaluable *The Life of Adam Smith* (Oxford, 1995), ch. 5. The interpretative gloss is mine.
[4] Stewart, 'Account of the Life and Writings of Adam Smith LD.D', pp. 271–2.
[5] Ross, *The Life of Adam Smith*, pp. 77, 423.
[6] E. C. Mossner, *The Life of David Hume*, 2nd edn (Oxford, 1970), pp. 144–5.

reasons that will shortly become apparent, I assume he must have read it before preparing his lectures on rhetoric and *belles-lettres* in 1746 and 1747 – what he would have found was a brilliant but incomplete essay in historicism which showed that it was possible to explain how we develop the cognitive skills on which sociable life depends from the experience of common life without presuming the existence of occult and theologically loaded assumptions about the organisation of the mind. In Hume's theory, man was to be seen as a creature of imagination and passion, a being whose understanding of the world was shaped by custom, habit, and the conventions of everyday life. Indeed, his theory pointed towards the radical sceptical conclusion that the 'mind' which regulated our understanding and the self itself were cultural constructs, mere bundles of impressions given coherence and continuity by customs and conventions. Ethically, however, this theory pointed towards a cool moral scepticism which Smith was to find unsatisfying. For Hume, the virtuous individual was a sociable agent whose respect for custom and convention was tempered by the knowledge that customs could all too easily degenerate into the superstitions and enthusiasms which had so often destroyed social order and progress. Such a person realised that virtue was an accomplishment which lay within the reach of every polite and sceptical citizen who was sensitive to the opinions of others and to the utility of his actions for the public good. In Hume's idiom, the Hutchesonian longing for virtue was little more than a form of enthusiasm which could be purged by politeness.

For Smith, Hume's philosophy had a serious philosophical weakness. As modern commentators know, it is difficult to explain his theory of knowledge without presuming the existence of a theory of language which is generally assumed but never developed. There can be no doubt that Hume was acutely aware of the importance of speech and language to his theory of mind. The *Treatise* is full of references to the importance of 'conversation' in shaping the mind. What is more, his famous discussion of the crucially important events which make us aware of the meaning and necessity of justice, speak of that concept as a 'language' which has to be learned by all of those who wish to live in organised societies. Indeed, in book III of the *Treatise* Hume seems to sketch the outlines of a natural history to show how we acquire the ideas of justice, political obligation, morality and beauty and religion on which sociability depends. We shall never know why Hume failed to develop the theory of language which would have given theoretical depth to his science of man; perhaps he felt that he had done enough to justify turning from the natural history of man to the civil history of his own country and to important questions about the preservation of liberty in contemporary

Britain. What matters here is that Smith's first major intellectual project consisted in developing what may be described as a post-Humean theory of language which he was to use to develop an 'experimental' and historicist account of the progress of sociability and morality. It was an enterprise which meant turning once again to France and to the remarkable thinking about the origins of language that emerged from that country in the later 1740s and early 1750s following the publication of Condillac's *Essai sur l'origine des connoissances humaines* in 1746.[7]

Condillac argued that the organisation of the mind could only be understood in terms of the organisation of language and that language was to be seen as a system of communication whose origins could only be explained in terms of the changing needs of primitive man. Using a device first used by Mandeville, Condillac speculated on how two solitary, vulnerable aboriginal children first learned to communicate by means of gestures and cries and in time developed the rudiments of language. Their primary instinct would have been to assign particular names to particular objects. However, 'il n'étoit pas possible d'imaginer des noms pour chaque objet particulier; il fut donc nécessaire d'avoir de bonne heure des termes généraux' and it was in the creation of these *genera* that primitive man first acquired the capacity for abstract thought and the capacity for language.[8] The crucial problem for Condillac, as it would be for Smith, was explaining the origin of this power of abstraction. Locke had argued that its roots lay in reason. Condillac, who regarded himself as a critic as well as a disciple of Locke, concluded that the power of reasoning, like that of memory, imagination and perception, had its origin in sensation, and in a capacity for connecting ideas: a 'liaison des idées'. Need had obliged aboriginal man to conceive general ideas. Need had given him the power of thought. In other words, need had given birth to 'mind'. As he put it:

Le bon sens, l'esprit, la raison et leurs contraires naissent également d'un même principe; qui est la liaison des idées les unes avec les autres; que, remontant encore plus haut, on voit que cette liaison est produite par l'usage des signes; et que, par conséquent, les progrès de l'esprit humain dépendent entièrement de

---

[7] The following discussion of Condillac is much indebted to two works by Hans Aarsleff, 'The Tradition of Condillac: The Problem of the Origin of Language in the Eighteenth Century and the Debate in the Berlin Academy before Herder', in his *From Locke to Saussure: Essays in the Study of Language and Intellectual History* (London, 1982), pp. 146–209; *The Study of Language in England 1780–1860*, new edition (London, 1983), pp. 13–43. See also E. M. Hine, *A Critical Study of Condillac's Traité des Systemes* (The Hague, 1979); J. Sgard, *Condillac et les problèmes du langage* (Geneva, 1982).

[8] *Œuvres philosophiques de Condillac,* ed. G. Le Roy, 3 vols. (Paris, 1947), I, p. 86: 'As it was impossible to invent names for each particular object; it therefore became necessary to have recourse to general terms.'

l'adresse avec laquelle nous nous servons de langage. Ce principe est simple, et répand un grand jour sur cette matière: personne, que je sache, ne l'a connu avant moi.[9]

Condillac drew two important conclusions from his theory, which Smith was to develop. In the first place, he was able to trace man's ability to reason to a precise moment in historical time, when his ability to take cognitive control of his environment was challenged and when he was forced to use words and signs in a radically new way. In the second place, Condillac was able to show how each individual fashioned a particular language of his own out of the linguistic resources of the world in which he found himself; 'je dis *son langage*', Condillac wrote, 'car chacun a le sien, selon ses passions'.[10] This meant that the intellectual progress of any nation was constrained by the limitations of its language. Indeed he thought that 'les nations ne peuvent avoir des génies supérieurs qu'après que les langues ont déjà fait des progrès considérables'.[11] Indeed,

On doit donc trouver dans une langue qui manque de mots, ou qui n'a pas de constructions assez commodes, les mêmes obstacles qu'on trouvoit en Géométrie avant l'invention de l'algèbre. Le français a été, pendant longtemps, si peu favorable aux progrès de l'esprit, que si l'on pouvoit se représenter Corneille successivement dans les différens âges de la monarchie, on lui trouveroit moins de génie, à proportion qu'on s'éloigneroit davantage de celui où il a vécu, et l'on arriveroit en fin à un Corneille qui ne pourroit donner aucune preuve de talent.[12]

Smith's thinking about the origins of language was probably first sketched out in Edinburgh in 1748 in the course of his lectures on rhetoric and *belles-lettres* and developed in Glasgow. However, it was not published until 1761 when it appeared in the *Philological Miscellany* as 'Considerations Concerning the First Formation of Languages'. It was later attached to the third and subsequent editions of the *Theory of Moral Sentiments* and was, said Stewart, an essay 'on which the author himself

---

[9] *Ibid.*, I, p. 36. 'Common sense, the contents of the mind, reason and their opposites share the same source; a principle which states that ideas are related, one to another; that, more profoundly, one sees that this relationship is the product of the use of signs; and that, as a consequence, the progress of the human mind depends entirely upon the skill with which we have made use of language. This principle is simple enough and one day will be considered of great importance: no one that I am aware of has recognised it before me.'

[10] *Ibid.*, I, p. 98: 'every man according to his passion has a particular [language] of his own'.

[11] *Ibid.*, I, p. 100. 'It is demonstrable that there can be no such thing as a superior genius, till the language of a nation has been considerably improved'.

[12] *Ibid.*, I, p. 100. 'In a language therefore, defective in words, or whose construction is not sufficiently easy and convenient, we should meet with the same obstacles as occurred in geometry before the invention of algebra. The French tongue was for a long time so unfavourable to the progress of the mind, that if we could frame an idea of Corneille successively in the different ages of our monarchy, we should find him to have been possessed of less genius in proportion to his greater distance from the age in which he lived, till at length we should reach a Corneille who could not give the least mark of his abilities.'

set a high value'.[13] The 'Considerations' was a characteristically unas-
suming but unobtrusively powerful response to Condillac's *Essai*. Like
Condillac, Smith wanted a theory of language that would throw light on
the operations of the mind. He told George Baird that such an approach
was 'not only the best System of Grammar, but the best System of Logic
in any Language, as well as the best History of the natural progress of the
Human mind in forming the most important abstractions upon which all
reasoning depends'.[14] He used natural history in the same way as
Condillac, speculating on the cognitive experience of aboriginal man and
concluding that language and the mind were the product of need.
However, he had little time for Condillac's ambitious attempt to construct a new account of the principles of grammar which was based on
sensation and 'la liaison des idées'. His own understanding of grammar
was conventional and derived from the Port Royal *Rhetorique ou l'art de
parler,* by Bernard Lamy, a book he had probably used in the Logic and
Metaphysics class at Glasgow. Smith thought that aboriginal man had
first learned to construct *genera* by using tropes to extend the range of his
vocabulary. Lamy had thought that all tropes were metonymies ('metony-
mie signifie un nom pour un autre') and had regarded the inventiveness
which human beings show in the use of tropes to express their own peculiar thoughts as one of the most striking characteristics of human
speech.[15] Smith agreed and thought that they had probably used a somewhat obscure form of metonymy known to grammarians as 'antonoma-
sia' which involved assigning 'one object the name of any other which
nearly resembles it, and thus to denominate a multitude by what originally was intended to express an individual'.[16] Thus we might say of a
great orator that he was a Cicero, or of a wise judge that he was a

---

[13] Stewart, 'Account of the Life and Writings of Adam Smith LD.D', p. 292. It is important
to remember that the version of the essay which was published in 1761 addressed not only
Condillac's thought on the origins of language, but that of those who had written about
the subject subsequently – Rousseau included. Smith summarised the elements of his
thought in narrowly Condillacian terms in his *Lectures on Rhetoric and Belles-Lettres*. I
have assumed that the elements of this argument were in place by 1748.

[14] *Correspondence of Adam Smith*, ed. E. C. Mossner and I. S. Ross (Indianapolis, 1987), pp.
88–9; cf. *Essays on Philosophical Subjects,* p. 274.

[15] 'La fecondité de l'esprit des hommes est si grande, qu'ils trouvent steriles les langues les
plus fecondes. Ils tournent les choses en tant de manières, ils se represent sous tant de
faces differentes, qu'ils ne trouvent point de termes pour toutes les diverses formes de
leurs pensées. Les mots ordinaires ne sont pas toujours justes, ils sont ou trop forts ou
trop foibles. Ils ne'en donnent pas la juste idée qu'on en veut donner': B. Lamy, *La
Rhetorique, ou l'art de parler* (Sussex Reprint, French Series No. 1, Brighton, 1969), p. 90.
Lamy's discussion of tropes is to be found in book II, ch. 2.

[16] 'Considerations Concerning the First Formation of Languages and the Different Genius
of Original and Compounded Languages', reprinted in *Adam Smith Lectures on Rhetoric
and Belles-Lettres*, ed. J. C. Bryce (Indianapolis, 1985), p. 204.

Solomon. The invention of this trope was an epic moment in human history for it was then that human beings had acquired the capacity for language and thought.

In the beginnings of language, men seem to have attempted to express every particular event, which they had occasion to take notice of, by a particular word, which expressed at once the whole of that event. But as the number of words must, in this case, have become really infinite, in consequence of the really infinite variety of events, men found themselves partly compelled by necessity, and partly conducted by nature, to divide every event into what may be called its metaphysical elements, and to institute words, which should denote not so much the events, as the element of which they were composed. The expression of every particular event, became in this manner more intricate and complex, but the whole system of the language became more coherent, more connected, more easily retained and comprehended.[17]

Smith's theory was a conjecture about the first and most important step in man's progress from rudeness to refinement, the moment in which he became a language user and acquired the capacity for discourse on which his subsequent development would depend. Like Condillac, he realised that every stage in his progress as a moral and sociable agent would be controlled by the structure and resources of the language of the society in which he lived. He also realised that the linguistic resources of a closed, static society, insulated from the outside world, would tend towards stasis and stagnation and would confine the intellectual, social, and moral impulses of its people. Condillac had deplored the linguistic confusion which must occur when two societies are brought into contact accidentally. Characteristically, Smith welcomed such contact on the grounds that it would put pressure on existing languages and on the inventive tropic powers of those who used them.

As long as any language was spoke by those only who learned it in their infancy, the intricacy of its declensions and conjugations could occasion no great embarrassment. The far greater part of those who had occasion to speak it, had acquired it at so very early a period of their lives, so insensibly and by such slow degrees, they were scarce ever sensible of the difficulty. But when two nations came to be mixed with one another, either by conquest or migration, the case would be very different. Each nation, in order to make itself intelligible to those with whom it was under the necessity of conversing, would be obliged to learn the language of the other. The greater part of individuals too, learning the new language, not by art, or by remounting to its rudiments and first principles, but by rote, and by what they commonly heard in conversation, would be extremely perplexed by the intricacy of its declensions and conjugations. They would endeavour, therefore, to

---

[17] 'Considerations', p. 218. Jo Donohu tells me that Smith may have drawn some of his thinking about tropes from C. Du Marsais' classic *Traité des tropes* (1730). I am very grateful for this reference.

supply their ignorance of these, by whatever shift the language could afford them.[18]

In this remarkable conjecture, which forms part of the conclusion of the 'Considerations', a conjecture which may well have been formulated as early as 1748, Smith outlined one of the planks on which his general theory of progress would henceforth rest. Closed societies had a tendency to stagnate linguistically, socially, economically. A general instinct for improvement would only be awakened when such a society was exposed to outside pressure. Only then would the further progress of civilisation be possible.

Smith's theory of language and his account of the conditions which impelled human beings to invent the tropes which transformed the resources of language was to structure his theories of rhetoric and *belles-lettres* and morals, and inform his thinking about the moral economy of polished and commercial societies. This was why he summarised the argument in the third of the lectures on rhetoric and *belles-lettres* and published the whole text in the second and subsequent editions of the *Theory of Moral Sentiments*. In the *Lectures on Rhetoric and Belles-Lettres* Smith dealt with the use of language in polished societies where citizens were practised in the art of discourse and sensitive to its persuasive powers. He argued, conventionally, that language will only persuade if it pleases, and less conventionally that it would only please if it was used 'naturally' and with a due sense of 'propriety'.

A wise man . . . in conversation and behaviour will not affect a character that is unnatural to him; if he is grave he will not affect to be gay; nor, if he be gay will he affect to be grave. He will only regulate his naturall temper, restrain [it] within just bounds and lop all exhuberances and bring it to that pitch which will be agreable to those about him. But he will not affect such conduct as is unnaturall to his temper tho perhaps in the abstract they may be more to be wished.

In the like manner what is it that is agreable in Stile; It is when all the thoughts are justly and properly expressed in such a manner as shews the passion they affected the author with, and so that all seems naturall and easy. He never seems to act out of character but speaks in a manner not only suitable to the Subject but to the character he naturally inclines to.[19]

Propriety was the concept on which Smith's theory of rhetoric depended. In a polished, spectatorial world men and women quickly learned to rely on

---

[18] 'Considerations', p. 220. This dimension of the argument, though not Smith's theory about the origin of languages, was explored by two of Smith's Glasgow pupils, Archibald Arthur, Thomas Reid's assistant and successor as Professor of Moral Philosophy at Glasgow, and William Richardson, Professor of Humanity 1773–1815, in an essay 'On the Confusion of Tongues', in *Original Essays and Translations by Different Hands* (Edinburgh, 1780), pp. 324–7, 359.   [19] *Lectures on Rhetoric and Belles-Lettres*, p. 55.

a sense of propriety that would socialise and individuate simultaneously. It was a lesson which implied that a pleasing and persuasive use of language would help to ease the tensions between *amour de soi* and *amour propre* on which sociability depended. Apart from casual but revealing remarks about the quasi-aesthetic pleasure we derive from using language with propriety and apart from observing that 'it is the custom of the people that forms what we call propriety', Smith seems to have said nothing systematic about the nature of propriety in the lectures.[20] That was left for the *Theory of Moral Sentiments* (1759) which was based on Smith's Glasgow course in moral philosophy. That course was run in parallel to the course on rhetoric and *belles-lettres*; indeed the treatment of the two subjects is complementary. Once again, Smith resorted to the use of natural history in explaining the way in which individuals acquire moral sentiments. He tells us about the moral progress of individuals who live in polished societies, who become as skilled in trading sentiments as they are in trading goods and sentiments. They are individuals who long for the approval of others but learn the hard way that self-approval brings more contentment than the applause of the world. They are individuals who learn to value propriety. And, strikingly, they are individuals who have learned to value fiction as a means of furthering their pursuit of approbation and *apathaeia*.

Smith wrote about this process of moral education as someone who valued Stoic ethics for their own sake, for their seemingly natural appeal to citizens in all ages, and for their value in encouraging sociability. As he put it: 'The never failing certainty with which all men, sooner or later, accommodate themselves to whatever becomes their present situation, may, perhaps, induce us to think that the Stoics were, at least, thus far very nearly in the right; that, between one permanent situation and another, there was, with regard to real happiness, no essential difference.'[21] The core of his theory lay in his famous account of the process of moral trading. It was in such encounters that individuals learned how to estimate the characters of others, here that they learned to see themselves as others saw them, here that they learned to value propriety and the consolations of Stoic ethics.

Characteristically, Smith realised the satisfaction of moral need was a matter of learning to deploy language effectively. *The Theory of Moral Sentiments* begins with a dramatic – even melodramatic – case study significantly adapted from the discussion of Stoic ethics in *De Finibus*.[22] It deals with our response to the agonies of a brother on the rack.

---

[20] *Ibid.*, p. 5. Cf. Du Marsais, 'C'est toujours le plus commun et le plus connu qui est le propre', *Traité des tropes*, p. 33.
[21] *The Theory of Moral Sentiments*, ed. D. D. Raphael and A. L. Macfie (Indianapolis, 1982), p. 149.   [22] *De Finibus* III, xxiii.

As we have no immediate experience of what other men feel, we can form no idea of the manner in which they are affected, but by conceiving what we ourselves should feel in the like situation. Though our brother is upon the rack, as long as we ourselves are at ease, our senses will never inform us of what he suffers. They never did, and never can, carry us beyond our own person, and it is by the imagination only that we can form any conception of what are his sensations. Neither can that faculty help us to this any other way, than by representing to us what would be our own, if we were in his case. It is the impressions of our own senses only, not those of his, which our imaginations copy. By the imagination we place ourselves in his situation, we conceive ourselves enduring all the same torments, we enter as it were into his body, and become in some measure the same person with him, and thence form some idea of his sensations, and even feel something which, though weaker in degree, is not altogether unlike them. His agonies, when they are thus brought home to ourselves, when we have thus adopted and made them our own, begin at last to affect us, and we then tremble and shudder at the thought of what he feels.[23]

The pressures that are placed on our cognitive and linguistic resources are made immediately obvious. Smith realised that the partialities of language make it impossible for us to enter into our brother's sufferings except by resorting to fiction, attempting to imagine what we would feel in his position and judging whether, in such circumstances, we would want to act as he does. For unless his behaviour satisfies that condition, we shall not feel that he has acted with propriety and we shall withhold our sympathy. To avoid that painful situation our brother will have no option but to respond in kind and make his own assessment of our conduct. And so the transaction will proceed until we reach a situation in which sympathy can be offered and reciprocated. A pleasurable state of mutual sympathy will have been achieved, a state which Smith thought offered the greatest pleasure society had to offer.[24] The encounter has been driven forward by moral need. The rhetorical skills of the two brothers have been tested to the utmost by their attempts to enter their respective cognitive and passional worlds and to negotiate a potentially rewarding moral transaction. In the process they will have created the illusion of 'knowing' each other.

However, it was when men and women found that they could no longer rely on the world to supply them with approbation and sympathy that they were obliged to resort to the greatest rhetorical ingenuities of all. In this situation, Smith observed they were in the habit of seeking the approval of a 'man within the breast', an 'abstract man', an 'impartial spectator' whose voice was the voice of propriety and whose judgement was to be valued over that of the world. In editions 2 to 5 of the *Theory of Moral Sentiments*, Smith offered a long, meticulously crafted analysis of

[23] *Ibid.*, p. 9.   [24] *Ibid.*, p. 13.

the social and moral experience which shows us the limitations of worldly approval and encourages us to look for alternative interior sources of approbation; it is an account which at every point presupposes an encounter regulated by the resources of speech and language.

When we first come into the world, from the natural desire to please, we accustom ourselves to consider what behaviour is likely to be agreeable to every person we converse with, to our parents, to our masters, to our companions. We address ourselves to individuals, and for some time fondly pursue the impossible and absurd project of gaining the good-will and approbation of everybody. We are soon taught by experience, however, that this universal approbation is altogether unattainable. As soon as we come to have more important interests to manage, we find, that by pleasing one man, we almost certainly disoblige another, and that by humouring an individual, we may often irritate a whole people. The fairest and most equitable conduct must frequently obstruct the interests or thwart the inclinations of particular persons, who will seldom have candour enough to enter into the propriety of our motives, or to see that this conduct, how disagreeable soever to them, is perfectly suitable to our situation. In order to defend ourselves from such partial judgements, we soon learn to set up in our own minds a judge between ourselves and those we live with. We conceive ourselves as acting in the presence of a person quite candid and equitable, of one who has no particular relation either to ourselves, or to those whose interests are affected by our conduct, who is neither father, nor brother, nor friend either to them or to us, but is merely a man in general, an impartial spectator who considers our conduct with the same indifference with which we regard that of other people. If when we place ourselves in the situation of such a person, our own actions appear to us under an agreeable aspect, if we feel that such a spectator cannot avoid entering into all the motives which influenced us, whatever may be the judgements of the world, we must still be pleased with our behaviour, and regard ourselves, in spite of the censure of our companions, as the just and proper objects of approbation. On the contrary, if the man within condemns us, the loudest acclamations of mankind appear but as the noise of ignorance and folly, and whenever we assume the character of the impartial judge, we cannot avoid viewing our own actions with his distaste and dissatisfaction.[25]

Philosophers sometimes write of Smith's impartial spectator as though it was a quasi-Hutchesonian faculty of the mind. It is nothing of the kind. Smith has shown here that the impartial spectator is another fiction generated by rhetoric, language, and the imagination. It is a testimony to fictive virtuosity of moral agents living in polished worlds and to the disciplined manner in which they construct fictions to serve their primary moral needs.

Nowhere was Smith's thinking more powerful than in his quasi-Mandevillian insights into the facility which human beings show for investing the language of common experience with new, tropic meanings.

---

[25] *Ibid.*, pp. 129–30n. Cf. *Correspondence*, pp. 54–5.

We are apt to value notions of propriety and justice for aesthetic rather than functional reasons. We find ourselves valuing trinkets for 'the aptness of the machines which are fitted to promote [production]' and not for their utility.[26] More generally, we are apt to view all the satisfactions of life in relation to 'the order, the regular and harmonious movement of the system, the machine or oeconomy by means of which it is produced'.[27] Indeed it was out of such illusions that we conjured up the Stoic image of the world as part of a divinely ordered and benevolent universe which offered the individual the consolation of *apathaeia* and society the prospect of sociability, order and improvement. 'And it is well that nature imposes upon us in this manner', Smith wrote. 'It is this *deception* [my italics] which rouses and keeps in continual motion the industry of mankind. It is this which first prompted them to cultivate the ground, to build houses, to found cities and commonwealths, and to invent and improve all the sciences and arts, which ennoble and embellish human life; which have entirely changed the whole face of the globe, have turned the rude forests of nature into agreeable and fertile plains, and made the trackless and barren ocean a new fund of subsistence, and the great high road of communication to the different nations of the earth.'[28] It was an insight 'that has not, so far as I know, been yet taken notice of by any body'.[29]

As Smith grew older and physically frailer, he seems to have become impressed by the difficulty of mastering the resentments of common life. In the *Lectures on Jurisprudence* he had spoken of the affronts that the progress of society and the growth of inequality bring in its wake and both here and in the *Wealth of Nations* he had been scathingly aware that government must naturally appear to many as an institution for preserving the property of the rich from the envy of the poor. In the sixth and last edition of the *Theory of Moral Sentiments* his faith in the civilising powers of commerce seems muted as he calls for a more austere, more Epictetan Stoicism to arm the modern citizens against the rigours of commercial civilisation. Whether these were lessons the writing of the *Wealth of Nations* had taught him is a question that lies beyond the scope of this essay. Nevertheless it is striking that, in the final edition of the *Theory of Moral Sentiments*, he became increasingly aware of the frailty of the judgements of the man within the breast when faced with the praise or blame of the world. Once again the crisis is seen in rhetorical terms as a failure of language which calls for new displays of tropic ingenuity. 'The man within seems sometimes, as it were, astonished and confounded by the

[26] *Ibid.*, p.180.   [27] *Ibid.*, p.183.   [28] *Ibid.*, pp.183–4.
[29] *Ibid.*, pp. 179–80. Smith's argument was designed as a critique of Hume's theory of utility.

vehemence and clamour of the man without' he wrote. Under these circumstances 'he discovers his connexion with mortality, and appears to act suitably, rather to the human than to the divine, part of his origin'. Under these circumstances, the 'humbled and afflicted man' had only one resource left to him, to resort to a final act of moral fiction, to appeal 'to a still higher tribunal, to that of the all-seeing Judge of the world, whose eye can never be deceived, and whose judgements can never be perverted'. And it was from him and him alone that we could look for justice and happiness in the world to come.[30] In the final months of his life, Smith had returned to a more austere, Epictetan Stoicism, spun out of the resources of language by recourse to a new form of theological fiction.

Smith's natural history had shown how individuals seek the satisfaction of their material and moral needs by exploiting the resources of worlds in which they find themselves, their understanding being constrained at every point by the limitations of language and by material circumstance. It was a natural history which was designed to make sense of the experience of individuals living in polished societies; unlike Robertson, Smith had little interest in barbaric or non-European societies. What is more, it was a natural history which argued that human beings will only be truly sociable and productive when they are free to exchange their goods, services, and sentiments and when their conduct is constrained by propriety rather than laws. For only then will they be able to aspire to a life directed by the impartial spectator, a life led according to the principles of Stoic virtue. In commercial society it will be easier for the many to live according to the direction of the impartial spectator than it was in the slave-orientated societies of antiquity, although the condition of the few who worked on the production lines of an advanced economy were a famous source of worry for the author of the *Wealth of Nations*. The species whose material and moral progress Smith charts in his historicised theory of human nature and in his account of the progress of civilisation is a species in search of the Stoic satisfactions which commerce has now made generally available. His historiography has made possible the birth of a new philosophic Whiggery.

---

[30] *Ibid.*, pp.131–2.

4   Adam Smith and tradition: the *Wealth of Nations* before Malthus

Richard F. Teichgraeber III

I

Because this essay addresses questions I think have been raised but not fully explored elsewhere, it may be best to begin with a careful explanation of my title. Part of my purpose here is simply to deepen and complicate our understanding of Adam Smith's *Wealth of Nations* by tracing the broad outlines of Smith's reputation in British thought and culture between the publication of the first edition of the *Wealth of Nations* in March 1776 and the appearance of the first edition of Malthus's *Essay on Population*, which appeared anonymously in June 1798. Well before his identification a generation later as the founding figure of the tradition of British political economy, Smith stood by himself as a thinker whose importance was seen as incontestable. Yet he was also followed in various directions. We know that both the revolt of Britain's North American colonies and the French Revolution had something to do with the mutability of Smith's reputation.[1] But so too did another development largely overlooked by students of his career: the sweeping transformation of the British publishing business that had taken place over the course of his lifetime and was to continue into the nineteenth century.

The broader issue that lies behind the observations I want to make is one hinted at in the first part of my title – namely, to ask how Smith's reputation in the late eighteenth century sheds light on the larger question of how and why the *Wealth of Nations* initially came to exercise authority in

I would like to acknowledge my indebtedness to Wilfred F. McClay, Stefan Collini, Richard Whatmore, and Brian Young, each of whom offered valuable comments on earlier versions of this essay.
[1] Donald Winch, *Riches and Poverty: An Intellectual History of Political Economy in Britain, 1750–1834* (Cambridge, 1996), part II, provides a careful overview of the conflicting uses of Smith's thinking in British debates about the meaning of the American and French revolutions. Also see Gertrude Himmelfarb, *The Idea of Poverty: England in the Early Industrial Age* (New York, 1983), pp. 42–144; Biancamaria Fontana, *Rethinking the Politics of Commercial Society: The Edinburgh Review, 1802–32*, ch. 1; and Emma Rothschild, 'Adam Smith and Conservative Economics', *Economic History Review* (February 1992), pp. 74–96.

British affairs. Perhaps the first thing that should be said by way of answer here is that until roughly two decades ago this sort of enquiry hardly seemed necessary. During the bicentenary year of *Wealth of Nations*, specialists and non-specialists alike seemed content to discuss Smith's reputation primarily as a matter of his pioneering exposition and espousal of the principles of liberal capitalism. There was also broad agreement that it was this role that had first gained him widespread recognition in the nineteenth century as the founding figure of the tradition of classical British political economy, and hence one of the main forerunners of both orthodox economics and Marx's analysis of nineteenth-century capitalism.[2]

The years since the bicentenary, however, have witnessed a remarkable effort to qualify – and in some cases completely to revise – this still familiar estimate. The main challenge has come from a new generation of Smith scholars who, on re-examining the sources and character of his ideas, have tried to replace the liberal-capitalist Smith with a figure whose main intentions and achievements must be understood in terms of a variety of distinctively eighteenth-century ideologies and concerns that he addressed throughout his work. Despite some significant differences in individual views, most of these new scholars agree that previous interpretations of Smith were imperfect because they failed to understand how his views on law and government served as the intellectual context within which he first developed his understanding of political economy and his arguments for free trade. They have argued, too, that we come much closer to understanding Smith's intentions in writing the *Wealth of Nations* if we take seriously his description of 'political economy' as one branch of 'the science of a statesman or legislator'. Whatever appeals the book may have had for later audiences, it seems clear that during his own lifetime statesmen and legislators were the readers Smith most wanted to entangle in his text and in the process persuade to leave behind old laws and preconceptions that blocked further economic development of their nations.[3]

---

[2] For a critical overview of Smith scholarship at the time of the *Wealth of Nations* bicentenary, see Donald Winch, 'Not by Economics Alone', *TLS* (12 March 1976), pp. 278–80.

[3] Duncan Forbes, 'Sceptical Whiggism, Commerce, and Liberty', in A. S. Skinner and T. Wilson, eds., *Essays on Adam Smith* (Oxford, 1976), pp. 179–201, and D. Winch, *Adam Smith's Politics: An Essay in Historiographic Revision* (Cambridge, 1978) – probably the two most original studies of Smith to be published in the last quarter-century – are the works that first set the revisionist scholarship in motion. Studies that built on and continued the project begun by Forbes and Winch include Knud Haakonssen, *The Science of a Legislator: The Natural Jurisprudence of David Hume and Adam Smith* (Cambridge, 1981); Istvan Hont and Michael Ignatieff, *Wealth and Virtue: The Shaping of Political Economy in the Scottish Enlightenment* (Cambridge, 1983); John Robertson, 'Scottish Political Economy Beyond the Civic Tradition: Government and Economic Development in the

The Adam Smith who emerges from the revisionist scholarship of the last two decades is sceptical and self-questioning, rooted more deeply in early-modern moral and legal thought than previously suspected, and fully aware of contemporary habits of mind and political practices he believed stood in the way of realising liberal economic doctrines. It should be said that much of the evidence to support this reading has always been there, and it was not entirely overlooked by a handful of earlier scholars also determined to distinguish Smith's thought from the legends that surround it.[4] Given my concerns here, however, one of the more interesting features of recent work on Smith has been the readiness of some leading scholars – in some moods – to say that, while we now possess a much fuller historical understanding of the origins and character of Smith's ideas, such an understanding provides little or no guidance in approaching what one might argue is the historically more important question of what became of his ideas after his death. Put another way, we are confronted with the interesting case of specialists who know that early in the nineteenth century the *Wealth of Nations* became one of those 'classic' texts people were often admonished to go back to, but who tell us that most of those who did go back then misconstrued what they found.

Two examples will suffice. One is Donald Winch, who has argued that 'much of Smith's science of the legislator died with him, and any account of the branch of it that constitutes [classical British] political economy must take account of that fact'. This claim is the outcome of an insistently historical approach to Smith's thinking that Winch has done as much as anyone to foster. Its significance here, however, lies more in his provocative refusal to accept that the case for Smith's authority as the founder of the nineteenth-century tradition of political economy is so obvious that it needs no careful justification and analysis. In fact, Winch also goes on to say that when such work is finally done it will tell us that not only did Smith's particular vision of political economy as a form of statecraft survive only in piecemeal form in the new tradition fashioned in his name by Malthus, Ricardo, and J. R. McCulloch, but also that in this process much of what was original and distinctive about Smith's thinking on economic questions was lost forever – or at least until the

Wealth of Nations', *History of Political Thought*, 2 (1983), pp. 451–82; Laurence Dickey, 'Historicizing the "Adam Smith Problem": Conceptual, Historiographical, and Textual Issues', *Journal of Modern History*, 3 (1986), pp. 579–609; Richard F. Teichgraeber III, *'Free Trade' and Moral Philosophy: Rethinking the Sources of Adam Smith's 'Wealth of Nations'* (Durham, N.C., 1986); Patricia H. Werhane, *Adam Smith and his Legacy for Modern Capitalism* (New York, 1991); and Jerry Z. Muller, *Adam Smith in His Times and Ours* (New York, 1993).

[4] Jacob Viner, 'Adam Smith and Laissez-Faire', in *The Long View and the Short* (Glencoe, Ill., 1958); J. Ralph Lindgren, *The Social Philosophy of Adam Smith* (The Hague, 1973).

current generation of Smith scholars managed to bring it back into the foreground.[5]

Argued in more extreme terms and on different grounds, this view of the fate of Smith's ideas also informs Gertrude Himmelfarb's study of changing conceptions of poverty during the onset of industrialisation in Britain. Apparently unpersuaded by revisionist interpretations, Himmelfarb upholds the liberal-capitalist perspective on Smith, contending that his ideas must still be taken as crucial to our understanding of the early stages of British industrial capitalism. On her account, however, Smith turns out to be an intellectual giant who was never allowed to play out his chosen role, because his essentially moral vision of a capitalist economy – one 'in which an "invisible hand" ensured that individual interests would conduce to the common good and individual competition would produce social harmony' – came to be neglected. Himmelfarb's explanation of why this justification of capitalism was overlooked says that readers of the *Wealth of Nations* never had a chance to judge its arguments accurately because of misleading circumstances in which the text was embedded after publication of Malthus's *Essay*. The notorious 'population principle' quickly undermined Smith's original expectations that economic growth would benefit all members of society. Where Smith saw the promise of social harmony in an economy where wages and population increased simultaneously, Malthus instead posited a struggle for existence which taught that poverty was a fact of life and that the poor would be doing well simply if they managed not to become poorer than they already were.

Himmelfarb concludes, somewhat predictably, that it is Malthus who must be held accountable for turning Smith's thinking about 'political economy' into one element of a 'dismal science', thereby depriving Britain's industrialising capitalist economy of 'the moral and social roots' Smith had tried to give it. But her account of the Smith–Malthus relationship also has two more novel implications. The first is that the very tradition of which Smith is so often said to be the founding figure must now be taken as something of a thick camouflage that makes Smith's progressive vision look exactly like those of lesser (and less hopeful) thinkers.[6] The other is the suggestion that under other historical circumstances Smith's

[5] Donald Winch, 'Science and the Legislator: Adam Smith and After', *Economic Journal*, 93 (1983), pp. 501–20. Yet also see Winch's chapter on Malthus and Ricardo in S. Collini, D. Winch, and J. Burrow, *That Noble Science of Politics: A Study in Nineteenth-Century Intellectual History* (Cambridge, 1983), pp. 63–90, which stresses, by contrast, the importance of a limited but still persisting interest in statecraft in both Malthus and Ricardo.
[6] Himmelfarb, *The Idea of Poverty*, pp. 101–44. For an alternative and less sanguine account of Smith's views on the relationship between economic growth and economic inequality, see Hont and Ignatieff, 'Needs and Justice in the *Wealth of Nations*', in *Wealth and Virtue*, pp. 26–44.

vision might have been seen for what it 'really' was. Exactly what circumstances those might have been, however, are never spelled out. As a result, we are left to guess about how Himmelfarb's brighter Smith could ever have stood on his own as an actual historical figure or how he might have come into play with the Smith who was revered yet entirely misunderstood by the proponents of political economy. Indeed, apart from counterfactual speculation about events that might have sooner made Smith the subject of rigorous historical scholarship, it is hard to imagine what they might include.

I have seized on two of the more pointed statements of recent historical re-interpretations of Adam Smith primarily to suggest why the moment has arrived to look closely again at the question of how and why the *Wealth of Nations* first came to exercise authority in British affairs. My exploration of these points will proceed by way of a few observations about the character of classical British political economy as an intellectual tradition, and then proceed to more detailed comments about Smith's reputation in British culture before it was tied firmly to the cause of that tradition.[7] In focusing primarily on the years before Malthus, I do not mean to challenge the assumption that the *Wealth of Nations* was actually the founding text of nineteenth-century British political economy. Strictly speaking, the positing of a Smith-founded tradition may be historically incorrect, but by the mid-nineteenth century it was consistent with what Smith's countless admirers and critics had come to see as an agreed-upon fact. The story I tell in this essay begins with a brief explanation of how that agreement came about, and argues (among other things) that it must be understood as something more than a historical mistake.[8]

II

Most consciously constructed traditions have as their founders figures who present a definite project for their heirs to work on – Hegel, Marx,

---

[7] I have learned much about the dynamics of intellectual and cultural traditions from Edward Shils, *Tradition* (Chicago, 1981); John Guillory, 'Canonical and Non-Canonical: A Critique of the Current Debate', *Journal of English Literary History*, 3 (1987), pp. 483–528; Jane Tompkins, *Sensational Designs: The Cultural Work of American Fiction, 1790–1860* (Oxford, 1985); Cathy N. Davidson, *Revolution and the Word: The Rise of the Novel in America* (Oxford, 1986); Robert von Hallberg, ed., *Canons* (Chicago, 1984); and Richard H. Broadhead, *The School of Hawthorne* (Oxford, 1986), ch. 1.

[8] It is worth noting, at the outset, that there are two distinguishable senses of the term 'tradition' at work in this essay. In the first, it refers to traditions – such as classical British political economy – that are consciously constructed by a particular community of interpreters. The definition of the second sense refers to traditions – such as 'liberal capitalism' – that intellectual historians construct after the fact. It is Smith's complex role in the first of these 'traditions' that is my main concern here.

Darwin, and Freud are obvious modern examples that come to mind here. But the particular tradition Smith is often said to have founded with the publication of the *Wealth of Nations* has something of an oddity for its source. Smith himself never recruited any disciples.[9] And while the *Wealth of Nations* did become something of a steady seller by the end of his life-time, there is surprisingly little evidence to suggest that its reception by contemporary readers was ever a matter of deep concern to him. Smith did not initiate any public or private campaigns to bring attention to his book. He accepted early criticisms and over-simplified appraisals of the *Wealth of Nations* with almost complete silence and equanimity, and passed over several opportunities to make his own views better known and accessible in a topical pamphlet or popular essay. In short, it appar-ently just never occurred to Adam Smith that he ought to help call a new tradition into being.

Nor was he a noticeably helpful guide for contemporary readers inter-ested in grasping his intentions in writing the *Wealth of Nations*. Historically, interpretation of the book begins with two of its awkward features: length and loose organisation. (Or, as Smith's publisher William Strahan politely put it, initial demand for the book had been far greater 'than I could have expected from a work that requires much thought and reflection . . . to peruse to any purpose'.[10]) It is perhaps no great surprise, then, to discover that despite steady sales over the course of his lifetime, the *Wealth of Nations* never figured in any impassioned debates or dramatic confrontations during the late 1770s and 1780s. Smith remarked in his introduction that he intended to outline a plan for a world economy whose principal object was growth, and at times he spoke of that plan as an 'obvious and simple system of natural liberty'. But the book he actually came to write – more like a small library than a single volume inviting its readers to start at the beginning and read straight through – greatly complicated the task of understanding all that he seemed to mean by that phrase. There is no 'obvious' or 'simple' explanation for the vast structure that Smith constructed to hang his plan on. Late eighteenth-century readers also confronted a work whose author chose not to expound his argument for free trade without regu-larly reminding them that, in his opinion, liberal economic doctrines seemed to run far ahead of actual political and social attitudes in late eighteenth-century Europe. While the *Wealth of Nations* offered a thor-ough exposition of the principles of free trade, it also assembled a careful

[9] The first two paragraphs of this section summarise points I have developed at greater length in my '"Less Abused than I Had Reason to Expect": The Reception of the *Wealth of Nations* in Britain, 1776–90', *Historical Journal*, 30 (1987), pp. 337–66.

[10] Quoted in John Rae, *Life of Adam Smith* (London, 1895), p. 286.

(and sometimes gloomy) inventory of traditional habits of mind and political practices that Smith saw as standing firmly in the way of efforts to realise such principles.

None of this, of course, ultimately prevented Adam Smith from being followed. But the peculiarities of the *Wealth of Nations* as a text also required his self-styled disciples to make a model of their founder that they could then follow. In 1816, for example, George Pryme justified the need for a course of lectures on political economy at Cambridge by explaining that the *Wealth of Nations* was 'but a confused assemblage of the most sound principles of political economy. To understand [Adam Smith] well, one must be habituated to arrange his ideas anew, and to reconsider them in that altered order.' Yet the 'necessity of this labor', Pryme concluded, 'puts him out of reach of ordinary laborers', and so a new course of lectures was urgently needed to supply the deficiency. Similarly, readers of McCulloch's famous 1828 edition of the *Wealth of Nations* encountered a volume in which one-third of the printed text was made up of McCulloch's own extensive notes and appendices, most of which were designed 'to make the reader aware of the fallacy or insufficiency of the principles Dr Smith has sometimes adopted'.[11]

It is possible that in the pantheon of great Western thinkers Adam Smith stands alone in the amount of critical abuse he received from those who first presented themselves to the world as his disciples. More will be said about the character and significance of this criticism at the end of this essay. Here I simply want to draw attention to a point that is now well established in the current guild of historically minded Smith specialists – and that is the relatively late date at which Smith's authority was invoked on behalf of 'political economy' as a distinct tradition. Forty years after the publication of the *Wealth of Nations* there seems to have been only one person – Malthus – whose main intellectual energies were devoted to political economy and who even thought of himself as a 'political economist'. Smith in fact never referred to himself as a 'political economist', and the phrase 'political economy' itself first appeared at the outset of book IV, not quite half-way through a text of almost half a million words.[12]

All that said, we should also be careful not to overestimate the importance of the historical distance that separated Adam Smith from his first self-appointed disciples. While nineteenth-century proponents and

[11] 'A Syllabus of George Pryme's Lectures on Political Economy' [1816], reprinted in Gary F. Langer, *The Coming of Age of Political Economy, 1815–25* (New York, 1987), pp. 197–208; Adam Smith, *An Inquiry into the Nature and Causes of the Wealth of Nations*, ed. and intro. J. R. McCulloch (Edinburgh, 1828; Edinburgh and London, 1838), pp. xliii–xlix.
[12] Langer, *The Coming of Age of Political Economy*, p. 2.

popularisers of political economy at best only partly understood all that Adam Smith was about, I see no reason to fault them for overlooking in the *Wealth of Nations* what they had no obvious reason to be interested in. Smith is no exception to the rule that the conscious structuring of a tradition demands the subordination of an individual author's intentions to the higher meaning of the tradition, and that this subordination usually proceeds by way of purging texts of their perceived irrelevancies and then assigning some readily understood central meaning to what remains. Approached from this angle, we also should not be surprised then to find that when proponents and popularisers of political economy looked back on the *Wealth of Nations* in the middle decades of the nineteenth century, they had little trouble in explaining why Smith stood as the founder of their tradition. Despite his many shortcomings, Smith had accomplished what all founder–discoverer figures are supposed to accomplish in the way of freeing himself from the false beliefs of his predecessors – i.e. 'mercantilism' – and leaving behind a new theory that became the main point of departure for the further development of a new tradition. The great achievement of the *Wealth of Nations*, McCulloch observed, was its masterly exposition of the benefits that arose from free trade, an exposition which he took to focus largely on uncovering the inconsistencies and absurdities of existing regulations that forced economic activity into particular politically defined channels.[13]

We know that a tradition comes to life when its creators successfully project their own ideals on to the texts that they choose to canonise. We also need to understand, however, why such a process inevitably comes to exclude other interpretations of those same texts. So again I would emphasise that there is no great puzzle in finding that nineteenth-century political economists celebrated the *Wealth of Nations* as a triumphant breakthrough from the dated assumptions of 'mercantilism' to a new 'science of wealth' that supported their commitment to free trade. (In fact, the view of the *Wealth of Nations* as a giant machine assembled primarily to drive home the doctrine of free trade dates back to 1777, although it was then first employed by critics of Smith's book.[14]) What is striking, and therefore deserves some explanation, is the confidence that informed this single-minded estimate, the apparently complete assurance that no other estimates of Adam Smith could be or ever would be made.

---

[13] *Wealth of Nations*, ed. McCulloch, pp. xliii–xlix; also see McCulloch's *The Principles of Political Economy with a Sketch of the Rise and Progress of the Science* (Edinburgh and London, 1825), arguably the first work to popularise successfully the view that 'political economy' represented a distinct intellectual tradition whose founder was Adam Smith.

[14] See my 'The Reception of the *Wealth of Nations*', pp. 350–4.

III

As I have noted already, the historical map into the *Wealth of Nations* provided by political economists and still so widely employed as to have the quality of self-evident truth in the 1970s, was drawn at the earliest some forty years after the book was first published. What came before it were several other descriptions of the significance of the text, only two of which I want to touch on here because they are particularly useful in helping us to understand how the political economists' version of Smith ultimately became such a long-lasting article of cultural belief. Historically speaking, the first of these is the Adam Smith who had already been placed in the rank of intellectual immortals several decades before the political economists gave him new lustre. The other is the figure who, in the first years of the 1790s, was one of the intellectual heroes of British sympathisers with the cause of the French Revolution. Since the second is a figure perhaps most completely different from the one we remember, I want to address him first.

A little-known anecdote can serve as a point of entry here. On 1 February 1793, ten days after the execution of Louis XVI, members of the House of Lords gathered to hear the Prime Minister, William Pitt, provide an outraged account of developments in Paris, followed by a call for the nation to prepare for war with the armies and the ideas of the French Revolution. In the discussion that ensued, the Marquis of Lansdowne rose to dispute Pitt's view of the meaning of what had transpired. The King had brought on his own death, Lansdowne remarked, by his continuing refusal to negotiate with the new government of France. He then went on to offer the following comments on Pitt's call for war against the ideas that had informed the creation of that new government:

With respect to French principles, as they have been denominated, those principles had been exported from us to France, and could not be said to have originated among the people of the latter country . . . The new principles of government, founded on the abolition of the old feudal system, were originally propagated among us by the Dean of Gloucester, Mr [Josiah] Tucker, and had since been more generally inculcated by Dr Adam Smith, in his work on the Wealth of Nations.[15]

---

[15] *Cobbett's Parliamentary History*, XXX, pp. 329–30, 1 February 1793. Better known as Lord Shelburne, William Petty, first Marquis of Lansdowne (1737–1805) dispensed patronage to many British liberal intellectuals and dissenters, including Bentham, Price, Priestley, and Tucker. He has also often been called Adam Smith's earliest disciple in Parliament. For a review of the evidence on this last point, see Kirk Willis, 'The Role in Parliament of the Economic Ideas of Adam Smith, 1776–1800', *History of Political Economy*, 11 (1979), pp. 528–32.

In the winter of 1793, Lansdowne was one of a rapidly diminishing number of Britain's political elite still sympathetic with the cause of the French Revolution (Britain declared war on France on 12 February), and it should be said that his attempt to enlist Adam Smith's authority in defending the French was immediately and forcefully challenged. Yet Lansdowne was by no means alone in finding a radical line in Smith's thinking. Throughout the 1790s, a remarkable number of British writers cited the *Wealth of Nations* as a guide and support for a fundamental challenge to the traditional order in Britain as well as in France. Particularly during the first years of this violent and tumultuous decade, liberal economic doctrines were generally seen as part of an even wider movement for social and political reform, as arguments first used against artificial economic restraints were now turned – as Lansdowne's remarks in Parliament suggest – against the forms of religious and hereditary privilege which still dominated all major European nations in the late eighteenth century.[16] Thomas Paine's invocations of Smith's authority are well known. Perhaps the most carefully developed 'radical' interpretation of Adam Smith appeared in Joseph Priestley's *Lectures on History and General Policy*, where Smith was cited frequently in criticism of the British government's restrictive religious and economic policies.[17] To the end of the 1790s, Smith also remained one of the heroes of all those, both inside and outside the established order, who opposed continuation of the French war and attacked any measure which contributed to its prolongation. In fact, the first abridgement of the *Wealth of Nations*, which appeared in 1797, was the joint effort of two well-known and outspoken liberals who drew special attention to book II, chapter 3, where Smith had demonstrated how excessive government spending on warfare diminished a country's economic productivity.[18]

[16] The most famous, yet also perhaps the most extreme, instances are Thomas Paine's *Rights of Man*, pt. I (1791), and the Marquis de Condorcet's *Sketch for a Historical Picture of the Progress of the Human Mind* (1793). More restrained statements of the hope that liberal economic reform pointed the way towards broader social and political change were recurrent in the British liberal press in the 1790s. See, for example, the explanation in the *Analytical Review* (Sept.–Dec. 1790), pp. 149–50, of why its readers should welcome France's becoming a 'free and commercial people':

> The genius of commerce is gone forth amongst the nations of the earth, everywhere carrying peace and plenty and freedom in her train. The old wars were for dominion, now they are for trade, and therefore will be fewer of them; because all war is destructive to trade. The first kings of the earth were tyrants and despots . . . now they are merchants and traders. The kingdoms of Europe may be said to have become warehouses; the courts, counting-houses; the prime-ministers, bookkeepers; and the secretaries of states, clerks and porters.

[17] See Richard Whatmore's essay in this volume; Joseph Priestley, *Lectures on History and General Policy*, 2 vols. (London, 1788; Philadelphia, 1803), II, pp. 209–11, 217, 240–1, 249, 323–5.
[18] Jeremiah Joyce, *A Complete Analysis or Abridgement of Dr Adam Smith's Inquiry into the*

There are other interesting details in this story. The important inter-pretative questions for my purposes here, however, are these: why did egalitarian and radical readings of Smith never manage to take hold in the 1790s? And what does this failure tell us about Smith's subsequent role in that tradition which did succeed in establishing its alternative but nar-rower interpretation of his political significance? At first glance, it seems that the chief reason radical readings of Smith did not survive is simply that they were not allowed to survive. In the wave of reaction that swept over Britain after 1793 the most radical voices in Britain – Paine and his followers – were sent into exile, and with them went a vision in which democratic egalitarianism had been combined with support for national economic development in a free market society.[19] More moderate voices were also carefully scrutinised for any hint of 'Jacobin' sympathy. For example, the great Scottish universities in Edinburgh and Glasgow, once progressive institutions where Smith had begun his intellectual career, were now subject to what a recent historian has called a psychological reign of terror. In this setting, 'Jacobinism' served as a term to condemn any thought of political and economic reform. As late as 1799, when Dugald Stewart ventured to teach the doctrines of Adam Smith and Malthus at Edinburgh University, a contemporary remarked that the mere term 'political economy' made most people start. For they still 'thought that it included questions touching the constitution of govern-ments; and not a few hoped to catch Stewart in dangerous proposi-tions'.[20]

The facts of political reaction and coercion also provide part of the background for understanding the development of efforts to disentangle

Nature and Causes of the Wealth of Nations (Cambridge, 1797). Joyce (1763–1816) was a Unitarian minister active in London radical politics. A close associate of members of the London Corresponding Society, he had been arrested (and then acquitted) on charges of treason in 1793 along with several leaders of the LCS. Joyce's work was pub-lished by Benjamin Flower (1755–1829) who was editor of the *Cambridge Intelligencer*, 1793–1803, and known as the guiding intelligence of one of the most truculent liberal newspapers of the day. See Michael J. Murphy, *Cambridge Newspapers and Opinion, 1780–1850* (Cambridge, 1977).

[19] Richard J. Twomey, 'Jacobins and Jeffersonians: Anglo-American Radical Ideology, 1790–1810', in M. Jacob and J. Jacob, eds., *The Origins of Anglo-American Radicalism* (London, 1984), pp. 284–99; Michael Durey, 'Thomas Paine's Apostles: Radical Emigres and the Triumph of Jeffersonian Republicanism', *William and Mary Quarterly*, 4 (1987), pp. 661–88. A second, somewhat more successful, attempt to draw radical social and political messages out of the *Wealth of Nations* would be made by proponents of 'working-class political economy' in the early nineteenth century; see Noel W. Thompson, *The People's Science: The Popular Political Economy of Exploitation and Crisis, 1816–34* (Cambridge, 1984).

[20] Richard B. Sher, *Church and University in the Scottish Enlightenment* (Princeton, 1985), ch. 8; Henry Cockburn, *Memorials of His Time* [1854], ed. and intro. Karl Miller (Chicago, 1974).

progressive economic views from any broader vision of social and political reform. The actions of the government and loyalist associations did not completely silence liberal sentiment in Britain after 1793.[21] But for the disillusioned liberals who remained a way had to be found to answer those who were ready to read 'Jacobinism' into their continuing efforts to achieve economic and religious change. In the realm of economic policy, help came from two sources who relied directly on Adam Smith in their efforts to define the moderate reformers' reply to conservative suspicions. The first was Dugald Stewart who, in retreating from his early sympathy with the Revolution, rejected the view that following Smith in a commitment to free trade logically entailed a larger commitment to democratic politics. The insights of the *Wealth of Nations* had shown clearly that:

> The happiness of mankind depends not on the share which the people possess, directly or indirectly, in the enactment of laws, but on the equity and expediency of the laws that are enacted. The share which the people possess in the government is interesting chiefly to the small number of men whose object is the attainment of political importance.

There could be no question, Stewart concluded, that the *Wealth of Nations* aimed at the improvement of society, but it did so 'not by delineating plans of new constitutions, but by enlightening the policy of actual [i.e. existing] legislators'.[22]

An Adam Smith who closed his eyes on broader constitutional questions could be taken as a guide and support for Britain's disillusioned improvers. So too could the Adam Smith they found amended by Malthus, who also enlisted Smith's authority at the very outset of his *Essay* in another effort to define more of the middle ground between reaction and revolution. Whatever its subsequent role in forming the central principles of political economy, the immediate impact of the *Essay* on what remained of the British liberal community was to provide hope by way of showing – albeit in dramatically new terms – that while certain

---

[21] J. E. Cookson, *The Friends of Peace: Anti-War Liberalism in England, 1793–1815* (Cambridge, 1982), argues persuasively that only during the year following an invasion scare early in 1798 did the British government succeed in terrorising the liberal press into inactivity. Cookson also shows that the activities of the British liberal press were more widespread and vigorous than ever before in the 1790s, thereby refuting the traditional view that the government and the loyalist associations achieved an almost total intimidation of the press. For a recent restatement of the traditional view, however, see Ian R. Christie, *Stress and Stability in Late Eighteenth-Century Britain: Reflections on the British Avoidance of Revolution* (Oxford, 1984), esp. ch. VI.

[22] Dugald Stewart, *Account of the Life and Writings of Adam Smith* [1793], reprinted in Adam Smith, *Essays on Philosophical Subjects*, ed. W. P. D. Wightman, J. C. Bryce, and I. S. Ross (Oxford, 1980), pp. 269–351. On Stewart, see Collini, Winch, and Burrow, *That Noble Science of Politics*, ch. I; and Fontana, *Rethinking the Politics of Commercial Society*, ch. 3.

reforms in economic policy remained urgent, their accomplishment need not lead to radical social upheaval.[23]

IV

Karl Mannheim and others have argued that coherent ideologies emerge only when and if they have been forced, by combat with new ideals, to give a theoretical account of themselves. And it is tempting to conclude that the tradition of classical political economy first came into view in the late 1790s as an ideological aid for British liberal reformers who sought to distance themselves from the more comprehensive ideal of 'liberty' embodied in the French Revolution. This view of things also gains support from a familiar assumption that says traditions are what other people, once powerful – or, as in the present case, soon to be powerful – invent to serve their own interests, but that careful investigation eventually allows us to open up and demystify. There are good reasons to wonder, however, about the extent to which the social and political functions of traditions tell us all we want to know about their origins and formation. To understand those developments, we need to understand the workings of a society's cultural institutions at the time when a new tradition first emerges. Or as Edward Shils has observed, while traditions serve ideological functions, they also have a 'physical existence' in the form of actual texts produced, distributed, and read (in some fashion) at particular moments in history.[24] And if we go back to the last decades of the eighteenth century with this consideration in mind, what we find is mutation less dramatic and violent than the American and French revolutions, but perhaps ultimately equally far-reaching in its consequences for Britain. Ask a modern-day cultural historian of that era to tell you about the setting into which Smith launched *Wealth of Nations*, and her answer would probably begin with the observation that his book was just a small

---

[23] Malthus certainly never regarded himself as any kind of pessimist. Although he faulted William Godwin for mistakenly attributing all social problems and injustices to human institutions, he did not doubt that some institutions in fact worsened or prolonged unacceptable economic hardships. Malthus echoed Adam Smith, then, in arguing that abolishing primogeniture could bring benefits by increasing the number of landowners and equalising property holdings. Malthus's credentials as a moderate reformer are carefully set out in Donald Winch, *Malthus* (Oxford, 1987) and *Riches and Poverty*, part III. For evidence that the first *Essay* was welcomed as the work of a moderate reformer, see the *Analytical Review* (August 1798), pp. 119–20; *Monthly Review* (September 1798), pp. 1–9; and Godwin's reply to Malthus in *Thoughts Occasioned by the Perusal of Dr Parr's Spital Sermon* [1801] in *Uncollected Writings (1785–1822)*, ed. J. W. Marken and Burton R. Pollin (Gainesville, Fla, 1968), pp. 299–345, where Godwin says of the *Essay*: 'Of this book and the spirit in which it is written I can never speak but with unfeigned respect.'

[24] Shils, *Tradition*, pp. 89–91, 143–52.

stream feeding into an unprecedented flood of new printed material. Let me conclude by suggesting some of the largely neglected ways in which this perspective deepens and complicates our understanding of events that have allowed *Wealth of Nations* to gain its enduring reputation.

It is only recently that we began to have an adequate understanding of the cultural organisation of British intellectual life during Adam Smith's lifetime. The older research of Richard Altick and Ian Watt – still the starting place for serious study of this subject – established that the second half of the eighteenth century was a time when a dramatic increase in the annual output of books paralleled a slow but steady growth in popular levels of literacy and book-reading, and also when a new abundance of books allowed for the successful introduction of new literary genres such as the novel, the cheap reprint, the anthology, and stories intended primarily for children.[25] Alvin Kernan, John Brewer, and other scholars returning to these pioneering studies of the rise of a 'print culture' have recently established the consequences of this change in more concrete terms. First of all, we can see now that the transition from scarcity to abundance in print culture ultimately changed the way in which books were read and used. Books in abundance eventually ceased to be special sources of revelation for their readers, since extensive exposure to many printed texts, rather than repeated intensive examination of the same ones, required a hastier and more casual style of reading simply to keep up with the greater abundance of printed material. The full potential of literacy was revealed not just in being able to read, but in being able to read many books.[26]

Changes in the extent and style of reading also had profound consequences for writers and the roles they could claim. One form of these consequences can be seen in the creation of a new institutional setting for writing: the rise of Grub Street, where the writer's role was transformed from gentleman amateur, at home in a world of courtly letters based on patronage, to at best a professional interested in pleasing the general reading public, and at worst a paid hack in the new print factories. As Kernan shows, Samuel Johnson and many of the other leading British

[25] Richard D. Altick, *The English Common Reader: A Social History of the Mass Reading Public 1800–1900* (Chicago, 1957); Ian Watt, *The Rise of the Novel: Studies in Defoe, Richardson and Fielding* (London, 1957), esp. ch. II.
[26] David D. Hall, 'The Uses of Literacy in New England, 1600–1850', in William L. Joyce, David D. Hall, *et al.*, eds., *Printing and Society in Early America* (Worcester, Mass., 1983), pp. 1–47; Alvin Kernan, *Printing Technology, Letters, and Samuel Johnson* (Princeton, 1987); Terry Belanger, 'Publishers and Writers in Eighteenth-Century England', in Isabel Rivers, ed., *Books and their Readers in Eighteenth-Century England* (London, 1982), pp. 5–26; and John Brewer, *The Pleasures of the Imagination: English Culture in the Eighteenth Century* (New York, 1997), part II.

writers of the time lived out the first stage of the destruction of a culture in which only a select few discussed 'literature' and its replacement by a new and much larger and more varied audience for letters, who were significant chiefly as buyers of books in the market place, and for whom all writing and publication was designed. Here those who sought access to this new reading public had to do so on terms that made literature desirable in relation to a variety of other still less expensive eighteenth-century commodities. Here too the very number of books available guaranteed, with few exceptions, that the fame and importance of writers would be fleeting, since reputations were measured primarily in terms of continuing success in the literary market place.[27]

Finally, we now also have a better grasp of why so many of the British elite in the late eighteenth century were profoundly uneasy about the consequences of increasing levels of literacy, an uneasiness that took the form of a 'literacy crisis' the exact opposite of that in our own time. Initially, the fear of the elite was based on the assumption that the spread of reading and writing, especially among the lower classes, endangered not only the established order in polite letters, but also the more important areas of religion and politics. That fear was of course confirmed by what took place in Britain in the early 1790s, as the sales of Paine's *Rights of Man* reached into the hundreds of thousands. It was also reinforced by the appearance of a new genre of political texts, pioneered by Paine and imitated by others, written in the ordinary vernacular of readers generally considered incapable of direct participation in political life. Access to print not only allowed the disenfranchised to know more about democratic ideals, it also gave them powerful new means of expressing those ideals in their own language and hence of aiding their dissemination.[28]

All these recent studies have greatly enriched our understanding both of specific changes involved in a vast expansion in the scale of publishing and reading that began in Britain during the second half of the eighteenth century, as well as the broader and more complex relationships between books, writers, and society at that time. But what does the transition to a print culture have to do with Adam Smith's *Wealth of Nations*?

---

[27] Kernan, *Printing Technology, Letters, and Samuel Johnson*, chs. II and III; Nigel Cross, *The Common Writer: Life in Nineteenth-Century Grub Street* (Cambridge, 1985).

[28] Olivia Smith, *The Politics of Language, 1791–1819* (Oxford, 1984), chs. I–III. It should be noted that the American Revolution had already given the British elite evidence that the spread of reading and writing might threaten the established order at home. Literacy in the North American colonies was extremely high, and political pamphleteers had an enormous influence in revolutionary America, with not the least of these popular agitators being Paine, especially in his *Common Sense* (1776). See Bernard Bailyn, *The Ideological Origins of the American Revolution* (Cambridge, Mass., 1967); John Brewer, *Party Ideology and Popular Politics at the Accession of George III* (Cambridge, 1976); and Colin Bonwick, *English Radicals and the American Revolution* (Chapel Hill, N.C., 1985).

A step-by-step recounting of every facet of the publishing and reception history of Smith's book during these decades would extend well beyond the boundaries of this essay. There is room here, however, for me to hazard a two-part precis of what this as yet unwritten chapter in British intellectual and cultural history might tell us. Part one would show that during his own lifetime Smith himself was largely immune to the vicissitudes of Britain's emerging print culture. While roughly a contemporary of Johnson, Goldsmith, and other new writers-for-hire, he was of course no Grub Street hack but worked instead as an author in the elite milieu of eighteenth-century 'literature'. The eleven editions of the *Wealth of Nations* produced by William Strahan in London between 1776 and 1805 were published as impressive and increasingly expensive folio or octavo volumes, with the title page of each edition informing readers that Smith was 'Formerly Professor of Moral Philosophy at Glasgow' and, after 1778, one of the Commissioners of Customs in Edinburgh. Moreover, as King's Printer and an MP, who was also the publisher of Gibbon's *Decline and Fall of the Roman Empire*, Strahan himself was much more than an ordinary tradesman. Such facts are important because they immediately suggest the high cultural status of the author and of his book at the time of its publication. They also tell us something more significant about the limited interpretative community in which the *Wealth of Nations* was first assigned meaning. The 'Dr Adam Smith' mentioned so often in late eighteenth-century writing was not simply an advocate of economic reform but also a figure who seems almost predestined to have made an enduring mark in the world of polite letters.[29] His immediate success in this realm doubtless also explains much about why he never felt any need to popularise his views or enlist disciples.

The first canonisation of Adam Smith, however, was ultimately threatened by the workings of a new print culture from which he perhaps escaped, but his book could not. This of course is where the second part of our story would begin. Because the evidence here points in so many directions, it would be foolish to offer confident pronouncements about what further research and analysis might reveal. One of the main questions that will need to be resolved, however, seems clear enough. In a

---

[29] It is worth noting that Smith himself moved comfortably in the upper levels of British society. In fact, the *Wealth of Nations* was the fruit of ten years of concentrated effort made possible in 1766 by the patronage of Charles Townshend, then Chancellor of the Exchequer. Townshend had lured Smith away from Glasgow in 1764 to serve as travelling tutor to his stepson, the third Duke of Buccleuch. When the Grand Tour was completed in 1766, Smith was rewarded with a pension for life of 300 pounds a year. 'Dr Smith's' high standing in the elite world of eighteenth-century literature is also evident in some of his obituaries. See, for example, *Gentleman's Magazine* (July 1790), p. 673, and *The Bee, or Literary Weekly Intelligence* (11 May 1791).

culture attempting to come to terms with an unprecedented abundance of books – a conservative estimate of titles published in London alone in the 1790s is 16,243 – what forces served to save the *Wealth of Nations* from obscurity?[30] If we restrict our focus to the period before the appearance of Malthus's *Essay on Population*, I think it would be misleading to say that those forces were already clearly at work. The *Wealth of Nations* did not enter the public domain until 1805, and ledgers maintained by Smith's publisher show that at most some 5,250 copyrighted editions were extant at the time of his death on 17 July 1790. (At least one pirated English-language edition was published during Smith's lifetime – in Dublin in 1785; but we do not know how many copies were produced or at what price.) In the realm of politics, there is no question that the *Wealth of Nations* became an important source of information and insight for British MPs debating questions of economic policy during the 1780s, but probably nothing more than that. There are no signs that Smith's book was taken as any kind of final authority in this arena, and the larger cultural significance of Smith's presence in parliamentary debates is also hard to assess. Even when elections to Parliament were contested, candidates rarely if ever said anything in public about the policies they stood for.[31] In this regard, it is also very hard to find invocations of Smith's authority in late eighteenth-century literary reviews that we are now used to thinking of as voices for the cultural ideals and economic interests of Britain's then still disenfranchised middle class. In fact, of the eleven copyrighted Strahan editions of the *Wealth of Nations* published between 1776 and 1805, only the first was ever reviewed. The reason for this, however, is perhaps no great mystery. By the end of the eighteenth century, British literary reviews were overwhelmed by the sheer number of books about which they sought to inform their readers. Still conceiving of their function chiefly as the recording of advances of knowledge in all fields of

---

[30] C. J. Mitchell, 'The Spread and Fluctuation of Eighteenth-Century Printing', *Studies on Voltaire and the Eighteenth Century*, 230 (1985), pp. 305–21. Threats of obscurity in a print culture take a variety of forms, the most important of which in Smith's case was that an aura of originality that surrounded the *Wealth of Nations* during his lifetime was lost in certain circles over the course of the 1790s. What Kernan describes as a process of demystification appeared to set in during the mid-1790s with the appearance of more readers who felt free to criticise the *Wealth of Nations* and even to make their own abridged editions. See, for example, John Gray, *The Essential Principles of the Wealth of Nations* (1797); Edward Tatham, *A Letter to the Right Honorable William Pitt ... on the National Debt* (1795); *Monthly Review* (August 1797), pp. 61–3; and *Recherches sur la nature et causes de la richesse des nations ... Traduction nouvelle, avec des notes et observations; par Germane Garnier* (Paris, 1802). Garnier observed that 'no performance of modern date, of half its merit, is so deficient in method and has so little *finishing*, as the *Inquiry into the Wealth of Nations*'.
[31] See Willis, 'The Role in Parliament of the Economic Ideas of Adam Smith, 1776–1800'; Teichgraeber, 'Reception of the *Wealth of Nations*, 1776–90'; F. W. Fetter, *The Economists in Parliament, 1780–1868* (Durham, N.C., 1980).

human enterprise, reviewers had a vast and rapidly expanding territory to cover. The upshot of their efforts were periodicals that provided descriptive (and increasingly swollen) catalogues of recently published books, yet offered little in the way of a systematic ordering of new knowledge.[32]

But what of the publication of the first edition of Malthus's *Essay*? If we choose to approach it as an important episode in the formation of the tradition of British political economy, it is peculiar in at least two respects. The first is that it presents the interesting example of an intellectual tradition coming to life at a moment when the cultural authority of its parent work had yet to be firmly established. Conflicting appeals to Smith's thinking during the decade of the French Revolution show that his reputation was not in eclipse in the late 1790s. But it would be a mistake to say that in 1798 Malthus invoked Smith's authority because it defined a particular and widely recognised intellectual project he too wished to work on. The other related oddity of the Smith–Malthus relationship is Malthus's decision to publish anonymously. By identifying himself with a long-standing European tradition of authorship that shunned monetary reward, Malthus clearly wanted the first edition of the *Essay* to be seen as the work of a person of enlarged views and unbiased opinions. As with Smith, however, he apparently did not recognise that he was also helping to bring a new tradition to life.

V

Two final points. I began by asking how Smith's reputation in the late eighteenth century sheds light on the question of how and why the *Wealth of Nations* first became an important reference point in British affairs. Clearly I do not subscribe to the notion that the *Wealth of Nations* was an instant 'classic', simply because its first readers included some who said it was a book whose arguments would withstand the test of time. When it comes to classics, one should always ask whose test of time is being applied. Close study of the early publishing and reception history of Smith's book, however, raises a second and more difficult question: does the hallmark of a true classic, as Jane Tompkins has suggested, lie in its capacity 'to reward the scrutiny of *successive* generations of readers, speaking with *equal power* to people of various persuasions'?[33]

---

[32] S. Botein, J. R. Censer, and H. Ritvo, 'The Periodical Press in Eighteenth-Century English and French Society: A Cross-Cultural Approach', *Comparative Studies in Society and History*, 23 (1981), pp. 464–90; Derek Roper, *Reviewing before the 'Edinburgh', 1788–1802* (Newark, Del., 1978).

[33] Tompkins, *Sensational Designs*, pp. 34–5 (emphasis added).

Perhaps this is so with most other 'great' books. But I do not think Tompkins' suggestion gets us started in trying to summarise the early history of the *Wealth of Nations*. Even with its modest early sales, it is clear the book enjoyed more respect and prestige in the eighteenth century's limited 'republic of letters' than it ever did in the realm of nineteenth-century political economy.[34] Yet at the same time there is little evidence that the book's first canonisation provoked the sort of careful, and often sharply critical, scrutiny it later received at the hands of nineteenth-century political economists, all of whom thought that in many areas Smith's book had *not* withstood the test of time. From this perspective, I also think we can see that the nineteenth century not only brought forward a new estimate of Smith's significance; it gave rise to a new procedure for arriving at that estimate as well. To put it schematically, the effort to establish a new identity for the *Wealth of Nations* as the founding text of the tradition of political economy was more a matter of creating a monument than of demonstrating the continuing validity and pertinence of Smith's thinking taken in its entirety. In fact, it is not too much to say that the purpose of reading the *Wealth of Nations* changed entirely, since the book's chief claim to immortality was now seen to lie in its presentation of certain – but by no means all – of the best insights of a tradition still in the process of defining itself and sorting out its true and false propositions.[35] In this setting, the *Wealth of Nations* became something of a museum piece. It held out the promise of broadening the minds of nineteenth-century students of political economy by making them more aware of the larger historical and moral significance of their studies. Yet there was no reason to believe such study would significantly improve the quality of their thinking about current theoretical disputes within the tradition.

In conclusion, where does this analysis of the early fate of the *Wealth of Nations* lead British intellectual historians? Back, I think, to an issue whose interest is chiefly intra-tribal, but has broader implications as well: the question of how closely our efforts to understand the influence and cultural significance of the *Wealth of Nations* should be seen as bound to

[34] The high standing of the *Wealth of Nations* in 'polite' British culture was not an unimportant part of the book's appeal to those who sought to fashion a new intellectual tradition in its name. McCulloch, for example, regularly spoke of the book's 'well-founded' and 'deserved' celebrity. But McCulloch's respect for Smith never entailed deference, because he saw Smith's most important achievement as a matter of having taken only *some* of the steps which led to the formation and study of political economy in its current phase.

[35] See Shils, *Tradition*, pp. 100–40, on the different significance of texts for 'humanistic' as opposed to 'scientific' traditions of thought.

Smith's text.[36] Quite closely, over the course of the last two decades, many specialists understandably have said, and their work has been immensely helpful in recovering lost dimensions of the *Wealth of Nations'* intellectual and cultural origins. Yet clearly Smith is still remembered, and continues to exert widespread influence, as the champion of ideas that inspired or confirmed changes he knew little or nothing about. Some intellectual historians would retort that, even so, legitimate scholarship ought to hold the line against anachronism, and thereby continue to work to distinguish Smith from his legends and to challenge the ideologue's claim to monopolise the 'real significance' of the *Wealth of Nations*. Well, yes and no. On this point, one could also argue that custodianship of Smith's reputation (or that of any other 'great' thinker) does not necessarily fall to historians alone. Nor should we try to understand the meaning and importance of the *Wealth of Nations* in isolation from its results, even when these include selective interpretation or outright misunderstanding. Indeed, it would be especially short-sighted for those of us who minutely study the history of Smith's ideas and career to neglect or dismiss the roles played by autodidacts, booksellers, publishers, journalists, and countless other arbiters of public opinion, all of whom, whatever their immediate purposes, have helped to keep the *Wealth of Nations* in circulation for well over two centuries. All of these arenas should be taken into account, I think, if we aim to come to terms with the remarkably long and complex cultural life of Smith's great and difficult book.

[36] Lawrence Buell, *The Environmental Imagination: Thoreau, Nature Writing, and the Formation of American Culture* (Cambridge, 1995), pp. 311–13, makes some broad points about the canonisation of Thoreau's *Walden* (1854) that I think also hold true for the *Wealth of Nations*.

Part II

5 Economy and polity in Bentham's science of legislation

David Lieberman

I

Recent study of British political thought in the decades between the American War of Independence and the Great Reform Act has produced a crowded picture dense with political traditions and doctrinal configurations. If earlier historical scholarship tended to focus on a limited number of famous contests (Burke against the Rights of Man; Whigs vs. Radicals over constitutional reform), we are now as likely to scrutinise High Church ecclesiology and Christian political economy; philosophic history and natural jurisprudence; Paleyite theological utilitarianism and evangelical social thought; shifting configurations of Dissent and Protest, and of Dissent and Patriotism; and finely shaded and carefully delineated varieties of Whiggism and Toryism.

In a manner perhaps surprising, this scholarship has left relatively untouched the figure of Jeremy Bentham, whose writings on law and politics had for earlier generations seemed an obvious and critical landmark for this period of British intellectual history. Often this (relative) neglect of Bentham is the intended aim of revisionist interpretation: the product of the well-rehearsed rejection of Leslie Stephen's image of utilitarianism as the natural heir of *English Thought in the Eighteenth Century* or of A. V. Dicey's depiction of Benthamism as the definitive blueprint for Victorian legislative reform. But some of this neglect may be considered the less intended by-product of the state of current Bentham scholarship. The great labour of the past generation – as centred on the publication of the new edition of Bentham's *Collected Works* – has been to produce a more accurate version of Bentham's thought itself, freed from the corruptions of Bentham's nineteenth-century editors, popularisers, and critics. Most of the important recent treatments of Bentham thus have involved a kind of interpretative rescue operation, in which (for example) Bentham's

I am indebted to Lindsay Farmer and Philip Schofield for their comments and guidance on an earlier version of this essay.

jurisprudence is rescued from the legal positivism of John Austin; his democratic theory is distinguished from the defences of representative government advanced by James and John Stuart Mill; his moral theory is salvaged from the several 'fallacies' in terms of which it standardly stood condemned.[1] For the intellectual historian, the result, somewhat para-doxically, is an ever-widening gap between the 'historical Bentham' (meaning the figure known in the nineteenth century through the vehicles of Dumont's *Traités de législation civile et pénale* and John Stuart Mill's revi-sions) and the 'authenticity Bentham' (meaning the figure now recovered from the manuscripts and new edition).[2] These days it often seems easier to place James Mill – the student of Dugald Stewart; the philosophical historian of British India; the polemicist of Philosophical Radicalism – than it does to locate the self-styled 'hermit of Queen Square Place'.[3]

This essay is designed to identify some of the places where it would be fruitful to link the newly 'rescued' Bentham and the extensively revised intellectual history of eighteenth- and early nineteenth-century Britain. To do so, I pursue some quite basic questions concerning the kinds of ideas about social conduct Bentham presumed in his legislative theory and programme; the question (to speak more grandly than my own treat-ment warrants) of the sociology informing Bentham's jurisprudence. This involves (in the first and second parts) taking up some well-established themes: the nature and extent of Bentham's debts to political economy, particularly as elaborated by Adam Smith in the *Wealth of Nations*; and the alleged 'economic' presuppositions of Bentham's treat-ment of human nature. And it involves (in the third part) introducing a more neglected dimension of Bentham's radical political programme: the role of public opinion and print culture in the operation of the democratic society elaborated in the *Constitutional Code*.

---

[1] See the important reconsiderations of Bentham's jurisprudence by H. L. A. Hart, *Essays on Bentham* (Oxford, 1982) and Gerald J. Postema, *Bentham and the Common Law Tradition* (Oxford, 1986); of his democratic theory by L. J. Hume, *Bentham and Bureaucracy* (Cambridge, 1981) and Frederick Rosen, *Jeremy Bentham and Representative Democracy* (Oxford, 1983); and of his moral theory by David Lyons, *In the Interests of the Governed* (Oxford, 1973) and Ross Harrison, *Bentham* (London, 1983).

[2] The complexities are illuminated by J. R. Dinwiddy in 'Bentham in the Early Nineteenth Century', in his *Radicalism and Reform in Britain 1780–1850* (London, 1992), pp. 291–313. See also the suggestive comments by John Robson, 'Which Was Mill's Bentham?', *Bentham Newsletter*, 7 (1983), pp. 15–26; R. D. Collinson Black, 'Bentham and the Political Economists of the Nineteenth Century', *Bentham Newsletter*, 12 (1988), pp. 24–36; and William Twining, 'Reading Bentham', *Proceedings of the British Academy*, 75 (1989), pp. 97–141.

[3] For the historical placement of James Mill, see Stefan Collini, Donald Winch, and John Burrow, *That Noble Science of Politics* (Cambridge, 1983), ch. 3. Bentham's self-description appears often in his correspondence; see, for example, *Correspondence of Jeremy Bentham*, vol. VII, ed. J. R. Dinwiddy (Oxford, 1988), p. 466.

According to a standard characterisation, the science of political economy supplied Bentham with his theory of society, and exercised a unique and pervasive impact on his moral and legal theory. Such an interpretation appears in any number of the accounts of modern political philosophy's surrender to economics, where Bentham's writings frequently serve both as an important contributor to and a major index of this celebrated historical declension;[4] and it echoes in those twentieth-century indictments of the cultural and social damage rendered by the Industrial Revolution which Donald Winch considers in his essay in this volume. And much the same characterisation figured no less prominently in some of the earliest and most influential of the efforts to take the measure of utilitarianism. Marx thus reported that 'political economy' was 'the real science' of Bentham's 'theory of utility'; Maine yoked together Bentham's legislative programme and Ricardian economics as the twin and mutually reinforcing sciences behind the recent thirst for innovative legislation; Dicey lectured that the 'disciples' of 'Adam Smith' and 'the Benthamites formed one school' and that their 'dogma of laissez faire' was 'practically the most vital part of Bentham's legislative doctrine'; and Halévy concluded his magisterial survey of Philosophic Radicalism with the judgement that the moral theory of the utilitarians was 'their economic psychology put into the imperative'. [5]

These days it has become easy work to challenge such confident Victorian pronouncements.[6] Such judgements standardly ran together a number of distinguishable claims: points about shared deductive and individualist methodologies; about shared policy recommendations and favoured law reform projects; and about the social classes who embraced these doctrines and policy initiatives. Moreover, we no longer can suppose (with Dicey or Maine) that the disciples of Adam Smith and the Benthamites in any sense exhausted or dominated the public debate over legislative reform, even in those settings where their influence was once so unambiguously discerned. And we would equally question the ease and casualness with which these accounts collapsed the distance between Smith's *Inquiry* and Ricardo's *Principles*. But while these important revisions and corrections would serve to undermine once routine claims about the affinities between classical political economy and Benthamic

[4] For a characteristic rendering of this theme, see C. B. Macpherson, *The Life and Times of Liberal Democracy* (Oxford, 1977), ch. 2.
[5] See Karl Marx, *German Ideology, Part One* [1845], in *Karl Marx: Selected Writings*, ed. David McLellan (Oxford, 1977), p. 185; Henry Sumner Maine, *Popular Government* [1885] (Indianapolis, 1976), p. 155; A. V. Dicey, *Law and Public Opinion in England* (1905; 2nd edn, London, 1914), pp. 126 and n. 147; Elie Halévy, *Growth of Philosophic Radicalism* [1901–4], trans. Mary Morris (London, 1972), p. 478.
[6] See Collini, *That Noble Science of Politics*, pp. 281–2.

utilitarianism, they leave in place more general questions concerning the relationship between the two bodies of thought. And here it seems important to keep hold of the most basic insight that political economy, in some significant manner, mattered to Bentham's legislative science.

Certainly, the science of political economy – the 'general theory' considering 'everything which concerns the wealth of nations' – was 'a branch of the science of legislation' Bentham was eager to embrace.[7] It was a body of speculation which formed part of the expertise required for the proper administration of the modern state;[8] and it was an area of knowledge in which Bentham sought to establish his own credentials. His best-known contribution to political economy, the 1787 *Defence of Usury*, was one of the few publications that earned for its author any public attention in the period before his reputation was secured through the medium of Dumont's 1802 redaction, *Traités de législation civile et pénale*. And Bentham plainly delighted in the (mistaken) report that his *Defence* had converted no less a figure than Adam Smith.[9] Smith's assessment of the work was critical: not only was Smith's endorsement of legal restraints on the rate of interest a major target of Bentham's essay; even more important, Smith, for Bentham, was the unrivalled authority in this branch of knowledge. He was 'the father of political economy'; his *Wealth of Nations* had 'not left much to do' for treating the 'causes and mode of [wealth's] production'.[10] Or, as Bentham put it in a manuscript of the 1790s: 'The parentage of Pluto's Wealth is no secret. He is the child of Earth by Labour . . . He has Earth for his Mother . . . Labour for his Father, and Adam Smith for his head Genealogist.'[11]

In recent years, Donald Winch has taught us to see in Smith's own 'science of a statesman or legislator', and in the political economy to which it contributed, a much more highly integrated and wide-ranging body of social speculation than previously had been recognised. And this

[7] Jeremy Bentham, *General View of a Complete Code of Laws*, in *Works of Jeremy Bentham, Published under the Supervision of … John Bowring*, 11 vols. (Edinburgh, 1838–43), III, p. 203. (*Works of Jeremy Bentham* hereafter cited as *Bowring*.) See also the definitions Bentham supplied in his *Manual of Political Economy* [1793–5], in *Jeremy Bentham's Economic Writings*, ed. W. Stark, 3 vols. (London, 1952–4), I, pp. 223–4.
[8] See Jeremy Bentham, *Constitutional Code*, vol. I [1830], ed. F. Rosen and J. H. Burns (Oxford, 1983), pp. 314–15.
[9] See Bentham's comments at the time of the 1790 publication of the second edition of his *Defence of Usury*, in *Correspondence of Jeremy Bentham*, vol. IV, ed. Alexander Taylor Milne (London, 1981), pp. 132–4, 208–9; and also the discussion of the work's reception by Stark in *Bentham's Economic Writings*, I, pp. 26–33.
[10] See Bentham, *The Rationale of Reward* (London, 1825), p. 70n, and *Institute of Political Economy* [1801–4], in *Bentham's Economic Writings*, III, pp. 321–2.
[11] Jeremy Bentham Manuscripts, University College London: UC.cliiia.107, cited in Douglas Long, 'Bentham on Property', in Anthony Parel and Thomas Flanagan, eds., *Theories of Property: Aristotle to the Present* (Waterloo, Ont., 1979), p. 241.

reconstruction of Smithian science, in turn, has enabled us to see the variety of ways in which this science was easily distorted and truncated, both in the heat of polemical battle (as in the case of Paine and Burke) and in the later efforts to appropriate his legacy in altered social settings (as in the case of Dugald Stewart and his students).[12] Winch's discussion provides a model for considering Bentham's own handling of Smith's teaching, where again one encounters a remarkably selective, partial and distorting appropriation of the Smithian system.

An obvious place to begin is with two (predictably) uncompleted attempts by Bentham to produce brief synthetic statements of 'the art of government in matters of political economy' or 'the art of directing the national industry to the purposes to which it may be directed with the greatest advantage'.[13] These are Bentham's *Manual of Political Economy*, composed in the period 1793–95, and the *Institute of Political Economy*, composed in the period 1801–4.[14] Both works proceed initially in terms of a contrast between the 'science' and the 'art' of political economy – a distinction which enabled Bentham to offer lavish praise for 'Dr Adam Smith' ('a writer of great and distinguished merit'), while at the same time justifying his own succeeding efforts in this field. Smith's 'object was the science: my object is the art'; 'this work', Bentham further explained, 'is to Dr Smith's, what a book on the art of medicine is to a book of anatomy or physiology'.[15]

Bentham's distinction between political economy as art and as science, as Winch has explained, figured critically in the struggles over Smith's legacy in the first decades of the nineteenth century, and it is tempting to read Bentham in light of these broader currents.[16] As with Dr Smith's other professed admirers, Bentham found the *Wealth of Nations* to be methodologically flawed for its failure to keep purely enough to its assigned role in the *science* of political economy; and as with others, Bentham found important gaps in the Smithian science (as in the neglect of population in the *Wealth of Nations*).[17] At the same time, it seems no less important to note the more idiosyncratic elements of Bentham's reaction.

[12] See Donald Winch, *Riches and Poverty* (Cambridge, 1996), chs. 5–8; and *That Noble Science of Politics*, ch. 1.
[13] *Institute of Political Economy*, in *Bentham's Economic Writings*, III, p. 307; and *Manual of Political Economy*, in *ibid.*, I, p. 223.
[14] The two works, as published in vols. I and III of *Bentham's Economic Writings*, need to be distinguished from the material appearing under the title, 'Manual of Political Economy' in vol. III of *Bowring*, which is an unreliable compilation of the two separate works; see *Bentham's Economic Writings*, I, pp. 49–50.
[15] *Manual*, in *Bentham's Economic Writings*, I, pp. 223–4; and see *Institute*, III, pp. 308, 318–22.   [16] See *That Noble Science*, pp. 49–54, 67–89.
[17] See *Manual*, in *Bentham's Economic Writings*, I, pp. 224–5, and *Institute*, in *ibid.*, III, p. 361n.

The distinction between science and art was standardly deployed in Bentham's legislative theory, where, as in the more particular case of political economy, he insisted that 'the only use of the science is the serving as a foundation to the art'.[18] The priority of practice over theory followed naturally from Bentham's utilitarian convictions, but not in a manner that prevented him from pursuing at remarkable length and depth more purely theoretical topics, as in the case of the intricacies of his theory of language and fictions, or the conceptual apparatus of jurisprudence he referred to as 'law metaphysics'.[19] What, perhaps, was peculiar about Bentham's engagement with political economy – at least initially – was the casualness with which he regarded its theoretical achievements, and the readiness with which he let the *Wealth of Nations* supply its authoritative pronouncement.[20]

In addition, the relationship between science and art in this context requires some elaboration, for it is easy to mistake what was involved in Bentham's effort to derive 'practical use' from the Smithian science. In some cases, what this involved was specifying entire areas of legal policy where the insights of the science could be directly applied. Thus, in that area of legislative science styled *The Rationale of Reward*, legislative art frequently adopted wholesale the insights of political economy. Under the heading of 'reward' Bentham considered the relatively exceptional situations in which the legislator influenced conduct not through the threat of punishment but through the inducement of benefit, most commonly where government secured services by rewarding labour. The guiding principle for how government was to price such labour was that 'in all cases in which no particular reason can be given to the contrary, the liberty of competition ought to be admitted upon the largest scale'; and this was a principle definitively established by Smith, whose application 'of it to the laws relating to trade has nearly exhausted the subject'.[21]

But the relatively straightforward move from economic theory to legislative practice in the case of *Reward* was exceptional. Most often the art of political economy demanded that the legislator accommodate the insights of the science within a legislative programme whose structure and objectives only in part concerned 'the wealth of nations'. As Bentham reported in a work devoted to setting out the basic architecture and rela-

[18] *Manual*, in *ibid.*, I, p. 224.
[19] See the treatment in my *Province of Legislation Determined: Legal Theory in Eighteenth-Century Britain* (Cambridge, 1989), ch. 13.
[20] See, for example, *Manual*, in *Bentham's Economic Writings*, I, p. 223n: 'Be the doctrine [of Smith] true or false, this concise sketch will serve at any rate to give a view of the state of the question upon all the topics of political economy that can come under the consideration of the legislature ... If the doctrine be erroneous, exhibited as it is here, it will not be difficult to correct the error.'   [21] *Rationale of Reward*, pp. 110, 118.

tionships among the component parts of a 'Complete Code of Laws', although it was easy to identify 'a science distinct from every other which is called *political* economy', he could not see 'that there can exist a code of laws concerning political economy, distinct and separate from all the other codes'. Rather, a collection of economical laws could 'only be a mass of imperfect shreds, drawn without distinction from the whole body of laws'.[22]

The general approach is clarified by reference to Bentham's treatment of the 'Principles of the Civil Code', a discussion which elaborated a system of legal rights and obligations (including, of course, a system of property rights) and the legislative principles guiding their distribution.[23] Here Bentham differentiated the fundamental object of the legal system – the promotion of happiness – into four subsidiary ends: subsistence, abundance, security and equality; he explained how all the functions of civil law could be identified in these subsidiary ends, and how they were to be respectively ordered and coordinated as legislative objectives. A large burden of the discussion was directed at establishing the primacy of security (and the prevention of frustrated expectations) in the principles of civil law. Unlike the other 'subsidiary ends' of legislation, security functioned not just as a component part, but more as a general pre-requisite and enabling condition for the effective pursuit and cultivation of happiness.[24] The capacity 'to look forward' in an 'expectation of the future' distinguished men from brutes; 'expectation' was the 'chain which unites our present and our future existence, and passes beyond ourselves to the generations which follow us'; 'the principle of security extends to the maintenance of all these expectations'.[25] In societal terms, it was again 'security' that provided the preconditions of successful coexistence. The preservation of security (and the prevention of frustrated expectations) was both the 'principal object of law' and 'entirely the work of law' –

---

[22] *General View of a Complete Code of Laws*, in *Bowring*, III, p. 203.

[23] Bentham treated civil law and the civil code at several stages of his career. The account developed here draws most heavily on his *Theory of Legislation*, which is the English translation of Etienne Dumont's redaction, *Traités de législation civile et pénale ... Par M. Jérémie Bentham, jurisconsulte anglois*, 3 vols. (Paris, 1802). For a full examination of this branch of Bentham's jurisprudence, see P. J. Kelly, *Utilitarianism and Distributive Justice* (Oxford, 1990).

[24] The importance of security in Bentham's moral and legal theory is stressed in two recent (and divergent) accounts of his utilitarianism and jurisprudence; see Postema, *Bentham and the Common Law Tradition*, chs. 5 and 12; and Kelly, *Utilitarianism and Distributive Justice*.

[25] *Theory of Legislation*, ed. C. K. Ogden (London, 1931), p. 111. See also Bentham's further discussion of the difference between security and the three other subsidiary ends, in *Correspondence*, VII, pp. 47–9; and in *Pannomion Fragments*, in *Bowring*, III, p. 225, where he emphasises how security, unlike the other ends, is not limited to 'matters of wealth'.

without the law creating an arena of security, there could be 'no abundance, and not even a certainty of subsistence; and the only equality . . . is an equality of misery'.[26]

In addition to establishing the primacy of security, the discussion of these differentiated 'subsidiary ends' enabled Bentham to account for the flexibility that necessarily attended the legislator's application of the general principles of the civil code. What was required by law to promote the goal of subsistence, for example, would rightly vary in conditions of scarcity as compared with conditions of moderate plenty or opulence.[27] Where Bentham advanced generic propositions concerning the relationships between these goals – such as the claim that prosperity naturally tended to greater social equality, or that communal ownership of land naturally retarded social improvements – he drew readily from the science of political economy. But the science of wealth did not itself provide the ordering logic for the civil code. Instead, when Bentham turned to analyse the legislative principles guiding the distribution of portions of wealth, he turned to a set of psychological properties termed the 'axioms' of 'mental pathology' which specified 'the knowledge of the sensations, affections, passions, and of their effects upon happiness'.[28] It was this scheme of mental axioms which grounded the case for equality as a legislative goal, and which guided the legislator's hand 'in the creation and distribution of proprietary and other civil rights'.[29]

The resulting body of legislative principles gave ample scope, where appropriate, to the insights of political economy, but within a legislative structure that ordered rights and obligations on a different basis. Thus, for example, when Bentham went on to consider the leading examples of attacks on security which were committed by government (and which his legislative principles served to condemn), he included policies, such as the 'forced reduction of the rate of interest', which were standardly covered 'as a question of political economy' on account of the damage such measures caused 'to wealth'. But in the setting of the principles of the civil code, such injurious regulations were regarded 'with a more immediate view to security', and condemned as measures which undermined the expectations of lenders without compensating benefit to borrowers. And given the perspectives of the civil code, such misguided

[26] *Theory of Legislation*, p. 109.
[27] See *ibid.*, pp. 128–33; and see also *Institute*, in *Bentham's Economic Writings*, III, p. 322n, and *Defence of a Maximum* [1801], in *ibid.*, III, pp. 247–302, especially p. 255.
[28] *Theory of Legislation*, p. 102. By the time of the 1789 publication of *An Introduction to the Principles of Morals and Legislation*, Bentham had come to regard the elaboration of these axioms as a major pillar of his legislative theory; see *An Introduction to the Principles of Morals and Legislation*, ed. J. H. Burns and H. L. A. Hart (London, 1970), p. 3n.
[29] *Morals and Legislation*, p. 3; and see *Theory of Legislation*, pp. 103–9.

regulations earned inclusion in a discussion equally devoted to measures of little direct relevance to political economy, such as the dissolution of convents and monastic orders.[30]

These same general principles of legislative science, moreover, guided Bentham's analysis when he turned more directly to the task of presenting 'the art' of political economy for the legislator. Both in the *Manual* and in the *Institute of Political Economy*, he presented modified versions of the subsidiary ends of legislation (subsistence, security, abundance, equality) to introduce and explicate the 'ends or uses of wealth'.[31] Even more important, by identifying the scope of political economy so emphatically with 'the art of directing the national industry to the purposes to which it may be directed with greatest advantage',[32] Bentham tended to associate its instruction chiefly with the legislative goal of abundance; that is, with but one of the lesser three of the four subsidiary ends of law. The consequence was a remarkably narrow art, comprising a remarkably meagre set of governing principles. As Donald Winch observed of the related setting in which Bentham appropriated Smith in making his case against colonies, 'The discussion is more dogmatic, and many of the subtle distinctions which were so much a feature of Smith's analysis have disappeared.'[33]

In the *Manual of Political Economy*, Bentham presented, 'as the groundwork of the whole', a principle taken from the *Wealth of Nations*: 'the limitation of industry by the limitation of capital'.[34] And the application of this principle generated a set of arguments in repudiation of the prevailing network of commercial bounties, drawbacks and prohibitions. 'Its chief conclusion', Leslie Stephen summarised, 'is that almost all legislation is improper.'[35] At first glance, Bentham's art of political economy appears to reveal, as Dicey put it, that 'laissez faire . . . was practically the most vital part of Bentham's legislative doctrine'.[36] But this is to miss the structuring elements of Bentham's legislative theory. The art of political economy was so limited because its parent science (for Bentham) was so focused on wealth. The limitations on what the legislator positively could do to promote abundance were quite distinct from the very substantial tasks the legislator faced in promoting security and subsistence. As Bentham explained in the *Manual of Political Economy* (and later explored further in his 1801 *Defence of a Maximum*), legislation restricting the price

---

[30] *Theory of Legislation*, pp. 141–3.
[31] See *Manual*, in *Bentham's Economic Writings*, I, p. 226 and n.; and *Institute*, in *ibid.*, III, pp. 308–12.   [32] *Manual*, in *ibid.*, I, p. 223.
[33] D. Winch, *Classical Political Economy and Colonies* (Cambridge, Mass., 1965), p. 29.
[34] *Manual*, in *Bentham's Economic Writings*, I, p. 225.
[35] Leslie Stephen, *The English Utilitarians*, 3 vols. (London, 1900), I, p. 309.
[36] Dicey, *Law and Public Opinion*, p.147.

and exportation of corn looked quite different from the perspective of 'security of subsistence' from the way it did with regard to the goal of promoting wealth.[37] Political economy did not teach Bentham to contemplate areas of social life which operated stably in the absence of law. Rather, it provided guidance on a social goal which did not rank uppermost in the Benthamic legislative science. The legislator's 'great purpose is to preserve the total mass of expectations as far as is possible from all that may interfere with their course', Bentham observed in a voluminous 1801 essay on paper money. 'In comparison with this, encrease of wealth is but a frivolous object.'[38]

Of course, in making his case for the legislative priority and social benefits of security, Bentham recognised and indeed emphasised the manner in which a properly designed and effectively-enforced legal regime of security of person and possession generally tended to promote the accumulation of wealth. 'Security is the seed of opulence', pronounced the *Institute of Political Economy*; and the pronouncement can be readily taken as a Benthamic formulation of a Smithian theme. Where Smith in the *Wealth of Nations* maintained that the 'laws and customs so favourable to the [security of tenancy of the] yeomanry have perhaps contributed more to the present grandeur of England than all their boasted regulations of commerce taken together',[39] Bentham in the *Institute of Political Economy* rejoined:

> What the legislator and the Minister of the Interior have it in their power to do towards encrease either of wealth or population is as nothing in comparison with what is done of course, and without thinking of it, by the judge, and his assistant, the Minister of Police.[40]

None the less, as we have seen, the case for legal security was not established on the basis of its contribution to wealth; and given the structure of Bentham's own legislative science, however eloquently Smith in the *Wealth of Nations* made the case for the stability of possession and the virtue of justice, these arguments were not directly within the scope of an art of political economy. (In Bentham's terms, these were parts of Smith's 'science of a statesman or legislator' not directly about political

---

[37] *Manual*, in *Bentham's Economic Writings* I, pp. 265–7; and *Defence of a Maximum*, in *ibid.*, III, pp. 284–90.   [38] *The True Alarm* [1801], in *ibid.*, III, p. 198.

[39] Adam Smith, *An Inquiry into the Nature and Causes of the Wealth of Nations* (1776), ed. R. H. Campbell, A. S. Skinner, and W. B. Todd, 2 vols. (Oxford, 1976), I, p. 392.

[40] *Institute*, in *Bentham's Economic Writings*, III, p. 323. See also *General View of a Complete Code of Laws*, in *Bowring*, III, p. 203: 'The most powerful means of augmenting national wealth are those which maintain the security of properties, and which gently favour their equalization. Such are the objects of the civil and penal law. Those arrangements which tend to increase the national wealth by other means than security and equality (if there be any such,) may be considered as belonging to the class of economical laws.'

economy.) Ironically, the organising categories of Bentham's legislative science did as much to cabin as to celebrate the Smithian science. This legislative architecture best explains the notably modest withdrawal of funds from the *Wealth of Nations* Bentham chose to make in first practising the art of political economy ('the limitation of industry by the limitation of capital'). And it perhaps also accounts for the apparent ease with which Bentham disregarded those parts of Smith's theory of law and government which repudiated just that kind of comprehensive, utilitarian reconstruction of public institutions which Bentham's own legislative theory so often promised.[41]

One major consequence of this Benthamic approach to political economy was that, in treating topics within its scope, his legislative theorising tended to swallow up the economics. (As even Stark was forced to acknowledge in introducing the final instalment of his three-volume edition of *Bentham's Economic Writings*, it was hard to be confident of the seriousness of Bentham's commitment to the field.[42]) The situation can be illustrated in many of Bentham's 'economic writings', but the example which deserves special attention here is the *Defence of Usury* – in part on account of its direct concern with Smith, and in part on account of the prestige it was subsequently accorded in the canon of classical political economy. Bentham's 1787 polemic against usury laws positioned the authority of 'Dr Smith' in a critical manner. The *Wealth of Nations* contained a defence of the laws against usury, and Bentham's counter-case was expressly pursued with the 'weapons' Smith had 'furnished' and taught his critic 'to wield'.[43] Bentham's insistence 'that there are no ways in which these laws can do any good' turned on the demonstration that the same general reasons Smith established against legal restraints on 'exchanges in general' equally and fully applied to exchanges of 'present money for future'.[44]

But although Smith's doctrines were at the centre of Bentham's case,

---

41   Smith's own legislative doctrines are treated, most recently, by Winch in *Riches and Poverty*, chs. 4, 6–7; see also Knud Haakonssen, *Science of a Legislator* (Cambridge, 1981). Bentham's relationship to the jurisprudence of the Scottish Enlightenment is illuminated by J. H. Burns in 'Scottish Philosophy and the Science of Legislation', *Royal Society of Edinburgh Occasional Papers*, 3 (1985), pp. 11–29.
42   See *Bentham's Economic Writings*, III, p. 47. My emphasis on these limits to Bentham's 'economic writings' is not to deny the increasing intricacy and ambition of these writings themselves, especially in the area of banking and monetary policy. The fullest review of these materials remains Stark's own introductions to his edition of *Bentham's Economic Writings*. For a contrasting treatment of the relationship between Bentham's political economy and his jurisprudence, see P. J. Kelly, 'Utilitarianism and Distributive Justice: The Civil Law and the Foundations of Bentham's Economic Thought', *Utilitas*, I (1989), pp. 62–81.   43   *Defence of Usury*, in *Bentham's Economic Writings*, I, p. 167.
44   *Ibid.*, pp. 142, 132.

what is no less striking is how much of *Defence of Usury* did not engage political economy at all. The analysis began with reference to Bentham's theory of language, with the argument that 'the sound of the word *usury*' was responsible for immediately biasing any careful scrutiny of the nature of bargains for money. The tract continued with a standard stock of claims Bentham deployed in his law reform proposals generally. The perpetuation of this misguided legislation, he explained, was symptomatic of the tendency 'in matters of law' for the inertial forces of 'authority' and 'prejudice' to sustain irrational institutions. The prominence given to Adam Smith on the title page of *Defence of Usury* in no way prevented Bentham from devoting one entire section of the work to William Blackstone and his *Commentaries on the Laws of England*; later passages took aim at another favourite target, Aristotle.[45] Two years following its first publication, Bentham described his *Defence of Usury* as a critical application of his principles of legislative classification, in this instance serving to expose a penal law which lacked the required justification in public utility.[46] The characterisation suited the work at least as well as the more familiar category of 'economic writing'. And it supplies apt testimony to the more pervasive manner in which Bentham's legislative theory loudly embraced but firmly contained the science Dr Smith had fathered.

II

Admittedly, those commentators who discerned the unmistakable triumph of economics in Bentham's thought rarely believed that the charge turned on the kind of careful reconstruction of the organising categories of Bentham's legislative science attempted above. All this, perhaps, is rather beside the point. Bentham's absorption of political economy occurred in a less avowed and more insidious manner, in terms of his most basic assumptions about individual behaviour and social action. The key construction, it is standardly argued, concerns Bentham's conception of human nature. 'With the dryest naiveté', Marx maintained, 'he assumes that the modern petty bourgeois, especially the English petty bourgeois, is the normal man. Whatever is useful to this peculiar kind of normal man, and to his world, is useful in and of itself.'[47]

My aim in this section of the essay is to take up the question of Bentham's treatment of human nature, and the more particular claim that this account presumed and valorised the prudent, appetitive behav-

---

[45] *Ibid.*, pp. 130, 157, 153–6, 158–9.   [46] See *Morals and Legislation*, pp. 4–5.
[47] Karl Marx, *Capital*, 3 vols. [1867], trans. Ben Fowkes (Harmondsworth, 1976), I, p. 759n.

iour of the market place: Halévy's 'economic psychology put into the imperative'.[48] Again, my hope is both to exploit and to propose lines of connection between some of the recent reinterpretations of Bentham's writings and the broader revisions in the intellectual history of Bentham's era. This latter scholarship has been particularly powerful in its scrutiny of the careers of those notorious conceptual constructs, 'rational economic man' and 'laissez-faire individualism'. Here we have been taught to recognise the range of sources for late eighteenth- and early nineteenth-century individualism which were not the products of Dicey's famous firm of 'Smith and Bentham'.[49] In the case of Smith, we have been shown the manner in which Smith's account of human prudence and the pursuit of wealth supported (rather than compromised) a moral theory which expressly rejected rival systems of ethics based on selfish and utilitarian accounts of human behaviour.[50] And in charting the debates and doctrines which linked and divided Philosophic Whigs and Philosophic Radicals in the first decades of the nineteenth century, we have learned not to focus exclusive attention on the 'principle of self-interest' which Macaulay so brilliantly elevated to pre-eminence in his famed assault on James Mill's political science.[51]

Bentham, no less than James Mill, has been taken as the very model of the attempt 'to deduce the science' – in this case, of legislation – 'from the principles of human nature';[52] and interpretative attention continues to be directed both at the content of this account and at its place within Bentham's theory of ethics. Much of this scholarship has been designed to rescue Bentham from the long-entrenched charges of basic philosophic error in linking hedonism and utilitarianism, and to modify earlier characterisations of his psychological hedonism. The broad thrust of this reinterpretation has been to distance Bentham's use and understanding of human nature from the approach adopted by James Mill in the *Essay on Government*; and to move Bentham closer to more typical, Humean conventions concerning the types of assumptions about human behaviour it was prudent to make for the purposes of designing institutions of law and government.[53]

[48] See the discussion above, note 5.
[49] See especially the contribution of Boyd Hilton in *The Age of Atonement* (Oxford, 1988).
[50] See Winch, *Riches and Poverty*, pp. 103–9.
[51] See Winch, *That Noble Science of Politics*, pp. 110–26.
[52] See Thomas Babington Macaulay, review of James Mill's *Essay on Government* [1829], in Jack Lively and John Rees, eds., *Utilitarian Logic and Politics* (Oxford, 1978), p. 124.
[53] Much of this work has been developed in response to accounts of Bentham's alleged 'naturalist fallacy' and to Halévy's interpretation in *Growth of Philosophic Radicalism* of Bentham's strategy for the harmonisation of individual and collective interests. In what follows, I am especially indebted to the discussion in Harrison, *Bentham*, chs. 5–6.

For the legislator, of course, the great priority concerned the *influencing* of human conduct rather than the refined conceptualisation of human nature. Still, legislative science could never proceed without some understanding of the human material upon which law worked; and the success of legislative art plainly depended, in good measure, on the accuracy of this understanding.[54] In designing laws and institutions, the legislator utilised punishment and reward so as 'to make it each man's *interest* to observe on every occasion that conduct which it is his *duty* to observe'; and in so building upon the foundation of 'personal interest', the legislator relied on that 'principle of action . . . most to be depended upon, whose influence is most powerful, most constant, most uniform, most lasting, and most general among mankind'.[55]

The claim that the sovereign mastery of pleasure and pain rendered all human conduct intrinsically self-interested appeared repeatedly throughout Bentham's writings (though 'self-interest' actually was a term he avoided). The insight that 'on every occasion, by interest in some shape or other is the conduct of every man determined'[56] promptly ruled out a variety of conventional Christian and classically inspired moral pieties counselling self-denial, self-sacrifice, or self-resignation. ('*Summum Bonum*: Consummate Nonsense' began the relevant section of Bentham's *Deontology*.[57]) And it equally ruled out institutional designs which relied on 'disinterestedness' as a qualification for positions of authority and public office.[58] But, as in the case of most eighteenth-century moralists, Bentham expressly distinguished the hedonistic psychology and the dynamics of 'self-preference' from a doctrine of selfishness or narrow self-love. All individuals readily associated their own pursuits of pleasure with the happiness of at least some others. Although 'the only interests which a man at all times and upon all occasions is sure to find *adequate* motives for consulting are his own', nevertheless 'there are no occasions in which a man has not some motives for consulting the happiness of other men'.[59] As his ethical theorising developed, Bentham came to place greater weight on the efficacy of benevolence (that is, acts undertaken to promote

---

[54] See Bentham's defence of the methodology adopted in developing his account of 'mental pathology' in *Theory of Legislation*, p. 103.

[55] *Pauper Management Improved* [1797], in *Bowring*, VIII, pp. 380–1.

[56] *Deontology* [1834], in Jeremy Bentham, *Deontology . . . A Table of the Springs of Action and Article on Utilitarianism*, ed. Amnon Goldworth (Oxford, 1983), p. 128.

[57] *Ibid.*, p. 134.

[58] See, among many examples, *Pauper Management Improved*, in *Bowring*, VIII, p. 381.

[59] *Morals and Legislation*, p. 284. See also the later formulation of 1822: 'though self-regard, the desire in man to feel himself happy, is in every situation the predominant desire and propensity in human nature, neither is social regard, sympathetic regard, the desire to see others happy, less extensively inherent in it'; Jeremy Bentham, *First Principles Preparatory to Constitutional Code*, ed. Philip Schofield (Oxford, 1989), p. 14.

'the happiness of others') in social life. And even at the level of institutional design, the legislator sought to mobilise the force of sympathy and what Bentham termed the 'moral sanction' in the effort to ensure that the 'ruling-few' exercised their power in the interests of the entire community.[60]

Ironically, in charting the operations of 'self-preference', Bentham came to voice virtually all the points of methodological difficulty better associated with the critique of Benthamic utilitarianism. Since the 'subjection of conduct to interest' applied equally in 'the case of the most extensively beneficent, generous, and heroic action that ever was performed' as it did 'in the case of the most mischievous or selfish',[61] serious ambiguities arose over quite what it meant to *explain* human behavior in terms of personal interest. The familiar statement, he warned, that an individual 'is never governed by any thing but his own interest' was 'indubitably true', but only in that 'large and extensive sense of the word interest (as comprehending all sorts of motives)'. At the same time, the claim was 'indubitably false in any of the confined senses in which . . . the word interest is wont to be made use of'.[62]

Equally critical difficulties emerged over the difference between real and perceived interests. Individuals successfully navigated their pursuit of pleasure and avoidance of pain 'wheresoever they have a clear view of their own interest'.[63] But this evidently allowed for various settings in which the requisite 'clear view' was noticeably obscured. In his writings on poor relief and indigence, Bentham seemed prepared to acknowledge entire sub-groups of the community who could not be relied upon effectively to pursue their own real interests. Less exceptionally, he recognised that even those who generally succeeded in pursuing their interests would occasionally lapse: 'never probably has any man existed who has not acted against his own interest'.[64] And finally, in his radical political theory, he emphasised the manner in which well-entrenched networks of 'interest-begotten prejudice' systematically served to confuse the 'subject-many' as to the extent to which their real interests were regularly sacrificed to the interests of a corrupt 'ruling-few'.[65]

[60] Bentham's institutional strategy for the mobilisation of the moral sanction remains in dispute among recent commentators; see the contrasting approaches of Postema, *Bentham and the Common Law Tradition*, pp. 383–402, and Philip Schofield, 'Bentham on the Identification of Interests', *Utilitas*, 8 (1996), pp. 223–34.   [61] *Deontology*, p. 128.

[62] Jeremy Bentham, *Of Laws in General* [1782], ed. H. L. A. Hart (London, 1970), p. 70n; and see the further discussion in Harrison, *Bentham*, pp. 142–7.

[63] *Morals and Legislation*, p. 40.

[64] *Deontology*, p. 129; and see the further discussion in Harrison, *Bentham*, pp. 162–5.

[65] See the valuable survey of this dimension of Bentham's political programme in Hume, *Bentham and Bureaucracy*, pp. 186–95.

Given such complexities, it becomes evident that the legislator, in presuming a stable and predictable universe of individual self-preference,
proceeded pragmatically and strategically. The individual was never
taken to be an infallible judge or perfect pursuer of his own interests. But
the legislator had sufficient insight into the processes of self-preference
for the purposes of law. To what extent, then, were such knowledge and
presumptions dependent on more specific Benthamic views, implicit or
explicit, concerning the nature of economically orientated conduct?

In considering this question, it is worth recalling that Bentham's legislative programme required not only a sufficient stability in social conduct
(such that law could harness duty to personal interest), it further required
no little sophistication on the part of social agents in planning and adjust-
ing their conduct in the light of anticipated pleasures and pains as these
had been positively manipulated through the introduction of legal sanctions. Probably the best-known example of this occurs in Bentham's discussion of the proper level of severity to be adopted in the penalties of the
penal code. Like many penal reformers in the second half of the eighteenth century, Bentham believed the application of his legislative principles would serve to bring a decisive reduction in penal severity by
introducing the requisite proportionality between levels of crime and
levels of punishment. Beccaria, in this context, had written of the need to
establish 'a scale of crimes' which comprehended 'all actions contrary to
the public good', placing these 'criminal' acts on a gradation between the
most pernicious ('those which immediately tend to the dissolution of
society') and the least pernicious ('of the smallest possible injustice done
to a private member of that society'), and then assembling 'a corresponding scale of punishments, descending from the greatest to the least'.[66]

Bentham's treatment of the same aspiration drew instead on the terminology of the market place. Cases in which sanctions proved ineffective or
counter-productively excessive (termed 'cases unmeet for punishment')
were 'cases where punishment is unprofitable'. On the other hand, in
cases 'meet for punishment', sanctions needed to be of a severity (or
'value') 'sufficient to outweigh that of the profit of the offence'. And in a
concluding summary of a chapter-long survey of the eleven principal
'properties to be given to a lot of punishment' (which included 'frugality'
as number 6), Bentham identified those properties 'calculated to
augment the *profit* which is to be made by punishment' and those calculated 'to diminish the *expense*'.[67]

This treatment of proportionality in punishment was typical of the

[66] Cesare Beccaria, *An Essay on Crime and Punishments* (1767; 3rd edn, London, 1770),
pp. 22–3.   [67] *Morals and Legislation*, pp. 163–4, 166, 186.

manner in which Bentham invoked metaphors of trade and accumulation in order to convey his understanding of individual psychology and social action. The discussion of mental pathology in the principles of the civil code (treated above), including the account of the diminishing marginal utility of surplus pleasure, modelled man's sensibilities to happiness entirely in terms of 'portions of wealth'.[68] In the *Deontology*, he explained the practice of beneficence by likening 'every act of virtuous beneficence' to a contribution 'to a sort of fund – a sort of Saving Bank', whereby the individual established a 'General Good Will Fund . . . from which draughts in his favour may come to be paid'.[69] In defending the laboured terminology and distinctions which comprised his account of the 'value of a lot of pleasure, how to be measured' in *An Introduction to the Principles of Morals and Legislation*, Bentham reassured his reader that his treatment was neither 'novel and unwarranted', nor different from the 'settled Practice of mankind'. Such calculating valuations of pleasures and pains occurred routinely, as in the valuing of 'an article of property [or] an estate in land'.[70] And in a later attempt to clarify the intricate calculations required to perceive the difference between the value of present pleasure and the value of an equal amount of certain but future pleasure, he proposed 'to form an estimate of this diminution, [to] take the general source, and thence representative, of pleasure, viz. *money*'.[71]

Yet even this extensive invocation of property and profit to give content to a generalised account of human behaviour did not lack its ambiguities. As Ross Harrison notes, in some early manuscripts of the 1770s Bentham explored the possibility of using money as the universal measure for the calculation and inter-personal comparison of states of happiness. But in his published works he identified problems inherent in such an approach, expressly denied that all pleasures and pains could be measured in monetary terms, and repudiated the 'vulgar error' that only money has value.[72] A passage from *An Introduction to the Principles of Morals and Legislation* is equally revealing. There Bentham directly took up the challenge that his strategy of guiding social conduct through a regime of proportionate penal deterrence was fundamentally misguided ('so much labour lost') because criminal acts were the work of passion and 'passion does not calculate'. In part, Bentham met the charge by rejecting its claims: 'the proposition that passion does not calculate, this like most of these very general

---

[68] See *Theory of Legislation*, pp. 102–9.   [69] *Deontology*, pp. 184–6.
[70] *Morals and Legislation*, p. 40.
[71] *Codification Proposal, Addressed ... To All Nations Professing Liberal Opinions* [1822], in Jeremy Bentham, *'Legislator of the World': Writings on Codification, Law and Education*, ed. Philip Schofield and Jonathan Harris (Oxford, 1998), p. 251. (I am indebted to Philip Schofield for alerting me to this passage.)
[72] See the valuable analysis of these contrasting positions in Harrison, *Bentham*, pp. 155–62.

and oracular propositions, is not true'. But, he also went on to observe that of 'all the passions' the one 'most given to calculation' was that corresponding 'to the motive of pecuniary interest' (that is, the pursuit of wealth). And since the mischiefs produced by this particular motive figured as the leading object of the penal law, criminal deterrence enjoyed 'the best chance of being efficacious, where efficacy is of the most importance'.[73] Once more, it might seem, Bentham turned to economically orientated conduct in order to redeem the behaviourist assumptions of his legislative project. But in this case, the logic of economic motivation and pecuniary interest did not supply the clarifying core of *generalised* social conduct. Rather, economic conduct was distinguishable from generalised social conduct by being the 'most given to calculation' (though its exceptionality proved a happy advantage to the penal law). In this setting at least, Bentham's reliance on the experienced calculator of economic benefits and burdens appeared as much the pragmatic construction of legislative science as did his more general utilisation of the logic of personal interest.

III

Bentham's social actor, in crucial respects then, functioned in a manner that evinced the calculating discipline of profit-seeking and market-exchange. In this sense, it is hard to imagine Bentham's legislative science functioning in a community which lacked the practice of truck, barter, and exchange. Where the familiar reduction of Benthamic man to 'economic man' proves incomplete and misleading is in the failure to notice the extent to which Bentham's account of human nature was itself the self-conscious construction of legislative art rather than the (putative) neutral statement of descriptive findings. But the emphasis on Bentham's 'economic psychology' is misleading also in another sense: in its tendency to overshadow other, no less critical assumptions about social conduct Bentham made in his legislative programme. In this final section I seek to explore one such set of assumptions: those concerning the operation of public opinion in Bentham's programme for representative government in the *Constitutional Code*.

One of the important (and long-overdue) accomplishments of the new edition of *Collected Works* has been to break the grip long exercised by *A Fragment on Government* and the first six chapters of *An Introduction to the Principles of Morals and Legislation* in the treatment of Bentham's thought. In the case of Bentham's political and constitutional theory, the edition

---

[73] *Morals and Legislation*, pp. 173–4.

has made available a series of important writings from the final decade of Bentham's career, when much of his legislative science was focused on the elaboration of a radical programme of constitutional democracy.[74] The study of Bentham's legislative science as applied to constitutional law has increasingly come to focus on these materials.

The political debates and polemics over parliamentary reform in the 1820s and 1830s tended to highlight the most immediately controversial elements of the Philosophical Radical programme: the calls for manhood suffrage and for the ballot. (In due course, the arguments advanced in support of these same reforms furnished the site for the observation of yet another 'economic' triumph over political philosophy: the 'economic theory of democracy'.[75]) In Bentham's own case, his views on the suffrage were notoriously extreme, even by Philosophical Radical standards. As Brougham explained to his fellow legislators in the House of Commons, 'Mr Bentham' would give the vote to any 'person of either sex [who] was able to put a pellet into a box, no matter whether he were insane and had one of the keepers of a mad-house to guide him'.[76] Still, recent scholarship has properly emphasised how much of Bentham's plan of democratic government depended on a range of institutional devices that extended well beyond the electoral process.[77] The 'ruling-few' needed to function under legal restraints as well as electoral accountability, while the 'subject-many' needed to wield the power of public opinion as much as the democratic franchise.

Bentham summarised his utilitarian programme of good government under the formula, 'Official Aptitude Maximized, Expense Minimized'. 'Official Aptitude' covered several capacities, including appropriate 'moral aptitude' which referred to the determination of an individual exercising political power to seek the promotion of 'his own happiness by giving encrease to the happiness of the greatest number'.[78] As with the other elements of desired 'official aptitude', the *Constitutional Code*

---

[74] These writings, as published in the new *Collected Works* edition, include: *Colonies, Commerce, and Constitutional Law: Rid Yourselves of Ultramaria and Other Writings on Spain and Spanish America* [1820–22], ed. Philip Schofield (Oxford, 1995); *First Principles Preparatory to Constitutional Code* [1822]; *Securities Against Misrule and Other Constitutional Writings for Tripoli and Greece* [1822–3], ed. Philip Schofield (Oxford, 1990); *Constitutional Code*, I; *Official Aptitude Maximized, Expense Minimized* [1830], ed. Philip Schofield (Oxford, 1993).

[75] See Alan Ryan, 'Two Concepts of Politics and Democracy: James and John Stuart Mill', in Martin Fleisher, ed., *Machiavelli and the Nature of Political Thought* (New York, 1972), and Terence Ball, *Transforming Political Discourse* (Oxford, 1988), ch. 6.

[76] Speech to the House of Commons, June 1818; quoted in Bentham, *Codification Proposal*, in *Legislator of the World*, p. 303.

[77] See especially the treatments of the *Constitutional Code* in Rosen, *Bentham and Representative Government*, and Hume, *Bentham and Bureaucracy*, chs. 6–8.

[78] *First Principles*, p. 14.

furnished a network of structures and procedures (or 'securities against misrule') for sustaining this commitment to utilitarian goals. In the case of 'moral aptitude', Bentham identified and extolled an institution he termed the 'Public Opinion Tribunal', giving it expansive responsibilities in his programme against the 'disease' of misrule.[79]

The Public Opinion Tribunal, in the highly technical expression of Bentham's mature constitutional writing, constituted 'a fictitious tribunal' or 'imaginary tribunal or judiciary', which applied 'the punishments and rewards' of 'the popular or moral sanction.'[80] As in the case of more conventional judicial bodies, the Public Opinion Tribunal received accusations and allegations of misconduct (here the acts of misrule committed by those exercising government power); heard counter-testimony in defence; weighed and evaluated assembled evidence; formed and publicised its determined conclusions; and finally gave 'effect and execution' to its judgement.[81] The punishments it imposed (its exercise of the popular or moral sanction) chiefly comprised the lowered popularity and weakened prestige on the part of those officials it found wanting in desired moral aptitude.[82]

As an institution of constitutional democracy, Bentham's Public Opinion Tribunal was even more democratic than the electorate. It would frequently function in the form of 'sub-committees', containing members of the community who turned their attention to particular issues or particular government actions; and such sub-committees might on occasion become dominated by an 'aristocratical section' opposed to the 'democratical' interests of the full Public Opinion Tribunal.[83] Nonetheless, there were no rules of qualification or requirements for joining; membership in the Public Opinion Tribunal was determined entirely by the individual choosing to participate in its operations. As a result, the Tribunal included in its ranks several of the sub-groups standardly disqualified from political life – foreigners and children, no less than unpropertied males and women. To the extent that the extra-legal processes of the Public Opinion Tribunal were modelled on more formal political bodies, its decisions constituted a uniquely popular vehicle of power. 'Public opinion may be considered as a system of law, emanating from the body of the people', declared the *Constitutional Code*.[84] And Bentham repeatedly stressed the efficacy of its sanctions:

[79] Bentham deployed the terminology of 'remedy' and 'disease' routinely in this context; see, for example, his 'preliminary explanations' to *Securities Against Misrule*, p. 25.
[80] *First Principles*, p. 283; and see *Constitutional Code*, I, pp. 35–9.
[81] See *Securities Against Misrule*, pp. 60–4.
[82] See *Constitutional Code*, I, p. 134n: 'Under the sort of law established and enforced by the power of the moral sanction – the penalty ... is forfeiture of a correspondent degree of popularity.'   [83] See *First Principles*, pp. 70–6.
[84] *Constitutional Code*, I, p. 36. (The passage continues, with the clarification: 'If there be no

[The English King] may kill any person he pleases, violate any woman he pleases; take to himself or destroy any thing he pleases. Every person who resists him while in any such way occupied, is, by law, killable, and every person who so much as tells of it, is punishable. Yet, without the form of an act of parliament, he does nothing of all this. Why? Because by the power of the Public Opinion Tribunal, though he could not be either punished or effectively resisted, he might be, and would be, more or less annoyed.[85]

Although the Public Opinion Tribunal constituted a 'fictitious tribunal', Bentham clarified its institutional forms and functions by discussing two of its existing and leading 'sub-committees': the common law jury and the newspaper press.[86] The jury evinced several of the institution's features: its similarities to a judiciary and its capacity to impede the abuse of political power. Newspapers, in contrast, bespoke the public, flexible and self-determining character of the Tribunal's membership and range of reference. Bentham's confidence in the power of newspapers to combat political misrule was remarkably displayed in a work he composed in 1822 addressed to the Islamic state of Tripoli. The essay presumed the continuation of arbitrary rule in Tripoli, and therefore turned to 'publicity' and 'Public Opinion' as the principal available 'check . . . to the power of the government'.[87] In this setting, Bentham celebrated the newspaper as 'the only effectual instrument' for mobilising and guiding such public opinion, further maintaining that in the preferable form of 'Representative Democracy' only the 'Prime Minister' exercised a more important function than 'this one sort of written instrument'.[88] Given this analysis, Bentham in the essay went on to develop a set of guidelines for best initiating and maintaining a newspaper press under Tripolitan conditions.

That Bentham should have been so attentive to these vehicles of public opinion may be thought unsurprising. As early as the 1776 *Fragment on Government*, he identified '*liberty of the press*' and '*liberty of public association*' as among the defining attributes of a '*free* government'.[89] Well before his final conversion to democratic politics, Bentham in a variety of settings advocated the mechanisms of publicity and public inspection as

individually assignable form of words in and by which it stands expressed, it is but upon a par in this particular with that rule of action which ... is in England designated by the appellation of *Common Law*.')   [85] *Ibid.*, p. 25.

[86] On the latter institutional form, see the helpful survey by Philip Schofield, 'Bentham on Public Opinion and the Press', in Dimity Kingsford-Smith and Dawn Oliver, eds., *Economical with the Truth: The Law and Media in Democratic Society* (Oxford, 1990), pp. 95–108.   [87] *Securities Against Misrule*, p. 125.

[88] *Ibid.*, pp. 44–5; see also *Constitutional Code*, I, p. 54: 'by the healing hand of Public Opinion, the rigour of Despotism may be softened'.

[89] See *A Fragment on Government* [1776], in *A Comment on the Commentaries and A Fragment on Government*, eds. J. H. Burns and H. L. A. Hart (London, 1977), p. 485.

vital resources against the abuse of power.[90] And, of course, freedom of the press and freedom of opinion, like manhood suffrage and the ballot, were basic parts of the wider Philosophic Radical programme. '[W]ithout the liberty of the press', James Mill argued in his paper devoted to the subject, 'it is doubtful whether a power in the people of choosing their own rulers ... would be an advantage.'[91]

But these important lines of continuity should not obscure the more idiosyncratic and radical dimensions of Bentham's constitutional project. Unlike other contemporary radical political reformers, Bentham never presumed that representative government in itself eliminated the vices of political corruption and the abuse of power. Rather, representative government presented the opportunity for introducing those devices which might effectively hinder the processes of misrule.[92] Among these, the organisation and circulation of public opinion was fundamental. Here the Public Opinion Tribunal did not function simply in support of the electoral system, furnishing the citizenry with the information it needed to make an informed judgement at the ballot box. Rather, public opinion was an on-going force in a democratic society, serving to encourage the utilitarian commitments of the 'ruling-few' and to discipline political power outside the formal institutions of law and the state. Moreover, it was not enough for the constitution of the democratic state simply to allow or even encourage the public scrutiny and discussion of its rule. The structures and procedures of politics needed to be articulated in a way that forced the governors to disclose their decisions and the interests they promoted before the public. Thus, the *Constitutional Code*'s elaborate bureaucratic structure which promoted efficiency and expertise at the same time served the goals of administrative transparency and rigorous accountability. 'The military functionary is paid for being shot at', Bentham explained; 'the civil functionary is paid for being spoken and written at ... Better he be defamed, though it be ever so unjustly, than that, by a breach of official duty, any sinister profit sought should be reaped.'[93]

While the Public Opinion Tribunal has been properly highlighted in

---

[90] Bentham's concern to identify techniques to ensure proper administrative aptitude and accountability through publicity, record-keeping and inspection first developed in connection with his proposed institutional projects of the 1790s, such as the panopticon prison and the pauper panopticons. On these materials, see the important discussions in Hume, *Bentham and Bureaucracy*, especially pp. 139–64, and Janet Semple, *Bentham's Prison: A Study of the Panopticon Penitentiary* (Oxford, 1993), especially pp. 134–47, 268–70, 319–21.

[91] James Mill, 'Freedom of the Press' [1823], in *James Mill: Political Writings*, ed. Terence Ball (Cambridge, 1992), p. 117.   [92] See *First Principles*, pp. 25–6.

[93] *Constitutional Code*, I, p. 40.

some of the most recent scholarship on Bentham's political theory, much less has been done to place it in context or to consider Bentham's approach in terms of the kind of 'trajectory of opinion' charted by John Burrow in his 1985 Carlyle Lectures.[94] Certainly there were clear echoes of the tropes of the more popular Painite versions of English radicalism in Bentham's juxtaposing public opinion to the showy but contentless pretensions of monarchic and aristocratic virtue. Likewise, the emphasis on public opinion's power and authority recalled the increasingly commonplace, at times conservative and even complacent later eighteenth-century rendering of Hume's famous dictum that 'it is . . . on opinion only that government is founded'.[95] What was more characteristically and distinctively Benthamic was the conceptualisation of public opinion in expressly juridical terms (public opinion as an 'imaginary tribunal or judiciary'), and the effort to identify an institutional form (albeit a 'fictitious' one) for harnessing its power systematically.

The Public Opinion Tribunal could only achieve the goals the *Constitutional Code* assigned it because of the eagerness of the democratic community not only to pay attention to the information about the conduct of politics that was presented to it, but to utilise this information actively and routinely for the critical evaluation of the conduct of political life. What, for Bentham, needed to be organised were the institutional forms for the coordination and dissemination of public opinion. But the citizen's capacity and disposition to exploit and maintain these institutions could be presumed. In these respects, the strategy for public opinion in the *Constitutional Code* seemed to take for granted quite specific and particular features of contemporary anglophone politics, whose novelty and varied impacts have been frequently emphasised in recent work on Hanoverian public life.[96]

Most obvious for the purposes of Bentham's constitutional designs was the dramatic and much-noted proliferation through the eighteenth century of newspapers and periodicals, along with sundry items of political ephemera, including prints, cartoons, pamphlets, tokens, and

---

[94] J. W. Burrow, *Whigs and Liberals* (Oxford, 1988), p. 66. See also the important explorations of the increasing appeal to public opinion in eighteenth-century political speculation in J. A. W. Gunn, *Beyond Liberty and Property* (Kingston and Montreal, 1983), ch. 7, and Keith Michael Baker, *Inventing the French Revolution* (Cambridge, 1990), ch. 8.

[95] Hume, 'Of the First Principles of Government' [1742], in *Hume: Political Essays*, ed. Knud Haakonssen (Cambridge, 1994), p. 16; and see Burrow, *Whigs and Liberals*, pp. 53–6, 60–5.

[96] Much of this discussion has been inspired by the frame developed in Habermas' *Structural Transformation of the Public Sphere*; the scale of this scholarship is now considerable. In what follows here, I am especially indebted to two recent, synthetic considerations of the cultural impacts of print media: J. Paul Hunter, *Before Novels* (New York, 1990), and John Brewer, *The Pleasures of the Imagination* (New York, 1997), chs. 3–4.

medals.[97] The rise of the newspaper press was itself but one element in
the more general elaboration of the institutions associated with an
increasingly vibrant and dense print culture, with its networks of London
and provincial printers and booksellers, coffee houses and reviews, and
commercial 'subscription libraries'. But the press and printed news-
sheets proved particularly significant in their relation to the political practices of the kingdom. In the first half of the century, particularly in the
great journalistic campaigns attending the 'rage of party' during the reign
of Queen Anne and the 'patriot' attacks on Walpolean 'oligarchy', the
periodic press was itself directed and sustained largely as an extension of
parliamentary politics and ministerial rivalries. But by mid-century, such
instruments of political information helped to create and support the
political culture of those excluded from direct parliamentary participation, including – as in the case of the Wilkite agitation of the 1760s – the
publication and increasingly extensive distribution of more radical critiques of established government structures. Later still, extra-
parliamentary bodies – such as the Committee for the Abolition of the
Slave Trade and its 1788 and 1792 petition campaigns – proved adept in
forcing issues upon parliamentary politics through the effective mobilisation of public opinion and the varied media of print and publication.[98]

While much of this process was dependent on changes in commerce
and economy, not least upon the enlarging consumer markets of 'middling' and provincial society, print and news were no less implicated in
changes of law and political value. The lapse of the Licensing Act in 1695
brought a final end to the system of pre-publication censorship and guild
monopoly through which publishing in England had previously been regulated. In its place, there gradually emerged a new, more porous legal
regime centred on the law of copyright and libel.[99] 'The liberty of the
press' joined the settled canon of rights 'essential to the nature of a free
state', even among those commentators no less alarmed by 'the licen-
tiousness' of the press and the dissemination of radical political doctrines.[100] In 1771, Parliament abandoned the prohibition of the direct

[97] On newspapers and politics, see the recent survey by Bob Harris, *Politics and the Rise of
the Press* (London, 1996). On the importance of the press and print-trade to the processes of extra-parliamentary and provincial politics, see John Brewer, *Party Ideology and
Popular Politics at the Accession of George III* (Cambridge, 1976), ch. 8, and Kathleen
Wilson, *The Sense of the People* (Cambridge, 1995).

[98] See, for example, J. R. Oldfield, *Popular Politics and British Anti-Slavery* (Manchester,
1995).

[99] On these legal developments, see Philip Hamburger, 'Development of the Law of
Seditious Libel and the Control of the Press', *Stanford Law Review*, 37 (1985), pp.
661–765, and Mark Rose, *Authors and Owners: The Invention of Copyright* (Cambridge,
Mass., 1993).

[100] See William Blackstone, *Commentaries on the Laws of England*, 4 vols. (1765–9),

reporting of its own proceedings, and parliamentary debates and votes quickly became the political staple of London and provincial newspages. British politicians now came of age in the knowledge that their deliberations and speeches would be as much *read* by an informed and interested public as *heard* by a select parliamentary audience. None of this, of course, approximated the patterns of dissemination secured by the mass-circulation press of the modern era. None the less, the circulation of political information had plainly become a most striking feature of eighteenth-century public culture. In his classic statement of the *Principles of Moral and Political Philosophy* of 1785, William Paley maintained that for him – as 'with most men who are arrived at the middle age and occupy the middle classes of life' – it was difficult to conceive any 'amusement and diversion' which brought 'greater pleasure' than that received 'from expecting, hearing, and relating public news; reading parliamentary debates and proceedings; canvassing the political arguments, projects, predictions, and intelligence, which are conveyed, by various channels, to every corner of the kingdom'.[101]

For Bentham's constitutional designs, as important as the increased publicity attending political practice were the varied kinds of information generated by the routine operations of parliamentary government. The British state in the eighteenth century emerged as the major collector and, by the late 1760s, printer of information about government practices, economy, and society.[102] The development was most dramatically evident in the detailed statistics concerning the state's expenditures and tax revenues which accompanied the annual fiscal legislation introduced to the House of Commons; and which itself featured centrally in the political effort by Parliament to control the executive and accurately monitor the ever-burgeoning national debt. The revenue system of excise and customs, and the political machinations over tax policy, led to the amassing of accounts concerning trades and commerce; public information on

facsimile reprint of the first edition (Chicago, 1979), IV, pp. 151, 153. By 'liberty of the press' Blackstone referred to absence of censorship prior to publication. The relative novelty of 'freedom of press' in discussions of English rights is emphasised by Lois G. Schwoerer in 'Liberty of the Press and Public Opinion: 1660–95', in J. R. Jones, ed., *Liberty Secured? Britain Before and After 1688* (Stanford, 1992), pp. 199–231; the later Hanoverian debate over the contribution of the press to English liberty is examined by Eckhart Hellmuth, 'The Palladium of All Other English Liberties', in Eckhart Hellmuth, ed., *The Transformation of Political Culture* (Oxford, 1990), pp. 467–501.

[101] William Paley, *Principles of Moral and Political Philosophy* (1785; 9th American edn, Boston, 1818), p. 298.

[102] The government practices and structures which encouraged the demands for political intelligence are considered in John Brewer, *Sinews of Power* (New York, 1989), pp. 130–4, 221–49, and Paul Langford, *Public Life and the Propertied Englishman* (Oxford, 1991), chs. 3–4.

current social conditions followed in the wake of more fitful parliamentary legislative efforts in such areas as poor law reform and policing in the metropolis. The largely local and particularistic character of Parliament's legislative activity, in turn, encouraged the development of channels of communication through which 'lobbies' and interest groups supplied the legislature with advantageous information and kept abreast of potentially damaging legislative proposals.

In his own radical political polemics, Bentham showed himself a skilled consumer of this mass of conveniently compiled and easily acquired political 'intelligence'. In 1830, he accompanied the publication of the first volume of the *Constitutional Code* with a collection of essays composed over the previous twenty years and assembled under the title, *Official Aptitude Maximized; Expense Minimized*. Two of the longest items in the volume were a pair of 'Defences of Economy', composed in critique of the Whig programme of economical reform associated with Edmund Burke's parliamentary initiative of 1780 and in critique of the Tory administrative reform programme elaborated by George Rose in a pamphlet of 1810. The two critiques sought to expose the manifold defects and corruptions on offer in these establishment schemes of retrenchment. In so doing, Bentham drew extensively on information concerning late eighteenth- and early nineteenth-century government expenditures (especially the system of 'pensions, sinecures, reversions') which was made available in such printed sources as the *House of Commons Sessional Papers* and the thirteen reports of the Commons' Committee on Public Expenditure (1807–12). These essays were later followed by another voluminous and complimentary polemic, *Indications Respecting Lord Eldon*, which denounced legislation of the 1820s covering judicial salaries and court fees at the central courts of Westminster Hall; and which, again, relied on information assembled in the reports of parliamentary sub-committees and published in the *Commons Sessional Papers*. The collection's penultimate item, the uncharacteristically brief essay 'On Public Accounting', responded critically to a recent report of a special commission on the practice of keeping public accounts, initiated by the Commons Committee on Public Income and Expenditure and published in the 1828 *Commons Sessional Papers*.[103]

Bentham's more developed and positive strategy for the organisation and publication of political knowledge was contained in the elaborate

---

[103] For such instances of Bentham's utilisation of parliamentary publications concerning government expenditures and record-keeping, see *Official Aptitude Maximized, Expense Minimized*, pp. 58–65, 112–15, 212–19, 293–301. The relationship between the *Constitutional Code* and *Official Aptitude Maximized, Expense Minimized* is summarised in the editorial introduction of the latter work; see pp. xv–xvii.

articles of the *Constitutional Code* setting out the state's 'statistic function', 'registration', and 'publication' systems. These provisions were designed to ensure the proper and efficient flow of information across the several distinct departments of government, and between government functionaries and the constituents of the Public Opinion Tribunal. As we have seen, the ultimate efficacy of such measures depended on the readiness of the democratic populace to absorb and utilise the information with which the provisions of the *Constitutional Code* required it to be supplied. Such a politically orientated, inquisitive, and critical populace might well be understood as the cumulative product of the specific practices of politics in eighteenth- and early nineteenth-century Britain. And, on occasion, Bentham acknowledged the more parochial dimensions of this specific political sensibility. 'For an English Minister to neglect the Newspapers', he noted in a manuscript comment of the 1770s, 'is for a Roman Consul to neglect the Forum'.[104] But, most often, these dispositions and capacities appeared as more generic and naturally occurring features of all political association. Human nature, as citizen, came to society already politically alert, eager for information, and determinedly vocal.

In this context, Bentham's writings addressed to Tripoli once more prove particularly revealing. In these essays, Bentham devoted unsurprising attention to the special circumstances and challenges created by Tripoli's arbitrary government and Islamic institutions. But in his treatment of the mobilisation of public opinion in Tripoli, there was little indication of any special task to cultivate the kind of political orientations and interests needed to sustain the Public Opinion Tribunal. Rather, most of his specific suggestions for the successful inauguration of newspapers in Tripoli involved quite practical devices – such as the regularity of publication and the variety of news content – designed to attract and maintain the largest possible readership.[105] What Tripolitan society chiefly required was the technology of public opinion, the printing press and the newspaper. Once these were introduced, the audience to consume the information newly provided would readily appear and exert its critical power.

Whatever else Bentham may have presupposed about human nature and social action in his legislative science, in his mature constitutional programme he presumed social actors fully disposed to constitute themselves members of the Public Opinion Tribunal. In his 1817 *Plan of Parliamentary Reform*, which became notorious for its endorsement of 'virtual universality of suffrage', one of the few groups Bentham excluded

[104] Jeremy Bentham Manuscripts, University College London: cxlix.7; cited in Semple, *Bentham's Prison*, p. 57.   [105] See *Securities Against Misrule*, pp. 46–50.

from the franchise was 'non-readers'. But he emphasised that this was a purposefully 'temporary' exclusion; indeed, that the exclusion would create new incentives to literacy.[106] The *Constitutional Code* made clear why literacy and printed information were so vital to Bentham's understanding of the dynamics of democratic government and the attributes of political man. It is an aspect of his thought that deserves far greater prominence in the treatment of his social assumptions. Hitherto we have been so devoted to finding behind Bentham's legislative theory a nation of shopkeepers, that we have neglected his commitments to a nation of newspaper readers.

[106] *Plan of Parliamentary Reform, in the Form of a Catechism* [1817], in *Bowring*, III, p. 464.

6 'A gigantic manliness': Paine's republicanism in the 1790s

Richard Whatmore

I

Thomas Paine's writings, like those of Adam Smith, have largely been associated with some of the major traditions of modern political thought: in Paine's case, liberalism, capitalism, and, most recently, social-democracy.[1] The republican turn in intellectual history has done much to liberate Paine's ideas from association with causes he would not have recognised. A number of studies have added to our knowledge by placing Paine's work in the context of various neo-Harringtonian, Commonwealth, Old Whig and natural-law traditions which have been found in late eighteenth-century political discourse.[2] One problem with this literature is that the term 'republican', so often one of abuse in the eighteenth century, is too pervasive. In particular, historians have not specified which states writers were talking about when using such terms, which makes a great deal of difference when describing a writer's political position. For example, it was possible to believe republics to be theoretically superior to monarchies while supporting the idea of Britain as a mixed monarchy which had little in common with historical republics. This was the view which Catherine Macaulay defended throughout her life, and which David Hume articulated in 'The Idea of a Perfect Commonwealth'. Equally, Richard Price and Joseph Priestley believed in

My thanks for criticisms of earlier versions of the paper to Istvan Hont, Kieran O'Halloran, Michael Sonenscher, Donald Winch, and Brian Young. The research was supported by a grant from the Nuffield Foundation. Translations from the French are my own, unless otherwise stated.

[1] John Keane, *Tom Paine: A Political Life* (London, 1995).

[2] A. Owen Aldridge, *Thomas Paine's American Ideology* (Newark, Del., 1984), chs. 10–11; D. A. Williams, *Paine and Cobbett: The Transatlantic Connection* (Kingston, 1988), pp. 40–70; G. Claeys, *Thomas Paine: Social and Political Thought* (London, 1989), esp. ch. 4, and 'Republicanism and Commerce in Britain, 1796–1805', *Journal of Modern History*, 66 (1994), pp. 249–90; J. Fruchtman, *Thomas Paine and the Religion of Nature* (Baltimore, 1993) and *Thomas Paine: Apostle of Freedom* (New York, 1994), ch. 12; D. Wootton, 'The Republican Tradition: From Commonwealth to Common Sense', in his *Republicanism, Liberty and Commercial Society, 1649–1776* (Stanford, 1994), pp. 1–44.

the ideal of a universal republic in which fraternity would reign, but neither described themselves as republicans when discussing Britain. At first glance, Paine's republicanism does not accord with that of any contemporaries who were not his disciples.[3] Paine was one of a very small number of Anglo-American writers who believed that Britain's mixed government did not suit her society. Indeed, he believed mixed government would ultimately be responsible for putting an end to Britain's national greatness. Most recent commentators have, as a result, described Paine as an innovative political voice in republican thought. One of the best studies goes so far as to conclude that Paine was the founder of a new form of republicanism both in America in 1776 and in France in 1791.[4] Others have questioned whether it makes sense to call Paine a republican at all in the 1790s, at least in the sense of belonging to a distinctive tradition of political argument. The rejection of the republican interpretation can mean a return to the 'bourgeois liberal' Paine, and another set of historically questionable definitions.[5] On the other hand, a popular nineteenth-century view of Paine has been revived, stemming from a claim that his peculiar, critical and libertarian ideas 'cannot be captured by a single model or tradition'.[6] This approach returns us to the original problem, which is easy to specify but difficult to resolve. Paine called himself a republican, yet his ideas do not accord with accepted interpretations of republican argument in late eighteenth-century Britain or North America.

The aim of this essay is to explain the distinctiveness of Paine's idea of a republic as he formulated it in the early 1790s, and to do so by reference to a republican tradition which *was* recognised by Paine's British contemporaries. Advantage is taken of several clues in Paine's major writings to develop the argument that Paine's achievement was to translate for a British audience certain French writers' ideas about the nature of modern republicanism. Paine was influenced by a French republican tradition which developed in the late 1770s and became prominent in political argument towards the end of the 1780s. The central claim of the writers involved was that transforming European monarchies into commercial republics without hierarchical ranks would create states more stable and powerful than existing monarchies of whatever type, including Britain's mixed monarchy. Paine's links with France are well known. The commencement of the first part of *The Rights of Man* describes a friendship

[3] On the latter see J. A. Alger, 'The British Colony in Paris, 1792–93', *English Historical Review*, 13 (1898), pp. 672–94; V. C. Miller, *Joel Barlow: Revolutionist. London, 1791–92* (Hamburg, 1932).
[4] Eric Foner, *Tom Paine and Revolutionary America* (New York, 1976), pp. 216, 237.
[5] Isaac Kramnick, 'Republican Revisionism Revisited', in his *Republicanism and Bourgeois Radicalism* (Ithaca, 1990).
[6] Mark Philp, 'English Republicanism in the 1790s', *Journal of Political Philosophy*, 6 (1998), pp. 235–62.

with Lafayette stretching back to 1777. The first page of the pamphlet stated an intention to refute Burke on behalf of Paine's many French friends who were actively involved in Paris. Paine first visited France in 1780, returned twice in 1787, and began a series of lengthy stays from June 1789. Through his links with the venerated Franklin, and because of the notoriety of *Common Sense* and the *Letter to the abbé Raynal*, Paine was fêted by the Parisian admirers of the American Revolution in 1787.[7] At this time, as he made clear in *The Rights of Man*, he became close to 'the Bishop of Toulouse's secretary', probably the anglophile abbé Morellet. He also became acquainted with Morellet's friend, Condorcet, and the anti-physiocratic circle of Jacques-Pierre Brissot and Etienne Clavière. Paine's subsequent links with such men, when a member of the Convention, almost brought him to the guillotine in 1793–4. Imprisoned in the Luxembourg for ten months, and anticipating execution, he refused to recant the form of republicanism he had articulated with them, in the journal *Le Républicain* and among like-minded contributors to the *Cercle Sociale* publishing house.[8]

The majority of historians have refused to examine Paine's political ideas from a French perspective.[9] Seemingly good reasons have been given. It is well known that Paine was initially ignorant of the language. Furthermore, he was notoriously disdainful of other writers' work. As one acquaintance put it, 'He knew all his own writings by heart and nothing else.'[10] The first part of *The Rights of Man* was written in England, as was much of the second. To many both books appear to be the product of local circumstance, obsessed as they are with the nature and future of the

---

[7] The *Mémoires secrets*, ed. L. P. Bachaumont, 37 vols. (1780–9) of 3 January 1783 referred to 'le célèbre auteur du sens commun' (XXII, 9). However, before his first visit of 1787 he wrote to Franklin that apart from Lafayette 'there are none I am much acquainted with'. On his arrival, his correspondence shows that this speedily changed: *Complete Writings*, ed. E. Foner, 2 vols. (New York, 1969), II, p. 1261. With regard to Paine's French links it is unfortunate that J.-P. Brissot failed to complete the commentary on Paine which he promised in his *Mémoires*, 2 vols. (Paris, 1912), I, p. 134. Given that Paine's friendship with Franklin was the source of most of his French contacts, a useful guide is A. O. Aldridge, *Franklin and his French Contemporaries* (New York, 1957). See also E. Badinter and R. Badinter, *Condorcet (1743–1794)* (Paris, 1988), pp. 227–31.

[8] G. Kates, *The Cercle Social, the Girondins and the French Revolution* (Princeton, 1985), pp. 162–4.

[9] Exceptions include A. O. Aldridge, 'Condorcet et Paine. Leur rapports intellectuels', *Revue de littérature comparée*, 32 (1958), pp. 47–65 and 'Condorcet, Paine and Historical Method', in L. C. Rosenfield, ed., *Condorcet Studies I* (Atlantic Highlands, N.J., 1984), pp. 49–60; G. Kates, 'From Liberalism to Radicalism: Tom Paine's *Rights of Man*', *Journal of the History of Ideas*, 50 (1989), pp. 569–87; B. Vincent, 'Thomas Paine: républicain de l'univers', in F. Furet and M. Ozouf, eds., *Le Siècle de l'avènement Républicain* (Paris, 1993), pp. 101–26; W. Doyle, 'Thomas Paine and the Girondins', in his *Officers, Nobles and Revolutionaries* (London, 1995).

[10] Cited in D. Freeman Hawke, *Paine* (New York, 1974), p. 226. The author of the comment was Etienne Dumont in his posthumously published *Souvenirs sur Mirabeau*, ed. J. Bénétruy (Paris, 1950), p. 180.

British state. Alternatively, because attacks on mixed government first made in *Common Sense* and *The Crisis* were reiterated in the major works of the 1790s, some historians have demanded a North American context to explain Paine's ideas. His writings have consequently been placed in the tradition of Commonwealth perceptions of Hanoverian rule as these were developed in the colonies.

As was noted above, Paine has been described as an innovator working within this tradition because he claimed that Britain would collapse unless she became a free state of a particular kind. Yet Paine openly disavowed the accepted themes of Country or Old Whig writers. Where they were fearful of commerce and manufactures, Paine declared himself to be 'in all my publications . . . an advocate for commerce'.[11] While few British writers considered Britain's mixed government as unsuited to that state, Paine believed that the only free state, whether small or large in size, was a republic without king or aristocracy. It was more important to eliminate hierarchical ranks than to enjoy the supposed civil rights of 'free-born' Britons. Limited monarchy had to be replaced by national sovereignty, creating very different ideas about social duties and political obligations. Far from spreading effeminacy, Paine associated his commercial republic with the moral transformation of the populace. It would institute what he called 'a gigantic manliness'. This complex term signified honesty of thought and deed, courage and the pursuit of rational modes of living; patriotism and dedication to the public good in all spheres of existence, especially trade and politics. The citizens of Paine's republic, the entire population of adult males, would replicate in civil society the virtues which had hitherto characterised disinterested dedication to the public good in political life alone. Although peaceful in nature, he believed that when challenged such a republic would defeat in war all mixed and absolute monarchical governments, even when ranged in leagues against it. In short, Paine's was a 'modern' form of republicanism, with little in common with traditional British or American perspectives. This does not mean that Paine was wholly original. He was aware of French interest in the possibility of transforming large European monarchies into modern republics from the late 1770s. Knowledge of republican ideas developed in France does much to illuminate Paine's beliefs and political identity.

II

To describe Paine as a modern republican underlines the difficulty of understanding this ex-Briton by reference to domestic traditions of polit-

---

[11] *Rights of Man*, Part Two, in *Political Writings*, ed. B. Kuklick (Cambridge, 1989), p. 196.

ical argument. It is also important to note that Paine's writings taken as a whole cannot be understood as different parts of a single ideology. Paine frequently stated that his ideas were all of a piece, and in later writings constantly referred back to *Common Sense*, which he perceived to be his own political testament.[12] Certain themes do span the first and the final writings, such as the critique of mixed government, the association of monarchy with ignorance and his defence of moderate wealth. Paine also developed and altered many of the views first articulated in the 1770s. If *Common Sense* and *The Crisis* are compared with the first part of *The Rights of Man*, for example, numerous differences emerge. The first was a product of circumstance. Although *Common Sense* praised 'the republican . . . part of the constitution of England', Paine nowhere sought to foment revolution in Britain or to challenge the form of government which appeared most suited to established European monarchies. The most he did was to remind Englishmen, as Hume had done before him, that their national vanity, based on comparison with the supposed tyranny of France, was without foundation. As he put it, 'the *will* of the king is as much the *law* of the land in Britain as in France'.[13] By contrast, *The Rights of Man* sought 'the happiness of seeing the New World regenerate the Old'.[14]

A more important difference concerns Paine's view of ranks. In the 1770s monarchy and hereditary succession were blamed for the ills of states, being the source of war, ignorance, and corruption. Paine ranked monarchy 'in scripture as one of the sins of the Jews'. In modern times he held it to have become 'the popery of government'.[15] In *The Rights of Man* Paine maintained these opinions, arguing that Burke's *Reflections* 'shortened his journey to Rome' in defending 'this vassalage idea . . . monarchy'. In addition, however, Paine attacked the aristocracies of Europe as being co-responsible for the decline of their states. Paine called aristocrats parasites, 'a kind of fungus'; rather than nobility, they represented 'No-ability, in all countries'. In a characteristic paragraph he once more used the example of the Jews to illustrate his point:

By the universal economy of nature it is known, and by the instance of the Jews it is proved, that the human species has a tendency to degenerate, in any small number of persons, when separated from the general stock of society, and inter-marrying constantly with one another.[16]

---

[12] It is significant that Lanthenas translated *Sens commun* and *La Crise américaine* in 1794. *Le Siècle de la raison ou recherches sur la vraie théologie et sur la théologie fabuleuse* appeared in the same year.   [13] *Common Sense*, in *Political Writings*, pp. 7, 15.
[14] Part One, dedication to George Washington. Paine's change of opinion can be traced to *Prospects on the Rubicon* which was probably written in France in August 1787 (*Complete Writings*, II, p. 621).   [15] *Common Sense*, pp. 9–11.
[16] *Rights of Man*, Part One, pp. 93–4, 105–13.

Where, in the 1770s, Paine had defined a republic as a state without monarchy, he now held that equality between ranks was essential to republican liberty. He stated the intention 'to exterminate the monster Aristocracy, root and branch', and demanded that Englishmen follow the French example by destroying their nobility. Abolishing primogeniture was to be the first iconoclastic act.

The third aspect of Paine's ideas which changed in the 1790s concerned his attitude to commerce. In *Common Sense* Paine declared that in North America 'our plan is commerce', claiming that liberty of trade would 'secure us the peace and friendship of all Europe'. Yet in the final section of the pamphlet, 'Of the Present Ability of America', neo-Harringtonian themes can be discerned. Commerce made for powerful states, but it was also believed to be a force for peace and fraternity based on reciprocal exchange, and as such was the enemy of aggressive patriotism. The fact that America was a largely non-commercial nation therefore increased rather than diminished her military capabilities. A spirit of patriotism derived from yearning for independence made the American soldier more than a match for his British counterpart:

> Commerce diminishes the spirit both of patriotism and military defence. And history sufficiently informs us that the bravest achievements were always accomplished in the nonage of a nation. With the increase of commerce England hath lost its spirit. The city of London, notwithstanding its numbers, submits to continued insults with the patience of a coward. The more men have to lose, the less willing they are to venture. The rich are in general slaves to fear, and submit to courtly power with the trembling duplicity of a spaniel.[17]

In *The Rights of Man*, Part Two, Paine expressed no fears concerning the sacrifice of military power to commercial well-being. Despite being a commercial republic, he considered France to be far stronger than Britain. Indeed, he was certain that the constitutional innovations of the National Assembly had resolved the famous eighteenth-century paradox about French power: a state superior in resources, numbers, size, and civilisation had been defeated in war by its inferior rival, Britain.[18] Paine always adhered to Charles Davenant's neo-Machiavellian claim that the form of government of a state determined its greatness.[19] As a conse-

---

[17] *Common Sense*, p. 35; also, 'Thoughts on the Peace', in *Letter to the Earl of Shelburne . . .*, 9th edn (London, 1792), pp. 23–5.

[18] For a statement of the paradox, see Arthur Young, *Letters Concerning the Present State of the French Nation . . . With a complete comparison between France and Great Britain...* (London, 1769), pp. 440–2.

[19] For Davenant's commentary on Machiavelli's maxim, 'That no cities have augmented their revenues or enlarged their territories, but while they were free and at liberty', see 'An Essay upon the Probable Methods of Making a People Gainers in the Balance of Trade' (1699) in *The Political and Commercial Works*, 5 vols. (London, 1771), II, p. 337; also, I.

quence, he believed the Revolution would ensure that France fulfilled her economic potential and would once again be militarily superior to her smaller neighbour.

A more optimistic view, which Paine expressed at the end of *The Rights of Man*, Part Two, stated that if the kind of republicanism he favoured was adopted in Britain, an alliance would then be made with the other commercial republics of Holland, France, and America. These states would be so powerful that they could dictate terms to every throne and altar. In particular, Paine advised them to force Spain 'to open South America to the rest of the world for trade'. He concluded that 'better times are in prospect . . . for the world . . . the insulted German and the enslaved Spaniard, the Russ and the Pole, are beginning to think'. Inaugurating the 'Age of Reason', Paine called his generation 'the Adam of a new world'.[20] The question that needs to be asked at this point is how far such ideas accorded with those of his radical British contemporaries.

III

It is accepted by most historians that the perceived decline of Britain from the time of the war with the North American colonies led to a revival of what has recently been termed a 'neo-Roman theory of free states', demanding the purification of the constitution by means of a return to fundamental principles.[21] Opinions differed on the nature of the required reforms, which ranged from tinkering with the powers of the crown to a radical affirmation of popular sovereignty.[22] Yet few writers believed it was necessary to reconstitute the political system. In general, British writers did not believe that the established constitution would destroy itself, any more than they believed that Britons had anything to learn from other European republics or monarchies.[23] Political thinking was largely carried out by reference to British history, and events in other parts of the world were understood in such terms.

Nowhere is this clearer than in the careful use of the term 'republican'

Hont, 'Free Trade and the Economic Limits to National Politics: Neo-Machiavellian Political Economy Reconsidered', in J. Dunn, ed., *The Economic Limits to Modern Politics* (Cambridge, 1993), pp. 41–99.   [20] *Rights of Man*, Part Two, pp. 200–3.
[21] Q. Skinner, *Liberty Before Liberalism* (Cambridge, 1998), ch. 1. See also P. Miller, *Defining the Common Good* (Cambridge, 1994), ch. 6.
[22] John Cartwright, *The Constitutional Defence of England* (London, 1796), pp. 119–24; see also I. Hampsher-Monk, 'Civic Humanism and Parliamentary Reform: The Case of the Society of the Friends of the People', *Journal of British Studies*, 18 (1979), pp. 70–89; A. Goodwin, *The Friends of Liberty* (London, 1979), ch. 2.
[23] J. G. A. Pocock, 'Edmund Burke and the Redefinition of Enthusiasm: The Context as Counter-Revolution', in F. Furet and M. Ozouf, eds., *The French Revolution and the Creation of Modern Political Culture*, 4 vols. (Oxford, 1990), III, pp. 19–43.

by radicals who believed reform was necessary. Such radicals believed that Britain's strength depended upon a mixed rather than a republican form of government. Even those, such as Catherine Macaulay, who believed that the seventeenth-century republican tradition had a role to play in late eighteenth-century politics, took pains to emphasise their support for a mixed form of government for late eighteenth-century Britain. This preference was determined by the necessity of social order. In addition, an established system of hierarchical ranks was required to prevent the rule of the ignorant or the rise to power of a corrupt demagogue. By contrast, republics were associated with a degree of material and civil equality which was dangerous to social peace and destructive of the most important virtue in the British radical canon: independence. Macaulay was explicit on this point. The 'whole art of true and just policy', was 'to preserve the natural subordination established by God himself'. Rather than being a republican, she preferred to think of herself, as her friend Thomas Hollis put it, as 'a true Old Whig, almost unic [*sic*]', sharing Hollis' belief that 'all commonwealths are founded by gentlemen'.[24] James Burgh emphasised that he opposed the creation of a republic in Britain because this would be 'throwing out all the three estates at once'. It was rather necessary 'not to abolish either king, lords or commons, but to preserve and re-establish them, on their original and proper foot'.[25] Richard Price used similar arguments to defend himself against the charge of republicanism in 1785; Britain simply had 'too many high and low' to countenance such a transformation.[26] In 1787 he gave his most detailed denial:

so far am I from preferring a government purely republican, that I look upon our constitution of government as better adapted than any other to this country, and in theory excellent . . . what I here say of myself I believe to be true of the whole body of British subjects among Protestant Dissenters. I know not one individual among them who would not tremble at the thought of changing into a democracy our mixed form of government, or who has any other wish with respect to it than to restore it to purity and vigour by removing the defects in our representation, and establishing that dependence of the three states on one another in which its essence consists.[27]

---

[24] Catherine Macaulay, *The History of England from the Accession of James I to that of the Brunswick Line*, 8 vols. (London, 1763–83), IV, p. 355n; Hollis, *Memoirs of Thomas Hollis*, I, p. 428, cited in B. Hill, *The Republican Virago* (Oxford, 1992), p. 167. See also C. Robbins, 'The Strenuous Whig, Thomas Hollis of Lincoln's Inn', in her *Absolute Liberty* (Hamden, Conn., 1982), pp. 168–205.

[25] James Burgh, *Political Disquisitions*, 3 vols. (London, 1774–5), III, pp. 297–9.

[26] Richard Price, *Observations on the Importance of the American Revolution* (London, 1785), p. 72n; *Additional Observations on the Nature and Value of Civil Liberty* (London, 1787), pp. 8, 20, 44.

[27] Richard Price, *The Evidence for a Future Period of Improvement in the State of Mankind* (London, 1787), in *Political Writings*, ed. D. O. Thomas (Cambridge, 1991), pp. 164–5.

The British radicals adhered to what was probably the only maxim shared by Smith, Montesquieu, Rousseau, and Voltaire: that republicanism was a doctrine for small states alone, because large states lacked the homogeneous political culture necessary to sustain popular institutions. Endorsing this view in the 1790s, Burke saw himself as the guardian of a fundamental political truth against a new, predominantly French, heresy.[28] The large republic of the United States did not challenge this assumption, even after federal powers were increased, because it was perceived to be a union of small states. It was altogether unique because its politics were not marred by the 'European' problems of an entrenched systems of ranks, an inegalitarian distribution of property, and a history of domestic and international unrest.[29] Christopher Wyvill made this point in his attack on 'the enthusiastic Politician' Paine, whose 'avowed purpose is to overturn and destroy our . . . Mixed Government, by King, Lords and Commons', and replace it with 'his wild project for the universal establishment of Republican Forms of Government'. It was fortunate, he believed, that 'the Proselytes to republican notions are few at present, and inconsiderable'.[30]

The most radical of the anti-Burke tracts, James Mackintosh's *Vindiciae Gallicae,* illustrates the differences between French and British perspectives on republicanism. Mackintosh supported the 'democratic character' of the French Revolution because of the peculiarities of French history. French and English governments had originally been similar in form, enjoying the benefits of Gothic representative institutions. In France, however, 'the downfall of the feudal aristocracy . . . before Commerce had elevated any other class of citizens into importance' caused noble powers to devolve on the crown. The resulting reign of the 'dissolute tyrant' Louis XIV ensured that 'the three great corporations of the Nobility, the Church and the Parliaments were tainted by despotism', degrading the people to 'political helotism'. Thus the Revolution in France had of necessity to be more democratic than that of England in 1688. In the latter 'the Clergy, the Peerage and Judicatures of England . . . qualified to partake of a more stable and improved liberty'.[31] Justifying 'democratic character' did not make Mackintosh a republican. He did not

---

[28] Edmund Burke, *Letter to a Member of the National Assembly* [May, 1791], in *Further Reflections on the Revolution,* ed. D. E. Ritchie (Indianapolis, 1992), pp. 65–6.

[29] Josiah Tucker's comment in *Cui Bono* (Gloucester, 1781), p. 117, is memorable and significant: 'As to the future Grandeur of *America,* and its being a rising Empire under one *Head,* whether Republican or Monarchical, it is one of the idlest and most visionary Notions, that ever was conceived, even by writers of Romance.'

[30] Christopher Wyvill, *A Defence of Dr Price and the Reformers of England* (London and York, 1792), pp. 8, 60–7.

[31] James Mackintosh, *Vindiciae Gallicae,* 2nd edn (London, 1791), pp. 18, 63–7.

support the idea of a general revolution across Europe, national sovereignty or the destruction of ranks as necessary to a free state. Rather, it
was essential for popular sovereignty to be affirmed in institutions compatible with the manners of the nation. This explains why, writing soon
after the publication of *Vindiciae Gallicae*, he opposed 'that spark of
Republicanism which moderation must have extinguished, but which
may, in future *conceivable circumstances*, produce effects, at the suggestion
of which good men will shudder'.[32] Unlike Paine, Mackintosh defended
the 'manly' legacy of 1688 and the 'senatorial nobility' which was then
established. He concluded: 'nothing can be more absurd than to assert
that all who admire wish to imitate the French Revolution'.[33]

The perspective of British writers on the Revolution in France was
shaped by the lack of a domestic tradition of reflection upon the possibility
of making republics out of large European states. Once more the example
of Richard Price is instructive. In correspondence with the Duc de la
Rochefoucauld and others, he made clear his view that the Revolution was
a means of making France more like Britain. In June 1790 he pointed out
that the celebration of the anniversary of the fall of the Bastille had been
accompanied by John Horne Tooke's toast 'that the English nation had
only to maintain and improve the constitution which their ancestors had
transmitted to them'.[34] Price's hope was that events in France would
inspire a revision of the 1688 constitutional settlement to emancipate
Catholics and dissenters and broaden representation. Existing ranks,
property rights, and civil distinctions would remain, creating a mixed form
of government in each nation. In turn this would secure international
peace and greater prosperity fuelled by uninhibited commerce. The publications of the Revolution Society in London envisaged similar effects, and
stressed their commitment to 'the Revolution, which seated our Deliverer
King William the Third on the Throne [and] do hereby declare our
firmest attachment to the civil and religious principles which were recognised and established by that glorious event'. They included Stanhope's
letters describing Louis XVI as a patriotic king, 'the RESTORER OF
FRENCH LIBERTY ... placed like the Kings of England ... at the head of
an enlightened people and free constitution of government'.[35]

[32] James Mackintosh, *A Letter to the Right Honourable William Pitt* (London, 1792), cited in
The Life of Sir James Mackintosh, 2nd edn, 2 vols. (London, 1836), I, pp. 79–82.
[33] Mackintosh, *Vindiciae Gallicae*, pp. 250–60, 293–302, 351.
[34] *Correspondence of Richard Price*, ed. B. Peach and D. O. Thomas, 3 vols. (Durham, N.C.,
1983–94), III, pp. 305–11; *Memoirs of John Horne Tooke*, ed. A. Stephens, 2 vols. (New
York, 1968), II, pp. 35–7.
[35] *The Correspondence of the Revolution Society in London, with the National Assembly, and with
various societies of the Friends of Liberty in France and England* (London, 1792), pp. 1–3,
10–11.

Many Englishmen shared the chauvinistic view of William Fox that the origins of the French Revolution could be found in Locke's *Two Treatises on Government* and the British tradition from Locke to Price.[36] Mackintosh was equally of the opinion that the Revolution of 1688 had inspired the French, being 'the first example in civilised Europe of a Government which reconciled a semblance of *political*, and a large portion of *civil* liberty, with stability and peace'. It created 'the school of sages, who unshackled and emancipated the human mind, from among whom issued the Lockes, the Rousseaus, the Turgots and the Franklins'.[37] At the commencement of the Revolution, a writer as Francophile as Helen-Maria Williams noted that the French 'imbibed the noble lesson which England has taught' and 'are become madly fond of the English'.[38] Before his death Price expressed a less nationalistic view, arguing that the French Revolution represented the fusion of the intellectual traditions of Britain and France against 'arbitrary power': 'Milton, Locke, Sidney and Hoadly in this country . . . Montesquieu, Fénelon and Turgot in France'.[39] Catherine Macaulay saw the French constitutional debates of the National Assembly as a perfect fusion of republican and monarchical political maxims. They had ingeniously combined 'the mere office of an executive governor, with the stability that is annexed to hereditary descent' and 'a truly popular constitution [founded on] the will of the people'. Yet, as in all of her writings, she took pains to justify restrictions on political liberty as compatible with the rights of man in the state of nature, since 'no one not inclined or by bodily infirmity not able to till the ground had a right to the fruits produced by the labour of others'.[40]

When France became a republic in September 1792 it was anathema to British radicals. Even David Williams, who had been made a citizen by the National Assembly, condemned the Convention 'collected principally from the dregs of France'. In 1793 he attempted to engineer links between Lord Grenville and the Girondins in the hope of establishing in France 'a constitution similar to that of Britain'.[41] Charles James Fox, in his attack on the policy of war being fostered by Pitt, declared that republicanism was 'the evil that I dread'. He defended 'Those who desire Reform . . . the middle order of men, who dread as much Republicanism on the one

---

[36] *The Interest of Great Britain Respecting the French War* (London, 1793), pp. 12–14.
[37] Mackintosh, *Vindiciae Gallicae*, pp. 326–35.
[38] Helen-Maria Williams, *Letters written in France* [1790] (Oxford, 1989), pp. 68–9.
[39] Price, *A Discourse on the Love of our Country* [November 1789], in *Political Writings*, pp. 180–2.
[40] Catherine Macaulay, *Observations on the Reflections of the Right Hon. Edmund Burke, on the Revolution in France* (London, 1790), pp. 78–9, 86, 95.
[41] David Williams, *Incidents in my own life which have been thought of some importance*, ed. P. France (Falmer, 1980), pp. 27–31.

hand, as they do Despotism on the other'.[42] The majority of radicals saw the creation of the republic as a retrograde step, which weakened France just as it ruined opportunities for domestic and international peace.[43] It could be explained as a reaction to the corruption of the monarchy, but its disastrous nature appeared to have been confirmed by the widespread reports of politically inspired assassinations and massacres, culminating in the policy of Terror. To most Britons, Burke's view of 1792 was correct: events in France underlined the superiority of Britain's mixed form of government, and the political traditions of independence and civil liberty which supported it.[44]

IV

Paine's exceptionalism with regard to the strength of modern republics, the equality of ranks, and the weakness of Britain, was made famous by the publication of the first part of *The Rights of Man* in February 1791. His ideas were so extreme in a British context that the radical printer Joseph Johnson refused to publish them, recalling the first copies when he realised their content. Certain themes of late eighteenth-century British political thought can nevertheless be found in his work. A debt was openly acknowledged to two writers in particular. The first Paine described as 'one of the best-hearted men that exists', and also 'a friend and republican'.[45] Richard Price's vitriolic attacks on corruption in government, the excessive influence of the monarch, and the dire consequences of an escalating national debt, all found a place in Paine's works. More distinctive was Paine's use of Price's defence of moderate wealth as the ideal for modern citizens, accompanied by a shared fear of growing poverty in Britain. With regard to commerce, it was probably from Price that Paine drew the argument that only certain forms of commerce were compatible with political and moral virtue. Price believed that a nation whose commerce was of this sort would be more economically successful than the mercantile state he perceived Britain had become. This view was repeated by Paine in *Common Sense*, which stated that 'oppression is often the *con-*

---

[42] *The Speech of the Right Hon. Charles James Fox, on the King's Speech ... December 13, 1792* (London, 1792), pp. 9–10.

[43] J. E. Cookson, *The Friends of Peace* (Cambridge, 1982), chs. 2, 7; C. Emsley, 'The Impact of the French Revolution on British Politics and Society', in C. Crossley and I. Small, eds., *The French Revolution and British Culture* (Oxford, 1989), pp. 31–62.

[44] Bentham was certainly of this view: see the illuminating work of J. H. Burns, 'Bentham and the French Revolution', *Transactions of the Royal Historical Society*, 16 (1966), pp. 95–114, and F. Rosen, *Bentham, Byron and Greece* (Oxford, 1992), ch. 3.

[45] *Rights of Man*, Part One, p. 53; 'Lettre à MM. Chabroud et Chapelier', *Le Républicain, ou le défenseur du gouvernement représentatif, par une société des républicains*, no. 2 (July 1791), p. 31.

sequence, but seldom or never the *means* of riches'.[46] The opposite was also true: 'though avarice will preserve a man from being necessitously poor, it generally makes him too timorous to be wealthy'. Britain's decline could therefore be traced to the corruption engendered by the mixed constitution, whose negative moral effects in turn reduced the forms of commerce conducive to wealth and virtue.

Price's support for the American republic and his faith in its future as an independent state also found echoes in Paine's work. Both men believed that republics were inherently more stable and peaceful than monarchies. They were also certain that human nature was heavily influenced by forms of government, and that the kind of transformation experienced by North America would regenerate the morals and manners of the general populace: in particular those of corrupt immigrants from European monarchies. Finally, they shared the ultimate goal of the creation of a universal republic which would guarantee peace in conditions of commerce and fraternity, where historic aspirations to universal monarchy had established peace by means of slavery and war. Price, however, believed that mixed government *was* compatible with economic success, and did not accept that liberty demanded the destruction of social hierarchy.

The other major influence on Paine among British writers was Adam Smith, whom he famously claimed for his own side in *The Rights of Man*, against the 'disorderly cast of [Burke's] genius . . . without a constitution'.[47] Paine's references to Smith were, as in this instance, frequently imprecise. It is possible to conclude that Paine's use of Smith was therefore misleading and that he interpreted him, if he read his books at all, as a supporter of free commerce and little more. However, it is notable that much of *The Rights of Man*, in which Paine discusses British 'improvements in agriculture, useful arts, manufactures and commerce', was modelled on book III of the *Wealth of Nations*. Paine followed Smith's argument that such progress had been made 'in opposition to the genius of government'. Equally, he blamed the 'spirit of jealousy and ferocity' between states for increasing poverty and reducing trade. More importantly, Paine appears to have used Smith's discussion of 'the natural progress of opulence' in his description of the 'unnatural' progress of political power in Europe. The story of the establishment of political liberty, its loss and the struggle to restore it, echoes the analysis of the establishment of the commercial stage of human society detailed by Smith in book III.

Paine's description of republican government as natural to man, and

---

[46] *Common Sense*, pp. 8–9.   [47] *Rights of Man*, Part One, p. 88.

the American and French revolutions as 'a renovation of the natural order of things . . . combining moral with political happiness and national prosperity', owed a great deal to Smith's idea of 'natural liberty'.[48] Where Smith placed the 'mercantile system', Paine placed monarchy; where Smith placed free commerce, Paine placed his republic. Other links have also been noted by historians, including opposition to primogeniture.[49] It is significant that while Smith considered the condition of the British poor to be above the condition of kings in uncivilised nations, Paine argued that civilisation was only possible in republics. In existing European monarchies the majority of the population found themselves 'far below the condition of an Indian'.[50] Political upheaval and a resulting moral transformation were in Paine's view the only options for any nation seeking to become genuinely civilised. Such opinions lead to the conclusion that Smith would have considered Paine as he did Price, 'a factious citizen, a most superficial Philosopher and by no means an able calculator'.[51]

V

Unlike Smith and Price, Paine believed Britain's mixed government to be a tyranny and a despotism, wholly unsuited to a populace claiming to be free born. He was under no illusion concerning the limits of British traditions of political thought and held them to be as bankrupt as attempts to harness public credit. Mixed government, he argued as early as *Common Sense*, was a contradiction in terms because 'the power which has most weight will govern'. In 1688 the English might have 'been wise enough to shut and lock a door against absolute monarchy', but at the same time they 'have been foolish enough to put the crown in possession of the key'.[52] The first part of *The Rights of Man* likewise concluded that the machinery of mixed government was oiled by corruption. Such views could have been drawn from a variety of historical sources, but it is noteworthy that such opinions are very difficult to find among contemporary British writers, however radical. Yet between the 1760s and 1770s they

---

[48] *Rights of Man*, Part One, pp. 137–41; Part Two, pp. 185–94.
[49] The best account of Paine's relationship with Smith, which makes many of these points, is Donald Winch's *Riches and Poverty* (Cambridge, 1995), esp. pp. 100–3, 128–31, 150–6.
[50] *Rights of Man*, Part Two, p. 195. The same claim was later made in *Agrarian Justice*.
[51] Adam Smith, Letter to George Chalmers, 22 December 1785, cited in Winch, *Riches and Poverty*, p. 124.
[52] *Common Sense*, pp. 7–8; on this attack see Claeys, *Thomas Paine: Social and Political Thought*, ch. 3.

were being vociferously propagated from Paris by the *économistes* or physiocrats.[53]

François Quesnay and his disciples across Europe and beyond were among the greatest anglophobes, and argued against the conventional wisdom of the relative prosperity of the British poor. More importantly for links with Paine, the mixed sovereignty which Quesnay associated with Britain's government was also an object of physiocratic hostility. In 1767 several works were published which illustrated this opposition. The first, Quesnay's own *Despotisme de la Chine*, condemned the disorder which accompanied any dilution of sovereign power:

> All the different ranks of the State can contribute in a mixed government to the ruin of the nation, through the discordance between private interests which divides and corrupts the tutelary authority, causing it to degenerate into political intrigues and abuses deadly to society.[54]

It was followed by equally vitriolic condemnations in the writings of Mercier de la Rivière and Nicolas Baudeau, who attacked mixed sovereignty as a practical impossibility in France or elsewhere, given the fact of material inequality between social orders and the size of the state.[55] Only an independent absolute monarch had the authority to stand above the fray of private interests and impose the 'essential laws of the natural order' against the military aristocracy debasing France. The step which Paine would not have taken, identifying Britain as an exemplar of an insecure popular 'republic', was made by Victor Riqueti de Mirabeau as early as *L'Ami des hommes*, in which he condemned 'a nation where the cries of the people too often prevail over reason'.[56] They did, however, also share the belief that Britain was in decline *because* of her mixed constitution. What made Paine distinctive was his argument that Britain would be surpassed, not by an agricultural monarchy governed by a 'legal despot', but rather by a new kind of republic. It would be a state more powerful, with a civil society more commercial, than any other in history.

The modern republic Paine ultimately envisaged was more egalitarian than other societies and also more commercial, creating a political

---

[53] 'Maximes de gouvernement économique' in *François Quesnay et la physiocratie*, 2 vols. (Institut National d'Etudes Démographiques, 1958 [henceforth, INED]), II, pp. 496–510.

[54] *Despotisme de la Chine*, INED, II, p. 919.

[55] Le Mercier de la Rivière, *L'Ordre naturel et essentiel des sociétés politiques* (London, 1767), pp. 139–50; Nicolas Baudeau, *Première introduction à la philosophie économique ou analyse des états policés* (Paris, 1767), pp. 385–406.

[56] Mirabeau, *L'Ami des hommes*, 6 vols. (La Haye, 1758–62), I, p. 131. He made the same point in his 'Eloge de Sully', *Ephémérides du citoyen*, 8 (1770), pp. 29–34.

community which was uniformly patriotic and inclined towards peace. Historic praise of the spirit of union to be found in absolute monarchies would in future be applied to large republics.[57] Such unity would, Paine believed, lead to victories if defensive wars became necessary. When France became a republic he advised its legislators that they had nothing to fear from the existing military powers of Europe. Modern republics would wage a new kind of war, 'a war of the whole nation . . . When a whole nation acts as an army, the despot knows not the extent of the power against which he contends.' Should the enemy successfully penetrate France, he would find himself 'in the midst of a nation of armies'.[58] The modern republic was more powerful than a mixed state, because it combined the unified authority of absolute monarchy with the civic commitment of an ancient republic. Paine only became fearful for the Revolution when the political culture became characterised by divisions between Paris and the provinces during the struggle in the Convention between Robespierre's Jacobins and the Gironde.[59]

The question was how such a political culture might be created. Paine's answer was to call for a national convention to legitimate the erection of republican political institutions. The term 'republican' was used in two senses: first, meaning the rule of the wise for the good of the public. As Part Two of the *Rights of Man* put it: 'Republican government is no other than government established and conducted for the interest of the public, as well individually as collectively.' A republic embodied the *Res Publica*, described by Paine as 'the public affairs of a nation'.[60] The association of the republic with the sovereignty of wisdom was of course an ancient tradition, particularly associated with neo-Platonic philosophy. Even Burke defended this use of the term.[61] It was stronger, however, in France, where writers from Bodin onwards used *république* in this sense. What made it attractive was its compatibility with the sovereignty of an enlight-

---

[57] John Brown, *An Estimate of the Manners and Principles of the Times, by the Author of Essays on the Characteristics, &c.*, 7th edn., 2 vols. (London, 1758), I, pp. 103–4: 'the national spirit of union . . . is naturally *strong* in *absolute Monarchies*, because, in the Absence both of Manners and Principles, the *compelling* Power of the *Prince* directs and draws every thing to one Point, and therefore, in all common Situations, effectually supplies their Place'.

[58] *Address to the people of France* [September 1792], in *The Writings of Thomas Paine*, 3 vols. (London, 1899), III, p. 99; *On the propriety of bringing Louis XVI to trial* [November, 1792], III, p. 117.   [59] *Letter to Danton* [May 1793], in *The Writings*, III, pp. 135–9.

[60] *To the Authors of Le Républicain* [July, 1791], in *The Writings*, III, pp. 5–7; *Anti-Monarchal Essay, for the use of New Republicans* [October, 1792], III, pp. 102–7.

[61] Burke, *Letter to William Elliot* [1795 May 26], in *Further Reflections*, p. 273: 'by the true republican spirit alone, monarchies can be rescued from the imbecility of courts and the madness of the crowd. This republican spirit would not suffer men in high place to bring ruin on the country and on themselves. It would reform, not by destroying, but by saving the great, the rich and the powerful.'

ened king. Indeed, it had been used in the seventeenth century to contrast the wisdom of French kings with the ignorance and excesses of the English republic.[62] Condorcet revived the term in physiocratic circles when he described Turgot as a republican of this stamp in the influential *Vie de Turgot* of 1782.[63] It also led him to describe the Declaration of the Rights of Man as the keystone of the Revolution, infusing ancient ideas about the rule of the public good into a political edifice founded on national sovereignty.[64] His intention was to give old republican maxims the force of law, and thereby constrain the powers of demagogues with dangerous ideas.[65] Although he shared these views, to Paine it was more important to use this sense of 'republic' to attack monarchy. It was the basis of his argument against the association of republics with small states. Small states should rather be monarchies, because the knowledge required to rule them was less extensive:

when it is attempted to extend this individual [monarch's] knowledge to the affairs of a great country, the capacity of knowing bears no longer any proportion to the extent or multiplicity of the objects which ought to be known, and the Government inevitably falls from ignorance into tyranny.[66]

Political representation was the great discovery of the moderns, which Paine, alongside the authors of *The Federalist*, believed would give republicanism new life. Representation made the political culture of the nation homogeneous and patriotic, while ensuring that the enlightened were called upon to govern. The resulting state would be impregnable:

So powerful is the Representative System; first, by combining and consolidating all the parts of a country together, however great the extent; and secondly, by admitting of none but men properly qualified into the government, or dismissing them if they prove to be otherwise, that America was enabled thereby totally to defeat and overthrow all the schemes and projects of the Hereditary Government of England against her.[67]

Paine favoured the broadest possible franchise at the base of the representative system, although he ignored women. For men, exclusion was only possible 'as a punishment for a certain time upon those who should propose to take away that right from others'.[68]

---

[62] J.-M. Goulemot, 'Le Mythe de Cromwell et l'obsession de la république chez les monarchistes françaises de 1650 à 1700', in J. Viard, *L'Esprit républicain* (Paris, 1970), pp. 107–110.
[63] Condorcet, *Vie de Turgot*, in *Œuvres de Condorcet*, ed. A. Condorcet O'Connor, 12 vols. (Paris, 1847–9), V, pp. 209–10.
[64] Condorcet, *Idées sur le despotisme*, in *Œuvres*, IX, pp. 148–9.
[65] Condorcet, *Déclaration des droits*, in *Œuvres*, IX, pp. 198–9, 206.
[66] Paine, 'Lettre aux auteurs du Républicain', *Le Républicain*, no. 2 (July 1791), p. 9.
[67] Paine, *A Letter to Mr Secretary Dundas* [6 June] (London, 1792), p. 5.
[68] Paine, *Dissertation on First Principles of Government* [1795], in *The Writings*, III, p. 267n.

Paine expressed faith in the progress of reason, in the capacity of a constitutional code to temper excesses, and the unity of opinion generated by republican patriotism. In numerous writings of the late 1780s Condorcet had given equal support to the first two claims. It was no surprise, therefore, that he was closest to Paine among supporters of the Gironde. After the king's flight to Varennes in April 1791 Condorcet was converted to the third tenet of Paine's creed. National unity, Paine convinced him, could only be maintained if the nation expelled Louis Capet. With J.-P. Brissot, Etienne Clavière and Achille Du Châtelet they created the journal *Le Républicain* to propagate their shared beliefs.[69]

The abbé Sieyès' critique of Paine and Condorcet's republicanism, in *Le Moniteur* of July 1791, brings the nature of these shared views into sharp relief.[70] Sieyès claimed not to understand why they called themselves republicans because the representative government they supported was compatible with a single monarch as chief magistrate or a committee of elected magistrates. Arguing in favour of the former, Sieyès stated that his preference for elected monarchy was superior to Paine's 'polyarchy', in part because of the speed of action associated with an executive of one person. Above all he feared that a senatorial executive would degenerate into an aristocratic tyranny. Paine and Condorcet therefore threatened 'social liberty' by favouring 'public life against private life'. Sieyès' aim, by contrast, was to establish a severely limited government: a criticism which those who praise the 'liberal' Paine might bear in mind. While the first part of *The Rights of Man* defended the 'rational order of things in the French constitution' of 1791, the second part had a different aim: to persuade the French to remove their king and create an elected committee of chief magistrates. Paine was therefore responding to Sieyès' criticism of this plan when he made the argument that a republic 'one and indivisible' would counter aristocracy by maintaining the material equality of the citizenry. The establishment of moderate wealth became a fundamental element of his political strategy, to prevent merchants, legislators, judges, or landowners from becoming a new nobility. This scheme, which some historians have anachronistically associated with the idea of a welfare state, became of fundamental importance because of Sieyès' criticism. The policy of pensions, annuities, a progressive income tax, and a civic education, all of which he was to defend to the end of his life, were heavily

[69] L. Cahen, *Condorcet et la Révolution Française* (Paris, 1904), pp. 248–69; K.-M. Baker, *Condorcet: From Natural Philosophy to Social Mathematics* (Chicago, 1975), pp. 304–6.
[70] Sieyès had challenged republicans to defend their views when he claimed 'il y a plus de liberté pour le citoyen dans la monarchie que dans la république' (*Gazette Nationale, ou Le Moniteur*, 6 July 1791, pp. 46–7). Paine responded with a letter dated 8 July which was published with Sieyès' response in *Le Moniteur* of 16 July (pp. 137–9).

indebted to Condorcet's ideas about social insurance and national instruction. Returning the compliment, Condorcet was able to provide Paine with evidence to flesh out his republican perspective on material equality in modern nations.

VI

The idea of a national convention was also the key to Paine's second characterisation of a republic. Such a convention embodied the sovereignty of the nation, which to Paine entailed not simply the abolition of monarchy but the more important destruction of social hierarchies: ranks would not be abolished but henceforth members of any rank would be equal to those of any other. The term rank thereby would signify an occupation rather than status. Equality between ranks was called by Paine 'equality of Rights . . . the true and only basis of representative government'.[71] Evils which plagued 'the old governments of Europe' could be traced to 'distortedly exalting some men, so that others are debased, till the whole is out of nature'.[72] Placemen, courtiers, and beneficiaries of civil lists would no longer exist; nor would distinctions between different groups within a community. Hierarchical ranks had been responsible, Paine believed, for the decline of Britain, whose taxes beggared the industrious because the landed aristocracy wielded authority and required public revenues to buy popular support. As a consequence 'the word "Commons", applied as it is in England, is a term of degradation and reproach, and ought to be abolished. It is a term unknown in free Countries.'[73] Without distinctions between ranks Paine was certain there would be 'no riots, tumults, and disorders . . . [nor] that class of poor and wretched people who are so numerously dispersed all over England'.[74]

The central message of the second part of *The Rights of Man* was that the Revolution in France was great because it was the first upheaval in Europe to recognise the importance of ending social hierarchies. Men had become 'of one degree'. There were 'no more titles, no nobility or aristocracy . . . the peer is exalted into the *man*'. The French would be rewarded with a society where 'the poor are not oppressed, the rich are not privileged. Industry is not mortified by the splendid extravagance of a court rioting at its expense.'[75] Low taxes would allow commerce to thrive while the nation would be better and more justly governed. It was a historical fact that 'the greatest characters the world has known rose on the

---

[71] Paine, *Dissertation*, in *The Writings*, III, p. 265.
[72] *The Rights of Man*, Part One, in *Political Writings*, p. 71.
[73] *Letter Addressed to the Addressers on the Late Proclamation*, in *The Writings*, III, pp. 61, 86–7.
[74] *Letter to Dundas*, p. 8.   [75] *The Rights of Man*, Part Two, in *Political Writings*, p. 159.

democratic floor'. Where Sieyès sought to maintain social hierarchies, embodied in the *marc d'argent* property qualification for 'active citizenship' in the first French constitution, Paine's aim was to regenerate humanity by reconstructing the social order. Ranks would not be associated with political or civil inequalities, and moderate wealth would protect this social constitution.

The union of national sovereignty with a commercial and patriotic society in which ranks would be equal was an idea which Paine popularised in British political discourse. Contemporaries recognised that it marked him out from other radicals. As Horace Walpole put it, Paine's answer to Burke 'deserves a putrid fever. His doctrines go to the extremity of levelling.' Commenting on Paine's debate with Sieyès, Walpole claimed it concerned 'the plus or minus of rebellion'.[76] In Burke's view, Paine had contributed to the creation of 'a seductive liberty' by the 'Revolution of doctrine and theoretick dogma', envisaging a universal republic through 'the creation of a commonwealth . . . and the abolition of monarchy, nobility, and church establishments . . . in each country'.[77] Like Paine, whose intellectual manoeuvres he understood, Burke emphasised the importance of levelling ranks and the creation of a homogeneous political culture which was terrifying in its patriotism. These points were echoed in hundreds of pamphlets.[78] Paine's prosecution for sedition by the British government in June 1792 was based on the claim that he 'reviled what was most sacred in the Constitution, destroyed every principle of subordination and established nothing in their turn'.[79]

Such ideas might have been alien to British political argument but they had a longer history in France. Calls for the abolition of ranks were made by Diderot in his *Vie de Sénèque* of 1778 and 1782.[80] They were popularised in revisions made by Diderot to the abbé Raynal's *Histoire philosophique des deux Indes* in the late 1770s and early 1780s. According to Diderot, proof that 'primitive liberty' could be restored by 'the general assembly of a great nation', could be found in North America. As a result, the new republic should be a model whose example ought to be followed by all European peoples who valued liberty. The secret of

[76] Letters to Mary Berry, 3 April and 26 July 1791, *Horace Walpole's Correspondence*, 48 vols. (New Haven, 1937–83), VI, pp. 239, 319.
[77] Burke, *Thoughts on French Affairs* [December, 1791], in *Further Reflections*, pp. 208–11.
[78] Most of which have been expertly analysed by Greg Claeys: *Thomas Paine*, ch. 6. See also J. A. Epstein, *Radical Expression: Political Language, Ritual and Symbol in England, 1790–1850* (Oxford, 1994), ch. 4.
[79] Cited in M. Conway, *The Life of Thomas Paine*, 2 vols. (New York, 1909), I, p. 344, from Paine's note in *Letter to Mr Secretary Dundas*, p. 2.
[80] Diderot, *Essai sur les règnes de Claude et de Néron, et sur les mœurs et les écrits de Sénèque pour servir d'introduction à la lecture de ce philosophe*, in *Œuvres complètes de Diderot*, ed. J. Assézat, 12 vols. (Paris, 1875), III, pp. 48, 71, 321–4.

American success was 'the equality of station' and 'universal ease' which 'has given rise in every breast to the mutual desire of pleasing'. America was already, Diderot believed, the most stable polity in the world because it enjoyed the purest manners: 'Gallantry and gaming, the passions of indolent opulence, seldom interrupt that happy tranquillity . . . the female sex are still what they should be, gentle, modest, compassionate, and useful.' Such manners would ultimately make the state an international power infinitely superior to Britain or France.[81] Paine's knowledge of Raynal's *Histoire* is certain from his *Letter to the abbé Raynal* of 1782, in which he complained that certain paragraphs were plagiarised from *Common Sense*. That Paine read the book is no surprise given the sheer number of editions of the *Histoire* published during this period and the popularity of Justamond's translations of 1776 and 1788. Like *Common Sense*, it was pessimistic about Britain's future prospects and blamed mixed government for the decline of the state. Whether Paine was influenced by any of Diderot's ideas about ranks and manners in his subsequent writings is impossible to discern; like Diderot, he was reluctant to list his sources. It is, however, an interesting speculation. A surer link is with Brissot and Clavière, who were members of a political circle, including Chamfort and Honoré Gabriel Riqueti de Mirabeau, which blamed the French nobility for the weakness of the state and the economy. In a series of publications from 1787, Clavière and Brissot called for the regeneration of humanity by means of republican government, the levelling of ranks, and a political economy of moderate wealth.[82] Paine would have been introduced to both authors in the late 1780s because of their links with Franklin and the *Société des amis des noirs*. By means of their *Société Gallo-Américain*, they were then seeking to propagate their belief that the republicanism of the American Revolution could be applied to large European monarchies. Alongside Condorcet, they were involved with Paine in the creation of the journal *Le Républicain* in 1791 and with Paine contributed to the Girondin journal *La Chronique du mois*. It is likely that they influenced Paine's perspective on ranks, particularly in the early 1790s.

---

[81] Diderot, *A Philosophical and Political History of the Settlements and Trade of the Europeans in the East and West Indies*, trans. J. O. Justamond, 6 vols. (London, 1798), VI, pp. 108–9; II, p. 90. Many of Diderot's contributions have been published in G. Goggi, *Pensées détachées* (Siena, 1976) and *Mélanges et morceaux divers* (Siena, 1973). Translations and commentary can be found in J. Hope Mason and R. Wokler, eds., *Diderot: Political Writings* (Cambridge, 1992).

[82] J.-P. Brissot and E. Clavière, *Point de Banqueroute, ou lettre à un créancier d'état, sur l'impossibilité de la banqueroute nationale, & sur les moyens de ramener le crédit & la paix* (London, 1787); *Observations d'un Républicain sur les diverses systèmes d'Administrations provinciales* (Lausanne, 1788); *De la France et des Etats-Unis ou de l'importance des Etats-Unis pour le bonheur de la France* (Paris, 1791).

When Paine's ideas are placed in the context of various French republican writings, which appeared to be a single tradition from a British perspective, he ceases to be a lone figure. With regard to the French Revolution, he also ceases to be the innovative thinker so many studies have portrayed. Paine's calls for the destruction of nobility, moderate wealth, and a republican alternative to mixed government were influenced by Price and Smith but probably developed under the tutelage of such writers as Diderot, Brissot, Clavière and, later, Condorcet. In the early 1790s Clavière and Brissot began to argue that the surest means to abolish nobility and make moderate wealth more widespread was the *assignat* paper-money project to persuade the French populace to embrace commerce. Against them, Paine favoured Condorcet's schemes for pensions and public instruction. After the death of his republican associates in the Terror, Paine's republicanism took another turn. This reflected his loss of optimism about the capacity of republican political institutions to maintain themselves in conditions of historical allegiance to monarchy, church, and nobility.[83] He began to argue that the only means of restoring the national unity essential to republican citizenship was to create a rational religion which would teach fraternity. Blaming the atheism of such men as Condorcet for their political defeat, he turned, with the old physiocrat Dupont de Nemours, to the religion of Theophilanthropy. The *Age of Reason*, published on Paine's emergence from the Luxembourg, sought to instil in citizens a patriotism capable of distinguishing between enthusiasm and fanaticism, where civic instruction, the civil constitution of the clergy, and the *assignats* had failed. Such works as *Agrarian Justice*, however, continued to promote the ideal of moderate wealth which was also the central theme of Condorcet's final republican manifesto, the *Esquisse d'un tableau historique des progrès de l'esprit humain*. *Agrarian Justice* was dedicated to the Directory and noted that 'the present constitution of the French Republic [is] the *best organised system* the human mind has yet produced'. His only fear was that the constitution of 1795 violated 'the equality of the right of suffrage' and in doing so diminished 'the enthusiasm that right is capable of inspiring'. In short, only universal manhood suffrage would create a state capable of defeating the monarchies which sought to destroy it. Yet Paine was involved in the Directory's plans for the invasion of England from 1798 and continued to believe that France would defeat Britain in war because of the manliness of the republican state. He donated money to facilitate the abolition of 'the tyranny and corruption of the English government'.[84]

---

[83] This can be traced to the letter to Jefferson, 20 April 1793, *Complete Writings*, II, pp. 1330–2.   [84] *Complete Writings*, II, pp. 675, 1403–5.

What is beyond dispute is that Paine successfully imported a French republican discussion of the limits of mixed government into a British political scene which had hitherto ignored it. Burke acknowledged this towards the end of his life. Rather than describing the French republic as the historical anomaly of the *Reflections*, doomed to collapse by civil war or the combined arms of Europe's monarchies, he called it a state of unparalleled power. The 'Republick of Regicide' appeared to have reversed the logic of public finance. Bankruptcy, 'the very apprehension of which is one of the causes assigned for the fall of the Monarchy, was the capital on which she opened her traffick with the world'. The patriotism and national unity of committed republicans had 'conquered the finest parts of Europe, distressed, disunited, deranged, and broke to pieces all the rest'.[85] Believing 'our Constitution is not made for this kind of warfare', Burke argued that Hume's euthanasia of the constitution was no longer absolute monarchy; rather, it was Paine's republic.[86]

---

[85] *First Letter on a Regicide Peace* [1796], in *The Writings and Speeches of Edmund Burke*, 10 vols. so far (Oxford, 1991), IX, pp. 188–93.
[86] *Fourth Letter on a Regicide Peace* [1795], in *The Writings and Speeches*, IX, pp. 98, 108, 119.

7 Irish culture and Scottish enlightenment: Maria Edgeworth's histories of the future

Marilyn Butler

I

Maria Edgeworth, like other leading creative writers in English of the 1790s, was a populariser of the late Enlightenment. She so plainly excelled in this role that she seemed proof against the masculinist prejudice towards clever women. Reviewers were respectful, even the hostile ones. The article on 'Intellectual Education' in Chambers' *Cyclopaedia* (vol. XVII, 1812) was devoted to her innovative child-centred, psychological teaching method. Francis Jeffrey, along with Etienne Dumont, Bentham, and a cluster of leading serious reviewers, considered she made fiction more truthful and more important than before. Why then had her reputation come under such fire, even in the first quarter of the nineteenth century, that after the 1830s her books were rarely re-issued and as a whole went out of print? Ruskin could still claim she wrote the most rereadable books in existence.[1] What makes such books no longer readable? This essay is about her serious successes, particularly her original and technically accomplished use of Scottish thinking in different types of writing. But it is also about the success of her opponents in destroying her popularity, largely through guilt by association: their remarkably enduring identification of her with unloved causes, such as irreligion, the popular Enlightenment, the plight of the poor, and Irish politics.

Within four years of her first major publication, *Practical Education* (1798), this Irishwoman had made her name on the continent as well as in Britain and America with knowledgeable and lively books in three different fields. She began with the educational writing and stories for children, her main literary preoccupation between 1782 and 1798, but in Britain was soon associated with her Irish tales and writings (from *Castle Rackrent* in 1800 to *Ormond*, 1817). In the era following the French Revolution she amassed an intellectually ambitious *œuvre* relating to England, three full-

---

[1] Ruskin had read her tales, and *Patronage*, 'oftener than any other books in the world, except the Bible': Letter to Henry Acland, n.d. [?1855]; Bodleian Library, Oxford, MS Acland, d. 72.

scale novels, *Belinda* (1801), *Patronage* (1814), and *Helen* (1834), and more than a score of tales, which were studies, mostly comic and satirical, of British and European societies, their interactions, and their national character. And by 1812 she was newsworthy.

To return to her readability: Edgeworth's style in her tales was praised from the outset for its entertainment value, derived from the fact that her stories and lessons are essentially conversational – the dialogues of characters who rarely dispute directly. Critics noticed that not only individuality but attitudes, characteristic of different backgrounds, classes and cultures, were identified and expressed with a new kind of accuracy and knowledge in these conversations. She had an ear for idiom and inflection: as a second innovation, she used it to introduce in the dialogue of upper-class characters a flow of quotation, or real-life allusions, as a means of conveying individuality and starting ideas. The effect is bookish, but also eclectic and witty rather than didactic. At her best, Edgeworth's characters are good company, having evidently spent their lives exchanging thoughts, ideas, and much miscellaneous reading in seventeenth- and eighteenth-century books, from the most learned and specialised to fairy tales, jokebooks, and periodicals.

Among the potential problems was the fact that, by early nineteenth-century standards, Edgeworth had an unusual intellectual range. Albeit through her characters, she referred to books by then widely considered vulgar, improper, or politically tendentious, and to relatively little that was 'women's reading'. She was well read in, for example, Machiavelli, Bacon, James Harrington, his editor Toland, Molière, Pascal, Sévigné, La Rochefoucauld, Voltaire, Rousseau, probably Hume, Smith, Hartley and his editor Priestley, Erasmus Darwin, Genlis, Marmontel, Kant (or his English critics), Staël, and Wollstonecraft. Their presence exposed her to criticism, though she often avoided naming more notorious writers, for example the last three, Machiavelli, and Rousseau. Laclos' *Liaisons dangereuses* was imitated in one scene in *Leonora*, but not identified.

Pickering and Chatto's new annotated twelve-volume edition of Edgeworth will, in other words, surprise those whose notions of lady-like early nineteenth-century discourse are formed by Austen – who is aware of Edgeworth and indeed imitates her, but with a consistent exclusion of general ideas.[2] The modern novel featuring a heroine was designated women's reading, and therefore effectively policed to keep out not merely impropriety but thought. By disavowing the word 'novel' near the beginning of her career in her Preface to *Belinda* (1801), Edgeworth managed, somehow unopposed, to adopt as her main medium a free version of the

[2] M. Butler, 'Simplicity', *London Review of Books*, 5 March 1998, p. 6.

French philosophical tale associated with Voltaire. Her main themes when she depicts the English upper classes are satirical and critical. She published most of her work in wartime, which gave her a topical target in the English weakness for francophilia – but an old-regime, libertine and frivolous Frenchness, rather than sympathy with the Revolution. The strongest line of critique in this vein emerges in the epistolary tale *Leonora*, 1806, the six-volume *Tales of Fashionable Life*, especially *Manoeuvring*, 1809, *Emilie de Coulanges* and *Vivian*, 1812, and lastly in *Patronage*, 1814; a focused criticism of institutions, echoing the views of Smith and Bentham, gathers strength in the last two. This is her serious vein, which is unlike the didactic or 'conduct' middlebrow writing of the period. More generally, the rapidity of her writing, the variety of her characters and her flow of allusion – the features which made her distinctive – also made her entertaining. As if by accident, she was leading her more bookish readers, men or women, to follow her into established public debates, or pick up, if they could, historical and European sources for her plots. To read her was to tune into the vast, open-ended conversation that was Hume's and Smith's metaphor for modern society.

II

It has never been any secret that Edgeworth had some links with the Scottish Enlightenment, specifically with Adam Smith. A difficulty hitherto has been to pin down what mattered to the Edgeworths in Smith's diverse *œuvre*, and above all what Maria Edgeworth recognisably used. She was famously handed *The Wealth of Nations* to read in 1782 at the age of fourteen, when after a six-year residence in England her father Richard Lovell Edgeworth gathered up his family and brought them home to Ireland. It was at this point, after exposure in England to the discussions on political economy, estate management, and (less often noticed) education stimulated by Smith's most famous book, that R. L. Edgeworth (RLE) reorganised his estate in County Longford on liberal and progressive grounds, redesigned the interior of the house as a school for his fourteen younger children, and recruited his clever eldest daughter to be his assistant, in estate matters more particularly.

RLE wrote of these projects, house and estate, as linked: 'I returned to Ireland with the firm determination to dedicate the remainder of my life to the improvement of my estate, and to the education of my children; and . . . of contributing to the melioration of the inhabitants of the country, from which I drew my subsistence.'[3] In 1782, the year when the Irish

---

[3] *Memoirs of Richard Lovell Edgeworth*, begun by himself, and concluded by his daughter, 2 vols. (London, 1820), II, p. 1.

Volunteer movement created the 'patriot' Dublin parliament, his experiments might have looked republican. For the Edgeworths, though, this date marked the launch of domestic and educational projects that were to involve the family as a whole from 1780 to the 1820s. Following the advice of a group of Scottish writers, including Smith, James Anderson, Kames, and William Ogilvie,[4] RLE had it in mind to improve the people rather than the land, by educating not just his own younger children but the children and adults living on the estate. In an address to a Longford county meeting on reform, he welcomed proposals for Catholic emancipation and forecast that improvements such as his would set national changes in motion. Once a tenant is no longer subjugated 'to a blind dependence on the owner of his farm, a yeomanry will by degrees arise, which will diffuse liberty and industry through every class of the people of Ireland'.[5]

Both programmes, schoolroom and estate, aimed at individual betterment through education. The emphasis on the individual echoes Adam Smith in his most important discussion of education, in book V of the *Wealth of Nations* (1776), where Smith may in turn have been indebted to the psychological 1770s' work of Priestley, above all Priestley's abridged edition (1775) of David Hartley's *Observations on Man* (1749). Priestley and RLE were fellow-members of the Lunar Society of Birmingham. Until now that link has accounted for the methodology and timing of the experimental system worked out in 1778–9 by RLE and his second wife Honora Sneyd, to be in turn developed by Maria Edgeworth and other adults of the family between 1782 and 1798, and further reinterpreted, reshaped, and transformed in Maria's educational manuals, dialogues, and children's tales. My initial proposition here, however, is that in its broader, more philosophical stance and its most distinctive practical features, the Edgeworths' method was partly based on practice, partly characteristic of liberal social thinking, especially Scottish thinking, of the 1770s.

The Edgeworth teaching method is based essentially on a simple, focused dialogue – initially between an individual adult and a child, but in Edgeworth's subsequent writing importantly between one child and another. Instruction is given sparingly in this child-centred system; an adult's reply to a child's question is typically another question. Much else is very informal. Classroom hours are short and books there to consult, rather than to be read through or learnt. Previous educationalists in the

---

4 James Anderson, *Observations of the means of exciting a Spirit of National Industry; Chiefly intended to promote the Agriculture, Commerce, Manufactures and Fisheries of Scotland* (Edinburgh and London, 1777), p. 424. Kames, *Sketches of the History of Man*, 2 vols. (1774); William Ogilvie, *Essay on the Right of Property in Land* (London, 1782). For another, later Scottish source, Simon Gray: see General Introduction, *The Novels and Selected Works of Maria Edgeworth*, ed. M. Butler and M. Myers, 12 vols. (London, 1999–2000), I, pp. xxviii–xxxiv.   5 *RLE's Memoirs*, II, pp. 50–1.

same tradition, Bacon, Locke, and Smith, already saw the young child from four to six or eight as naturally curious: an observer, experimenter, or budding philosopher. The Edgeworths confirmed this from their daily lessons, and worked out a teaching method in the light of practical experience. The child has a short attention-span: an Edgeworth lesson, short anyway, stopped when the child lost interest. A single difficulty prevents it from understanding: they got the children to talk, while the adults held back from delivering instruction. Children were best left to observe and reflect for themselves, and to devise their own experiments. These were striking innovations in science teaching, from which the family's daughters, more numerous and cleverer than the sons, benefited.[6] But the basic building block, the dialogue or conversation, was also being interpreted more generally as a principle of household communality.

The Edgeworths' practice was to live as a group, children included, reading, writing and talking together in the largest room (the library). Visitors to Edgeworthstown, the Genevan professor and journal editor M. A. Pictet in 1801 and the Irish lawyer Charles Kendal Bushe in 1810, praised the communal system warmly.[7] They did not notice that it literalised the 'conversation' Hume in his *Essays* and Adam Smith in his *Theory of Moral Sentiments* (1759) set such store by, which in fact becomes a model for civil society itself: quiet, reasoned, bipartisan, the desired modern ideal after the armed factions and fanaticism of seventeenth-century religious wars.

RLE's changes on the estate – leasehold reform, farming for profitability, the scrapping of tenants' feudal obligations, the granting of a plot to smallholders on which to grow vegetables or keep an animal – derived from a combination of liberal writing on estate management and more radical efforts to resuscitate Harringtonian land reform.[8] None of this is well explained by the Edgeworths; it is the opposite with the interest RLE took in the parish school and even in 'hedge schools', an interest in local children and sometimes adults as individuals rather than producers.

---

[6] 'Memory and Invention', *Practical Education*, 2nd edn, 3 vols. (1801), III, pp. 82ff, esp. pp. 111–15; cf. Mitzi Myers, 'Aufklärung für Kinder: Maria Edgeworth and the Genders of Knowledge Genres', *Women's Writing*, 2 (2) (1995), pp. 113–40, specifically p. 117.

[7] Marc-Auguste Pictet, *Voyage de trois mois en Angleterre, en Ecosse et en Irlande* (Geneva, 1802), pp. 193–4; Charles Kendal Bushe, Letter to his wife, 16 August 1810; E. OE. Somerville and Martin Ross, *Irish Memories*, new edn (London, 1925), pp. 49–52; quoted in Marilyn Butler, *Maria Edgeworth: A Literary Biography* (Oxford, 1972), pp. 212–13.

[8] E.g. Nathaniel Kent, *Hints for a Gentleman of Property* (1775), an enlightened manual on rationalising a medium-sized estate (income about £2,000); Kames was a source for leasehold reform, but RLE found his tenants resistant. *RLE's Memoirs*, II, pp. 23–5. Ogilvie, the neo-Harringtonian advocate of the redistribution of land, was a wild card in relation to RLE's estate practice, but in Edgeworth's Irish fiction popular land-hunger is a recurring motif.

From the outset he evidently engaged in the kind of conversation well illustrated in the *Essay on Irish Bulls*, when he is described on horseback overtaking a 'gossoon' or messenger-boy, and setting him a problem in mental arithmetic as he runs.[9]

In the three later Edgeworth tales each of the estates in the story has a school: the first, in *Ennui*, is run by a Scotsman, an avowed admirer of Adam Smith, the second, in *The Absentee*, by a couple, the Burkes, who adopt a distinctive mode of civility when in conversation with the people of the estate:

> He said . . . he tried to make all his neighbours live comfortably together . . . by giving them opportunities of meeting socially . . . he had so much to do, he said, that he had no time for controversy. He was a plain man, made it a rule not to meddle with speculative points, and to avoid all irritating discussions; he was not to rule the country but to live in it, and make others live as happily as he could.[10]

The unpublished correspondence confirms that the Edgeworths used similar protocols when talking to tenants, to avoid speculative points and irritating discussions.[11] Family conversation ran on similar lines. Both were probably derived from a source such as the passage in the *Theory of Moral Sentiments* where Smith seriously observes that children in a well-functioning family respect their parents, and the parents respect the children.[12] In addition, while the Edgeworths rarely write about economics or the 'market place', their work, particularly Maria Edgeworth's, engages deeply and pervasively with Smith's relatively brief discussion on education.

In her instructive article on Smith's and Condorcet's liberal and individualistic theories of education, Emma Rothschild observes that on this topic Smith's views were notably unlike the 'cold' economic thought – utilitarian, materialist, rationalist and determinist – of Condorcet's critics then and now.[13] Though no friend to state intervention in education generally, Smith made an exception on behalf of poor children, because he saw in them the victims of one of the central features of the commercial system, the division of labour. If they start work when very young, say

---

[9] *Essay on Irish Bulls* (1802), ch. xii, 'Irish Wit and Eloquence'; passage cut in 3rd edn (1808) and subsequent editions; Edgeworth's *Works*, I, pp. 385–6.

[10] *The Absentee*, ch. ix; ed. H. Van der Weire and K. Walker, *Works*, V, p. 104.

[11] Cf. letter of Maria Edgeworth to Mrs Graham (n.d. [1814]), where she describes her attempt to tell people on the estate that Napoleon has abdicated: 'As they have not it seems been supplied at this crisis with their Secret gazettes they will doubt the authenticity of ours . . . "It's only minding his nets he'll be & it won't be long afere he'll catch the world again."' Dumont papers, Bibliothèque Nationale, Geneva, MS Constant 46.

[12] *Theory of Moral Sentiments*, p. 222; quoted by Emma Rothschild, 'Condorcet and Adam Smith on Education and Instruction', in Amelie Oksenberg Rorty, ed., *Philosophers on Education: Historical Perspectives* (London and New York, 1998), pp. 209–26, esp. p. 220.

[13] Rothschild, 'Condorcet and Adam Smith', pp. 209–10.

between six and eight, have no further education, and throughout life do dull, repetitive jobs, making no use of their intellectual faculties, they are 'mutilated and deformed [in an] essential part of the character of human nature'. Torpor of mind renders them 'not only incapable of relishing or bearing a part in any rational conversation, but of conceiving any generous, noble or tender sentiment, and consequently of forming any just judgement concerning . . . the ordinary duties of private life'.[14] It is precisely the happiness and personal rewards of middle-class private life that Smith believes the poor should share, and characterises not primarily as possessions but as lifelong private pursuits: the sciences, geometry, and 'conversation' (which at this time also means interaction) with friends and family.

Rothschild's article provides a valuable key to the writings of the Edgeworths, in and beyond the topic of education, by pinpointing a late eighteenth-century 'left-liberal' concept of the role of mass education in modern society, one which implicitly views the poor child as a citizen, but more obviously and strikingly as an individual; for Smith, too, advocated the psychological approach, aiming at self-reliance, which was the hallmark of the Edgeworth educational method. On the poor, Adam Smith's views were unusual, so that the Edgeworths' convergence with them is all the more telling. In pursuit of a free school system for every Irish child, RLE served for six years as a member of the committee set up by the Irish Board of Education in 1806 under the chairmanship of William Stewart, the Anglican Archbishop of Armagh. A still more creative response can be seen in Maria Edgeworth's writing for children which, whether in tales or pedagogic dialogues, is strikingly accessible, often uses poor children in humble settings as protagonists, and represents them as a whole as genuine heroes and heroines, sturdier and more enterprising than their middle-class equivalents.[15]

But Smith and Condorcet also left the Edgeworths a legacy that came to haunt Maria Edgeworth's career. Smith's insistence that the poor should be encouraged to think and to converse was made more provocative by a corollary, that their thinking should not be moulded, still less controlled, by the teacher; and least of all by church and state with the aim of making the people obedient. It was an Enlightenment axiom that for two centuries religion had been the prime cause of Europe's endemic civil strife and misery. While pretending he made this recommendation in

[14] Smith, *Wealth of Nations*, ed. R. R. Campbell and A. S. Skinner (Oxford, 1979), pp. 788, 782.
[15] Notable stories about entrepreneurial poor children in *The Parent's Assistant*, 2nd enlarged edn (1800), include 'Lazy Lawrence', 'The Orphans', 'The Basket Woman', and 'The False Key'.

the interests of public quiet, Smith skilfully brought up the lesson of history: 'The more they are instructed, the less liable [the people] are to the delusions of enthusiasm and superstition, which, among ignorant nations, frequently occasion the most dreadful disorders.'[16] Condorcet incensed Robespierre by adding that the same could even be said of France's own sacred cow, the new constitution, which should be taught in school only as a fact. 'To excite in its favour a blind enthusiasm which makes citizens incapable of judging it [would be] to violate freedom in its most sacred rights, under the pretext of teaching how to cherish it.'[17]

In 1798 Maria Edgeworth had completed a work which still had the title RLE had given the project he initiated with Honora in the 1770s – *Practical Education*. It was then in the form of a slim volume of lessons for beginning readers. The quite different second version was a two-volume manual for parents educating their children entirely at home, with a chapter each for a range of syllabus subjects, such as grammar, arithmetic, and mechanics, and others for general topics, such as toys and books. There was nothing on religion, except a sentence in the preface to say that it had been omitted, along with politics, 'because we have no ambition to gain partizans, or to make proselytes, and because we do not address ourselves exclusively to any sect or to any party'.[18] Most comment, in for example the *Analytical, Critical* and *Monthly Reviews*, passed over this gap. But the *British Critic*, founded earlier in the decade by Anglican clerics, wrote a pithy denunciation in a single paragraph of 'education *à la mode* . . . and not a word on God, Religion, Christianity, or a hint that such topics are ever to be mentioned'. The same paragraph reappeared in the widely circulating *Gentleman's Magazine*.[19] Relieved, presumably, that it was no worse, the Edgeworths decided not to change their policy on religion when a third edition was called for in 1801, although they knew that some friends, such as the Genevan Calvinist Pictet, regretted the omission. They merely strengthened the moral advice in certain places, and as a concession to the religious lobby altered the title to *Essays on Practical Education*.

The respected Mrs Trimmer in the *Guardian of Education* was not appeased. She acknowledged the 'great ingenuity and practical knowledge displayed in this work, but feared for the morals and religion of pupils taught by it'.[20] But a book meant for private middle-class use was a minor matter. Within a few years mass popular education did become an issue; what was taught mattered above all; and the notion of deliberately

[16] Smith, *Wealth of Nations*, p. 788.   [17] Quoted Rothschild, 'Condorcet', p. 218.
[18] *Practical Education*, Introduction to first edition (1798), p. xvii.
[19] *British Critic* 15 (1798), p. 210 and *Gentleman's Magazine* 70 (1798), p. 459.
[20] Sarah Trimmer, *Guardian of Education*, 5 vols. (London, 1802–6), II, p. 171.

not teaching religion or morals was now eccentric, and highly unpopular. Rothschild has shown how Smith's by now notorious views on the matter were censured by his editor William Playfair, who rebuked Smith in the eleventh edition of the *Wealth of Nations* (1805).[21] I shall return to the effect on Edgeworth's career of this part of Smith's legacy in a later part of the essay.

III

Maria Edgeworth's Irish tales have not hitherto been considered in relation to the Scottish Enlightenment. Indeed, at the present time much of the most energised new comment on her comes from academic departments that place her in Anglo-Irish or post-colonial literature; it is the English connection that is attended to, and from a specific point of view. The Irish historian Tom Dunne began a vogue with his lecture of 1984, 'Maria Edgeworth and the Colonial Mind'; since then he has argued that her writing is a leading expression of Protestant Anglo-Irish landlordism and of a commitment to continued English governance, while RLE's keyword, 'improvement', stands in Dunne's view for Anglicisation.[22] The critic Seamus Deane falls in with the practice of reading the fiction by way of the family affiliation, while adding 'spins' of his own. His even stronger emphasis on Protestantism, for example, leads him to merge Edgeworth with the Evangelical Hannah More, and to attribute what he takes to be Edgeworth's failures as an Irish writer and would-be historical novelist to her sectarian predisposition to chastity and sobriety.[23] The sophisticated new historicist Catherine Gallagher discusses Edgeworth as the final case-study in her book on eighteenth-century women writers and political economy, *Nobody's Story*. Gallagher surely has too narrow an idea of what, in the period, such an interest might have entailed: Edgeworth 'had been taught to believe in the "productivist" economic theories of the political economists, who stressed that human labor created value, and she applied their theories to her own work as an author'.[24] Gallagher does not see the link to a different Smith in a passage she quotes from *Professional Education*, on the need to think and read for oneself – even

[21] Rothschild, 'Condorcet', pp. 212, 219–20.
[22] Tom Dunne, 'Haunted by History: Irish Romantic Writing, 1800–1850', in Roy Porter and M. Teich, eds., *Romanticism in a National Context* (Cambridge, 1989), p. 22, and '"A Gentleman's Estate should be a Moral School": Edgeworthstown in Fact and Fiction', in Raymond Gillespie and G. Moran, eds., *Longford: Essays in County History* (Dublin, 1991), esp. pp. 97, 116.
[23] Seamus Deane, *Strange Country: Modernity and Nationhood in Irish Writing since 1790* (Oxford, 1997), pp. 30–48.
[24] Catherine Gallagher, *Nobody's Story* (Oxford, 1994), p. 257.

though Edgeworth is urbanely insisting that this is *even* true when reading the *Wealth of Nations*.[25] Edgeworth's refusal as a leading educationalist to teach religion became contentious, especially to the religiously committed. Her second borrowing from the Scottish Enlightenment was less obviously objectionable: it was the evolving 'science of man' after 1800, as represented by Dugald Stewart's *Elements of the Philosophy of the Human Mind* (1792) and political lectures (from 1799), and by contributors, among them Stewart's former pupils, to the *Edinburgh Review*. The modern world has been changed into a vital interactive system, thanks largely to print, with its ever-widening reach; its agents of change will not be protest or violence, but the spread of culture and the pressure of opinion; these, in Stewart's optimistic (and long) view, have set in motion an evolutionary process of gradual but certain improvement. In his chapter on Stewart and the *Edinburgh Review*, to which this part of the discussion owes much, Donald Winch observes that 'improvement' is Stewart's translation of the French-revolutionary word, 'perfectibility'.[26] I hope to show how Edgeworth, in step with the Edinburgh literati, adopted culture (rather than economics) as the basis of her view of society, and how she built upon this base the literary innovation for which she is best known – the first fictional representation of a national group, the Irish.

The Edgeworths were aware of Dugald Stewart by the mid-1790s from his *Elements*. The era's change of emphasis towards language, systems of communication (including telegraphy and cryptography), and the role of the press appears distinctly, described as a stage of thinking beyond Smith, in RLE's learned paper on his invention, a telegraph, delivered to the Royal Irish Academy on 27 June 1795. With characteristic optimism he gave this talk in anticipation of the first-ever message to be telegraphed that August – with great symbolic appropriateness – from Scotland to Ireland.[27] In 1796 RLE was in Edinburgh, arranging that his son Lovell should board with Stewart's family and receive tuition from him; the next son, Henry, also lived with the Stewarts from 1801. Personal links were

---

25 *Ibid.*, p. 264, quoting from [R. L.] Edgeworth, *Professional Education* (London, 1809), p. 297. Despite the title page, Maria Edgeworth wrote the work.

26 Donald Winch, 'The System of the North: Dugald Stewart and his Pupils', in Stefan Collini, D. Winch, and J. Burrow, *That Noble Science of Politics* (Cambridge, 1983), pp. 25–61, specifically p. 39.

27 'An Essay on the Art of Conveying Secret and Swift Intelligence', *Transactions of the Royal Irish Academy*, 6 (1797), pp. 95–139. In the course of devising a codebook for his telegraph, RLE became interested in the project of a universal [or philosophical] language, an idea pursued in the mid-seventeenth century by John Wilkins, an early member of the Royal Society, and afterwards by Fontenelle and Leibniz. The latter wanted to make 'an alphabet of human thoughts', a step towards a philosophical language. 'Secret and Swift Intelligence', p. 122.

formed for life when RLE, Maria, and Mrs Frances Edgeworth visited Edinburgh in March–April 1803 on their journey home from Paris to Edgeworthstown, and set up a correspondence mainly conducted by Maria Edgeworth and Mrs Stewart. Equally important were the contacts made with Jeffrey and the *Edinburgh Review*.

It is an additional point of interest in what follows, therefore, that the sons would have been attending Stewart's influential new lectures on politics from 1799, and undoubtedly conveying something of them to Edgeworthstown. Before this, the family in January 1799 staged a new play by Maria, a comedy called *Whim for Whim* written to take their minds off the horrors of the Rebellion of 1798 and its aftermath, but also to justify aims such as egalitarianism, education, and progress. One of the two liberal protagonists, Opal, a young man who moves rapidly between mentors such as Condorcet and (more certainly) Kant, reluctantly gives up his hopes of joining the Illuminati; but the curtain nevertheless comes down on Opal's resilient cry, 'I shall study Common Sense!'[28]

Edgeworth's most celebrated book and first study of Ireland, *Castle Rackrent*, was almost wholly written between 1793 and 1798. It is a fictionalised family memoir, which is intricately based on real Edgeworth family documents, describing seventeenth-century characters and events within a circle about six miles in diameter in their corner of Longford. I shall, therefore, omit further discussion of it here as it predates the turn towards language and cultural systems evident in an equally inventive, if now neglected, second book on Ireland. RLE and Maria Edgeworth agreed to write the *Essay on Irish Bulls* as a joint endeavour in 1797, though the actual writing was probably done in 1801–2, prior to publication in May 1802. The basic idea had first occurred to Swift, who conveyed it in October 1730 to Lord Bathurst:

A certain wag, one of my followers, is collecting materials for a tolerable volume of English Bulls, in revenge of the reproaches you throw upon us for this article . . . All these are to be gathered, others invented, and many transplanted from here to England . . . And there must be a long Introduction proving the native Irish rabble to have a better tact for Wit than the English, for which philosophical causes shall be assigned and many instances produced.[29]

Except that they wrote a long essay rather than compiling a collection, the Edgeworths followed each suggestion with remarkable fidelity, including Swift's sardonic aims, to clear the Irish of the charge of stupidity and to make the bull or accidentally comic blunder seem the property of the English.

[28] *Whim for Whim*, Act V, sc. iv; Edgeworth's *Works*, XII (forthcoming 2000).
[29] Swift to Lord Bathurst, October 1730; *Swift's Correspondence*, ed. Harold Williams, 5 vols. (Oxford, 1963), III, p. 411. Edgeworths' reference in *Irish Bulls*, ch. II, cut in 3rd and subsequent editions; see *Works*, I, p. 374.

More fundamentally and philosophically, though, the Edgeworths' version explores personal and national identity, not just of the Irish but of all the people of the British Isles. Dugald Stewart is given a pre-eminent part in the work, in a new introduction (1808), as the representative Scottish thinker, a colleague to Locke (England) and Burke (Ireland).[30] For the first time an Edgeworth text achieves the effect an Irish scholar has described as 'quilting',[31] which, to be successful, has to aim for distinctness among the parts, a degree of pattern, and harmony in the whole. The pieces of the quilt are reported conversations; the quilt as a whole, discourse itself. The discrete pieces, typically the names of books, writers or an idea, can be arranged logically under headings though they occur randomly in the book:

(a) Conversations: formal dialogues (e.g. in two late chapters, 'The Bath Coach Conversation', involving an Englishman, a Scotsman, and an Irishman); informal encounters with talkers of all classes, including the mathematical Irish messenger-boy; dialect, thieves' cant, ribald jokes; wagers, coin-tossing, pugilism.

(b) Utopias: e.g. Lucian's fantastic voyages to the moon, More's *Utopia*, Harrington's *Oceana*; Ireland from ancient times: Hesperides, Atlantis.

(c) Three inset narratives, each featuring an Irish hero in a different popular genre: viz. a school story ('Little Dominick'), a sentimental Irish ballad ('The Irish Mendicant'), and 'The Irish Incognito', a hybrid genre using Lucian, the picaresque novel and stage farce.

(d) Wars, wars of words, invented conspiracies. Irish civil wars, e.g. 1688, 1798; French Revolution. Current English battles against the French, 1799–1801. Seventeenth-century English conspiracies and slanders, typically anti-Catholic, e.g. the 'Popish Plot' of Charles II's reign; Richard Musgrave's *Memoirs of the Different Rebellions in Ireland*, 1801, alleging that all were led by Catholic priests. The savage orders, involving torture and execution, given during the '98 Rebellion by Lord Clare, Ireland's leading law officer.

(e) Early Celtic or British mythology; lines to Garden of Eden, usually attributed to the Welsh. Wm. Ireland's play, *Vortigern*, 1796; Blackmore, *Prince Arthur*, 1695; Howard, *The British Princes*, 1669. Irish historians: O'Halloran, etc.

(f) Role-models and heroes. Scottish soldiers, Abercromby and Moore, distinguished for humanity in 1798 Rebellion. Irish writers of both sexes, Catholics and Protestants (list on last page of text); popular heroes: pugilists and conmen, such as the bottle conjuror.

[30] 'Introduction', *Irish Bulls*, new in 3rd and subsequent editions; *Works*, I, p. 74.
[31] W. J. McCormack, 'The Tedium of History: An Approach to Maria Edgeworth's *Patronage*', in Ciaran Brady, ed., *Ideology and the Historians* (Dublin, 1991), pp. 77–98, esp. p. 96.

(g) Learned jokes, puns, puzzles. Debates on personal identity: can a baby be changed at nurse? Pun: William of Ogham (for Occam) in list of real and alleged Irish writers, last page of text.

(h) Books about books and language. Dictionaries, encyclopaedias, etc. Scottish essayists and professors, debating the history of literature and culture, rhetoric, dialect, 'the low': especially Beattie, Kames, Blair, the (Catholic) advocate of dialect, James Adams.

Setting out the different strands in summary form makes it easier to see that they have social discourse itself as their common thread, not as sometimes suggested the bull, nationhood, or national character. Contemporaries would moreover have been struck by the comprehensiveness of this portrayal of 'conversation'. The pleasant uncontentious dialogue in the Bath Coach between philosophers of the three nations recalls Hume's 'easy and sociable age' at its best, and their discussion of personal identity ranges back through Western culture to Plato. Yet the modern populace, though sometimes easy and playful is also given to insults and murderous attacks; even more significantly, the people get at least equal time, and the Irish extra time. The high and low strands help weave together a new, enlarged civil society and British nation.

This is both a manifesto and an extreme example of Edgeworth's new method and new subject, modern culture itself. There is no British culture as such. Four distinct peoples inhabit the British Isles: English, Scottish, Irish, and Welsh, each with a history and cultural traditions, oral and written. Regardless of government and its institutions, it is from their cultural particularity that they define themselves against the others. By using their multi-stranded text to illustrate and convey this hybrid culture, the Edgeworths dispense with the tiresome notion of national character or more accurately caricature. While not doing equal justice to all four nations, they do enough to differentiate the four, and identify two as more interesting. The Welsh (represented by a pedantic, overbearing, and regressive schoolmaster) are preoccupied by genealogy and mythological history; many of the English citations are legal and historical. The Scots play a larger part, for they have written the best work on culture (not economics), as illustrated by Beattie, Blair, Kames, Burns, and the Smith of the *Theory of Moral Sentiments*. The Irish appear particularly productive culturally, since they excel in a variety of comic kinds – jests, bulls, confidence tricks, classic stage comedy, the picaresque novel, much satire, burlesque, fraud, lies, fantasy, utopias.

The Edgeworths avoid giving a standard explanation for Irish particularity, such as Montesquieu's environmental one: they merely give the Irish proverb, they are 'dipped in the Shannon'. The text's citations from ancient literature and from Plato, Aristophanes, Lucian, Herodotus,

Horace, Molière, Voltaire, and Anthony Hamilton, dignify comedy itself. Like the three charming inset stories, each in a different comic genre, they reinforce the cultural profile of Ireland, which is not only a land of exuberance and laughter but of literature, romance and enchantment, in keeping with the ancient-world reputation of this western outpost of Europe.

The *Essay* is then a sophisticated learned 'anatomy', much indebted in manner as well as matter to the French Enlightenment, especially to Voltaire and, quietly but pervasively, Swift.[32] Though the *Essay* predates the *Edinburgh Review* by five months, it has a family resemblance to that most characteristic medium of the day, the journal. It illustrates vividly how the Irish, Scots, and English exist for themselves and for their neighbours largely by way of print culture and the stereotypes, turns of phrase, newsworthy events, and personalities that are to be found in books and newspapers. There is moreover a strong underlying note of Stewart's progressivism and optimism, both in the philosophic dialogue between the Englishman, the Scotsman, and the Irishman, and in the random deployment of so much literature and learning before an eclectic crowd of characters – as though they all have access to a whole world of ideas, if they have the will and the time.

Finally, the book is progressive in its Irish politics, through the consistent thread of parody directed at the bigot Musgrave, and some impertinent running jokes about Protestant fanaticism. In the *Essay*, the Union is a fact: it need not mean the absorption of the Irish into the English. Instead the clear focus on the Irish and the Scots brings out the gifts of both, and hints hopefully at a future alliance to provide a counterweight to the centralising impulses of metropolitan England. As earlier beneficiaries or victims of union with England, the Scots have worked out strategies for preserving their national identity, such as Stewart's notion of a nineteenth century of gradual social progress, achieved by cultural rather than political means. This scenario empowers literati, wherever they are, and weakens the hold of politicians in London. Equally, and perhaps for young readers, the two heroes and role-models of *Irish Bulls* are the Scottish soldiers General Sir Ralph Abercromby and Major-General John Moore, who during the 1798 Rebellion denounced the severity with which a Dublin backed by London deployed troops and militia against the rural Catholic population; afterwards the same men distinguished themselves against the French in Holland and Egypt. Compliments to two Scotsmen carry criticism of English management in war.

The authors from the outset distance themselves from Englishness.

---

[32] *The Tale of a Tub, The Modest Proposal, The Drapier's Letters, Genteel and Ingenious Conversation in three dialogues* and *The Story of the Injured Lady, being a true picture of Scottish perfidy, Irish poverty and English partiality.*

Swift's original idea, faithfully carried out, is to turn the tables on Ireland's big neighbour, at all levels. 'John Bull', or the mass of the English population, is itself strictly bovine, and on Adam Smith's authority: it was the poor of *civilised* society who were made torpid and deformed by the division of labour.[33]

The three later Irish tales – *Ennui* (1809), *The Absentee* (1812), and *Ormond* (1817), the most powerfully interesting fiction yet, 'if fiction it can be called'[34] – were deeply admired by virtually all reviewers for their convincingly factual observation of Irish life. They had a second aspect which reviewers found it harder to pinpoint. They were not standard novels, but philosophic tales, which meant, according to one of the leading French practitioners, Marmontel, that the writer and the reader remained detached, reflecting on a pastoral, archaic world from a standpoint knowingly modern.[35] Much in the style of the *Essay on Irish Bulls*, different strands of Irish story and experience bring out a hybrid society. Irish history since 1169 enters through the use of leading Irish family names – 'Old Irish', 'Old English' or medieval, and 'New English' (from Elizabeth's reign on, that is post-Reformation). Gaelic Ireland enters when characters refer to old practices, legends, and folklore, or when Edgeworth deploys traditional plot-motifs. The later tales begin like standard novels, a combination of fictional travels and a young man's education, or *bildung*; once on Irish soil, events seem magical and allegorical. *Ormond* particularly uses parallel plots from world literature and history. Such reminders accustom readers to a non-naturalistic or 'philosophical' form.

The first of these new-model Irish tales, *Ennui*, was mostly written in 1804–5, immediately after Edgeworth's first visits to sophisticated circles in France and Scotland. It concerns an Irish peer, the Earl of Glenthorn, brought up from early childhood in England, who is persuaded by a visit from his Irish foster-nurse, Ellinor O'Donoghoe, to visit Ireland. Once there he lives like a feudal lord, and among other adventures becomes caught up in the '98 Rebellion. He then discovers from Ellinor that he is not after all the hereditary earl, but her own son, whom she exchanged for the lord's baby while she was nursing them both. He resigns his title and previous family name (O'Shaughnessy), and as Christy O'Donoghoe trains for seven years to become a lawyer. Eventually, his successor and foster-brother, the blacksmith–earl, becomes disillusioned and also resigns, to return to his forge. Our hero marries Cecilia the heir-at-law to the estate, and adds her name to his.

---

[33] Rothschild, 'Condorcet', p. 210, drawing on Smith, *Wealth of Nations*.
[34] Croker, *Quarterly Review*, 7 June 1812, pp. 329–42, esp. p. 330.
[35] J.-T. Marmontel, author of *Contes Moraux*, 2 vols. (Amsterdam, 1763), includes an essay on the tale in European tradition in his *Elements de littérature* (1789).

Ennui gives a dream-like, folkloric and cunning version of the Rebellion, interwoven with recent memories of the actual Rebellion's harsh suppression (the Yeomanry's violent treatment of the blacksmith was a common occurrence), and with the people's adventure yarns, as they turned the '98 immediately into legend. It also tells a complex political narrative, heavily indebted for its thick historical references to a two-volume *History of Ireland* (1803) by the English Catholic lawyer Francis Plowden, who tells the story of English governance in Ireland from 1169 in order to expose its consistent failure to make Irish Catholics equal citizens under the law. Read alongside *Ennui*, Plowden fills in the family background behind characters' names: Lady Geraldine will be a Fitzgerald, earls of Kildare and afterwards dukes of Leinster; Cecil Devereux, the descendant of a protégé of Elizabeth's minister, William Cecil, Lord Burghley, and her general in Ireland, Robert Devereux, Earl of Essex. Plowden also gives a preliminary account of Gaelic Ireland, along with its mythology, ancient kings, surviving pagan practices, and institutions such as the foster-nurse, who was Gaelic Ireland's bonder of families and septs, and English-governed Ireland's potential political infiltrator.

When he travelled to Killarney, Glenthorn if wide awake could have picked up the legends of its High King in Gaelic times, the O'Donoghue, who at the end of his reign walked out on and then under the waters of the Lake, having promised, Arthur-like, to return when his people needed him. The erstwhile Glenthorn, after shedding his English name, and undergoing a long labour leading to his real life's task, returns to the estate in his true form as O'Donoghoe Delamere, or from under the lake. For English readers this ending is heavily encrypted, indeed downright misleading, since Cecilia's names have so many other associations (with Burghley again, with a Fanny Burney heroine, and with the patron saint of music and harmony). No allusion is necessarily irrelevant, none excluded. Edgeworth offers not solutions, but a further option: an Irish future in which repossession of the land will come. Both *The Absentee* and *Ormond*, moreover, repeat the same distant promise. The alert reader will have uncovered an informed and critical history of Ireland; doing so is pleasurable, a reward for familiarity with books or reviews of books. If Irish, she will pick up the prophecy of a very different future – and if a pupil of Stewart, she will not expect it yet.

IV

The Scots were not the first to teach Edgeworth the value of networking. The professor from Geneva, M. A. Pictet, who visited Edgeworthstown in

1801, was already using selections from *Practical Education* and the other educational writings in the journal he co-edited, the *Bibliothèque britannique* (1798), which translated current British scientific and educational writing into French. The years from 1798 to 1802 were critical ones for the Calvinist Genevan republic, beginning with the French invasion of the Swiss cantons and followed by their incorporation into first a greater French republic, and subsequently an empire. It was Pictet who arranged for RLE and Mrs Frances Edgeworth, Maria, and her step-sister Charlotte to visit Paris (where he had an official post representing Geneva). He secured them introductions between October 1802 and February 1803 to French and Franco-Swiss scientific and banking salons, which included ex-encyclopaedists and current journalists, such as André Morellet and J. F. Suard (the former sent in 1805 a French appendix to the *Essay on Irish Bulls*). From this point Edgeworth was in effect drafted into a liberal and provincial opposition to Napoleon's metropolitan France, a Protestant, north-European network given definition and a liberal political and historical theory not only by the university circles who brought out the *Bibliothèque* but by Germaine de Staël's household at Coppet, including the key figures of Staël herself, Sismondi, A. W. Schlegel, and Constant.

Subsequent Edgeworth tales set in England, especially *Leonora* (1806), *Manoeuvring* (1809), and *Patronage* (1814), plainly belong to this propaganda warfare intended for other cosmopolitan liberals. *Leonora* is a story of spying and subversion, associating France not with progress but with the libertine old regime. *Patronage* has as its hero the German Count Altenberg, embodiment of Staël's portrait of northern culture in *L'Allemagne* (1810) – liberal, free, profoundly individualist and devoted to domestic and private life:[36] a compliment to Staël reinforced by the echo of Staël's liberal, republican Italian novel, *Corinne* (1808), which has a British hero. The Swiss also had a long-time resident in London in Etienne Dumont, Bentham's friend and ablest early interpreter.

In 1805 Dumont began a thoughtful intellectual correspondence with Edgeworth which continued into the 1820s, long after his return to Geneva. It was he who suggested the difficult topic of professional education, an onerous assignment on which Maria Edgeworth spent the best part of two years from 1806. The highly political and critical thinking about English institutions that went into this little-read work is reflected in Edgeworth's unexpectedly severe handling of the English political and parliamentary system in *Vivian* (1812) and *Patronage*, and the older professions of the church, the law, and medicine in the latter. Her depiction

---

[36] Cliona O'Gallchoir, 'Maria Edgeworth and the Rise of National Literature', Ph.D. thesis, Cambridge University, 1998.

in *Patronage* of an England in the grip of aristocratic influence aroused a chorus of disapproval from the various professions. On the other hand, Bentham championed the book anonymously as 'A Pupil of Miss Edgeworth's' in the Hunt brothers' *Examiner* precisely for its anti-aristocratic and anti-establishment satire. In private he was urging, according to Dumont, that she should not retract a line.[37]

A friendly association with the *Edinburgh Review* began in 1804 and worked itself out in review articles, not all of which can be noticed here. Two of the inner core of reviewers handled between them all the Edgeworth books that the *Edinburgh* reviewed: Francis Jeffrey, who in fact reviewed Edgeworth six times – *Popular Tales, Leonora,* and both series of *Tales of Fashionable Life,* the first including *Ennui,* and the second including *The Absentee*; and Sydney Smith, who reviewed *Essays on Irish Bulls, Professional Education,* and *Patronage.*[38] This was no stitch-up, since Sydney Smith very apparently had no personal liking for RLE. He poked fun at him, as tiresome and intrusive, in the reviews on *Irish Bulls* and *Patronage,* and wrote inattentive, uninformative accounts of the books he was sent, excessively padded with quotation.

Jeffrey, on the other hand, did admire Edgeworth from the moment he discerned her sense of mission in *Popular Tales* to reach out to a wide com-mercial-class audience. This preference made him dislike the epistolary novel *Leonora,* written in response to Wollstonecraft's *Maria or the Wrongs of Woman* (1798) and Staël's *Delphine* (1802). He chided her for the tale's fashionable and women-centred concerns, and urged her to return to the middle classes, where she could do more good. This must have been a dis-appointment to Edgeworth, for she had worked hard to craft *Leonora,* and set great store by it. Just as its women characters, all intellectuals, debate with one another, the tale as a whole debates with women writers in Paris (Helen Maria Williams, Genlis), with Staël, now in Switzerland, and with Swiss and French women encountered in the salons.

Besides, *Leonora* was the fruit of Edgeworth's first encounter with the *Edinburgh Review.* The opening letters, a debate between the self-oriented would-be philosopher, Olivia, and Leonora's mother, echo the first

---

[37] 'Il ne voudrait pas souffrir qu'on retranchât le moindre chose, il trouve les objections puériles.' Letter of Dumont to Maria Edgeworth, 14 February 1814; University College London, MS Bentham 174; see Butler, *Maria Edgeworth: A Literary Biography,* p. 496n and pp. 221–3. Cf. John Dinwiddy, 'Bentham as a Pupil of Miss Edgeworth's', *Notes and Queries* (June 1982), pp. 208–10. Condorcet, Jeffrey, Dumont, and Bentham all observed that novel-reading could offer a better introduction to society than other forms of instruction.

[38] 4 (July 1804), pp. 329–37; 8 (April 1806), pp. 206–13; 14 (July 1809), pp. 375–88; 20 (July 1812), pp. 100–26; 2 (July 1803), pp. 398–402; 15 (October 1809), pp. 40–53; 22 (1814), pp. 416–34. For reception see the introductions to each novel or tale in Edgeworth's *Works* (1999–2000).

articles in the first two numbers (October 1802 and January 1803) of the *Review* on, respectively, subversive Illuminati and Kant. Furthermore the tale as a whole owes its streetwise topicality to Edgeworth's energetic culling of many reviews carried by the *Edinburgh* up to the end of 1804, especially in the fields of European court memoirs (by Mirabeau, Kotzebue), good and bad travel writing (by Holcroft, Barrow), morals (Paley, Jacques Necker and Mme Necker), and sentimental writings, mainly novels, by the Parisian women already named.[39] *Ennui*, drafted in the years *Leonora* was written, 1804–5, draws on the same sources for the polished opening chapters set in England, and for Ireland owes much to Plowden's *History of Ireland*.[40] Jeffrey, who had himself written the first article in the number, was perhaps ill placed to spot the familiarity of her materials. But Edgeworth seemed immediately life-like and culturally up-to-date to early readers, especially other readers of the *Edinburgh Review*; they had all ingested its confident account of the competing idea-systems of present-day Britain and Europe. The journal, its readers, and Edgeworth as a writer made a circle that she knowingly closed, by telling her story as a set of virtually autonomous sketches, nearly independent of plot and characterisation, which lent themselves to quotation at length. She was rewarded by longer reviews than other novelists in her heyday, until Scott, who adopted the same technique, appeared on the scene in 1814 with *Waverley*.

With *Ennui*, at least, the first of the *Tales of Fashionable Life*, Jeffrey felt she had chosen the right course – and, in another probably hasty review, he praised her with an extravagance that a re-reading, or a disinterested editor, would normally have prevented. He envied her 'for having done more good than any other writer, male or female, of her generation' by writings 'beyond all comparison, the most useful of any that have come before us since the beginning of our critical career'. The current group of tales are 'actually as perfect as it was possible to make them'. He was equally extravagant in preferring *Ennui*, though here he used a comparison which must have outraged many readers: 'a story more rich in character, incident and reflection, than any English narrative with which we are acquainted; as rapid and various as the best tales of Voltaire'.[41]

Jeffrey's favour made it certain that others would review *Ennui*. But both he and the *Edinburgh Review* had made many political and religious enemies by 1808–9; this extravagant praise by Jeffrey himself gave them their opening. In what was originally a mild, well-disposed article by H. J. Stephen, William Gifford, the editor of the rival *Quarterly Review*,

---

[39] For the first six, see *Edinburgh Review*, 5, p. 78; 4, p. 84; 5, p. 259; 1, p. 287; 1, p. 382; 3, p. 490.   [40] *Edinburgh Review*, 5 (1804), pp. 152–67.
[41] *Edinburgh Review* 14 (July 1809), pp. 375, 380, 379.

inserted four stern paragraphs complaining of the absence of religion in Edgeworth's work. The duel of the two journals over Edgeworth brought into the fray two sectarian journals that did not usually review novels, the Anglican *Christian Observer* and Evangelical *Eclectic Review*. Both now addressed Jeffrey's review as well as Edgeworth's writing. The *Eclectic* protested 'it is a grand point of incompetency if she is totally ignorant what the human race exists for'.[42] The *Christian Observer* remarked that Edgeworth was the 'protégée' of a periodical of bad moral and religious principles, and that its 'high tone of panegyric will do her essential injury . . . the applauding critic and the applauded lady should be reduced to their proper levels.'[43] Both returned for the rest of the series, including *The Absentee*, in 1812. A new volume of Chambers' *Cyclopaedia* contained the long entry on 'Intellectual Education', which was almost entirely focused on Edgeworth's important contribution to the field. But – an ominous sign – it too raised the absence of religion.

Education was by now a social issue, often a daily occupation, for large numbers of middle-class women particularly. Opinion on schooling was already polarised in England along sectarian lines by 1810–11, between adherents of the Anglican Bell and the Quaker Lancaster systems; in Ireland the schism was the older one, between Catholic and Protestant. The Irish Board of Education chose RLE for the commission they set up in 1806 under the chairmanship of the Anglican primate, William Stewart, to make recommendations for a national school system. RLE's views as well as his energy can have been no secret locally or in London.[44] In the event RLE wrote the commissioners' fifth report and had letters appended to the third and the fourteenth (final) report (October 1812). By this time RLE's relations with the primate were good, and the report came out temperately liberal, in favour of two independent school systems, one Catholic and one Protestant, each advised on their religious syllabus and teaching by clergy of their own persuasion. If this had been implemented, rather than shelved till 1831, the new system would have superseded the Protestant Charter Schools, which were set up with the aim of converting Catholics, and therefore an object of Catholic suspicion. When at last in 1816 RLE set up his own boys' school at Edgeworthstown under his eldest son Lovell, the school ran for seventeen years, half fee-paying and half free, half Protestant and half Catholic; religious instruction was given to the boys on Saturdays by the clergyman of the family's persuasion.

---

[42] *Eclectic Review*, 6 (October 1810), p. 880.
[43] *Christian Observer*, 8 (December 1809), p. 781.
[44] Some, including perhaps Croker, must have known of or suspected the Edgeworths' authorship of a review of John Carr's *Stranger in Ireland*, *Edinburgh Review*, 10 (April 1807), pp. 40–60, which supported Catholic emancipation and separate schools.

By this time it was plain RLE had not long to live. To please him, Maria Edgeworth embarked on a work he could share in, which she also turned into his memorial. This was the three-volume set, *Harrington* and *Ormond* (1817), each tale named after its protagonist, both titles politically suggestive because, like so much of Edgeworth's fiction, they revisit the seventeenth century. *Harrington* recalls James Harrington, author of *Oceana* (1656), the leading utopian republican treatise of Commonwealth England; though primarily concerned with anti-Semitism, it analyses intolerance and persecution, their psychological roots and their long English history. *Ormond* suggests James Butler, first Duke of Ormond(e) (1610–88), the Stuarts' ablest servant in Ireland; alternatively his grandson the second Duke, who also served four Stuarts from Charles II to Anne, but after the accession of George I fled to France, to join the Stuart court in exile for the rest of his life. Like *Irish Bulls* and the other Irish tales, *Ormond*, largely by invoking historical names, brings to mind older narratives, the internecine religious wars not only of Ireland but of France, by recalling writings and lives of the long seventeenth century, from Spenser to Fénelon. The two titles, on the face of it implying sectarian balance, mask two stories directed in early nineteenth-century conditions at civic harmony and equal treatment.

Because this is above all her tribute to her father, RLE appears like a shapeshifter in many guises throughout *Ormond*: as the hero himself, a young man whose second love was the right one, and who came back from a visit to the France of Rousseau and the encyclopaedists to claim her;[45] as 'King' Corny, paternalistic landlord, educator, and tireless amateur mechanic on a remote County Longford estate;[46] and as Herbert Annaly, a modern improving landlord in the RLE style.[47] In the usual symbolic resolution, Ormond chooses to buy Corny's estate and to live among his Gaelic Catholic tenants; he marries Florence Annaly, whose family name is that of the Edgeworths' county, Longford, in Gaelic and Catholic times, before it was renamed in 1570.

The ending has to be decoded by the Annalys' given names. Florence must be named after the leading medieval Italian republic. By 1817 Florence was likely to evoke Sismondi's seven-volume historical study of republicanism (completed 1817), which was also a liberal protest against modern French imperialism and militarism. But the tale *Ormond* is centrally concerned with Irish landlordism in history;

45 RLE returned from France on hearing of the death of his first wife (Maria's mother), and after seeing his small children went straight to Honora Sneyd to propose.
46 One of the people of the estate, Moriarty, has thrown a floral tribute to Corny in the bog, an allusion to RLE, who mapped and reclaimed bogland.
47 Annaly seeks to educate both adults and children on his estate.

and if the sister's name, Florence, is linked with her brother's name, Herbert, different trains of thought are established. Edgeworth surely intends an allusion to the leading Elizabethan 'undertaker' or plantation-manager, Sir William Herbert (d. 1591), who while resident in Munster on his estate at Castleisland, 1587–9, publicly quarrelled with another Anglo-Irish landowner, as the fictional Herbert does, over the neighbour's involvement in smuggling. Sir William Herbert's learned interests make him a resonant figure within Edgeworth's collage: a friend of the avant-garde John Dee, an admirer of Sidney's Arcadian writing, the member of a circle in his native Monmouthshire which was evidently interested in sixteenth-century Florentine neo-platonism. At least Herbert married the daughter of a local landowner called Griffiths, who had named his child Florence. Herbert made his and Florence's only daughter Mary his heir, provided she married a Herbert – which would keep her within his own intellectual and literary Welsh circles.

Sir William Herbert had one characteristic, however – zealous Protestantism – which does not fit the tolerant Herbert Annaly. As so often Edgeworth allows one name to suggest two people, the second being William Herbert's son-in-law, Edward (1583–1648), best-known as Lord Herbert of Cherbury, though he was also Lord Castleisland in the Irish peerage. An ambassador, soldier, courtier, adventurer, poet and Renaissance man, Edward Herbert's most remarkable work is his Latin treatise *De Veritate* (Paris, 1624, first translated into French 1639), an original and perceptive examination of our modes of establishing truth, which leads into a sceptical discussion of revealed religion. In the context of the fearsome religious wars of his day, and of his friendships when in Paris with Grotius and Gassendi, Herbert emerges a critic of Protestant sectarianism, rather than of religion as a whole – for he too engages with neo-platonism, and writes eloquently on the immortality of the soul. His observation that all major religions maintain the same five major precepts, recognised by the intuitive 'common sense' of all peoples in all ages, makes him a pioneer of toleration and a forerunner both of Thomas Reid and Kant. Before this he came under attack, usually from Protestants: the Nonconformist divine Richard Baxter in 1674 and more memorably the Aberdonian divine John Leland, who dubbed him in 1754 'the father of English deism'. Well into the next century Herbert figured in negative reviews of modern scepticism. His name was in any case more current then than now because Horace Walpole in 1764 made a current classic of his lively if eccentric memoirs, which he had probably intended for private perusal by his family. In short, to hint even cautiously at Edward Herbert as the hero's main mentor and future inspiration was undoubtedly to throw down a gauntlet to partisan reviewers.

By 1820 the *Quarterly Review* was three years into an effective campaign against liberals, materialists, and 'infidels', with Byron and Shelley as prominent targets. John Wilson Croker, a Protestant and the ablest Irish reviewer in London, had already written one of the warmest and best-informed reviews of *The Absentee.*[48] He now urged John Murray to send him RLE's *Memoirs*, saying that he had a personal object. Croker performed up to his best standard of deadliness, by retelling RLE's life story logically, knowledgeably, and in such a way that he ridiculed and denigrated RLE the man. It was a prelude to Croker's seven-page finale, an accurate listing of a dozen brief references in Maria Edgeworth's second volume of her father's religious position, followed by a harsh summing-up. Croker sets out to destroy the Edgeworths' credibility as educationalists, by demonstrating not merely that RLE was a deist, but that both father and daughter repeatedly equivocated in the hope of making the public believe they were not. Maria Edgeworth had been caught in a trap she anticipated when her father made her promise to complete his *Memoirs*. She was incapable of denying his opinions, still more of misquoting him, especially after *Ormond*. In the *Memoirs* she had been able to prove nothing more than RLE's goodwill to religion in general, and this gave their enemies all the evidence they needed.

In the following year the *Quarterly* sent Richard Whately, future Archbishop of Dublin, Austen's *Persuasion* and *Northanger Abbey* (1818) to review. Whately, impressed perhaps by the Revd Henry Austen's introductory memoir praising his sister's piety and family values, inserted a passage which disparagingly compared the work of Edgeworth, from which Christianity was omitted. Edgeworth had still two impressive books to come: *Harry and Lucy Concluded* (1825), perhaps her educational masterpiece, and *Helen* (1834), her best novel. Given the lofty standards set for family reading from now till mid-century, it is hard to believe many families were drawn to Austen for her religion. But Edgeworth's reputation slid below Austen's: she was a figure from a past age, highbrow, worldly wise and secular, and there were now no journalistic champions to hand. It was not just that the *Edinburgh Review* had few answers to the *Quarterly* when working this vein; the *Edinburgh* had always been, from the *Quarterly* side, part of the target.

---

[48] *Quarterly Review*, 7 (June 1812), pp. 329–42.

8 Improving Ireland: Richard Whately, theology, and political economy

Norman Vance

I

Despite the work of Boyd Hilton and others, it is possible, even now, to neglect the role of religion in Victorian reform movements. It is also possible to defer too much to Irish exceptionalism, the deeply ingrained sense that, whatever might be said or done about public policy in England, it was always going to be irrelevant and wrong for Ireland. As other essays in this and its companion volume, *History, Religion, and Culture*, demonstrate, Scotland and France play an important role in British intellectual history, but nineteenth-century Ireland should not be forgotten as testing-ground, catalyst, and sometimes source of British political and social thought. Ireland demonstrated some of the worst problems of a pre-industrial economy in the earlier nineteenth century, but parts of Great Britain were still essentially pre-industrial at the same period. Consideration of the career of Richard Whately (1787–1863) makes possible a more nuanced understanding not only of the continuing interdependence of religion and public policy but of the interaction of Great Britain and Ireland under conditions of distress, disorder and possible improvement.

Whately, Englishman, Fellow of Oriel and Archbishop of Dublin, came from a family of improvers. His uncle, Thomas Whately, MP, wrote a celebrated treatise on landscape gardening, *Observations on Modern Gardening* (1770; 5th edition 1793). The younger Whately improved gardens, in which he grew exotic and experimentally grafted plants, improved his Suffolk parish, renovating the school and adding 250 seats to the church, and improved Oxford's ailing St Alban Hall, which he served as Principal (1825–31).[1] He also attempted, less successfully, to

---

[1] For Whately and gardening see E. J. Whately, *Life and Correspondence of Richard Whately, DD*, 2 vols. (1866; new edn 1868), p. 70; for Whately in his parish see Whately to Edward Hawkins, 27 D[ecember] 1822, Oriel College, Oxford, MS 342 and information from the present incumbent of St Mary's, Halesworth, Suffolk, Father Leonard Doolan, to whom I am indebted. Fr Doolan suggests the additional seating in the church may have been supplied by building a gallery which has since been removed. For Whately at St Alban Hall see E. J. Whately, *Life*, p. 38.

improve the Church of Ireland and the mental and moral landscape of the United Kingdom of Great Britain and Ireland. The variousness of his combative reformist campaigns against what he saw as ignorance and stupidity in England and Ireland has not helped his reputation in the twentieth century.[2] It is difficult to see Whately whole and to keep both his English and his Irish career simultaneously under review, though both were controversial and distinguished. Part of the problem is that his life and work constantly transgress conventional boundaries, chronological, geographical, and discursive, in ways that fruitfully signal the insidious capacity of such boundaries to foster anachronism and misunderstanding or at least partial understanding. Whately argumentatively survived Swing Riots in Suffolk, Famine years in Ireland and political defeat in the House of Lords (on admitting Jews to parliament). Tactless and forthright, a liberal in conservative Oxford, a modern Englishman indifferent to Irish antiquities, thanklessly dedicated to the peace of Ireland when there could be no peace, superficially cold among Irish hotheads, perpetually inclined to say the right thing at the wrong time or in the wrong place, he contrived to be simultaneously ahead of and behind his contemporaries. A child of – as well as in – the eighteenth century, a rationalist in a romantic era, he attacked Hume with his own weapons, intelligently praised old Archdeacon Paley and younger Jane Austen (but not, damningly, Maria Edgeworth) as Christian moralists, and lived long enough to take an intelligent interest in Darwin, in advance of most of his clerical colleagues.[3]

Large and unconventional, even uncouth (the contemporary wit Sydney Smith said he looked like a Yorkshire ostler), given to spinning round dangerously on one leg of his chair while in animated conversation,[4] he was variously famous or notorious in his day as a white-coated Oxford eccentric ('the White Bear'), a teacher, a logician, a political econ-

[2] W. O. Chadwick is amusing but unsympathetic in *The Victorian Church*, 3rd edn, 2 vols. (London, 1971), I, pp. 42–3, 53–4, 133, 169, etc. Desmond Bowen's treatment is rather severe in *The Protestant Crusade in Ireland* (Dublin, 1978), pp. 109–10, 290–7, etc. There is only one modern biography, D. H. Akenson's *A Protestant in Purgatory* (Hamden, Conn., 1981). I am grateful to Professor Akenson for making a copy of this book available to me.
[3] For Paley see *Paley's Moral Philosophy: with Annotations by R[ichard] W[hately]* (1859); for Jane Austen and Maria Edgeworth see [R. Whately] 'Modern Novels' [mainly *Northanger Abbey* and *Persuasion*], *Quarterly Review*, 24 (January 1821), pp. 352–76; for Darwin see R. Whately, 'On the Origin of Civilization' (1854) in *Lectures Delivered before the YMCA in Exeter Hall* (1855), p. 12, alluding to Darwin's account of his discoveries aboard the *Beagle*, and Whately to Edward Hawkins, 13 April 1860, Oriel College, Oxford, MS 334 alluding to *The Origin of Species*.
[4] For Sydney Smith's comment and evidence of unprepossessing manners see the comments (dated July 1833) of Sir Denis Le Marchant, secretary to Lord Brougham, in *Three Early Nineteenth Century Diaries*, ed. A. Aspinall (London, 1952), p. 363. For Whately's way with chairs see W. J. Fitzpatrick, *Memoirs of Richard Whately*, 2 vols. (1864) I, p. 98.

omist, a liberal churchman, a penal reformer, an educational reformer, and – in his spare time – a gardener. But he seldom merits more than a footnote or a sentence, not necessarily complimentary, in standard general histories of nineteenth-century England and Ireland. More specialist historians take some interest in him, particularly historians of education and economics.[5] But Whately's educational and economic thought, like everything he was involved with, is intimately bound up with his theology and his way of discharging his clerical office in both England and Ireland. That interconnectedness in a still United Kingdom, and the role of academic clergy in shaping public policy often enacted or promoted by their friends and pupils, are still too easily missed by secular or narrowly national historians.[6] But much is to be learned from the Oxford Professor turned Irish Archbishop, friend (and critic, complaining of 'simpleton Whigs') of Whig administrations and of Edwin Chadwick the sanitary reformer, successor to his former pupil Nassau Senior – an architect of the 1834 Poor Law – as Drummond Professor of Political Economy at Oxford.[7]

Equally unimpressed by evangelical fervour and Tractarian ecclesiology, Whately was a moralist and a scripture teacher rather than an innovative theologian. He saw himself as an enemy of dogma and party spirit, though his sustained hostility to the emergent Tractarian or, as he insisted on calling them, 'Tractite' party in Oxford had the effect of making him at least negatively partisan. In politics he again tried to eschew party, again not entirely successfully: he was promoted by the Whigs and so associated with them, but his politician uncle would have counted as a Tory and he

---

5 For Whately and education see Fergal McGrath, SJ, *Newman's University, Idea and Reality* (London, 1951), pp. 36–9, D. H. Akenson, *The Irish Education Experiment* (London, 1970) and J. M. Goldstrom, 'Richard Whately and Political Economy in School Books, 1833–80', *Irish Historical Studies*, 15 (1966–7), pp. 131–46; for Whately and economics see Salim Rashid, 'Richard Whately and Christian Political Economy at Oxford and Dublin', *Journal of the History of Ideas*, 38 (1977), pp. 147–55, Peter Mandler, 'Tories and Paupers: Christian Political Economy and the Making of the New Poor Law', *Historical Journal*, 33 (1990), pp. 81–103 and T. Boylan and T. P. Foley, *Political Economy and Colonial Ireland: the Propagation and Ideological Function of Economic Discourse in the Nineteenth Century* (London, 1992), *passim*, all in a sense following the pioneering work of R. D. C. Black in *Economic Thought and the Irish Question 1817–1870* (London, 1960). I am grateful to Professor Black for his generous help with the present essay.
6 But see Richard Brent, 'God's Providence: Liberal Political Economy as Natural Theology at Oxford 1825–62', in M. Bentley, ed., *Public and Private Doctrine* (Cambridge, 1993), pp. 85–107, A. M. C. Waterman, *Revolution, Economics and Religion: Christian Political Economy 1798–1833* (Cambridge, 1991) and Boyd Hilton, *The Age of Atonement: The Influence of Evangelicalism on Social and Economic Thought, 1785–1865* (Oxford, 1988).
7 Whately to [Revd H. H.] Dickinson, 13 April 1837, among uncatalogued Whately Papers in the Representative Church Body Library, Dublin (hereafter RCB MSS). For Whately and Edwin Chadwick see S. E. Finer, *The Life and Times of Sir Edwin Chadwick* (London, 1952), pp. 29, 36.

saw himself as neither Whig nor Tory,[8] prefacing his interventions in public debates with disclaimers of particular political allegiance.

He felt able to do this because his enduring interest in political economy was as much clerical and pastoral as political. As a Suffolk clergyman he soon found he needed to understand the economics of life on the land, 'how corn & cattle sell, & how tithes ought to stand', as he reported rather grumpily to his friends back in Oxford.[9] He had already enjoyed intellectual comradeship with other clerical economists such as his close friend Edward Copleston, another Fellow of Oriel, later Bishop of Llandaff, author of controversial pamphlets on the currency and unemployment. Another intellectual precursor, acknowledged in his Oxford lectures on political economy, was John Bird Sumner, a Poor Law Commissioner with Nassau Senior in 1834, later Archbishop of Canterbury. Sumner had written *A Treatise on the Records of the Creation, and on the Moral Attributes of the Creator* (1814) which moved from eighteenth-century theological concerns with 'theodicy', or justifying the ways of God to man, and Natural Theology, in the direction of political economy, approached through consideration of the moral economy of the created world and the wisdom and goodness of its creator. The specific problem in theodicy of reconciling the unruly passions of humanity with human welfare in a divinely ordered world had already been addressed by Archdeacon Paley, whose work Whately admired. It has been shown that Paley's optimistic conclusion that, subject to the restraints of reason and self-government, human passions can conduce to maximising human happiness, had a major influence on the political economy of Malthus and the idea of 'moral restraint' as a check on population, fundamental to the thinking behind Poor Law reform in the 1830s with which Whately was very much in sympathy.[10]

But where Sumner became increasingly identified with the Evangelical party in the Church of England Whately tried to steer clear of party considerations. He urged 'Christian Conduct towards Opponents' in an era of ferocious ecclesiastical controversy within and between churches and was quite prepared to admit in his early Bampton Lectures on *The Use and Abuse of Party Feeling in Matters of Religion* (1822) that endless arguments about the nature of the true church were rather beside the point when the institutional unity of the church ceased to exist the moment the

---

[8] See R. Whately, ed., *Remains of the Late Edward Copleston, DD* (1854), p. 31: where Copleston was a 'decided Tory' Whately says 'I myself, who have never been either [Whig or Tory], nor adopted the creed of any party, have been intimately acquainted with several worthy and patriotic men of every party.'

[9] Whately to Hawkins, 27 D[ecember] 1822, Oriel MS 342.

[10] Waterman, *Revolution, Economics and Religion,* esp. pp. 146–8.

gospel spread beyond the 'precincts of Judaea'. His controversial but attractively modern conviction that Roman Catholics and Protestant dissenters as well as Anglicans should be regarded as securely within the gospel covenant lay at the heart of his ecclesiastical outlook in both England and Ireland and was equally sensible for both places.[11] Even before he went to Ireland he seems to have looked forward to the end of the Anglican church establishment as a liberation. Like his pupil and fellow-economist Nassau Senior, he felt strongly that if the state supported Christianity it should fund Catholic and dissenting clergy as well as Anglicans, particularly in Catholic Ireland where the state-endowed Protestant Church of Ireland was bitterly resented by both Catholics and dissenters.[12] As a theologian Whately was committed to the traditional task of demonstrating the underlying wisdom of God's dispensations, and it was difficult to demonstrate either wisdom or fairness in arrangements sanctified by the state religion which caused so much resentment. Unfortunately Whately's own views were already provoking resentment in conservative circles in England even before Lord Grey (on the recommendation of Lord Brougham) persuaded him with some difficulty to leave Oxford in 1831 for the grimmer ecclesiastical battlefields of Ireland.

Whately's own metaphors were nautical as well as military: he accurately perceived the desperate condition of the established church in Ireland, perpetually 'under a heavy fire', 'a ship which is drifting on the rocks in a storm & cracking at every seam'. He saw his task as urgent for the good of the church in England and Ireland both: 'unless very strong & speedy measures be adopted, the Church here, & subsequently in England . . . I shall probably *survive*'.[13] He was almost right about the Church of Ireland at least: it survived him, but only just, and was disestablished in 1869, just six years after his death.

D. H. Akenson's study of his life and work, *A Protestant in Purgatory* (1981), registers the frustrations and difficulties of more than thirty years in Ireland but perhaps understates the positive achievement and underlying continuities of Whately's career which the present essay seeks to address. He was consistently, if sometimes brutally, strenuous, sensible

---

[11] R. Whately, *The Use and Abuse of Party Feeling in Matters of Religion*, 4th edn (1859), pp. 86, 16n.

[12] For Whately's thinking on church establishments while still in England see the anonymous *Letters on the Church, by an Episcopalian* (1826) usually attributed to him and accepted as his by his daughter and biographer. For Ireland, see Whately to Nassau Senior, January 1835, noting the absurdity of maintaining (through the *regium donum*) but not educating dissenting ministers while educating (at Maynooth) but not maintaining Roman Catholic priests, Lambeth MS 2164 f. 140; Whately to Hawkins, 29 April 1845, defending the controversial Maynooth Grant subsidising the training of the Catholic priesthood in Ireland, Oriel MS 258.

[13] E. J. Whately, *Life*, pp. 62–4; Whately to Hawkins, 11 October [1831], Oriel MS 182.

and far-sighted, but in Ireland, a country reputedly deficient in all these qualities, impoverished, administratively dysfunctional, and riven with prejudice and vested interest, popularity even for a reformer more diplomatic than Whately could not be expected on either side of the grave. Tractarian Oxford and belligerently Protestant Ireland, each certain of the other's error, united only in their (reciprocated) distrust of Whately, insisted on dogma or dogmatisms. But, disconcertingly for some, Whately was both deeply religious and temperamentally agnostic, scrupulously aware of matters of which 'we may safely remain in ignorance or in doubt during our time of trial here on earth', and disposed to advise against being 'wise above what is written'.[14] He put it even more bluntly in a private letter:

> My heterodoxy . . . consists chiefly in waiving a good many subtle questions agitated by various '-ans' & '-ites', & '-ists', & in keeping clear of sundry metaphysical distinctions relative to the mode of existence of the divine & the human mind, which are beyond my comprehension, & which I am disposed to think would have been brought down to the level of it by Scripture, had they been necessary parts of a saving faith.[15]

His predecessor in Dublin, Archbishop Magee, had been closely associated with an abortive 'Second Reformation' aimed at the conversion of Catholic Ireland, but Whately was conspicuously indifferent to such activity, observing of the proselytising Achill Mission in the far west that 'for nonsense & virulence no R. Cath. can exceed some Protestants'. He dissociated himself from the view of the Bishop of Ossory and his clergy that the Universal Church would condemn the doctrines of Rome, pointing out rather dryly that this would hardly be decided before the end of the month, but if it was Protestants would be substantially outvoted on the question.[16] In religious terms he believed in conscience and scripture but not in the flamboyantly aggressive preaching common among evangelical Irish Protestants such as Charles Kingsley's fictional Revd Panurgus O'Blareaway or Revd Tresham Gregg, eccentrically aggressive author of *Protestant Ascendancy Vindicated* (1840) and leader of the Dublin Protestant Operative Association, whom an exasperated Whately deprived of his official appointments and tried to prevent from preaching in his archdiocese in 1842.[17] Though he could be witty and entertaining

---

[14] [R. Whately] *A View of the Scripture Revelations Concerning a Future State Laid before his Parishioners by a Country Pastor,* 2nd edn (1830), p. 50; R. Whately, notes on Archbishop King's *Discourse on Predestination* appended to *The Use and Abuse of Party Feeling,* p. 357.

[15] Extract from (Whately's) letter (n.d.) to 'Revd E. P.', RCB MSS.

[16] E. J. Whately, *Life,* p. 232; Whately to Hawkins, 8 November 1850 and 19 February 1851, Oriel MSS 300, 301.

[17] For Kingsley's caricature of the type see his early novel *Yeast* (serial version 1848; published in book form 1851), chs. 7 and 10; for Gregg, see Bowen, *Protestant Crusade in*

on social occasions, his own preaching was coolly, even chillingly, rational and expository, completely lacking in the rhetorical exuberance and lively venom to which Irish congregations and courtrooms had long been accustomed. In secular terms, which for him were also essentially religious and moral, he believed in toleration, education, and classical political economy, but all of these got him into trouble with Irish Catholics and Protestants alike. If martyrs are persecuted witnesses to unpopular insights he was Ireland's only Malthusian martyr.

Ireland has had more than its share of saints and martyrs, some more plausible than others. Whately is not usually included among them, but William Alexander, Bishop of Derry, pronounced his obituary in these terms. Alexander was sufficient of a realist to accept that at least on the surface it was difficult to see much obvious saintliness, or much evidence of the popular devotion which saints command. But with some effort one could discern at least grudging respect:

> . . . better than his loftiness of station,
>   His power of logic, or his pen of gold,
> The half unwilling homage of a nation
>   Of fierce extremes to one who seem'd so cold.

Somewhere underneath the rugged manner and the sharp wit there were indeed the patient suffering and the unwavering courage of martyrs and saints:

> Rest then, O martyr, pass'd from anguish mortal;
>   Rest then, O saint, sublimely free from doubt;
> Rest then, O patient thinker, o'er the portal,
>   Where there is peace for brave hearts wearied out.[18]

This tribute conforms to the official pieties expected of clergymen, particularly when writing about an ecclesiastical superior, but it shows some insight into the life and times. Whately was indeed a brave heart who had earned his rest. He had suffered more than his share of the slings and arrows of Ireland's 'fierce extremes' and his last years had been darkened not only by illness but by the death in the space of two months of a newly married daughter and his wife.[19] Opponents of his unbending views on

Ireland, 1800–70, pp. 108–13 and J. H. Samuels, *A Report of the Arguments of Counsel, with the Judgement of the [Consistorial] Court in the Case of the Office of . . . the Archbishop of Dublin against Rev. T. D. Gregg* (Dublin, 1848).

[18] William Alexander, 'Death of Archbishop Whately', in *St Augustine's Holiday and other Poems* (1886), pp. 166–7. There was a much more ambiguous tribute in Samuel Ferguson's 'Epitaph on Archbishop Whately' quoted by Boylan and Foley, *Political Economy and Colonial Ireland*, p. 129.

[19] He reported the death of his daughter Blanche after eleven weeks of suffering on 4 March 1860 and the death of his wife on 25 April 1860. Oriel MSS 1122, 1123.

political economy, the Poor Laws and national education in Ireland occasionally felt he would be a wiser man if he doubted more, but his freedom from doubt, perhaps exaggerated for obituary purposes, was obtained at the price of strenuous intellectual effort, because he had from the outset rejected the rival securities of evangelical fundamentalism and Catholic or Anglo-Catholic dogma and tradition and had worked out an accommodation of orthodox political economy to orthodox Christianity at a time when they were often felt to be mutually antagonistic and equally if differently contentious.

II

Early in his career the temptations to doubt represented by Hume's still well-known tenth chapter 'Of Miracles' in the *Enquiry Concerning Human Understanding* (1748, but with a new edition in 1817) had been fairly easily disposed of in *Historic Doubts Relative to Napoleon Buonaparte* (1819). If one took seriously Hume's insistence that wise men proportioned their belief to the evidence, and extended Hume's sceptical argument about the evidence for New Testament miracles to current (or very recently current) affairs, one would come to doubt the sometimes contradictory or improbable, largely hearsay evidence for the life and very existence of Napoleon. The wickedly appropriate epigraph, from Burke, seemingly testifies to an old-fashioned Enlightenment confidence in reason in all parts of life: 'Is not the same reason available in theology and in politics? . . . Will you follow truth but to a certain point?'

In some ways this confidence, or the appearance of it, remained with Whately throughout his career as churchman and public man, but the relationship to eighteenth-century rationalism and free enquiry is more oblique and complicated than at first appears. The quotation comes from Burke's ironic impersonation of Bolingbroke, his *Vindication of Natural Society, by a Late Noble Writer* (1756). Burke had treated Bolingbroke as Whately treated Hume, turning his own rationalism against him in a *reductio ad absurdum* by defending nature against artifice at all costs, effectively demonstrating that if revealed (as opposed to natural) religion and its associated 'artificial' or man-made institution the church seem to be vulnerable to rationalist attack, as Bolingbroke the Deist had claimed, then the artificial institution of civil or political society is equally vulnerable. The connection between the two was clearly spelt out in Burke's text: 'Civil Government borrows a Strength from ecclesiastical; and artificial Laws receive a Sanction from artificial Revelations. The Ideas of Religion and Government are closely connected . . .'[20] Burke's implicit moral is that it is foolish and reductive to insist on the criterion of the natural for necessarily artificial social and religious institutions, and Bolingbroke and other writers such as Rousseau in his *Discours sur . . . l'inégalité* (1755) stand reproved for the attempt. Like Sumner before him, Whately as moralist and theorist of civil society and political economy had no more patience than Burke with Rousseau's idea of an originally benign State of Nature. He dismissed the notion as only found in 'poems and romances, and in the imagination of their readers'.[21]

But Burke's *Vindication* is at bottom profoundly conservative, romantically privileging custom and tradition, however absurd or inequitable in practice, in the manner of the subsequent *Reflections on the Revolution in France*. Is this what Whately the reformer really wanted? One wants to say 'obviously not', but a question remains. His remorseless logic and massive 'common sense, which often rose to genius', according to his successor in Dublin, Archbishop Trench,[22] present him in an attractively quasi-modern light, but they were more circumscribed than he might have cared to admit by the force of circumstances and the limitations and preoccupations of his age, class, and cloth. The Burkean undertow must not be disregarded. In 1819, the year of Peterloo as well as of *Historic Doubts*, as in 1830 in rural Suffolk and the 1840s in Ireland, a distressed and frightened country, threatened with agrarian violence and insurrection, wanted to be reassured that Hume was wrong, that the Burkean restraints imposed by traditional religion and, by extension, the traditional, hierarchical social order could still be relied on in turbulent times. As a clergyman of the Church of England as by law established Whately was part of that order, however critical of it he may have been from within. He took some of his political economy from Malthus, also a clergyman, and Malthus had incorporated the concept of moral restraint as a check on population into the second (1803) edition of his *Essay on the Principle of Population*, arguably as a kind of belated anti-Jacobin or counter-revolutionary gesture, though this view has recently been vigorously challenged.[23] In *Historic*

---

[20] Edmund Burke, *A Vindication of Natural Society*, in *Burke: Pre-Revolutionary Writings*, ed. Ian Harris (Cambridge, 1993), p. 16.

[21] J. B. Sumner, *A Treatise on the Records of the Creation and the Moral Attributes of the Creator*, 2 vols. (1816), II, ch. 3, p. 42 (the whole chapter, arguing that inequality of ranks and fortunes is the situation best suited to the improvement of human faculties, is in effect a refutation of Rousseau's *Sur l'inégalité*); R. Whately, 'On the Origin of Civilization' in *Lectures Delivered before the YMCA*, p. 5.

[22] R. C. Trench, *Letters and Memorials*, 2 vols. (1888), II, p. 27.

[23] So Waterman, *Revolution, Economics and Religion*, p. 145, but see Donald Winch, 'The Reappraisal of Malthus: A Comment', *History of Political Economy*, 30 (1998), pp. 353–63, esp. p. 361.

Doubts Whately offered his first – and liveliest – defence of the orthodoxy and mystery on which his church was founded against a still flourishing tradition of frequently politicised radical scepticism which went back even before Hume to John Toland's *Christianity not Mysterious* (1696). After what had happened in France since 1789, Toland, Bolingbroke, and Rousseau, Burke's *bêtes noires,* seemed all the more dangerous. Anxiety about possible revolution in England was the order – or disorder – of the day, and Whately was not immune. The essentially conservative orthodoxy and the sense of interdependence of church and state which prompted the attack on Hume were subsequently reinforced by his early experience of parish ministry. This in turn shaped his whole outlook and his attitude towards poverty and preserving the peace of Ireland, before, during and after the Famine, in ways that have been insufficiently recognised.

Whately was Rector of Halesworth in Suffolk between 1822 and 1831, dividing his time rather awkwardly between Halesworth (where the damp affected his wife's health) and Oxford for much of this period. But this relatively limited experience of parish work was in an area where farmworkers had been particularly adversely affected by the advent of threshing machines and the new commercial agriculture, and sporadic violence had resulted. Unemployment was the main problem: the workhouses were frequently overcrowded and disease-ridden. Rioters had partly destroyed the local workhouse, known as 'Bulcamp Hell', even before it was finished in 1765. Unemployed labourers had caused disturbances in the locality in 1816 and again in 1822 and there was an outbreak of machine-breaking and tithe and wages riots in 1830 associated with the 'Swing Riots' elsewhere in the country. Much of the hostility had been directed against parsons whose tithe or tax on agriculture was seen as making a bad matter worse and labourers and farmers had joined together to agitate for a reduction in the tithe.[24]

All of this confirmed Whately's tendency to insist on law and order even when sympathetic to the causes of unrest. But it also confirmed him in his hostility to tithes: 'had I *felt* on the subject as I do now, I sh[oul]d certainly never have taken orders'.[25] He was to find tithes even more a bone of contention in Catholic Ireland where non-payment was widespread. Almost his first act as Archbishop of Dublin, in January 1832, was to give evidence on the matter to a Select Committee of the House of

[24] For agrarian disturbances in the vicinity of Halesworth, see Revd J. B. Clare, *Wenhaston and Bulcamp, Suffolk* (London, 1906), pp. 49, 53, A. J. Peacock, *Bread or Blood: A Study of the Agrarian Riots in East Anglia in 1816* (London, 1965), pp. 78, 81, and E. J. Hobsbawm and George Rudé, *Captain Swing* (London, 1969), pp. 83f, 152–61.
[25] Whately to Hawkins, 27 D[ecember] 1822, Oriel MS 342.

Lords. As he observed afterwards, tithe commutation was essential to 'pacify Ire[lan]d, & preserve the Church'.[26] Rural England as well as rural Ireland needed to be pacified. In 1830 he warned his parishioners that rick-burning and agrarian agitation in hard times were likely to destabilise 'the whole state of society': in France, he insisted, such chaos had eventually led on to the absolute tyranny of Napoleon. Education was important, he insisted, if only as a means of what would now be called social control. People need to be educated into resisting rabblerousers, a view which had some currency in Ireland as well.

The sort of persons who are generally seduced into crime by wicked and design-ing leaders, are usually the most ignorant and uneducated. And accordingly, I find that the riots had their beginning in Kent and Sussex; where the labouring classes are more uninstructed than in any part of England I have ever been in.[27]

The origins of his enduring commitment to popular education, most apparent in his partly frustrated campaigns for a non-sectarian national education system in Ireland, can be seen in his Suffolk experiences.

Rural disorder and parish life in Suffolk also stimulated his increasingly professional involvement with the new science of political economy, often seen at the time as a radical and secular preserve. In reviewing the pub-lished lectures on political economy of his friend and former pupil Nassau Senior he registered his anxiety lest 'the cultivation of this branch of knowledge [might] be left by the advocates of religion, and of social order, in the hands of those who are hostile to both'.[28]

Religion and social order went together practically as well as ideologi-cally. As Archbishop of Dublin he was required to function, in the absence of the Lord Lieutenant, as one of Her Majesty's Lord Justices, and on at least one occasion, in November 1839, the etiquette associated with this position prevented him from attending a public meeting in Dublin to give direct expression to his principled objection to govern-ment policy on transportation and penal colonies. He did, however, send his chaplain, Revd H. H. Dickinson, to speak for him.

His leading position (subordinate only to the Archbishop of Armagh who was primate of all Ireland) within the deeply unpopular Protestant

[26] *Evidence of His Grace the Archbishop of Dublin as taken before the Select Committee of the House of Lords appointed to inquire into the Collection and Payment of Tithes in Ireland* (1832); Whately to Edward Copleston, 16 October 1836, Lambeth Palace MS 3163 f. 11v.
[27] [R. Whately], *A Letter to his Parishioners on the Disturbances which Have Lately Occurred. By a Country Pastor* (1830), pp. 10, 11. Compare the judgement of Boylan and Foley, *Political Economy and Colonial Ireland*, p. 128, that 'a main function of the national schools was to combat the effects of the rhetoric of agitators on the public'.
[28] [R. Whately] 'Oxford Lectures on Political Economy', *Edinburgh Review*, 48 (September 1828), pp. 170–1.

state church in largely Catholic Ireland to some extent obliged him to defend as well as improve the *status quo*. While temperamentally he was attracted by the wit and iconoclasm of open-ended rational discourse in the eighteenth-century manner, he was also constrained by the need to rescue his foundering church. He believed in knowledge, but not entirely for its own sake. The imparting of knowledge had to be strategic. It should not be withheld – particularly if the withholding might be noticed. As he observed in a letter,

> I have always found that men's minds are in most danger of being dangerously & permanently unsettled when they have been kept in ignorance of something wh[ich] they may hereafter discover, & wh[ich] they may think their teachers sh[oul]d have told them.[29]

Horace Walpole, who had admired and annotated Thomas Whately's *Observations on Modern Gardening* (the annotations were included in the 1801 edition) had provided a hint and a title for Whately's *Historic Doubts* with his own *Historic Doubts on the Life and Reign of King Richard III* (1768), but Walpole, an eccentric free spirit, not a churchman, was free to indulge himself and to proceed when it suited him in a spirit of disinterested historical enquiry.

In a sense Whately never had that freedom, though he may not have fully realised it. Despite their tone of dispassionate rational exposition, none of his numerous publications can be regarded as completely disinterested scholarship, historical or otherwise. Part of the trouble was that at bottom he did not really believe in history nor in fundamental change, nor in the historically contingent nature of his own position. He was sympathetic enough to the demoralising effect of ill government on the Irish people but still tended to feel that structural problems, whether of doctrinal difference or dysfunctional social arrangements, in Ireland or in England, could be explained in terms of ignorance and error rather than historical development. The imperfections of an unchanging human nature were the real problem. His treatise on *The Errors of Romanism traced to their Origin in Human Nature* (1830) carried as an epigraph the observation of Ecclesiastes (1:9) that 'there is no new thing under the sun'.

Unlike his former protégé John Henry Newman, but like many of his contemporaries, he was also largely unaware of, or chose to disregard, the precise historical circumstances and developments which had led to the increasingly unstable Anglican compromise and its insecure and problematic relationship with the volatile and changing social order of nineteenth-century rural England and Ireland. The logic of the Act of

---

[29] Whately to Hawkins, 16 March 1847, Oriel MS 281.

Union with Ireland was that Ireland should be, or become, essentially the same as England, amenable to the same legislative initiatives. Whately's official position as Archbishop more or less required him to believe this, and Whately the professional logician could turn this to advantage at times. In 1850 the formal restoration of the Roman Catholic hierarchy in Britain, the so-called 'Papal Aggression', unleashed a wave of populist anti-Catholicism which Whately, unlike many of his own clergy, found unpleasant. He was obliged to make some kind of formal response to this and to the Ecclesiastical Titles Bill, proposed in response to this popular sentiment, which rather spitefully prevented Catholic bishops from assuming titles already held by Anglican bishops in England. Whately felt the measure would only generate a sense of grievance, 'like firing at a mob with blank cartridge, which enrages without repelling'. Deadpan, he insisted that failure to extend the Bill to Ireland would constitute a viola-tion of the terms of the Act of Union. He knew perfectly well that this would be politically quite unacceptable and hoped it might make the government think twice about what it was doing in England.[30] At least from the perspective of the Act of Union, Ireland's problems could be optimistically seen as removable or improvable difference from normative or ideal Englishness. Whately felt that problems such as (by English stan-dards) overpopulated rural districts could be solved through assisted emi-gration, but nationalist Ireland has never forgiven him for making Irish children sing 'The stately homes of England', for expressing his educa-tional ideal as making of every pupil 'a happy English child', and for keeping patriotic Irish literature and history out of the curriculum.[31]

For Whately, Plato and Aristotle, Bacon and Shakespeare, Jane Austen and Paley (none of them Irish but that was purely incidental) were all witness to universal truths, applicable in all times and places. He saw himself as a scientist, effectively, and refused, at least officially, to see any-thing really distinctive about his own time and place which might unsci-entifically colour his outlook. This applied to his ethics and his biblical exegesis but most of all to his political economy, which gave rise to the criticism that he was insensitive to the special conditions of Ireland and to the (debatable) need for a special Irish political economy. He would have insisted that the general principles of political economy were robust enough to be unaffected by local circumstances, however extreme. As Nien-he Hsieh has pointed out, there was a conspicuous absence of examination questions concerning the Famine on the papers set for the

---

[30] *Life*, II, pp. 232–3; Whately to Samuel Wilberforce, 1 February 1851, Bodleian MS Wilberforce c. 10 f. 103.
[31] W. J. Fitzpatrick, *Memoirs*, II, pp. 176–7; F. S. L. Lyons, *Ireland since the Famine* (Glasgow, 1973), p. 89.

Whately Chair of Political Economy which he founded, giving support to the view that for better or for worse the Famine did not significantly alter the austerely scientific outlook of political economy as he understood it.[32] Whately's unacknowledged, more or less unconscious identification of the universe with England, and the church universal with something rather like the Church of England arises in part from the anglocentric confidence or bravado of a vanished age. Even his once-famous textbooks on logic and rhetoric, ostensibly timeless and value-free, incorporate, and are enlivened by, liberal Anglican special pleading, usually in more or less just causes, in the examples and illustrations. He illustrates the fallacy of irrelevant conclusion, or knowing all the answers but not the questions, which he claims is common among the uneducated, by referring to continuing debates about religious toleration. The point at issue, he claims, is not which religion is better or best but whether one man has a right to compel another to profess his religion, or whether those who profess the true faith (unblushingly presumed to be Anglican Christianity) have any right to monopolise secular power and civil privileges. It was in precisely those terms that he intervened in a House of Lords debate in 1833 and unsuccessfully urged upon perhaps under-educated peers that Jews should be admitted to parliament (this did not finally happen until 1858).[33] The logical fallacy of *petitio principii* or begging the question, already assuming, though deviously or muddle-headedly not stating distinctly, the truth of the point ostensibly in question, is described in a footnote as characteristic of the infidel Gibbon: 'His way of writing reminds one of those persons who never dare look you full in the face.' The eighteenth-century satirist Bernard Mandeville had provocatively argued against educating the labouring classes on the grounds that 'if a horse knew as much as a man, I would not be his rider'. This is given as an example of false analogy, at least as applied to men possessing civil rights as opposed to slaves: Whately's lifelong commitment to the cause of popular education, both in his Suffolk parish and in Ireland, appears here as a matter of logic and plain common sense and justice rather than of controversy as it was at the time.[34]

---

[32] For the appropriateness of the political economy of Whately and others to the Irish situation see Thomas A. Boyland and Timothy P. Foley, '"A Nation Perishing of Political Economy"?', in Chris Morash and Richard Hayes, eds., *Fearful Realities: New Perspectives on the Famine* (Dublin, 1996), pp. 138–50. For the Whately professorship examinations see Nien-he Hsieh in 'The Conspicuous Absence of Examination Questions Concerning the Great Irish Famine: Political Economy as Science and Ideology', *European Journal of the History of Economic Thought*, 6 (1999). I am grateful to Dr Hsieh and Professor R. D. C. Black for the opportunity to read this paper before publication.

[33] R. Whately, *Elements of Logic* (1826; 7th edn, 1840), pp. 256–7; see Whately on 'Emancipation of the Jews', Lords Debates, 1 August 1833, Hansard 3rd ser. 20, cols. 226–35.

[34] R. Whately, *Elements of Logic*, p. 227; *Elements of Rhetoric* (1828; 7th edn, 1846), p. 95.

Proper teaching was Whately's solution to all difficulties. He was very anxious to establish a special Ordination College in Dublin to ensure his clergy were properly instructed, though this ran him into bitter and prolonged controversy with Trinity College, Dublin.[35] The textbooks on logic and rhetoric, like his little books of *Easy Lessons* on political economy and other subjects for Irish children, like his Oxford college teaching and lectures on political economy, like his village sermons and lectures in the parish, like his charges to his clergy in Ireland and his careful examination of ordinands and professorial candidates in economics,[36] were all part of a sustained programme of benignly tendentious education and enlightenment. The programme was unsympathetic to innovations such as trade unions and broadly supportive of the existing model of law and order and habits of industry and prudence.

All of this rested on an anti- (or pre-)Tractarian assumption that the Anglican clergyman's principal role was that of authoritative teacher rather than mass-priest. Whately always claimed Christianity was unique among religions in not having a priesthood. Instead, it had ministers. The office of minister, instituted by Christ, was to instruct the people, 'to teach and lead them to serve Him themselves'.[37] By extension, the role of bishop or archbishop should be to teach and support clerical teachers, and Whately felt that was where his talents lay. Oriel had been the leading Oxford college in Whately's day partly because it had provided opportunities to develop or 'bring on' brilliant young Fellows, elected by competitive examination. Whately compared his position to that of his friend Edward Hawkins, Provost of Oriel, seeing himself charged with the parallel responsibility of catching his clergy young and 'bringing them on' as teachers.[38] This low view of the priesthood, widely advocated throughout his writings, is 'scientifically' vindicated in the *Logic* in passing, in a sly little discussion of verbal versus real questions illustrated by the New Testament Greek terms *hiereus* and *presbyteros*. Both tend to be translated 'priest' (which etymologically comes from *presbyteros*, literally 'elder'), although according to Whately only the former, not used in the New Testament except of Christ Himself, carried Old Testament associations of sacrificial as opposed to ministerial function.[39]

---

[35] Details of Whately's struggles to establish an Ordination College and of the hostility to it can be found in the often undated correspondence of the Whately Papers, *c.* 1834–*c.* 1840, among the RCB MSS.

[36] It is clear that he took the examination of professorial candidates, as of ordinands, very seriously (Whately to Hawkins, 1 June 1846, Oriel MS 274).

[37] R. Whately, *Essays on Some of the Peculiarities of the Christian Religion* (1825; 3rd edn, 1831), p. 368.

[38] Whately to Hawkins, 21 November 1832, 15 April 1833, Oriel MSS 196, 193.

[39] *Logic*, p. 323f.

Ministers of the established church traditionally sustained local schools, as Whately had done in Suffolk, as well as teaching from the pulpit. Schools were desperately needed in Ireland, as indeed they were in England, and thanks largely to Whately Ireland became the testing-ground for a national education system before one was developed in England. Speaking of the country as he found it in 1832, Whately groaned that 'The mass of ignorance, conceit, rashness, prejudice, & corruption that I have to encounter, no words can describe.' Endemic ignorance and prejudice could yield only to mass education. There was already some educational provision, notably the Kildare Street Schools established in 1811, but it was often associated with Protestant societies committed to teaching the Bible and converting Catholic Ireland, so the Catholic hierarchy was extremely hostile. To improve matters Whately became a Commissioner for Education and played a significant role in developing and writing textbooks for a new, basically secular, agreed national curriculum which included a little non-sectarian scripture. By 1840 he thought this programme of national education, bitterly attacked, mainly by Protestants and to a lesser extent by Catholics, for being either insufficiently or inappropriately religious, was beginning to pay off: 'We expect about 500 additional schools under the Board in the course of the year; having already nearly 2,000. The country is becoming in several places civilised & pacified under their influence to a degree that no one c[oul]d have anticipated.'[40] For Whately personally it was all to end in tears in 1853: after twenty years of defending the national system against the Protestant critics who condemned it as 'this bantling of Romanism', Whately discovered that some of the District Model Schools were quietly dropping the carefully prepared non-sectarian textbooks such as *Scripture Lessons* which Whately himself had compiled, finally severing the link between education and religion which was so important to him. He felt he had to resign as Commissioner, though the work of national education continued.[41]

This strenuous educational endeavour firmly allied Whately with the forces of 'modernisation' in Ireland, a process sponsored by progressive nationalist figures such as Thomas Davis who thanked God in 1845 that there were now four hundred thousand Irish children in the National Schools with which Whately was so closely associated.[42] Modernisation

[40] Akenson, *The Irish Education Experiment,* p. 388; Whately to Hawkins, 21 November 1832; Whately to Hawkins, 4 March 1840, Oriel MSS 196, 241.
[41] See, for example, the Education (Ireland) Debate in the House of Lords, 19 March 1833, in which Whately participated (Hansard 3rd ser. 16, cols. 778–826, esp. col. 786) and R. Whately, *Address to the Clergy of the Dioceses of Dublin and Glandalagh and Kildare on the Recent Changes in the System of Irish National Education* (1853).
[42] Thomas Davis, 'Habits and Character of the Irish Peasantry', *Nation,* 12 July 1845,

was, however, rather ambivalently regarded by Irish writers and sentimental Catholic nationalism because of its association with English and
Protestant initiatives and its tendency to reform out of existence Irish folk
ways and the oral traditions embedded in the apparently obsolescent Irish
language, even though Whately's *Easy Lessons on Money Matters* was
made available in an Irish-language edition. The Tyrone novelist William
Carleton, a slightly precarious convert to Protestantism, vividly recalled
pre-modern Catholic Ireland in his *Traits and Stories of the Irish Peasantry*
(1832) but he actually reprinted some of Whately's practical teaching for
farmers and embodied his strenuous gospel of ceaseless industry and economic prudence in his cautionary tale *Parra Sastha, or the History of Paddy
Go-Easy and His Wife Nancy* (1845). Paddy's improving neighbour, the
shrewd hard-working Presbyterian farmer Denny Delap, has all the
Whateleian qualities except Anglicanism. Insofar as Whately's teaching
mission involved political economy it could be seen not only as Protestant
but as unspiritually materialist in Catholic eyes, which may help to
explain the observation of Whately's deviant disciple John Henry
Newman that, considered in isolation from religion and morality, political
economy was 'at once dangerous and leading to occasions of sin'.[43]

Whately was professionally against sin and saw no necessary conflict
between the material and the spiritual. He felt political economy could be
rescued for conventional morality and roundly attacked Mandeville's
provocative hypothesis that private vice, aristocratic or otherwise, could
conduce to public benefit or national wealth.[44] But he was no leveller. For
all his quasi-democratic modernity, plainness of style, and common-sense
accessibility, the pre-industrial hierarchical habit of thought stayed with
him. The underlying intention sometimes seems to be to rescue rather
than to transform hierarchy and a radically dysfunctional social order,
particularly in Ireland, through the robust exercise of a species of intellectual paternalism.

The vindication of order and keeping in order had an unfortunate tendency to go together. Some of Whately's junior clergy must at times have
resented being treated as obdurate undergraduates resisting instruction,
'both too ignorant to teach & too conceited to learn' as he put it in a letter
to a former colleague in Oxford. 'I shd not mind their bad taste &

reprinted in *Prose Writings* (1890), p. 182f. Davis, Carleton, and modernisation are discussed in Norman Vance, *Irish Literature, a Social History* (Oxford, 1990).
[43] J. H. Newman, *The Idea of a University* [1852] ed. Martin J. Svaglic (Notre Dame, Ind.,
1982), pp. 64–5.
[44] R. Whately, *Introductory Lectures on Political Economy* (1831), p. 45. Mandeville's *Fable of
the Bees, or, Private Vices, Public Benefits* (1714) is also discussed, without being directly
named, in *Easy Lessons on Money Matters* (1842); see also E. J. Hundert's essay in this
volume.

bombast if they did but *instruct*, or try to instruct their hearers; but they never think of attempting it.'[45] In the same way his hungry Suffolk parishioners must have occasionally resented the lectures and sermons which told them how they should think and what was good for them and for their country. It would have been little consolation to them that the House of Lords was in effect treated in much the same way. A clergyman in the diocese of Oxford who presumed to advise Whately how to do his job as Archbishop was ingeniously if harshly snubbed when Whately forwarded the letter to his own diocesan bishop, Samuel Wilberforce, not one of Whately's friends, with the observation that Wilberforce too had a right to benefit from this advice and, if it was defective or inappropriate, to administer any instruction which the clergyman himself might require.[46]

But the intention was to exercise his teaching function to create space within the established order of things for enlightened rational discussion and reform, seeking to accommodate constantly changing circumstances to underlying first principles. This strenuous project led Whately to profess and propagate the new or newly formulated science of political economy to the extent of simplifying his Oxford lectures on the subject into schoolbooks for Irish children. It represented a special case of what he saw as the energetic explanatory function of the church in every age in relation to the divine economy. The observation that no creeds or detailed guidance as to ecclesiastical practice were provided in scripture seemed to Whately not a regrettable oversight but a wise dispensation of providence. The church, or rather individual churches, needed to be free to develop their own traditions. Whately's view of tradition, developed in the light of his friend Edward Hawkins's sermon on the subject,[47] allowed for considerable latitude. The Roman Catholic Church is not explicitly mentioned but Catholic and Anglo-Catholic over-reliance on the authority of ancient tradition from the time of the Church Fathers is implicitly condemned: no development or adjustment would be possible if the church simply and mindlessly hung on to ossified set forms of belief without taking the time and trouble to think through the meaning of the gospel and demonstrate the dispensations of a benign providence in and for a given age and country. Whately argues the Almighty deliberately withheld detailed instructions to stimulate this rational activity.[48]

---

[45] Whately to Hawkins, 18 March [1832], from Dublin, Oriel MS 188.
[46] Whately to Wilberforce, 4 April 1846, Bodleian MS Wilberforce c. 8, f. 116.
[47] Edward Hawkins, *A Dissertation upon the Use and Importance of Unauthoritative Tradition as an Introduction to the Christian Doctrines* (Oxford, 1819).
[48] R. Whately, *An Essay on the Omission of Creeds, Liturgies and Codes of Ecclesiastical Canons, in the New Testament* (1831).

There is an interesting parallel in his unconventional view that only God could possibly understand and appropriately punish the moral culpability of the sinner, leaving to human authority the opportunity to use prison sentences not only for purposes of deterrence but to stimulate good work habits, likely to reduce the chances of reoffending. He suggested it would be appropriate to express prison sentences in terms not of time to be served but sums of money to be earned at fixed rates and paid over on release to fund a more virtuous life. Prisoners should have freedom to work as hard as they wished and the incentive, which would also be character-forming, would be that the harder they worked the sooner the required sum of money would be earned and so the sooner they would be released.[49] Character-forming habits of industry could also be fostered among the more virtuous poor. While it was obviously desirable to make provision for cripples, idiots, and the blind, deaf and dumb, the able-bodied should have every incentive to work. When radical reform of the established Church of Ireland was mooted in 1832, Whately did not favour redistribution of church revenues to poor relief, not so much out of vested interest as from a sense that as with the 'pauper system' of the unreformed Poor Law in England the effect of this could be to increase distress by discouraging industry, forethought, and charity, degrading the pauper into a slave fed according to need rather than exertion.[50]

III

For Whately, ever practical, salvation on earth as well as in heaven called for unremitting effort rather than passive reliance on external (or eternal) support. He was adamantly opposed to the old system of outdoor relief, on the grounds that this would discourage effort and increase unemployment by increasing the poor rates which were a tax on the employers of labour. Long before he went to Ireland he had practical experience of the operation, and inadequacy, of outdoor relief under the unreformed Poor Law. By a local Act of 1764 the Suffolk parishes had been grouped together for Poor Law purposes into larger units, each with a workhouse or 'house of industry', and the workhouse for the Blything Hundred, which included his Halesworth parish, was not far away, at Bulcamp. According to the Blything Union Minute Books, Whately was appointed as one of the Directors on 11 April 1822. It did not take him long to find

---

[49] R. Whately, *Thoughts on Secondary Punishment, in a Letter to Earl Grey* (1832).
[50] *Evidence of His Grace the Archbishop of Dublin as taken before the Select Committee of the House of Lords appointed to inquire into the Collection and Payment of Tithes in Ireland*, pp. 53, 95.

fault with the system. In 1823, well before succeeding to the Drummond Chair of Political Economy at Oxford, he wrote an indignant *Letter to the Directors of the House of Industry at Bulcamp*, against making any allowance to unemployed labourers. The Poor Law system in Suffolk was only 'a bounty on idleness . . . a bounty on theft', he complained. In various parts of England, but particularly in Suffolk, the practice had grown up of supplementing or supplying wages out of the poor rate, sometimes directly employing paupers at wages lower than the prevailing rate. In consequence, whether idle or industrious, labourers had come to expect the same level of wages as a right, and farmers had every encouragement to manipulate the regulations, cutting down on labourers who were thus forced on to the parish and running their farms with inadequate labour which could be supplemented at peak periods by a body of labourers taken off the parish on a temporary basis.[51]

This experience of outdoor relief in England did nothing to make Whately think it could work in Ireland. He was a member of the 1836 Commission of Inquiry in Ireland which had concluded that 'we cannot recommend parochial employment or out-door relief for the labourers of Ireland. We cannot recommend a system which offers bounties on improvidence.'[52] Since outdoor relief had been discontinued in the unpopular 1834 Poor Law in England, in which Whately's pupil Nassau Senior was much involved, it is tempting to think that once again English experience, English thinking, and English legislation were being insensitively and inappropriately forced upon recalcitrant Ireland. But in this case, as with the national education question, Irish problems and the Irish experience contributed to policy in England rather than the other way round. Senior knew Ireland well. He had visited the country in 1819 and his shrewdly practical observations on the need for tithe reform and state support for Catholic priests, frequently repeated, influenced, or at least were echoed in Whately's views when he became Archbishop. In 1831 Lord Howick, son of the Prime Minister, asked Senior to report on Poor Laws in Ireland and the inadequacy of formal provision for the unemployed and the destitute. The resulting *Letter to Lord Howick* suggested that it would be most inappropriate to extend to Ireland the existing English system of poor relief, including outdoor relief, since it tended to increase population by diminishing the responsibility of marriage, and diminished industry by making subsistence independent of exertion. As his earlier observations of the tithe system would have taught him, collecting money for any statutory purpose was always difficult in impoverished

---

[51] Quoted by Peacock, *Bread or Blood*, p. 36.
[52] Poor Law (Ireland) Debate, Hansard 3rd ser. 91 (March 1847), col. 431.

Ireland, as much for economic as for political reasons. It was often noted at the time that income tax, land tax, and assessed taxes had never been levied in Ireland because of collection problems. So there was absolutely nothing to be said for a system of poor relief on the English model likely to require the maintenance of ever-increasing numbers of paupers from a fund more likely to diminish than increase with declining agricultural productivity, even if the poor rate could be collected in the first instance. The Irish experience prompted this devastating critique of the Old Poor Law in England, which he soon had an opportunity to reform after his appointment in 1832 to the Royal Commission whose report laid the foundations for the New Poor Law of 1834.[53]

Whately had kept closely in touch with these developments and when he served on the 1836 Irish Commission he was aware of the problems which Senior and his fellow-commissioners had tried to cure. Given the extremity of the Irish situation he recommended sponsored emigration, which both he and Senior were deeply interested in as a general solution to problems of unemployment in Britain, but nobody listened. It is worth pointing out that once again it would have been the Irish experience that prompted this kind of thinking in relation to both English and Irish rural unemployment, since long before the Famine there was an established pattern of (unassisted) emigration from Ireland, particularly from the north and particularly to the American colonies.

Whately still believed in emigration, and still deplored outdoor relief, when the potato famine caused unprecedented suffering and misery in the 1840s. He had initially felt that better organisation of Irish resources would solve the worst problems, but he and Senior corresponded regularly about Irish matters and it was Senior, with a better grasp of arithmetic, who persuaded him that Ireland simply could not support its existing population with its own produce. Starving Ireland was a Malthusian nightmare, and Whately, advised by Senior, was forced to conclude that:

A well organized and vigorous system of emigration, and of colonization combined with it . . . will be, I am convinced, the only mode of relieving Ireland – unless we wait for the operation of famine and pestilence – from that now superabundant population which presents an insuperable obstacle to its ultimate improvement.[54]

---

[53] For Senior, Ireland and Poor Law reform see S. Leon Levy, *Nassau W. Senior 1790–1864* (London, 1970), esp. pp. 45–6, 74–8, 82, 218, and Nassau Senior, *A Letter to Lord Howick on a Legal Provision for the Irish Poor; Commutation of Tithes, and Provision for the Irish Roman Catholic Clergy* (1831). For correspondence with Whately about sustaining the population on the produce of the land see Senior to Whately, n.d., RCB MSS.

[54] R. Whately, *Substance of a Speech Delivered in the House of Lords on Friday 26 March 1847 on the Motion for a Committee on Irish Poor Laws* (1847), p. 35. This speech contains Whately's most detailed account of his own attitude and practice during the Famine.

Ireland has never forgiven Whately for opposing outdoor relief during the Famine when it might have saved lives and brought short-term alleviation of distress. But his opposition to outdoor relief, like everything else about him, was moral and practical rather than dogmatic. He believed in natural causes and refused to believe that famines were divine visitations or punishments about which nothing could be done.[55] But he also genuinely believed on the basis of his Suffolk experience that outdoor relief on the old discredited model, even in conditions of calamity, would be demoralising and impractical, fearing that even if the necessary money could be raised the cost of outdoor relief could swallow up the entire rental of Ireland, as the cost of outdoor relief had notoriously swallowed up the entire rental of Cholesbury in England. Landlords would have no incentive to keep land burdened with an impossible poor rate, and no resources to pay labourers. A bankrupt country might never recover the capacity to employ labour at living wages.

Whately was neither heartless nor uncharitable, but charity had to be rational, by his lights. Thinking of the future, and of the possibility of rational economic policy in Ireland, he endowed the Whately Chair of Political Economy at Trinity College out of his own pocket, supported the Irish Statistical Society which promoted scientific economics, and he unobtrusively contributed generously to the relief of distress, on rational principles, by offering as much additional paid employment in his own grounds as he could afford, paying at a little below the current going rate so as not to draw labourers away from economically profitable and socially beneficial employment with neighbouring farmers. As he observed rather dryly, most of his neighbours were unable to do the same even if they wanted to because they were too heavily burdened with poor rates to afford it.

His theory and his practice were not absurd or ungenerous, though they may seem dated now. Morality, welfare, rational economics, and respect for self-reliance and human dignity, however incompatible, are still natural objects of state policy and natural concerns of clergy and laity, English and Irish. Whately's unacknowledged achievement was to keep all these objects in mind, to learn from both his English and his Irish experience, and to develop, and sustain in appalling circumstances, a coherent and principled vision of possible improvement.

---

[55] R. Whately, *National Blessings and Judgments Considered in a Discourse Delivered before the University of Oxford, May 29, 1822, with an Appendix Containing Remarks on the Present Crisis* (1831), p. 35, and Bowen, *Protestant Crusade*, pp. 291–2. This relates to the earlier Irish famines of 1822 and 1831.

Part III

9   Political and domestic economy in Victorian social thought: Ruskin and Xenophon

Jane Garnett

I

'The household has been treated by economists with curious negligence.' Writing in 1911, Mabel Atkinson, tutor in economics at King's College of Household and Social Science, proceeded to argue that, from Adam Smith, classical, neo-classical and historical economists were equally to blame. 'Economists . . . [who] have generally been men . . . with their eyes fixed on trade and the mechanism of trade, very naturally neglected that section of life in which values, material and immaterial were being continually created, but for use alone, not for commercial purposes.' In defining wealth, economists had certainly come to admit that it included collective and immaterial well-being (as Marshall had in book 2, chapter 2 of his *Principles*), but they characteristically then reverted to discussing wealth as though it consisted of material exchangeable commodities; whereas, 'clearly the real income of a family is increased if children have access to good free schools or ample open spaces'. Atkinson was writing to promote the scientific status of household administration in the higher education of women, and also to urge the need for more systematic practical research on consumption habits of different social classes. But she concluded by hoping that:

the principle of household management may in turn react on economic science, and may show to its professors that value in use, though more difficult to detect and estimate than value in exchange, has been unduly neglected both in theory and in practice. If, to the management of our towns – which are, after all, only our homes on a larger scale – were applied the principles used by a good housekeeper in ordering her home, then cleanliness, beauty and convenience would increase around her. A science of economics so modified would recall to a scholar the original meaning of the word; for what, after all, did the craft of οἰκονομική, as first developed by Xenophon and Aristotle, mean but just 'the management of the home'?[1]

---

[1] M. Atkinson, 'The Economic Relations of the Household', in A. Ravenhill and C. J. Schiff, eds., *Household Administration: Its Place in the Higher Education of Women* (London, 1910), pp. 123–206, at 123–30, 205–6. For discussion of Atkinson's place in the development of education in household science, see N. Blakestad, 'King's College of Household and Social Science, and the Household Science Movement in English Higher Education c. 1908–39', unpublished Oxford University D.Phil., 1994.

Mabel Atkinson's hope – so far as the theoretical development of economics goes – was to remain largely unrealised until the last couple of
decades, when economists have begun to ask fresh questions about the
nature of economic goods, and to challenge models based on rational,
individualistic profit-maximising behaviour in the market. In the last
quarter of the twentieth century disciplinary boundaries are being
crossed, reconstructed, and in some cases reasserted in ways which in
part echo late nineteenth-century processes of definition, and in part
suggest new ways of approaching the history of those debates.
Economists have begun to talk again to moral philosophers, and scholars
of the ancient world (of Indian and Hebrew civilisations as well as Greece
and Rome) have also been raising broader comparative questions about
economics. There has been a renewed focus on the rhetoric of economics.[2] Feminist economists have explored some of the ways in which asking
questions about gender can confront the assumptions on which the discipline of economics has been built. In so far as this work has been historical, much of it has been concentrated either on analysing the treatment of
women's labour by the canonical economic theorists, or on retrieving the
economic writings of women.[3] Less attention has been paid to the ways in
which debates about the relationship between the ideas of domestic and
political economy worked in the past in structuring critical social and
moral questions. It is on such questions of epistemology and of metaphor
that I want to focus here. A specific intersection of contexts in the
mid/late nineteenth century seems to me to be worth examination: the
centrality to Victorian debate of Greek cultural and intellectual para-
digms and the concern to establish securely the disciplinary status of
political economy. Considerations of gender were fundamental to each
context – both apparently simplifying the interconnection and suggesting
important complications.

Most significant for establishing a new critical approach to the house-

---

[2] See, for example, A. Sen, *On Ethics and Economics* (Oxford, 1987); A. Sen and M.
Nussbaum, eds., *The Quality of Life* (Oxford, 1993); B. B. Price, ed., *Ancient Economic
Thought* (London and New York, 1997); A. Klamer, D. McCloskey and R. M. Solow, eds.,
The Consequences of Economic Rhetoric (Cambridge, 1988).

[3] See especially, M. A. Ferber, and J. A. Nelson, eds., *Beyond Economic Man: Feminist
Theory and Economics* (Chicago, 1993); J. A. Nelson, 'Gender, Metaphor and the
Definition of Economics', *Economics and Philosophy*, 8 (1992), pp. 103–25; N. Folbre and
H. Hartmann, 'The Rhetoric of Self-Interest: Ideology and Gender in Economic
Theory', in *The Consequences of Economic Rhetoric*, pp. 184–203; M. Pujol, *Feminism and
Anti-Feminism in Early Economic Thought* (1992; Cheltenham and Northampton, Mass.,
1998 edn); P. Groenewegen, ed., *Feminism and Political Economy* (Aldershot, 1994); J.
Rendall, 'Virtue and Commerce: Women in the Making of Adam Smith's Political
Economy', in E. Kennedy and S. Mendus, eds., *Women in Western Political Philosophy:
Kant to Nietzsche* (Brighton, 1987), pp. 44–77.

hold in the Victorian period was Xenophon's *Oeconomicus*, in which, as in his *Memorabilia*, he had gone beyond using the *oikos* as an analogy for the *polis*, and treated it as a microcosm of the *polis*, different only in size, not in kind. This focus is in fact clearly different from that of Aristotle, whose argument that the good life could only be lived in the *polis* helped to reinforce the resilient assumption that the foundations of power lay solely in the public sphere, and that domestic power was less important. (Plato, too, used *oikonomia* in the narrow sense.)[4] The *apparent* equivalence of their binary oppositions between household and political society, however, gave scope for conflation of interpretation, and made it more difficult for critical voices to emerge. This point was reinforced by the association with women of writings on the household (from Harriet Martineau's *Household Education* to the more widespread genre of advice manuals which proliferated in the mid-century). A review article on ancient political economy in the *Westminster Review* in 1857 began by observing that every era regarded history with a different eye: since it was typical of the mid-Victorian age to be focused on material interests, people turned to ask of the Greeks, 'whether, amongst their various renowned philosophies and ethics, they also had any philosophy and ethics of the shop'. The writer went on (citing Xenophon in passing) to say that a closer attention to the Greeks in this respect would in fact offer a counterweight to materialism, as well as to Christian sentimentalism and 'Teutonic' tendencies to 'over-work and mere-work'.[5] In Victorian Britain, however, Greek economic thought as such seems to have received much more limited treatment than it did on the continent. A culture so keen to press analogies between Athens and Britain was highly selective in the type of analogies which it wished to draw. These limitations, however, are themselves suggestive. Contemporary concerns about the role of women were reflected in discussions of social life in Greece, where the restrictions on citizen-women in Athens (whether these were internalised or criticised) could lead all too easily to the reinforcement of a simple private/public dichotomy.[6] The legacy of some aspects of Greek culture – as interpreted by the Victorians – lasted well into this century, as Frank Turner has critically illuminated in his *The Greek Heritage in Victorian Britain* (New Haven, 1981). However, in Turner's own index there is no entry for women, family, household, or

---

[4] S. B. Pomeroy, *Xenophon Oeconomicus: A Social and Historical Commentary* (Oxford, 1994; 1995 edn), p. 240.
[5] 'Ancient Political Economy', *Westminster Review*, 68 (1857), pp. 1–32.
[6] See, for example, J. P. Mahaffy, *Social Life in Greece* (London, 1874), pp. 258–61; H. Blumner, *The Home Life of the Ancient Greeks*, tr. A. Zimmern (London, Paris and Melbourne, 1893).

economic ideas. This essay will focus in particular on Xenophon, and on John Ruskin's presentation of him. By offering some contextualisation of the reading of Xenophon in the second half of the nineteenth century, I hope both to underscore the radically constructive economic approach which it offered to Ruskin (and to emphasise its significance for the development of his thought); and, further, to suggest that the reasons why Ruskin's reading was contested or, more often, sidestepped, are themselves of real interest in understanding the theoretical trajectory of political economy in this period.

II

The first English translation of the *Oeconomicus* in the nineteenth century was that by Alexander Wedderburn and W. Gershom Collingwood, commissioned by and revised by Ruskin, and published in 1876 as the first volume of his never-completed Bibliotheca Pastorum.[7] The later 1870s and 1880s saw a series of editions and translations, both in England and on the continent – especially in France and Italy, where Xenophon was taken up by the school of Le Play, as he was by the Catholic critical economic thinkers at Louvain in the same tradition such as Charles Périn and Victor Brants.[8] Although aspects of Ruskin's reading of Xenophon have been acknowledged, there has been no real discussion of this edition and his preface, nor of its relation to the Bibliotheca project and to his economic thought as a whole. Yet for Ruskin it had sufficient significance to be chosen to introduce 'the series of classic books which I hope to make the chief domestic treasure of British peasants'[9] – the fundamental educational project which he had begun in *The Political Economy of Art* (1857), and continued – via *Unto this Last* (1860/62) – in *Sesame and Lilies* (1864), the lectures promised in 1857 on 'the political economy of literature'. As Ruskin wrote to Charles Eliot Norton in March 1876: 'I'm just doing a most careful preface to Xenophon – mapping Greek columns and relig-

[7] References to Ruskin's works will be from the Library edition edited by E. T. Cook and Alexander Wedderburn, 39 vols. (1902–12), hereafter Ruskin, *Works*.

[8] See D. R. Morrison, *Bibliography of Editions, Translations, and Commentary on Xenophon's Socratic Writings, 1600–present* (Pittsburgh, 1988); V. Brants, *Xenophon Economiste* (Louvain, 1881); G. Platon, 'Un Le Play Ateniese del IV. secolo a.C. o L' "Economia Politica" di Senofonte', *Nuova Rivista Storica*, 1 (1917), pp. 271–93; 2 (1918), pp. 450–70; and 3 (1919), pp. 43–63. See also the discussion in Albert Augustus Trever's Chicago Ph.D., published in 1916 as *A History of Greek Economic Thought*, which was infused with a Ruskinian frame of reference.

[9] The reference to 'peasants' has too often been taken literally as a means of pigeon-holing Ruskin's ideas as irredeemably nostalgic and regressive. See, though, Ruskin, *Works*, XXVII, pp. 260–1; 'in a healthy society artist and manufacturer are "developed states of the peasant"'.

ion all over Europe, and am giddy with the lot of things that focus, now, out of past work.'[10]

Xenophon's *Oeconomicus* (translated by Wedderburn and Collingwood as *The Economist*) consists of a complex structure of dialogues within a dialogue: that between Socrates and Critobulus giving way to Socrates' reported conversation with Ischomachus, the type of the perfect 'gentleman', a major part of which is discussion of Ischomachus' relationship with his wife in the management of the *oikos*. Incorporated within the dialogue with Critobulus is a reported conversation of the Persian king Cyrus, who is the other model of character and behaviour which Socrates presents. Within Ischomachus's discussion of his conversation with his wife are reports of the advice given to them by their father and mother respectively. The text begins with questions of fundamental definition: what is the purpose of economy? what is property? Property is defined as only what is useful, by analogy with knowledge, and with control over one's passions. Immediately the context is established for a right understanding of *oikonomia*. Xenophon's text is structured in a way which was entirely congruent with Ruskin's own cast of mind and rhetorical approach to persuasion: the reader is drawn in, carried along and repeatedly refocused on the central points by means of a series of overlapping metaphors. The administration of the Persian empire, which is discussed first, serves as a paradigm for the management of the household of Ischomachus and his wife (cf. the analogy drawn between public institutions and private households in the prologue to the *Cyropaedia*). The rhetoric is designed to build up to the model of the ideal household, which is to serve as the core of the metaphorical structure. The text is not a treatise on the mechanics of housekeeping, but a philosophical argument about the concentric circles of the economy – local and imperial. Cyrus's orderly park – in the Greek, *paradeisos*, from the Persian word for a walled garden, given as 'paradise' in the Ruskin edition – is a model for the orderly household. The king is a model for Ischomachus' wife, who is to be figured as a queen bee. Each is distinguished from a tyrant: to win over those who work for you and to exploit the possible connections between all parts of life is the aim of the ideal ruler – in husbandry, state government, economy, and war. Just as bees were believed to be associated with the divine, Persian kings were held to be mediators between their subjects and the gods, and Ischomachus' wife won the loyalty of her servants. The right use of language (under the aegis of Heaven) is itself a form of power – a solemn responsibility of the persuader. At the end of his preface,

---

[10] *The Correspondence of John Ruskin and Charles Eliot Norton*, ed. J. Bradley and I. Ousby (Cambridge, 1987), p. 379.

Ruskin's rhetorical device is to present the text as valuable for its 'simplicity of language and modesty of heart' – its appropriateness to its subject
matter, which should be within the compass of everyone's understanding,
and which it is hence the responsibility of everyone to understand. For
Xenophon, as for Ruskin, education is the basis of all social institutions:
everyone in the *oikos*, from the wife to the slaves, housekeeper and
foreman is educated, and thereby can develop (by contrast with
Aristotle's static view).

The resonances of gender in Xenophon's text are multi-layered, in
ways which also found an affinity with or indeed helped to suggest
Ruskin's own writings 'cross-gender' (in Dinah Birch's phrase).[11] It is a
text about the qualities of the true 'gentleman' (literally 'beautiful and
good'), a type of manliness which is counterposed to effeminacy and to
slavishness. Ruskin recognised the need to stress that this was not to
suggest any correlation between subordination and womanliness: a point
which was commended by a reviewer of the edition as being both important and contrary to superficial readings.[12] In chapter I Socrates refers to
a man using his money to buy a mistress (hetaira) 'by whose influence his
body would be worse, his soul worse, his household worse; how could we
then say that his money was any benefit to him?' A different word for mistresses is used a few lines further on, when Socrates describes 'deceiving
mistresses, who pretend to be queens of pleasure' (compare *Unto this
Last:* the Lady of Pleasure, who is opposed to the Lady of Saving, the
Lady of Health[13]). In chapter IV the banausic arts (which Ruskin glosses
as those which deprive the artisan of his fair measure of exercise, sun-
shine, and fresh air) are defined as those which may make men slavish and
effeminate. None of these associations is a fixed attachment to a particular sex or a particular class. Masters can be slaves to their passions; slaves
can be judged 'gentlemen' (ch. XIV. 9–10); women can acquire 'masculine qualities' (for example of formal discussion; of judgement: viz. ch.
VII. 10; ch. IX. 15; ch. X. 1). Nobility of character does not imply the
acquisition of 'masculine' qualities in any straightforward sense.
Marriage is presented as a moral and business partnership (to which each
brings property, and in which a connection is made between the care of
children and of property); and

in that both alike must give and receive, Heaven bestowed upon both powers of
memory and attention in a like degree, so that you could not determine whether
of the two excels therein. So also for the ruling of their spirits, where so they
should, they had equal opportunity given them; and it was granted to the stronger

[11] D. Birch, 'Ruskin's "Womanly Mind"', *Essays in Criticism*, 38 (1988), pp. 308–24, at 315.
[12] James Davies in *Academy*, n.s. no. 269 (1877), pp. 575–6.
[13] Ruskin, *Works*, XVII, pp. 75, 85.

therein, be it the man or the woman, to inherit the greater portion of the good arising therefrom. (vol. XXXI, pp. 57–8).

The analogy of the hive and human society was a Greek commonplace; but it is significant that, whereas Aristotle consistently makes the leader of the hive male, Xenophon very specifically here follows through his metaphor by making the leader female.[14] The theme of kingship and queenship is, of course, one which Ruskin constantly elaborates, drawing on a wide range of classical and medieval reference. But a close consideration of Ruskin's engagement with Xenophon underlines the degree to which, far from resorting to neat binary oppositions, he is constantly confronting such conventional tropes and moving from one to another in order to expose the narrowing and distortion which results from resting on one particular metaphor.

Both Robert Hewison and Nicholas Shrimpton have argued compellingly for the critical and ironic quality of Ruskin's writing in his lectures 'Of Kings' Treasuries' and 'Of Queens' Gardens' in *Sesame and Lilies* (1864), and have indicated the significance of Xenophon for the construction of the argument.[15] Far from supporting the confinement of women to the home (conventionally conceived in a narrow and limiting way), the relationship between *oikos* and *polis* offered a metaphor for the requisite infusion of 'female' values into the market place and the state. Ruskin was certainly making this point. But he went further: he continually found that the metaphors which he was using were misinterpreted, often being assimilated with what they were intended to attack, hence the need to refocus them, adding in further layers of imagery and allusion to cut across them and to break up the endless tendency to sink back into simplification; a method in some ways analogous to the Socratic method of teaching. In the same way Ruskin produced new editions of his work in different combinations, and with particular instructions as to how they should be read. For example, when he argued that *Sesame and Lilies* should be read alongside *Unto this Last*, this was to point up more strongly the economic metaphor of the former and to try to prevent its being read simply as a tract on the desirable social roles of literal men and women.

[14] Cf. Pomeroy, *Xenophon*, p. 278.
[15] R. A. P. Hewison, 'Some Themes and their Treatment in the Work of John Ruskin, 1860–1871, with Special Reference to *Unto this Last*, *Sesame and Lilies* and *The Queen of the Air*', unpublished Oxford University B.Litt., 1972; N. Shrimpton, 'Economic, Social and Literary Influences upon the Development of Ruskin's Ideas to *Unto this Last* (1860)', unpublished Oxford University D.Phil., 1976. Earlier writers on Ruskin's economic thought dismissed his reading of ancient authorities as either irrelevant or as simply following eighteenth-century convention. For these positions, see J. T. Fain, *Ruskin and the Economists* (Nashville, 1956), pp. 102–3; J. Sherburne, *Ruskin, or the Ambiguities of Abundance* (Cambridge, Mass., 1972), pp. 100–7.

The variation of metaphor and of juxtaposition was a crucial rhetorical strategy. The preface to *The Economist* exemplifies this practice. Indeed the key-stone of the preface discusses possible variant interpretations of a line of Horace in order to make a point about receptivity and right reading, espe-cially in relation to religious inspiration: the only right approach is that of the 'centrally powerful reader [who] imagines it to be possible that he may himself know no more of God than Horace did; – discovers and acknowl-edges in his own mind the tendency to self-deception, but with it also the capacity of divine instruction'. The moral lessons of Xenophon's text are introduced by a series of triads. First, Ruskin divides the Greek living soul into three orders: 'the vocal, or Apolline, centred at Delphi; the construc-tive, or Athenian, centred at Athens; and the domestic, or Demetrian, centred at Sparta. These three spiritual powers taught the Greeks (in brief terms) Speech, Art and Conduct . . . The Delphic Power is Truth . . . The Athenian Power is the Grace of Deed . . . The Spartan Power is the Grace of Love'. Each in turn corresponded to a historical focus: the Delphic Power to the Greek theocracy; the Attic to 'the laws of human government . . . founded on industry and justice . . . fulfilled in chivalric heroism'; the Demetrian to Sparta – and ultimately to Rome (and the German empire; i.e. thence by association to modern Britain). Each type is further glossed. Sinai and Delphi, the Hebrew and the Hellenic, are brought together as equivalent religious powers; the Athenian Power is generalised as determining the methods of art and laws of ideal beauty. 'The Demetrian, or Moral, Power [note: a female goddess] set before men the standards of manly self-command, patriotic self-sacrifice, and absolute noblesse in scorn of pleasure, of wealth and of life, for the sake of duty; and these in a type so high, that of late, in degraded Christendom, it has begun to be inconceivable.' 'Such being the classic authority of the three states, it cannot but be wise for every statesman, and every house-holder, in the present day, to know the details of domestic life under this conclusive authority in Art and Morals.' Ruskin establishes Xenophon's status as someone who maintained an assumption of principles and of spiritual powers in the face of rationalistic challenges and moral decay. He celebrates him as an admirer of Spartan virtues (at a point in the nine-teenth century when admiration for Athenian democracy was at its height).[16] His work is seen as the more valuable for being poised between 'the warrior heroism of nascent Greece, and the home-heroism of pac-ified Christianity in its happiest days'. This sense of creative tension is

---

[16] See E. Rawson, *The Spartan Tradition in European Thought* (Oxford, 1969; 1991 edn), pp. 353, 359.

paralleled by the motif of the five cities of which all should have knowledge, and each of which has a crowning quality and a representative
which leave a seed for the future amidst the decay of the civilisation: 'For
Athens, Marathon and Phidias; For Rome, Her Empire, and Virgil; For
Florence, The laws of commerce, and Dante; For Venice, The laws of
state, and Tintoret; For London, The laws of home life, and
Shakespeare'. Of the three truths of Xenophon's text, the ideal of domestic life – 'the loving help of two equal helpmates, lord and lady' – is the
crowning one, overlaid on the definition of wealth and the ideal of kingship.[17] The transitions do not form a straightforward chronological progression, of the type which Herbert Spencer had suggested in his idea of
the transition from a military to an industrial society. They are not auto-
matic, and cannot be taken for granted.

The assumption of spiritual authority and the need for openness to
divine instruction Ruskin held to be an abiding truth, present in all true
civilisations and to be Xenophon's primary requirement for education in
oikonomia.[18] Just as, in the *Memorabilia*, 'it is no question with Xenophon
. . . nor does he suppose it to be a question with the reader, whether there
are gods or not; but only whether Socrates served them or not'.[19] The
Bibliotheca Pastorum was intended to include works representative of
the values of each of his five cities. In the event it is significant that the
next book chosen was Sidney's paraphrase of the Psalms, which, Ruskin
commented, 'differs wholly from such modern attempts in . . . that it
aims straight . . . at getting into the heart and truth of the thing it has got
to say', continually exposing what is latent or unclear in the original. The
very familiarity of the Bible and Prayer Book language makes people less
alert to the meaning, just as the terms which political economists use are
deceptively straightforward.[20] Ruskin also wanted to expose the hypocri-
sies of 'Judaic Christianity' (by which he meant men's assumption that
they alone possess the true faith). He seems to have intended
Xenophon's *Economist* to be followed in the series of classic books by a
novel by the popular Swiss writer Albert Bitzius (alias Jeremias
Gotthelf), *Ulric the Farm Servant*. This work was eventually translated by
Julia Firth, edited by Ruskin and published in parts between 1886 and
1888, as a sequel to his edition of Francesca Alexander's *Roadside Songs of*

---

[17] Ruskin, *Works*, XXXI, pp. 7–29.
[18] Compare R. Jenkyns, 'Ruskin and the Interpretation of Greece', *The Ruskin Gazette*, 1
(1989), pp. 9–15 at 14 on Ruskin's rejection of a simple schematism which opposed
Hellenism and Hebraism.   [19] Ruskin, *Works*, XXXI, p. 20.
[20] *Ibid.*, XXXI, pp. 116; 118; compare William Smart, *A Disciple of Plato: A Critical Study of
John Ruskin* (Glasgow, 1883), p. 39. Smart observes of *Fors*, 'One might say of them what
Ruskin says of the teachings of heaven: "they are given in so obscure, nay, often in so iron-
ical a manner, that a blockhead necessarily reads them wrong".'

Tuscany. A sympathetic review of Gotthelf's work in 1863 brings out very clearly the reasons why Ruskin felt an affinity with him, and why the moral values presented in *Ulric* were believed to complement those in *The Economist*. Gotthelf's authority is established by the fact that he was not a professional author, but a Protestant pastor, a prophet, possessed by 'a living faith, a vitalizing power', for whom 'flowers and stones by the road-side all have their lessons of use or beauty'. The reviewer began by juxtaposing the superficial topos of Switzerland as a haven of idyllic simplicity with the frustration and rage against social grievances, which drove Gotthelf to write: the relations between farmers and labourers; the deplorable condition of national education; immorality and intemperance.[21] In his preface to *Ulric* Ruskin presented Gotthelf – 'a combination of Scott and Sydney Smith' – as setting out an ideal of peasant character at a point when it threatened to be corrupted by trade and foreign travellers. The work was a counterpart to *The Economist* in that it dealt with the relationship of master and servant, husband and wife: its heroine, Freneli, is described in terms very similar to those used to describe Ischomachus' wife.[22] For Ruskin aspects of Swiss life represented an ideal, though never an uncomplicated one, just as aspects of Tuscan peasant life were to do. The significance of the eventual pairing of *Ulric* with the *Songs of Tuscany* was to challenge simplistic dichotomies between Protestantism and Catholicism: to place 'in parallel light the more calculating and prosperous virtue of Protestant Switzerland' to the Tuscan peasant character animated by sincere Catholicism. Complacency about the intimacy of the connection between Protestantism and economic progress was seen by Ruskin as one of the most deplorable concomitants of the Victorian ideology of political economy, especially when it helped to reinforce the separation of the values of the commercial world and the home. In *Fors* (Letter 57), in September 1875, just as he was preparing the edition of Xenophon, Ruskin reported having been sent by the Belgian economist Emile de Laveleye his pamphlet on Protestantism and Catholicism. De Laveleye had evidently – and rightly – imagined that there might be some affinity between his thought, critical as it was of the premises of classical political economy, and that of Ruskin. But Ruskin railed at him for this work, in part because he privileged the pursuit of liberty, but more so 'for reviving the miserable question of a schism between Catholicism and Protestantism, which is entirely ridiculous and immaterial; and taking no note whatever of the true and eternal schism, cloven by the very sword of Michael, between

---

[21] *British Quarterly Review*, 38 (1863), pp. 304–21. See also J. Gotthelf, *Wealth and Welfare* (London and New York, 1866); *The Soul and Money* tr. G. Vere (London, 1872).
[22] Ruskin, *Works*, XXXII, pp. 490–504.

him that serveth God, and him that serveth him not'.[23] It was an interesting irony that the critical approach to economic principles of de Laveleye, who did not formally convert to Protestantism until 1878 (although he had been moving that way for many years before), was initially shaped by his Catholicism, and especially by his period of study with François Huet, the Catholic Christian socialist at the University of Ghent.[24]

III

We do not know when exactly Ruskin first read Xenophon. It is clear that after the hostile critical reaction to his *Cornhill Magazine* essays, during the latter half of 1861 and again in 1862 Ruskin turned to renewed detailed study of a series of classical texts, including Xenophon's *Memorabilia* and *Oeconomicus*. Much has been made of a letter of 5 November 1861 to suggest that Ruskin did not read Xenophon before this point, and indeed that other literary influences were more profound: 'I fully intend finishing Political Economy, but otherwise than as I began it. I have first to read Xenophon's *Economist* and Plato's *Republic* carefully, and to master the economy of Athens. I could not write now in the emotional way I did then.'[25] But the context of this letter suggests rather that the emphasis should be on 'carefully': Ruskin was characteristically probing the best way in which to gain the attention of his readers and to claim a persuasive authority. His frustration at the difficulties of doing so is powerfully expressed in a letter to Norton of August 1861: 'no one much comforts me but Socrates . . . what message I have given is all wrong; has to be re-said – in another way, and is – so said – almost too terrible to be serviceable'.[26] Although there is no direct acknowledgement of Xenophon in *The Political Economy of Art* (1857), the first lecture in particular is constructed around the definition of economy as the administration of a house, which is summed up as the art of managing labour, the description of the economist as the mistress of a household, the association of the queenly housewife and the queenly nation, the metaphors of

[23] *Ibid.*, XXVIII, pp. 402–3.
[24] Emile de Laveleye's *Le Protestantisme et le Catholicisme dans leur rapports avec la liberté et la prospérité des peuples. Etude d'économie sociale* (Brussels, 1875) was translated into English in the same year with a preface by Gladstone. De Laveleye's polemical association of Protestantism with liberty and prosperity was informed by his hostility to Belgian Ultramontanism, as well as being associated with his personal development away from Catholicism.
[25] Specially by Hewison, 'Some Themes', p. 25; D. Birch, *Ruskin's Myths* (Oxford, 1988), pp. 55–8. The letter is quoted in *Works*, XXVII, p. xlix.
[26] *Correspondence of Ruskin and Norton*, p. 66.

order and the garden, the analogies of farm, fleet, army, and nation. The 1857 Preface itself, with its famous denial that Ruskin had read any political economy, owes its rhetorical effect to Xenophon. At the beginning of chapter XVI of the *Economist*, Ischomachus says: 'I would show you that there is no real difficulty in what is called the great riddle of husbandry by people who, though they possess the most thorough and accurate knowledge in theory, have absolutely no practical experience of it.' Here Xenophon was underlining the philosophical rather than technical nature of his work by barbed reference to writers of agricultural manuals. The point is picked up again in chapter XX, in which it is emphasised that carefulness rather than knowledge is the secret of true success. By this stage the reader should feel confident that, without arcane specialist knowledge, but with proper application, he can farm, just as he could perform other civic duties. So Ruskin constructs his argument, incidentally moving almost imperceptibly from 'economical principles' to 'political economy' as defined by modern authors:

> profound study is not, in this case, necessary either to writer or readers, while accurate study, up to a certain point, is necessary for us all. Political economy means, in plain English, nothing more than 'citizen's economy' ... Nor are its first principles in the least obscure ... The statements of economical principles given in the text, though I know that most, if not all, of them are accepted by existing authorities on the science, are not supported by references, because I have never read any author on political economy, except Adam Smith, twenty years ago. Whenever I have taken up any modern book upon this subject, I have usually found it encumbered with inquiries into accidental or minor commercial results ... by the complication of which, it seemed to me, the authors themselves had been not infrequently prevented from seeing to the root of the business.[27]

The 'root of the business' was the question of primary definitions, and of analytical method. Ruskin's targeting of John Stuart Mill in his *Cornhill* essays was deliberately provocative. It was a recognition of the fact that Mill was the most prominent and authoritative representative of political economy, and maintained the hypothesis of 'economic man'. Ruskin also felt that Mill's *Principles* were in some respects the more dangerous for making a distinction between the laws and conditions of the production of wealth (which he held to partake of the nature of physical truths) and the distribution of wealth (which he allowed to be a matter for human institution).[28] This critical distinction seemed to Ruskin to risk encouraging moral compartmentalisation.[29] His constant

---

[27] Ruskin, *Works*, XVI, pp. 9–10.
[28] J. S. Mill, *Principles of Political Economy, with some of their applications to Social Philosophy*, in *Collected Works of J. S. Mill*, ed. F. E. L. Priestley and J. M Robson, 33 vols. (Toronto and London, 1963–91), II, p. 199.   [29] Ruskin, *Works*, XXVIII, p. 374.

reference in *Unto this Last* to 'popular' economists, on the other hand, underlined his conviction that it was the ideological hegemony of the working assumptions of political economy which was the main target. As Mill himself had observed in his essay on the definition of political economy (written first in 1836 and published in revised form in 1844 in *Some Unsettled Questions of Political Economy*) the use of such analytical abstractions as he was advocating was problematic: 'such is the nature of the human understanding, that the very fact of attending with intensity to one part of a thing, has a tendency to withdraw the attention from the other parts'.[30]

The mid-century debate focused upon the scientific status of political economy, and came to a head in a blistering address by J. K. Ingram (Professor at Trinity College, Dublin) to the British Association, which was threatening to evict economics for being insufficiently scientific. Ingram both attacked the way in which political economy had been pursued and offered a Comtist future for economics as part of a properly scientific sociology. He acknowledged the significance of Ruskin's critique, and, like Ruskin, argued that Mill, whilst far from narrow in his perspective, was inconsistent in whether 'economy' was a department 'carved' out of the general body of the science of society, or a different sort of question preparatory to social philosophy. Ingram picked up on the fact that when Senior referred to the dubious advantage to a labouring family of the employment of mother and children in non-domestic work, he thought it necessary to 'apologise for having introduced such remarks, as not, perhaps, strictly within the province of political economy'. Ingram's comment was: 'This is the very pedantry of purism; and the purism is not merely exaggerated, it is really altogether out of place.' He then emphasised that it was not just at a practical level but at the level of theory that different branches of social philosophy needed to be intertwined. This was crucial for both the intellectual authority and the image of political economy. He went on to argue that the treatment of labour as an abstraction was both philosophically and practically suspect. It had repelled working men from the study of political economy.

It is too often forgotten that before all things a man is a member of society – that he is usually head of a household, and that the conditions of his life should be such as to admit of his maintaining the due relations with his family – that he is also a citizen, and requires for the intelligent appreciation of the social and political system to which he belongs a certain amount of leisure and opportunity for mental culture.

---

[30] J. S. Mill, 'On the Definition of Political Economy', *Essays on Economics and Society*, in *Collected Works*, IV, p. 332.

It was not true that education was only relevant for productive efficiency, and labour – for example in respect of legitimate constraints on its mobility – was clearly not a commodity just like any other. Ingram proceeded to make a socially conservative but conceptually more radical point about the ways in which the abstractions of political economy also masked issues of gender:

> By a further abstraction, the difference of the social vocations of the sexes is made to disappear, in economic as well as political reasoning, by means of the simple expedient of substituting for *man* in every proposition *person* or *human being*; and so, by little else than a trick of phraseology, self-support is made as much an obligation of the woman as of the man. It is true that ungenerous sentiment has much to do with the prevalence of these modes of thought; but what it is most suitable to insist on here, is that the science on which they rest, or in which they find justification, is false science.[31]

For Ingram, writing from the perspective of Dublin, classical political economy might more readily be seen to be interpretable as hegemonically 'masculine' in an alien sense, to which the social values of the family were to be juxtaposed.

The issue of the employment of women – especially married women – outside the home was a vexed practical question, which also confronted assumptions about the role of the domestic sphere in a market economy. The *Saturday Review*, under the heading 'Queen Bees or Working Bees?', used the crudest language of political economy to argue against the training of women for a profession:

> Married life is woman's profession; and to this life her training – that of dependence – is modelled. Of course by not getting a husband, or losing him, she may find that she is without resources. All that can be said of her is, she has failed in business; and no social reform can prevent such failures. The mischance of the distressed governess and the unprovided widow, is that of every insolvent trader.[32]

Such an argument represented one clear version of the separation of spheres, to which Ruskin's writings and use of Xenophon could be read as a direct response – one in fact also not incompatible with the arguments which Mill put forward at the end of chapter 2 of *The Subjection of Women*, although they obviously proceeded from a totally different starting point. The notoriously anti-feminist *Saturday Review* was hostile to all such approaches in ways which drew on gendered stereotypes in formulating its language of condemnation: the Ruskin who wrote *Unto this Last* was 'a mad governess', 'a flirt who has ceased to be pretty', 'reproaching his

---

[31]   J. K. Ingram, *The Present Position and Prospects of Political Economy* (London and Dublin, 1878), pp. 9, 14, 18, 19.
[32]   'Queen Bees or Working Bees?', *Saturday Review*, 8 (1859), pp. 575–6, at 576.

neighbours with querulous female virulence'.[33] The *Saturday Review* became almost hysterical itself in its attack on what it saw as Ruskin's transgression of the proper boundaries of political economy. Other critics of the type of position adopted by the *Saturday Review* drew on Greek archetypes to challenge facile stereotypes of the values of the English home. Eliza Lynn Linton began an article on domestic life by referring to the Athenian distinction between the wife (uneducated and confined to the home) and the hetaira (the companion or mistress who could be highly educated, but who could not marry, and who entertained men outside the home). Her assertion was that 'men take this division of functions and multiplication of persons as the best and wisest model of human society possible to be fashioned'. She proceeded to explode the ideal of the home as a refuge from the troubles of the world, underlining the general lack of creative interaction between members of a middle-class family, between a father and his children or between a husband and wife.[34] James Donaldson, writing in the *Contemporary Review* in 1878–9 on the position and influence of women in ancient Greece, explored the same division of women's roles, and attributed to this the decay of Athens.[35] Here the Victorian admiration for Athenian culture was undercut; just as Xenophon's ideal of the household was recognised to be a challenge to the norm of Athenian life. The association of Athenian culture with Victorian liberalism – exemplified in Grote's massive *History of Greece*, which Mill so admired and Ruskin so deplored – led to the reinforcement of other related assumptions about the economy and about public and private spheres. As Frederic Harrison pointed out, there was a certain irony in this, in that ancient Greek civilisation demonstrated that the desire for wealth was not universal, as well as indicating that such a desire was not invariably associated with high intelligence.[36] The irony was mostly lost.

Indeed, the continuing debate about the scientific status of political economy barely confronted these associations. Ingram himself, who published in 1888 an enormously popular *History of Political Economy*, was highly selective in his following through of historical comparison. Essentially the conceptual scope of economic thought was little changed. He referred to Sismondi's admiration of Xenophon's *Oeconomicus* 'for the spirit of mild philanthropy and tender piety which

[33] *Saturday Review*, 9 (1860), pp. 582–4, at 582. See also Birch, 'Ruskin's "Womanly Mind"', p. 313.
[34] [E. L. Linton], 'Domestic Life', *Temple Bar*, 4 (1862), pp. 402–15, at 402–3, 412.
[35] Reprinted in J. Donaldson, *Woman; her Position and Influence in Ancient Greece and Rome, and among the Early Christians* (London, New York and Bombay, 1906).
[36] F. Harrison, 'The Limits of Political Economy', *Fortnightly Review*, 1 (1865), pp. 356–73, at 359.

breathes through it'; but then commented that 'it scarcely passes
beyond the bounds of domestic economy'. Even on Aristotle, whom he
praised, he commented that he did not give as much attention to economic subjects as one would like. 'When wealth comes under consideration, it is studied not as an end in itself, but with a view to the higher
elements and ultimate aims of the collective life.'[37] Palgrave's *Dictionary
of Political Economy*, undertaken in the 1890s in conjunction with the
foundation of the *Economic Journal* as the mouthpiece of Marshallian
economics, contained no entry for Family or Household. It too retained
a conventional sense of what should constitute the scope of economics.
In the article on 'The English School of Political Economy', the influence of Carlyle and Ruskin was deemed important, although it was necessary 'to keep in mind the distinction of economic theory from a mere
record of facts or a mere utterance of philanthropic aspiration'.
Xenophon's *Oeconomicus* was distinguished very sharply from a treatise
on political economy. 'It contains much good sense and sound morals,
and gives a conception of the domestic life, but little or nothing that is
economic in the technical sense.' Under 'Morality . . . in relation to
Political Economy', it was opined that 'the theory of morals of the economist need not be original or peculiar; it may not even be very clearly
conceived'.[38] Most significantly, in discussing the establishment of the
Economic Journal and its rival the *Economic Review*, organ of the Oxford-
based Christian Social Union, the comment was that the *Economic
Review* was 'not so strictly economic'. (In its review of Palgrave the
Economic Review in turn criticised its lack of attention to the relationship
between ethics and economics.)[39] In the appendix on 'The Growth of
Free Industry and Enterprise' at the end of his *Principles*, Marshall dismissed the notion that the Greeks could be of any economic interest,
since they 'knew little or nothing of the economic problems which are of
absorbing interest to our own age'.[40] At the beginning of the work, there
were unresolved slippages as to how far in fact his goal was to widen the
range of concerns and motivations behind economic decisions.
Although he considered a definition of labour which would incorporate
that work done for an end other than its immediate tangible rewards, he
reverted to arguing that it should only include activities which generated
income. His desire to protect women's altruistic roles as mothers nur-
turing human capital led to his separation of the domestic from the

[37] J. K. Ingram, *A History of Political Economy* (Edinburgh, 1888), pp. 14–15.
[38] R. H. I. Palgrave, *A Dictionary of Political Economy*, 3 vols.(London and New York,
1891–4), I, p. 735; III, p. 681; II, p. 813.
[39] Palgrave, *Dictionary*, I, p. 736; *Economic Review*, 7 (1897), p. 553.
[40] A. Marshall, *Principles of Economics*, 2 vols. (1890; London, 1961 edn), I, pp. 729 ff.

market, and hence to the reinforcement of the dominant ideological assumptions about the nature of economic questions.[41]

Even J. A. Hobson, standing as a radical critic of this essential continuity of marginalist economics with its classical predecessors, and agreeing with Ruskin that 'sentiment' was a fundamental basis of economic considerations, sought to utilise insights gained from Ruskin with reference only 'to economic phenomena as they are usually understood'. In his *Work and Wealth* he left it an open question whether political economists were justified in severing the marketable from the non-marketable, but argued that Ruskin's perception of the intimacy of the relations between the commercial and the non-commercial had led him to enlarge the context of economic questions too far.[42] He made the point that consumption was still chiefly within the family, and hinted that there was something of a paradox: whilst man was becoming narrower and narrower on the producing side, he was connecting more widely and variously on the consuming side. But possible implications of this were not really pursued, and Hobson did not develop discussion of the conceptual relationship between the household and the market.

Although he also wanted to make Ruskin conform to his own scientific conceptions, Patrick Geddes engaged much more closely with this aspect of his thought:

Since the activities of a community are the sum of the separate activities of its units, and since production exists for and is determined by consumption, political economy is from the present physical point of view, the generalised aspect of domestic economy, a proposition which Mr Ruskin, following the Greek economists, has traced into valuable detail, but which ordinary writers are wont comparatively to ignore.

Those economists who argued that Ruskin's references to medieval values or to Plato and Xenophon were sentimental and inappropriate to scientific argument were, Geddes showed, themselves missing the point. Ruskin's emphasis on quality of labour and utility of production in a sense wider than the purely material was related to Darwinian ideas of domestication: 'production and occupation, then, are judged, not by their immediate material result to particular individuals, whether queens or drones of the social hive; but by the aggregate result in a better or worse adapted environment'. Up-to-date science was on Ruskin's side; whilst on the other was 'too often sheer blindness to the actual facts of human and social life – organism, function and environment alike – concealed by illusory abstractions, baseless assumptions and feeble metaphors'.[43] Geddes

[41] *Ibid.*; compare pp. 24 and 27; 58.
[42] J. A. Hobson, *Work and Wealth* (1914; London, 1933), pp. 11–12.
[43] P. Geddes, *John Ruskin, Economist* (Edinburgh, 1884), pp. 28, 31–7.

precisely met Mabel Atkinson's requirements for the development of economic science; however, his impact was not to be on the mainstream of
economic theory, but on the conceptually detached environmental movement. He remained a maverick, his only institutional attachments being
as Professor of Botany at University College, Dundee (1889–1914) and
later as Professor of Civics and Sociology at the University of Bombay
(1920–23), which delimited the nature of his authority in a rapidly profes-
sionalising intellectual world.[44] In some respects, of course, later nineteenth-century critiques of classical economics helped to give an impetus
to the formation of separate disciplines (such as sociology, civics, social
work) dealing with the wider social context of economic activity. Mabel
Atkinson's household science was one such. At the same time the revival
of Christian moral philosophy in the last quarter of the century reinforced
an organic and holistic approach to economics as a branch of ethics, as
the Catholic economic philosopher (and admirer of Ruskin) Charles
Devas emphasised.[45] However, each of these developments could in fact
reinforce conceptual distinctions and help to disguise the epistemological
continuities in mainstream economic thought.

Ruskin liked the model of the household precisely because in the
household it was by definition not possible to abstract economic from
social relationships. But this was also what made it a difficult model to
handle. By synecdoche the necessary particularity of the microcosm was
associated with what was held to be the particularism of women's
outlook, which could therefore – as many felt – not have authority in the
wider economic debate. It was an emphasis which was all too easily
reduced to being a ratification of current social practice, rather than suggesting critical ways forward. W. B. Hodgson, educationalist and populariser of political economy, urged the need especially for girls to be
educated in (orthodox) economic principles, to enable them to fulfil
better their roles as consumers and philanthropists.[46] In the
Englishwoman's Journal in the early 1860s Bessie Rayner Parkes wrestled
with this topos in relation to the principles of political economy and the
practice of women's employment and sphere of usefulness. In line with
the broader liberal implications which it carried, she identified herself
with Mill's distinction between economic and social laws, although she
explored some of the practical problems of alignment (especially vis-à-vis

---

[44] See also P. Geddes, *An Analysis of the Principles of Economics* (Edinburgh, 1885); H.
Meller, *Patrick Geddes: Social Evolutionist and City Planner* (New York, 1990).
[45] C. S. Devas, *Political Economy*, Stonyhurst Philosophical Series, 3rd edn (1910; 1st edn,
1892), pp. 661–2.
[46] W. B. Hodgson, *On the Importance of the Study of Economic Science as a Branch of Education
for all Classes* (Edinburgh, 1860), pp. 40–1.

Christianity). She came up against a critical impasse: if theories about masses of men were always being superseded, how much more difficult it was to argue from abstractions upon the nature of women; 'for a woman's life is certainly more individual . . . more centred on one house, one circle'.[47] This again threatened to essentialise and thereby marginalise the conceptual scope of the household. By 1910 Mabel Atkinson was able much more confidently to sustain an argument for the broader implications of the economic relations of the household. In developing a discussion of domestic service, as an example of a little-studied sector of the economy, she suggested some of the reasons for its unpopularity in terms of conditions of work and quality of life. She was unabashed in proclaiming these to be sentimental considerations, which, she said, 'count more decisively with women than with men'.[48] But this message could seem to be being directed particularly at women, when it needed to be reaching men. E. J. Urwick observed in his introduction to a textbook, *Economics, Descriptive and Theoretical* edited by Atkinson and Margaret McKillop, that its approach was fundamental for the creation of a sense of citizenship. But to achieve this it needed to reach the widest possible audience. Because it included material on the household not normally found in economics textbooks, it would appeal to girls; for precisely this reason he would recommend it particularly to young men.[49] In saying this, of course, he was doing no more than laying bare the problem. The markedly British desire to make economics an exact science, with reference to well-established liberal, individualistic, ultimately Protestant assumptions was secure at a theoretical level, despite modifications at the margin. Ruskin's engagement with Xenophon continued to find its specific affinity rather with Catholic economic thought on the continent, where there had never been such a preoccupation with distinguishing the science and art of political economy, or with policing disciplinary boundaries. And Marchant's 1923 Loeb edition of the *Oeconomicus* turned to laughing at Ischomachus for instructing his wife on the virtues of keeping their pots and pans in order.[50]

---

[47] B. R. Parkes, 'Social Economy' in *Essays on Women's Work* (1865), pp. 219–20; cf. *Englishwoman's Journal*, 12 (1863), pp. 73–80. See also J. Rendall, '"A Moral Engine"? Feminism, Liberalism and the *Englishwoman's Journal*' in J. Rendall, ed., *Equal or Different: Women's Politics 1800–1914* (Oxford, 1987).

[48] Atkinson, 'The Economic Relations of the Household', p. 187.

[49] M. McKillop and M. Atkinson, *Economics, Descriptive and Theoretical* (London, 1911), pp. xi–xiii.

[50] *Xenophon in Seven Volumes. Volume IV: Memorabilia and Oeconomicus*, with an English translation by E. C. Marchant (Cambridge, Mass. and London, 1979; reprint of 1923 edn), p. xxvi. Marchant figured Ischomachus as Xenophon, and 'the little lady' (a phrase which captures well the tone of the translation) as his wife Philesia. Marchant's reading of the text as a whole was literalistic and patronisingly dismissive.

10   State and market in British university history

Sheldon Rothblatt

I

The historian's function is often that of restoring complexity to a past reality which some bold and excessively binary conceptual scheme has made too simple. In the present case, the conceptual villains are the terms 'state' and 'market', and the reality in question is the understanding of the development of British universities, principally in the early and mid-nineteenth century. The long reign of interventionist government in Britain, as elsewhere in Europe after 1945, effectively postponed critical discussion of the role which markets played, and continued to play, in shaping the patterns of higher education. The dramatic reversals of this policy in the course of the 1980s made it too easy for academics in Britain in particular to speak as though a long and uninterrupted, and largely benign, relationship between the state and 'its' universities had been rudely shattered by a wholly new insistence on introducing the play of market forces. Both the earlier orthodoxy and the more recent response tended to tell the story in over-simple terms; in particular, both worked with a reified and unhistorical notion of the opposition between 'state' and 'market' as fixed and mutually exclusive terms. This essay seeks to provide a more nuanced account of their reciprocal relationships during a key period in the shaping of universities in Britain.

In reality, the idea of the market, and of markets themselves, are relevant to any discussion of what has been termed the disintegration of the Georgian 'confessional state' in the early nineteenth century. This was followed by a long period of the re-shaping of the instruments of government in accordance with the presumed temper and spirit of the age. The variety of intellectual responses which this development provoked has been the subject of numerous recent studies focusing on such figures as the Coleridgeans, the Philosophic Radicals, the classical economists,

I want to record at the outset my indebtedness to Donald Withrington of Aberdeen University. His writings on Scottish university history and our conversations have heavily contributed to the ideas expressed in this essay.

224

political and economic liberals, Tory paternalists, and various lines of evolutionary Whiggism (several of these studies have been by contributors to this and its companion volume, *History, Religion, and Culture,* notably, of course, by Donald Winch and John Burrow themselves, but also by others such as Boyd Hilton and William Thomas). Some of these studies allude to the polarity between government, understood as the higher authority responsible for the success and health of the nation, and markets, seen as an impersonal means of distributing positional goods. The argument of this essay is to confirm that while such polarities were undoubtedly a prominent feature of Victorian intellectual history, there remains a second narrative involving a national debate on the university's obligations to society that led unexpectedly to a partnership between government and markets. Furthermore, it was this different and apparently unlikely alliance that provided a new but secular legitimacy to government in an age when liberal anti-statism appeared to be in the ascendancy.

Words like 'government' or 'state' are for the purposes of this essay useful abstractions. The effective instruments of government or the state are manifold and multifarious: the crown, the privy council, the cabinet, parliament, political parties or groupings, the civil service, the judiciary, local and regional governments. All can and have been written about as separate agencies and actors. A wholly faithful account of government activity in the nineteenth century would have to reflect the interdependencies and even rivalries that existed among these constituent elements of Britain's polity.[1] Clearly such an account cannot be managed within the parameters of a single chapter. But these complexities should be borne in mind.

Simply stated, a market is an arena in which negotiation and exchange take place. Thus viewed, the market is amoral (therefore an ethical problem for some thinkers). It does not 'dictate' the terms of accommodation, although each party to a negotiation will attempt to influence the outcome in its own favour. The great theorist of the market, Adam Smith, warned against all monopolies, including the university's domination of educational markets. (He was at one in this respect with other members of Dr Johnson's celebrated London 'Club', such as Edward Gibbon.) 'Monopolists very seldom make good work', he wrote, 'and a lecture which a certain number of students must attend, whether they profit by it

---

[1] For example, the different role that parliament and the privy council played in the early history of the London University. See Sheldon Rothblatt and Martin Trow, 'Government Policies and Higher Education: A Comparison of Britain and the United States, 1630–1860', in Colin Crouch and Anthony Heath, eds., *Social Research and Social Reform: Essays in Honour of A. H. Halsey* (Oxford, 1992), pp. 193–4.

or no, is certainly not very likely to be a good one.'[2] Exchanges can be complicated. One side, even if it does not suffer from a disadvantage, may grow weary of haggling, and both may be operating within larger cultural constraints such as those long ago termed the 'moral economy' in which custom and the customary determination of value play a major role.

II

At the beginning of the nineteenth century there were two university systems in operation in Britain, each providing different models for structure, curriculum, financing, and governance. The English model had evolved on a collegiate basis, a form of higher education once common and to be found in Scotland, but by 1800 Scottish higher education was no longer collegiate or centred on tutorial teaching ('regenting') but professorial, although this took several forms. In general, the two senior universities of England were similar in organisation and ethos, if not exactly in curricular emphasis, but the four or five Scottish universities contained differences that were the subject of Scottish educational debate (Aberdeen and Marischal were not joined until mid-century to form a single University of Aberdeen). The numbers going on to higher education in both parts of the kingdom were tiny by mass education standards (usually defined as about 15 per cent of the eligible student age cohort), but the issue that divided them was not so much the size of the student population in attendance as the question of potential access as measured by cost and social class. Recent work reiterates on a general scale what has long been known from the history of Oxford and Cambridge, that in the early-modern period universities were invaded by, and increasingly catered to, the richest students from the best, often landed, families, introducing or reinforcing class and status distinctions that had been present if in different forms in the medieval university.[3] Furthermore, it is very likely that in the middle ages the vast majority of low-income students, if they entered universities at all, remained for usually no longer than a year.

The existence of a wealthy student population in England had consequences that have been much discussed in historical writings: a low level of academic achievement, poor discipline, extravagance, and disregard for the importance of degrees since they were not considered essential for

---

[2] Adam Smith to William Cullen, 20 September 1774, in Letter 143, *Correspondence of Adam Smith*, ed. E. C. Mossner and I. S. Ross (Oxford, 1987), p. 174. I am indebted to Donald Winch for this reference.
[3] Maria Rosa de Simone, 'Admission', in *A History of the University in Europe*, II, ed. Hilde de Ridder-Symoens, (Cambridge, 1996), pp. 312–16.

subsequent careers. While not in a majority, bloods and wastrels by their very presence invariably influenced the general educational environment, especially in an age when clerical preferment often depended upon, or was presumed to depend upon, good connections with families of rank and privilege. In order to reach another student population, and at the same time to alter the prevailing atmosphere of academic indifference, late Georgian dons became increasingly interested in meritocratic policies replacing, or supplementing, an 'internal' measure of worth ('character') with an external one. Competition for recognition entered Oxford and Cambridge. Scholarship and prize competitions, rankings, later fellowship examinations were recognised by contemporaries as a fundamental shift in how personal relationships were to be assessed. Were these introductions a supply-side innovation, best understood as such, market probes to see if the new educational product would sell? The history of the Cambridge tripos and the Oxford honours schools suggests as much. The numbers of examination-takers in what had been introduced as a voluntary system rose only slowly in the early nineteenth century, indicating soft demand. The supply initiatives were therefore of a trial and error variety, testing the effects of parental wishes, prior schooling, expectations, and cost.

Over the last twenty years evidence has accumulated that indicates a very substantial set of market factors operating within the educational parameters of the unreformed college system.[4] The absence of certain decisive constraints on curricular choice in the eighteenth century – viz. low completion rates indicating the inutility of a degree, perfunctory examinations at college and university level, a stratified social system of ascribed ranks and purchasable privileges, and an unsettled network of secondary feeder schools – led to a subsidiary or unofficial system of course selection and instruction. Undergraduates were relatively free to attend professorial lectures of interest to them without concern for the consequences of final Schools examinations. The most important feature of the teaching of the unreformed collegiate university was an extensive programme of private instruction or coaching, generally described by historians as a nuisance and a corrupting influence on academic standards, not to mention an outright scandal since students were virtually required to pay twice for instruction. But in this instance there can be little doubt that coaching was a market response, demand-led, providing undergraduates with a variety of needed (or imagined) assistance. Coaching had other virtues. Young teachers were energised and gained experience.

[4] Lucy Sutherland brought attention to many of them, and plentiful examples now appear in the new history of Oxford University. See L. S. Sutherland and L. G. Mitchell, eds., *The History of the University of Oxford* (Oxford, 1986), V, esp. chs. 15–20.

Experiments occurred in tutorial instruction, and friendships formed between teacher and taught. Some coaching activity was related to the examinations culture growing up first in Cambridge, but some of it was not so much 'coaching' as private instruction in subjects not offered in the regular curriculum, for example, modern languages or certain branches of experimental science. The colleges were confused by this development, attempting to stop the practice while also arranging for precisely such supplementary instruction to please parents. But they also saw that private instruction utilised surplus labour and drained off the potential discontent of otherwise unemployable Fellows.

Simultaneously, especially after 1790, a student sub-culture arose and flourished, producing many of the extra-curricular features for which university student cultures have since become known, such as clubs, societies, intellectual sets, reading parties and recreational as well as competitive sports. All the indications are that these activities at the universities arose from below.[5] In the schools extra-curricular activities, also originating from below, or imported through pupil channels from rural sports and pastimes, were nevertheless appropriated for other purposes. J. A. Mangan demonstrated some time ago that in the public schools athleticism in the nineteenth century was encouraged from above, by headmasters, who saw a chance to strengthen school loyalties and attachments and accordingly advertise their wares to parents in search of suitable schooling.[6]

Some forty years ago Nicholas Hans[7] called attention to the spread of private schooling in the late Enlightenment, much of which, as we know from him but also from prior writings on the educational activities of the denominational Protestants, was a reaction to the grammar school monopolies maintained by the Church of England. The usual response of historians to the quarrels that marked grammar school history – the charges of financial misdealings, poor management, the misappropriation of scholarships, the entrepreneurial activities of masters, particularly with regard to taking boarders who were not on the foundation – has been Whiggish. The grammar schools, it is argued, were as unreformed and

[5] Sheldon Rothblatt, *The Revolution of the Dons: Cambridge and Society in the Nineteenth Century* (London, 1968; reprinted Cambridge, 1982); Rothblatt, *The Modern University and its Discontents: The Fate of Newman's Legacy in Britain and America* (Cambridge, 1997), ch. 3. In the 1850s the *British Quarterly* argued the case for increasing not curtailing private tuition at the ancient universities on the grounds that curricular innovation would be encouraged. See W. R. Ward, 'From the Tractarians to the Executive Commission, 1845–1854', in M. G. Brock and M. C. Curthoys, eds., *The History of the University of Oxford* (Oxford: Clarendon Press, 1997), VI, part 1, pp. 319–20.
[6] J. A. Mangan, *Athleticism in the Victorian and Edwardian Public School* (Cambridge, 1981), pp. 74ff.
[7] Nicholas Hans, *New Trends in Education in the Eighteenth Century* (London, 1951).

subject to personal mismanagement as the universities and simply in need of a drastic overhaul.

Undoubtedly abuses were rampant. But it also appears that market opportunities were available. Masters (and trustees) saw a chance to improve their incomes by offering curricular choices that may well have been outside their statutory mandates but not expressly forbidden, taking advantage therefore of changing local markets for education and trying to bypass antiquated restrictions. Private schools proliferated. Most of them were of uncertain and brief tenure, with an unsteady clientele as parents of a great variety of income levels searched for institutional forms of instruction to complement or duplicate education received at home or through tutors. But they were formidable competition for the grammar schools, which followed their lead, introducing subjects such as modern languages, accounting, history, geography, or mechanical drawing.[8] One cannot say too strongly how important the open market for lower forms of education was in the eighteenth century and how differentiated that market was, corresponding to every level of taste, religion, and family circumstance.[9]

Market response helps us account for the confusion between higher and lower forms of education before the middle of the nineteenth century. Universities, in need of student fees, simply accepted all comers. Historians of English and Scottish (and American) education have long been aware of the unsteady line dividing secondary from tertiary. Extraordinary overlap existed, to such a degree that in Scotland (and again America) the lexical differences between 'school' and 'university' or 'college' were almost non-existent. Indeed, age overlap had been the reigning situation for centuries and was embedded in the circumstances that led to the rise and development of the medieval university. The 'lower faculties' which featured the seven liberal arts, the mathematical and language emphases of the trivium and quadrivium, were really of secondary level, attracting teenagers who for the most part never finished a first degree. The 'superior faculties' for professional education were reserved for those who had the financial means, sponsorship, or class standing permitting a longer stay at university, with the reward (for some) of entry into liberal occupations. The age spread in British universities, combining schoolboys with undergraduates reaching maturity, was a standing disciplinary problem for Scottish and English universities until well into the nineteenth century; and only Oxford and Cambridge, experiencing a rise in age of entry throughout the eighteenth century, managed to reduce the spread. Nevertheless, the level of teaching in the

---

[8] Rothblatt, *Dons*, p. 37.   [9] Rothblatt, *Modern University*, ch. 6.

colleges did not automatically adjust and failed to recognise that the standard of elite secondary schooling was improving. One of the constant complaints of students at Oxford and Cambridge in the second third of the nineteenth century was that college tuition resembled the drill and discipline of school, meaning usually the reforming grammars and improving public schools. Oxbridge tutors were in many cases slow to respond to the challenges presented by undergraduates who arrived with better preparation than earlier. But this indicates how accustomed the colleges were to working with the academic materials normally available to them. There was little standardisation of academic norms in the schools or in the other modes of educational provision available, no agreed-upon entrance examination, with masters of colleges and tutors admitting on a variety of criteria, not necessarily fully academic, and in general allowing demand for access to determine supply.

The issue of market-related higher education broke open with the controversies surrounding the formation of the London University in the 1820s. This galvanised the Oxbridge monopoly as almost no recent issue had done; and the polemical controversies that ensued suggest the first public acknowledgement in England of the challenges of market-driven higher education. Every historic precedent had been apparently violated. First, the new university was 'godless'. It lay outside the obedience of the Church of England and was non-denominational, even admitting Jews (they had been instrumental in the new foundation's creation). Second, the university founders were cost conscious and defined a catchment area for the university that suited commuters and obviated the necessity for expensive accommodations. Third, the main thrust of the curriculum was 'applied', that is to say, preparation for medical careers. Furthermore, extensive provision was made for flexibility in timetabling, remedial instruction, and special tutoring where needed, indicating both the strength of the consumer but also the continuing uncertainties of prior schooling. This latter led to a decision to create a feeder school, a strategic decision that would be typical of new foundations both in England and in the United States. A fourth indication of an appeal to markets was the decision, in keeping with the non-residential character of the institution, to avoid imposing any particular discipline on the conduct of undergraduates outside the classroom (and often enough, in the case of medical students, not very much within it). So flagrant were these violations of the historic understanding of a university that the next major battle would be over the definition of a 'university' itself, which came in 1836 with the privy council decision to create a 'royal university' empowered, in a peculiar historical decision, to establish degree-granting examinations while leaving non-degree instruction to constituent colleges and programmes. A later reform opened examinations to virtually anyone, anywhere, bypassing the teaching colleges and placing the burden of preparation entirely upon the shoulders of the degree-seeker. (The strongest controversies of the last decades of the nineteenth century were over the establishment of a 'teaching university', that is, one in which the 'providers' of education in the colleges would control the examination system.) Thus at the outset the constituent colleges were denied the one feature that strengthened their control over educational demand. We do not as yet have a very good understanding of when and how degrees became important in the nineteenth century, since degree-takers at Oxford and Cambridge remained relatively few in number until much later. But we must assume that they were reasonably important for the communities that the first London colleges served, especially since medical education and medical standards had emerged as an important professional and social consideration.

A battle was joined, issuing in an interesting compromise between the forces of supply and demand, with the state assuming a new and apparently unfamiliar role as a regulator of academic standards. The state imposed itself on a long-developing and quite extensively organised educational consumer culture extending from every level of education upwards, from the most modest charitable schools for the poor, to various forms of popular and vocational education, secondary schools at many pricing levels and a new institution brazenly referred to by its founders as a 'university' – actually a university college but with a medical school. Educational markets had proved themselves to be extremely volatile, featuring, at lower levels, numerous short-term experiments. The Protestant dissenting academies, at one time almost regarded as a serious threat to the Oxbridge monopoly – although they never could be – did not last much into the new century. The fortunes of the few that did survive have been the subject of new studies, with Mansfield College becoming part of the Oxford federation of colleges in our own day.[10]

The London pattern was employed in Ireland and in the newer foundations of the nineteenth century (except Durham), the regional or civic universities, all established by private initiative (although in some cases with help from Oxford and other universities), but with such variations as seemed suitable to founders and supporters. All were subsequently grouped into an examining university (except Birmingham, founded as a 'unitary' university), which was a major step in detaching them from local control, weakening local boards of trustees, pushing them into the twentieth-century category of 'national' universities and allowing the vacated spaces to be occupied by non-university polytechnics.

---

[10] Elaine Kaye, *Mansfield College Oxford: Its Origin, History and Significance* (Oxford, 1996).

But one of the most interesting parts of this development, hitherto dominated by accounts of what happened in England, is the Scottish story, for what occurred in Scotland, as explained in a recent analysis by Donald Withrington, anticipated the English outcome with respect to the role of the state. The Scottish situation beautifully illustrates the relationship between supply and demand in university history. It explains why exclusive reliance on markets was problematical when viewed from the perspective of the leaders and shapers of higher education.[11] The London story was really in crucial respects the Scottish story. Indeed, scoffers were not unaware of this, accusing the godless London University (whose prop and support was Lord Brougham, the flamboyant Edinburgh lawyer and one of the original Edinburgh Reviewers) of being a Scottish colony in the metropolis.

The social and educational differences between the two university systems were the subject of an odd attack initiated from Edinburgh that has been much written about in university history. It is an 'odd' attack because despite the attention of historians it has not yet been clearly explained just what the Scottish professors and intellectuals had to gain from encouraging a national debate among the British elite on the purposes and meaning of a university education. The timing of the attack, however, seems to be correct, for by 1800 Scottish intellectual and academic achievements were sufficiently renowned throughout Europe to provide the confidence necessary to initiate a kingdom-wide controversy. The formation of a body of Scottish thought around ideas of progress provided Scotland with a historical explanation for its emergence as a modern and enlightened nation.[12] And the Scottish university communities could with justification claim that they had a major and decisive role in shaping the structure and curriculum of North American colleges and universities. The oldest of them, Harvard, had embraced the Scottish School of Common Sense in the early nineteenth century.

A central issue was the curriculum, broader and less specialised in Scotland, more general and philosophical, as George Elder Davie argued in a controversial book.[13] It was acknowledged that Scottish undergraduates did not receive as much of a classical education as they might, but also that the Scottish version was not so exclusively language-based (hence, given the technical character of linguistic concentration, not as 'rigorous'). In return it was asserted that English undergraduate studies

---

[11] Donald Withrington, 'Ideas and Ideals in University Reform in Early Nineteenth Century Britain: A Scottish Perspective', forthcoming in *The European Legacy*.
[12] See the essays by Nicholas Phillipson and Dario Castiglione in this volume.
[13] George Elder Davie, *The Democratic Intellect: Scotland and Her Universities in the Nineteenth Century* (Edinburgh, 1961).

were narrow and thus constraining. The second issue was access. A special Scottish mythology was drawn upon relating to the poor boy or the 'lad o' pairts' coming up from the parishes with the help of an effective ladder system of education.[14] While the opportunity system may not have been quite as pronounced as Scottish pride maintained, it was nevertheless true that the higher education delivery system was flexible and provided scope for remedial education. While the issue of standards did not figure prominently in the fight between the Oxford and Scottish debaters, partly because the Oxford honours schools examinations had not yet become widespread enough for an argument from quality to be utterly convincing, it was sufficiently present to break out at any time.

In the Scottish system of higher education, as in the English, degrees were not universally important in the early nineteenth century. Partly for this reason, but partly as a tactic to disarm establishment opposition, the founders of the London University had initially downplayed their interest in degree-giving. The prevailing attitude in Scotland was very much what one would encounter in the United States in much of the nineteenth century, namely, that some higher education was better than none at all and those whose means or situation prevented the pursuit of a degree should nevertheless be given ample opportunity to make choices. The common Oxbridge view was that degrees were only useful occupationally. For those whose livelihood was secure, a few years away from home provided a valuable 'public' residential experience well designed to serve the interests of a governing elite. By contrast, Scottish students were free to find their own accommodations at cost levels suitable to their purses and to drop out or in as they desired. Curricular adjustments, to include remedial education, were made by professors, and supplementary instruction was available for a fee (as in the English universities). So while Oxbridge students were socialised away from family and locality as part of an elite rite of passage, Scottish students remained connected to a wider Scottish populace.

Discipline tightened at Oxford and Cambridge during the period of the French Revolution and its aftermath, university authorities attempting to placate widespread outside disapproval of undergraduate conduct through greater college supervision. But Scottish academics were generally indifferent to the total life of their students, including their religious practices; and such lassitude, or apostasy, was insupportable from an Oxbridge perspective. But then Scotland did not profess to have an elite system of education aimed at socialising the future social and political

[14] David A. R. Forrester, 'The "Lad o' Pairts": A Study of the Literary Myth', in Jennifer Carter and Donald Withrington, eds., *Scottish Universities, Distinctiveness and Diversity* (Edinburgh, 1992), pp. 156–62.

leaders of society but rather one, which, while not yet in any sense a mass access system, was nevertheless obviously 'national' in its objectives. Scotland was an economically poor society whose future lay, according to those who managed its educational provision, with its brain power. It was a socially stratified society but hardly as divided as England. Its puritan, democratic heritage fought against the kind of exclusivity known south of the Tweed.

It would appear that Scotland's market-related university system was perfectly suited to the character of its society, and that a high dropout percentage and low degree acquisition rate were not particular concerns as long as entry for the worthy and striving was available. And yet it was precisely the Scottish universities that were the first subject of inquiry by a reform-minded royal commission and the Scottish universities that were first to feel the potential authority of the state. We must therefore join Withrington in looking further into what seems to be the paradox of a successful university system (successful in its historic aims and maintenance of a social contract), bold enough to attack the richer universities to the south, but subject to sufficient criticism to call into being the first university royal commission of the new century.

The first solution to the paradox (a point made with some force by Robert Anderson[15]) is that the Scottish crown had long possessed a financial interest in the financing of the universities, as well as in the system of parish schools. While professorial income derived largely from student fees, it was topped up by subventions from the crown, which also funded new chairs and buildings and maintained the old. No one apparently disputed the right of the crown to intervene in education in the national interest, and the crown had being doing so more or less since the beginning of the nineteenth century, if not earlier. The real point, therefore, was not the proper role of governments in formulating, or enforcing through royal visitation, higher education policy decisions, but the basis on which intervention was authorised. Was there a problem – that is to say, a problem common to all the Scottish universities, since there were major differences between them regarding professorial commitments to teaching – large enough to warrant intrusion from the centre?

The perceived problem was governance, and this was the same problem that would arise later with respect to Oxford and Cambridge, where administrative hierarchies, the Hebdomadal Council in the first and the Caput in the second, were unyielding barriers to continuous adaptation as new circumstance might require. Governance was also an

---

[15] R. D. Anderson, *Education and Opportunity in Victorian Scotland: Schools and Universities* (Oxford, 1983), appendix II.

issue that led to the establishment of the Royal University of London in 1836, with its body of Fellows empowered to administer examinations as the cheapest means for regulating the curriculum of the colleges. In Scotland it was the professorial-run senates that were singled out as oligarchical culprits. Consequently, the first step leading to outside investigation was the withdrawal of faith in the professors and their depiction as a closed guild that turned a national trust into a vested interest. In this environment, the office of rector, an elected position dominated by the professoriate, received a new stimulus for the exercise of its historic visitorial authority.

One major and revolutionary consequence of the recommendations contained in the Royal Commission report of 1830 was to transfer senate powers over financial matters to regional communities acting as 'university courts'. But this was done with regard to the market basis of much Scottish education. From an elite perspective, the most vulnerable part of the Scottish university system was the large numbers of occasional students who purchased what they needed but never completed the requirements for a degree. And while this was a concern of reformers, especially in the context of a quarrel with the English system over 'standards', beyond attempting reforms that might make the degree course more attractive, no interference with traditional demand-led opportunities was envisioned. Such a course would have meant imposing rising fees for a student population without adequate means. The crown itself did not at this juncture in history entertain the possibility of providing wide-scale subsidies for truly penurious students (as in the senior universities of England, bursaries did exist). It was certainly not the mood of the first half of the nineteenth century to encourage anything that might approach mass levels of access, not from a sense that such would be undesirable but from a (realistic) appreciation of the limited market demand for degree-level work. However, present or future demand needed to be met with enhanced opportunities and allowed to seek its own levels by a policy guaranteeing popular admission. Universities needed to have the flexibility to adopt policies in accord with clearly expressed public sentiment. To do so meant discarding the accumulated *ancien régime* baggage, even at the expense of established churches, which had in fact happened in Scotland and was eventually to happen in England.[16] This kind of educational policy was, therefore, akin in higher education to what would become known as the 'imperialism of free trade': the elimination of monopoly supports, agencies, and institutions.

A new era of Scottish history now commenced, being preceded by a

---

[16] Withrington, 'Ideas and Ideals'.

decade or more of vigorous discussions of Scottish national identity, dependent, as such discussions normally are, on contrasting North Britain with the dominant culture to the south. The Act of Union left a legacy of weak government but strong family and communal institutions: a reluctance, for example, to eliminate outdoor relief or subject it to strong central supervision. 'From Highlands to borders, the middle ranks of Scotland learnt to distrust the aristocratic families which ran the state.'[17] Yes, but those same middle (or middling) ranks, however they regarded their aristocratic superiors, were not necessarily supporters of a non-interventionist liberal state. They still expected that government would assist their universities when circumstances were right, and they still believed that a body of royal commissioners would understand that in Scotland access to universities was a critical historical feature of Scottish culture and social policy.

Historical analogies are rarely precise, and they are often misleading. But they can also be interesting in drawing our attention to certain main lines of development. Government policy towards education in the second third of the nineteenth century can be described in present-day terms as a form of privatisation, putting institutions more at the mercy of markets while reserving the right to re-intervene should the outcomes surprise the ultimate holders of a nation's purse-strings.[18] It was expected that higher education change would in this way produce a differentiated system of college and university instruction, each type of institution catering to different demand sectors. This is indeed what occurred up to a point (that point would need elaboration outside the scope of this essay). It was occurring very explicitly in such enterprises as the Woodard schools, whose founder created different types of schools for different social class categories. He did so not to perpetuate class divisions but to recognise market realities.[19] The outcome may be the same but the reasons are not.

As the historiography of the Victorian university tends to emphasise the role of government, some further reflections on that role are in order, especially in a market connection.

---

[17] R. J. Morris, 'Victorian Values in Scotland and England', in T. C. Smout, ed., *Victorian Values* (Oxford and New York, 1992), pp. 32–41.

[18] The allusion is to certain entrepreneurial activities and funding decisions, policy affecting audit, assessment and research and teaching exercises occupying today's higher education breaking news.

[19] Brian Heeney, *Mission to the Middle Classes: The Woodard Schools 1848–1891* (London, 1969), p. 91. Woodard believed that private initiative should remedy the failure of the Church of England to provide adequate schooling. Troubled by the active role of the state in reforming the ancient universities, he also expressed his fear of where government activity might lead and refused to give evidence to the Taunton Commission.

III

Whether or not the old order died in the year 1832, it is certainly the case that the 'confessional state' subsequently underwent a massive reconstitution. In place of the former oligarchies and collections of placemen, there was a slow but very certain movement to redefine the sources of moral legitimacy in government. Since this could no longer rest on virtual representation, or *noblesse oblige*, we find in those stimulating decades of the early and mid-Victorian period a number of initiatives that would in time produce a new code of legitimacy and a new social contract between governed and governing. Expressions of national interest, a desire for greater involvement in government, and wider civic recognition apparent since at least the 1770s, bubbled up from below, from classes, groups, and regional interests. Some historians have speculated that the state was tempted to exploit that interest in national affairs, enhanced by subsequent wars, better communications, and the intermingling of landed elites from English and Celtic regions. The circumstances were ripe for the formation of a surveillance state and an officially sponsored nationalism. But Linda Colley argues persuasively against this view. There was no compelling reason, she maintains, to exploit national attachments. On the contrary, there was every reason to avoid doing so, at least before the 1830s. Enthusiasm might easily get out of hand (a long-standing fear).[20]

Yet public interest in the affairs of state was strong, if not always specific or unified, and the public's desire for inclusion, its demand to be consulted or informed was met by the creation of what Oz Frankel has called an 'information culture'. Examining the means and methods by which commissions of inquiry created or helped create such a 'culture', he notes in detail how eager were the new bureaucrats or proto-bureaucrats to involve public opinion in their investigations of social abuses. Their techniques were many and varied and are marked by a singular openness. Meetings were announced well in advance, agents were sent into the field to encourage attendance, questionnaires and opinion-taking were standard, and site visits were reported in vivid detail to give both a sense of fact and verisimilitude. Obscure working-class communities – obscure to middle-income readership – figured prominently in the reports, much as Henry Mayhew and the social investigators of the mid-Victorian period acquainted incredulous readers, as do anthropologists, with the bizarre habits and lives of East Enders. A variety of rhetorical forms were employed in the writing of reports to make them as popular as a Dickens

---

[20] Linda Colley, 'Whose Nation? Class and National Consciousness in Britain 1750–1830', *Past and Present*, 113 (November 1986), pp. 103–9, 117.

novel, even to rescue reports from bureaucratic oblivion by bestowing upon them the authority of authorship and personality.[21] Condensed accounts, newspaper versions and cheap forms of publication, as well as mailing lists, were used in order to gain the widest dissemination and to build up public support for potential legislation. In sum, public knowledge of events was regarded as a critical step in solving social problems and in promoting a conception of public knowledge itself.[22] There were to be no claims about the mysteries of governance in high places.

One motive was to provide a moral basis for a state separating from its religious arm. A major side effect of this extensive, well-publicised activity was to encourage nationwide sentiment by incorporating accounts of regional and district behaviour in documents issued from a central authority in the metropolis. The centre, in other words, absorbed the provinces. In a sharp and focused analysis, Gary Cox has also maintained that regionalism was one casualty of franchise reform, while arguing a corroborating point with respect to the role of opinion in the creation of new instruments of governance. In his view, the evolution of cabinet government was virtually forced upon politicians by an electorate twice enlarged through reform acts. Redistricting, as well as the expanded franchise, broke the hold that the political class held over the hustings. Voters as well as politicians seemed to prefer party labels as a guide to the casting of votes and the channelling of opinion. Cox maintains that the enfranchised took the initiative and 'chose' party to discipline cabinet and parliament.[23] Perhaps voters too, from some instinctual sense, feared the anarchy that might ensue from a parliament that was a collection of independent private members and a cabinet that was really little more than a loosely organised committee. Cabinet government therefore was not just the creation of the career politicians who needed to consolidate executive authority in the wake of a decline in the powers of royal government. Neither was it a response to the chaos of the 'golden age of parliament' when party discipline was so weak that voting outcomes could not be predicted and MPs exhausted one another with endless speeches in efforts at persuasion (and grandstanding). It was the logical derivative of voter preference, if expressed unevenly. But this is how voting in a representative democracy works. Voters constitute a market, and votes are cultivated in that market (even purchased!) by candidates offering their attributes as

---

[21] Richard Selleck's biography of one such well-known proto-bureaucrat captures the tone of the new generation with panache. See his *James Kay-Shuttleworth: Journey of an Outsider* (Ilford, Essex, 1994).

[22] Oz Frankel, 'Reporting Society: Royal Commissions of Inquiry and the Culture of Social Investigation in Early-Victorian Britain', forthcoming in *The European Legacy*.

[23] Gary W. Cox, *The Efficient Secret: The Cabinet and the Development of Political Parties in Victorian England* (Cambridge, 1987).

products. (Edmund Burke said attributes were sufficient, but we remember that his Bristol address was occasioned by the electors actually demanding a legislative commitment.)

This is another example of the intricate connection between a market for products and services and the actual or potential suppliers. And to make a similar point with another example, turn-of-the-century students at Oxford and Cambridge were not explicitly demanding more and better examinations, and more discipline, and more academic work in a period when the dons were often perplexed by a new style of undergraduate. But many of the best students indicated, by their conduct and initiatives, even if indirect, that they were interested in a richer and more stimulating as well as more varied collegiate experience. They also indicated by their conduct that they were capable of a high degree of self-management and self-regulation and would not, as did another part of the student population, resent competition as a spur to and measure of achievement. The question for the dons was how to read and interpret undergraduate conduct and how to use it as a basis for the introduction of measures consistent with their own academic definitions.

IV

Moral legitimacy could no longer reside on a basis of confession. From the late 1820s right on through to Jewish emancipation in the 1850s and 1860s, church and state had become increasingly differentiated, the church reviving its own ecclesiastical parliament and Broad Churchmen searching for new forms of unity. The retreat from a historic union had proceeded in piecemeal fashion. It is false to assume that it proceeded without difficulties. Indeed, the quarrels and disagreements were fundamental and critical, protracted and detailed, but the sequence of events, seen in hindsight, was relentless. The removal of political disabilities for dissenters ended the Anglican hegemony; the emancipation of the Roman Catholics ended the Protestant ascendancy, and the entrance of Jews into political life effectively terminated the Christian constitution. En route, Anglican defenders of a historic alliance managed to retain certain advantages, so that it was not until 1835 that dissenters were allowed to marry without undergoing an Anglican ceremony. Church rates, used to maintain parish churches, were not abolished until 1868. University Tests, oaths of subscription to the Thirty-Nine Articles at Oxford and Cambridge, did not end until 1871; and compulsory chapel lingered on in certain colleges, certainly in the newly founded Anglican colleges of Selwyn and Keble.

As we might expect, the end of a Christian constitution was especially contested. Jewish emancipation, as David Feldman argues, was played out against a larger concern for the nature of the constitution and the definition of citizenship in a state responsive to an electorate that had increased beyond historical comprehension and was no longer effectively paired with an established church. It was agreed that the moral basis of the state had to be recreated but on a national basis. How then to define 'nation' and moral obligations? For example, if Jews were to become citizens (and not merely 'subjects'), would they use public recognition to retain a particular kind of exclusivity and communalism – a matter of concern to any number of debaters – or would they agree to become 'British' and cease (except privately) to be 'Jewish'?[24] But the same issue could arise with respect to Scotland and Ireland, and with regard to non-Anglicans generally. In other words, the plural basis of Victorian society was not so sufficiently established in constitutional theory, or in the culture of the governing elite, that questions concerning the unity of the state could be disregarded.

These remarks lead the way to a consideration of how the universities themselves were implicated in the reformulation of establishment institutions. Once again we are led to the thought that the Scottish universities are the key to understanding subsequent developments. Their quarrel with the 'English' universities, begun in the new literary–political periodicals of the century, started a public discussion that carried on until – until when? Until a state-supported higher education system emerged largely at the behest of the universities in the twentieth century. This battle spilled over the kingdom's boundaries into the empire and into the American higher education system, so deeply influenced by Scots in the eighteenth century, where in the next century, and thereafter, universities (derived from Scotland) and liberal arts colleges (derived from England) competed for the right to define an undergraduate education appropriate for a republic.

The Scottish universities, not nearly so religiously exclusive as Oxford and Cambridge, in cooperation with the royal commissioners, had legitimated the idea of a university with limited allegiance to established religions. Well might the ancient university regime worry about Scottish influence over English universities. Every new university of the century except Durham was Scottish in teaching and curricula (even the Anglican King's College in London). Flexible admissions criteria, low cost, professorial rather than expensive tutorial instruction, broader curricula with provision for the introduction of new 'modern' or 'practical' subjects were

---

[24] David Feldman, *Englishmen and Jews: Social Relations and Political Culture 1840–1914* (New Haven and London, 1994), pp. 19–48, 353–78.

standard features. A counter-strategy of conservative academic opinion formed in response to attempts to prevent a non-denominational London University from having a degree capability. Its primary effort was to differentiate colleges from universities. A 'college' was to be considered 'private', and as a private institution it would be free to exact an Anglican obedience from students and Fellows, leaving only universities as 'godless'. John Henry Newman followed the history of the London University with anger and resentment. In his autobiography he denounced the penetration of liberal ideologies and religious toleration into the collegiate quadrangles. On the basis of this closely regarded past, he constructed his 'idea' of a university.[25]

The strategy to preserve colleges as private enclaves of ecclesiastical loyalty and obedience failed. The state demanded the right to revise Oxbridge collegiate statutes to placate liberal public opinion, opening many if not all closed scholarships and fellowships and, in several stages, removing religious oaths and tests and other barriers to matriculation, graduation, and the tenure of fellowships. College finances were rendered more flexible as binding statutes were invaded by the state's power to revise fiduciary arrangements. So, as in Scotland, the state had recognised the 'just' complaints of the excluded, and had made it possible for the universities, with the aid of a more imaginative use of resources, to interpret demand and supply education in ways consistent with changing academic values. Despite state intervention, the ancient universities were now more autonomous in the disposition of their income than ever before.

The universities were on their way, their slow way to be sure, to what George Marsden has recently called 'established unbelief'.[26] The fights over public sector schooling in the 1870s were warning enough of how a religious war could paralyse the universities. Scholars are familiar with the stories of eminent Victorians who became agnostics yet maintained a continuous interest in the possibility of supernatural intervention through 'psychical research'. But that was a side issue; and by 1900 leading intellectuals and writers of another generation could not comprehend this last and desperate effort to prove the existence of the Unknown. A more universal issue for the universities was how to define the national interest, how to support a struggling conception of the nation-state through teaching and scholarly inquiry. The answers varied. One answer lay in the writings of philosophical Idealists particularly strong at *fin-de-siècle* Oxford. The Arnoldians (and Leavisites later) spoke of 'culture'. Yet another response could be found at the newly established London School

---

[25] Rothblatt, *Modern University*, chs. 1 and 5.
[26] George M. Marsden, *The Soul of the American University: From Protestant Establishment to Established Unbelief* (Oxford and New York, 1994).

Sheldon Rothblatt

of Economics with its mission of social amelioration. At Cambridge the teaching of politics migrated from one tripos to another, resisting pressure from the specialists and resolutely remaining a training ground for potential mandarins.[27] Within all universities a continuous and never-ending battle of the books commenced between those subjects serving particular markets and occupations and those professing to take a broader, liberal outlook.

A university needed an 'idea', Newman had once said, a central purpose, as he fearfully watched all such efforts disintegrate in an era of competing ideologies. The universities answered, however, that they had an idea. It lay in the centrality of examinations as a measure of merit, the 'Cambridge or Federal Principle',[28] the junior university's gift to the state but a gift whose growth and success owed much to an emerging 'demand' for quality education. The state, exercising its authority over trusts and endowments, and its visitorial power over internal issues of governance, guaranteed public support for universities.[29] In turn, the universities, knowing that the state would support their newly designed meritocratic policies, bestowed moral authority on government as the ultimate protector of civilisation. Dickens had summoned up the terrifying portrait of the Scottish schoolmaster, M'Choakumchild, slaughterer of the innocents, armed with the cruel weapons of educational utility and market economics. The images, and the denunciation of utilitarians by romantics of which Donald Winch writes, have lasted until our own day.[30] Yet there is another Scottish tale, equally imaginative but based on a far different set of historical materials and featuring an alliance between state and market. The example of the Scottish royal commissioners resonated throughout university–state relations until the state, prodded by the universities for a stronger financial role and itself arriving at a new definition of the national good through interventionist and later collectivist policies, became the sole buyer of university services. The partnership between state and market softened until another new state emerged in the last tumultuous decades of the twentieth century.

---

[27] Stefan Collini, Donald Winch, and John Burrow, *That Noble Science of Politics* (Cambridge, 1983), p. 343.   [28] Rothblatt, *Modern University*, ch. 5.
[29] Ward, 'Executive Commission', p. 319, is astonished that the state was so benign.
[30] Donald Winch's essay in this volume.

11   Mr Gradgrind and Jerusalem

Donald Winch

I

No sympathetic reader of Dickens's *Hard Times* is likely to credit Mr Gradgrind with the ability to build Jerusalem among the dark satanic mills of Coketown. Dickens did not, of course, share William Blake's visions: his own version of Jerusalem would probably have been a cheerier, less corrupt, and more efficient version of the society in which he lived and prospered. Nevertheless, he certainly hoped that the combination of utilitarianism and political economy embodied in the Gradgrind caricature would provide his readers with a thought-provoking statement of the problems of life in the Coketowns of his day.[1] Judging by the legacy of the image he created, Dickens succeeded beyond his own intentions and inclinations.

By inscribing *Hard Times* to Thomas Carlyle – the leading abominator of the worship of Mammon, the scourge of the 'cash nexus' and of the 'dismal science' that appeared to reflect or celebrate these features of modern life – Dickens was aligning himself with a powerful anti-utilitarian current in the debate on the 'condition-of-England' question, another of Carlyle's coinages. He did so effectively enough for John Ruskin, a fellow-admirer of Carlyle, to commend the novel to his own readers when he decided to unmask the fallacies of the *soi-disant* science of political economy in *Unto This Last* (1862).[2] All three authors were still sufficiently

As on many previous occasions, I am grateful for the detailed attention paid to earlier drafts of this essay by Stefan Collini. I am equally grateful for the critical comments of Laurence Lerner and David Pocock.
[1] '[*Hard Times*] contains what I do devoutly hope will shake some people in a terrible mistake of these days, when so presented. I know it contains nothing in which you do not think with me, for no man knows your books better than I.' Letter to Carlyle, 13 July 1854 in *The Letters of Charles Dickens*, 10 vols. (Oxford, 1965–98), VII, p. 367.
[2] '[Dickens] is entirely right in his main drift and purpose in every book he has written; and all of them, but especially *Hard Times*, should be studied with close and earnest care by persons interested in social questions.' First published in *Cornhill Magazine* (1860), and repeated in *Unto This Last* (1862); see *The Works of John Ruskin*, ed. E. T. Cook and A Wedderburn, 39 vols. (London, 1902–12), XVII, p. 31n.

in tune with one another to collaborate in opposing the campaign to pros-
ecute Governor Eyre in 1865–6. The campaign was being mounted by
John Stuart Mill and his 'radical' associates, and it provided Carlyle and
Ruskin with an opportunity to repeat their criticisms of the canting qualities of the science with which Mill's name was then so firmly linked.[3]
Dickens could also describe himself as a 'radical', and yet, as Humphrey
House argued many years ago, there must be some doubt as to how firmly
Dickens can be recruited into any intellectual grouping.[4] Having encapsulated, for his own purposes, the contrast between a utilitarian and what has
come to be thought of as a 'romantic' outlook on life, Dickens was later
found by his coadjutors to be unequal to the task of drawing the right conclusions. Hence Ruskin's mature judgement that Dickens was 'a pure
modernist – a leader of the steam-whistle party *par excellence*'.[5]

This problem invites the attention of the intellectual historian as well as
of the literary scholar. It concerns the power of symbolic representations
to define allegiances and form part of a canon that remains, if only by tireless repetition, a significant part of Our Island Story. Instead of returning
directly to the nineteenth-century schism between Romantics and
Utilitarians, the main focus of this essay will be on the legacy of the
Gradgrind caricature during the second half of the twentieth century. For
it has been via a number of interpreters of that legacy that the original
schism has been transmitted to us, acquiring additional features in the
process. The central figures chosen here to illustrate a highly influential
mode of transmission are F. R. Leavis, Raymond Williams, and Edward
Thompson. Jerusalem can be linked with Gradgrind in their cases
because each of them entertained earthly visions that could only be articulated by returning to the scene of nineteenth-century crimes – crimes of
sentiment as well as intellect of the kind that Dickens sketched, however
inadequately, in *Hard Times*.

Dickens's inadequacy as standard bearer for the causes later associated
with *Hard Times* can be detected in his treatment of Gradgrind himself.
Not only was Dickens prepared to acknowledge the kindly instincts that
lay beneath this 'man of facts and calculation', but he allowed him to
undergo a painful process of redemption. In one of his suspiciously frequent attempts to mollify those who might take the caricature amiss,
Dickens wrote: 'I often say to Mr. Gradgrind that there is reason and
good intention in much that he does – in fact, in all that he does – but that
he over-does it. Perhaps by dint of his going his way and my going mine,

---

[3] 'Radical' was Ruskin's term. For his charges against political economy during the campaign see *Works*, XVIII, pp. 437–45, 550–4.
[4] See Humphrey House, *The World of Dickens*, 2nd edn (Oxford, 1942; reprinted, 1960).
[5] Letter of 19 June 1870 written after Dickens's death: see *Works*, XXXVII, p. 7.

we shall meet at last at some half-way house.'[6] Far less forgiveness, far less willingness to believe that there were *any* half-way houses has been shown by twentieth-century readers who have accepted Gradgrind as the embodiment of a repellent mentality. With this came the catastrophic interpretation of Britain's experience of urban industrialisation, with political economy and utilitarianism being treated as complicit with the worst aspects of this experience. Gradgrind thus became a scapegoat for past errors and a persisting obstacle to any humane conception of a future social order, with the further implication that Jerusalem would be constructed on the high moral ground that stood above vulgar economic facts and calculations.

II

As so often happens with caricatures, what Gradgrind has been taken to symbolise has expanded to include dimensions Dickens could not have envisaged and would probably have been alarmed to contemplate. The commonest form of inflation has been the use of Coketown's MP, the would-be social and educational reformer, as shorthand for any ruthless Victorian employer, thereby confusing his role with that reserved for Bounderby in the novel.[7] Retaining their separate identities enables two other possibilities to be registered. First, by not preventing his daughter Louisa from marrying the odious Bounderby, Gradgrind completes the ruin of her life that began with her unimaginative education at his hands at home. Second, the marriage can be taken as an emblem of union between utilitarianism and industrial employers, thereby creating an alliance between an apologetic political economy and the interests of an exploiting class. While the first of these possibilities belongs squarely within the realm of Dickens's moral imagination, it is by no means clear that the second does.

Mid-twentieth-century interpreters, from F. R. Leavis onwards, have been more confident in attributing broader ideological significance to the marriage. Leavis regarded *Hard Times* as 'the supreme document in creative literature, where Victorian Utilitarianism and its part in Victorian civilisation are in question'.[8] As a consequence, perhaps, he judged the

---

[6] Letter to Henry Cole, 17 June 1854, in *The Letters of Charles Dickens*, VII, p. 354.
[7] For a surprising example see Eric Hobsbawm's statement that: 'The indictment against early nineteenth-century capitalism becomes no less black if we assume that every capitalist was like Dickens' Brothers Cheeryble, and that there were no Gradgrinds at all.' 'History and the "Dark Satanic Mills"', as reprinted in his *Labouring Men: Studies in the History of Labour* (London, 1964), p. 115.
[8] See his introduction to *Mill on Bentham and Coleridge* (London, 1950), p. 34, first published under the more informative title, 'Mill, Beatrice Webb and the "English School"', *Scrutiny*, 15 (1949), pp. 104–26.

Louisa–Bounderby marriage to be 'a just observation about the affinities and practical tendency of Utilitarianism'. The 'comprehensive vision' that Dickens expressed for the first time in *Hard Times* was 'one in which the inhumanities of Victorian civilisation are seen as fostered and sanctioned by a hard philosophy, the aggressive formulation of an inhumane spirit'.[9] Benthamism exemplified this 'indifference to essential human interests', with 'disastrous consequences' for those interests.[10]

With the help of Elie Halévy's account of philosophic radicalism, Leavis identified the ancestry of utilitarianism as running from Newton to Adam Smith before being passed to Bentham. It constituted 'an important line of intellectual history' that achieved fruition in 'laissez-faire individualism'. Thus characterised, it could be connected, quasi-Marxian fashion, with 'the classes associated with the expanding capitalist enterprise of eighteenth-century England' who regarded paternalistic forms of government as an obstruction to their interests. Having secured the Reform Act of 1832, the Benthamites and the middle classes they represented proceeded to oppose 'the sharing of its privileges and the reduction of its power'. Their most solid achievement was the new Poor Law of 1834, which became the

symbolic embodiment of all that was most rationally and righteously inhuman in orthodox Utilitarianism, with its implacable Malthusian logic. Utilitarianism, in fact provided the sanction for the complacent selfishness and comfortable obtuseness of the prosperous classes in the great age of Progress: they were protected by righteous rationality from the importunities of imaginative sympathy.[11]

Righteous rationality and imaginative sympathy provide the backdrop to Leavis's rehabilitation of *Hard Times*, though in analysing the novel he concentrated more on the educational theme than the industrial ones. The Sleary circus embodies 'fancy' and 'wonder' in contrast with the sterile numeracy of the Gradgrind regime, providing a 'spectacle of triumphant activity that, seeming to contain its end within itself, is, in its easy mastery, joyously self-justified'.[12] A parallel insight by D. H. Lawrence is added immediately, and readers of Leavis would have recognised that what was being commended here was a version of George [Bourne] Sturt's *The Wheelwright's Shop* (1923), one of the classics chosen by Leavis and Denys Thompson for use in the teaching of English in schools in *Culture and Environment: The Training of Critical Awareness* (1933).

As a disillusioned Ruskinian socialist, reflecting on his experience in

⁹ See F. R. Leavis, *The Great Tradition* (London, 1948), p. 228.
¹⁰ Leavis, *Mill on Bentham and Coleridge*, p. 31.   ¹¹ *Ibid.*, p. 34.
¹² Leavis, *The Great Tradition*, p. 228.

the 1880s, Sturt provided a direct link between nineteenth- and twentieth-century versions of the conflict between Utilitarians and Romantics.
Under the influence of Ruskin's *Fors Clavigera*, Sturt had believed that
'man's only decent occupation was in handicraft'. Yet when he took
charge of the wheelwright's shop, and attempted to run it along profit-
sharing lines, without regard to cost estimates and what competitors
could offer, neither his workmen nor his customers were willing to collaborate with his 'Ruskinian absurdities'.[13] The book is, therefore, not
merely an evocation of a world that was passing in the early years of the
twentieth century, but a precise economic diagnosis of why the enterprise
failed as a result of resistance to technological change and the encroach-
ment of competitors on what had previously been a local monopoly.
Unsurprisingly, this was not the side of Sturt's book that Leavis and
Denys Thompson noticed; they saw it more as a 'memory of the old
order' that could act as 'the chief incitement towards a new' – adding
rather forlornly, 'if ever we are to have one'.[14] While recognising that there
could be no return to a pre-machine age, Leavis consistently declined all
challenges to delineate his own version of Jerusalem. Such a task was
incompatible with the function of criticism. Yet by choosing to remain
silent on the nature of the new order, Leavis's vision continued to be
treated as nostalgic lament – much to its originator's annoyance.[15]

Some of the above is based on Leavis's introduction to Mill's essays on
Bentham and Coleridge, a work intended as an extension of arguments
mounted in *Education and the University: A Sketch for an 'English School'*
(1943). Mill's essays, plus the *Autobiography*, were commended as the
kind of 'extra-literary' sources best calculated to broaden the study of
nineteenth-century English literature at Cambridge. Indeed, Mill was
favoured over the prose writings of Coleridge, Carlyle, and Ruskin,
despite the 'enduring honour' attached to 'Ruskin's destructive analysis

[13] See G. Sturt, *The Wheelwright's Shop* (Cambridge, 1993), pp. 12, 53, 200.
[14] F. R. Leavis and D. Thompson, *Culture and Environment* (London, 1933), p. 97.
[15] Resistance to the demand to 'show our colours', whether coming from the left or right of
the political spectrum, was defended in the 1930s; see for example 'Under which King,
Bezonian?', *Scrutiny*, 1 (1932), pp. 205–14. Although Marxism was a prominent target for
Leavis during this period, he did make one significant concession: 'Let me say, then, that
I agree with the Marxist to the extent of believing some form of economic communism to
be inevitable and desirable, in the sense that it is to this that a power-economy of its very
nature points, and only by a deliberate and intelligent working towards it can civilisation
be saved from disaster.' See *For Continuity* (Cambridge, 1933), pp. 184–5. But the chief
problem remained one of developing 'an autonomous culture, a culture independent of
any economic, technical or social system as none has been before' (p. 168). What form
'economic communism' would take was never made clear, but the rejection of 'Morrisian
archaizing' and 'garden-suburb handicraftiness' was sustained in *Nor Shall My Sword*
(London, 1972), pp. 81, 85; and the dislike of any nostalgic tag upheld in letters to the
press; see *Letters in Criticism by F. R. Leavis*, ed. J. Tasker (London, 1974), pp. 100–1.

of orthodox political economy' – an analysis better read in J. A. Hobson's secondary account than in the original.[16] Notwithstanding 'the restrictive rigours of his father's educational experiment', Leavis judged Mill to be 'no unqualified Benthamite'. The encounter with Coleridge and Carlyle had made Mill a sensitive interpreter of the intellectual currents of his age.

'Technologico-Benthamite' became Leavis's compendium term for everything about the modern world that needed to be countered by the values embodied in his version of the 'English School'. More broadly, the campaign against technologico-Benthamism was Leavis's response to the cultural decline which had accompanied mass civilisation, a process that began with the industrial revolution and was continuing apace in the twentieth century. It is clear then that the niceties of Victorian intellectual history and the benefits to be derived from extra-literary studies were merely part of that much larger battlefield on which, in 1962, Leavis was to confront C. P. Snow, the latest apologist for Gradgrind values. In dividing the world into two cultures, scientific and literary, Snow had characterised 'literary intellectuals' as Luddites in their attitude to the industrial revolution and the rising living standards associated with economic growth. *Nor Shall My Sword* (1972) brought Leavis's causes together by enlisting all his heroes, from Blake to Lawrence (while, incidentally, abandoning Carlyle, Ruskin, and Morris, those who *might* be guilty of Luddism), and by encompassing all those modernist enemies who were guilty of upholding 'statistico-egalitarian reductivism'.[17]

III

By then, however, Leavis's enhanced summation of the schism between Romantics and Utilitarians had been taken up by others who can legitimately be described as his successors. Raymond Williams' *Culture and Society* (1958) surveyed the 'traditional great debate' provoked by urban industrialisation from 1780 to 1950, taking in Leavis himself en route. *Hard Times* was credited with an understanding of the 'dominant philosophy of industrialism', with some dubious real-life identifications of the objects of Dickens's satire being added. Whereas Leavis detected the grim presence of James Mill in the Gradgrind system of education

---

[16] *Mill on Bentham and Coleridge*, p. 36; see also J. A. Hobson, *John Ruskin, Social Reformer*, 3rd edn (London, 1904).

[17] *Nor Shall My Sword*, pp. 107–8, 110, 119–20, 149, 151. On this phase of Leavis's career see Stefan Collini, 'The Critic as Anti-Journalist: Leavis after *Scrutiny*', in J. Treglown and B. Bennett, eds., *Grub Street and the Ivory Tower* (Oxford, 1998), pp.151–76. On the Snow–Leavis debate see Collini's introduction to the reprint of C. P. Snow, *The Two Cultures* (Cambridge, 1993), pp. xxiii–xxv, xxix–xliii.

inflicted on his son, Williams was 'certain that Dickens had the son's *Political Economy* very much in mind in his general indictment of the ideas which built and maintained Coketown'.[18] Less enthusiastic than Leavis, however, Williams saw the novel merely as one of a number of its kind, 'more a symptom of the confusion of industrial society than an understanding of it', though he conceded that it was a significant symptom and, more vaguely, a 'continuing' one.

Culture and Society owed much of its early success to its claim that recovery of a critical tradition could provide resources for a truly common culture that would incorporate working-class achievements based on the ideals of solidarity and community.[19] Williams rejected the 'Coleridgean' or minority view of culture, and with it those exclusively literary connotations associated with Leavis's deployment of the great tradition. He also rejected the nostalgic and reactionary implications of the idea of a lost 'organic community' – a theme pursued in his other writings on *The Long Revolution* (1961) and *The Country and the City* (1973). Jerusalem was still a vision to be actively pursued, or more accurately, perhaps, to be pursued by political activists, provided they were unencumbered by the cultural pessimism and elitism associated with Leavis. After *Culture and Society*, partly as a result of the resounding success of the book, Williams embarked upon a more overtly political career as leader of the left, mending his fences with the newer forms of Marxism that came into fashion in the late 1960s, though never with quite enough scientistic rigour to satisfy the zealots who entered New Left circles after 1968. The label accurately applied to Williams' early position was 'left Leavisism'.[20] Those who employed it on his Marxist left, however, were more dismissive of Leavis, adding charges that Williams' modifications to the original

---

[18] R. Williams, *Culture and Society* (1958; London, 1961), p. 105. No evidence is cited in support of this certainty; the date given for publication of Mill's *Principles of Political Economy* is wrong; and the succeeding comment citing one of Mill's reactions to Dickens ('that creature') leaves the impression that this was Mill's response to *Hard Times*, no evidence for which exists. The remark was in fact Mill's response to Dickens's ridicule of the 'rights of women' in an earlier novel, *Bleak House*; see letter to Harriet Taylor, 20 March 1854 in *The Later Letters of John Stuart Mill, 1849–1873*, ed. F. E. Mineka and D. N. Lindley, 4 vols. (Toronto, 1972), I, p. 190. He added that it was 'the only one of [Dickens's novels] I altogether dislike'; and his comment on the death of Dickens was that he regarded it as 'like a personal loss, even to those who only knew him by his novels'; see letter to Charles Eliot Norton, 26 June 1870, *ibid.*, IV, p. 1740.

[19] For Williams' own retrospective view of *Culture and Society* see *Politics and Letters: Interviews with New Left Review* (London, 1979), pp. 97–132; and Stefan Collini, 'The Origins of Cultural Criticism?: The Culture-and-Society-Tradition Revisited', unpublished paper.

[20] Williams described the object of the journal he edited in 1947, also called *Politics and Letters*, as being to 'unite radical Left politics with Leavisite literary criticism'; see *Politics and Letters*, p. 65.

continued to be tainted with a series of 'isms' that belong to the polemics of new and old New Left politics at that time: romantic populism, moralism, subjectivism, culturalism, and literary idealism.[21]

Edward Thompson, the figure who joined forces with Williams as the joint leader of the intellectual left in the early 1960s, was to be on the receiving end of similar criticisms, and his responses were much less conciliatory than those given by Williams.[22] In his own review of Williams' work Thompson regretted the absence of the element of 'struggle' in the idea of 'culture', speaking ironically of 'The Tradition' as 'a procession of disembodied voices' whose meanings had been 'wrested out of their whole social context'. This was a politer form of a more common Marxist charge, namely that Williams had paid insufficient attention to the class location and reactionary opinions of some of his bourgeois cast. What, for example, were such noted anti-progressives as Burke and Carlyle doing as part of The Tradition? Why had Williams evaded any encounter with Marx and Marxism, or indeed 'with an historian, an anthropologist, a sociologist of major stature'? Did that account for the impression that the forces at work behind the creation of the tradition were being treated impersonally? Thompson also asked why there were 'no good or bad men in Mr Williams' history, only dominant and subordinate "structures of feeling"'? No-one could possibly charge Thompson with failing to make such moral discriminations in his own work. Nevertheless, these criticisms of Williams were 'comradely' in the best sense; they respected common aims and contained an insight into the differences between the trajectories of their respective autobiographies – Williams' journey from working class to middle class being, so to speak, reversed in Thompson's case.[23]

As a formative influence, they also had Leavis in common. Thompson drew attention to his own debt to Leavis in one of his last writings, an introduction to a reprint of Sturt's *The Wheelwright's Shop* published in 1993. Before he went up to Cambridge to read English he had been introduced to Sturt by a Leavisite schoolteacher. Another of the bonds that linked Williams and Thompson was a shared interest in 'the Romantic critique of

---

[21] See for example T. Eagleton, 'Criticism and Politics: The Work of Raymond Williams', *New Left Review*, 95 (1976), pp. 3–23.

[22] See especially the title essay and 'The Peculiarities of the English' in *The Poverty of Theory, and Other Essays* (London, 1978), written in 1978 and 1965 respectively. These essays can be compared with Williams' semi-apologetic answers to the questions posed by his New Left interviewers in *Politics and Letters*.

[23] See Thompson's review of Williams' *Long Revolution*, *New Left Review*, 9 and 10 (1961), pp. 24–33 and 34–9. Thompson later stated that the theoretical differences between his position and that of Williams at this time were so sharp that he wanted to be relieved of the reviewing task; see 'The Politics of Theory' in R. Samuel, ed., *People's History and Socialist Theory* (London, 1981), p. 398.

Utilitarianism'.[24] This common preoccupation originated with Leavis and was nurtured by their apprenticeship as adult education teachers under WEA auspices. Unknown to each other, they both taught courses involving literature and history along Leavisian lines, with *Hard Times* featuring among the romantic texts, and with *Culture and Environment* providing a means of organising the teaching material.[25]

IV

Gradgrind certainly became early mental shorthand for Thompson. The opening chapter of his first book, *William Morris*, is entitled 'Sir Launcelot and Mr Gradgrind'. It was published in 1955, a year before Thompson left the Communist Party over the Soviet invasion of Hungary. Although there are interesting differences between the original and revised editions, the portrait of Gradgrind serves the same purpose: to introduce the enemy Morris found it necessary to combat. Thompson's praise for *Hard Times* as a portrait of the enemy is a magnified version of Leavis, but with the same overtones of class conspiracy when speaking of political economy and the Victorian bourgeoisie:

Dickens's picture may be a caricature: but it is of the best order of caricature, which delineates the essential lines of truth. Mr Bounderby, the coarse and avaricious mill-owner of *Hard Times*, was giving way to his more sophisticated cousin, Mr Gradgrind. Gradgrind not only has power and wealth: he also has a theory to justify and perpetuate exploitation. The Victorian bourgeoisie had constructed from bits of Adam Smith and Ricardo, Bentham and Malthus a cast-iron theoretical system, which they were now securing with the authority of the State and the Law, and sanctifying with the blessings of Religion. The laws of supply and demand were 'God's laws', and in all the major affairs of society all other values must bend before commodity values.[26]

Although Thompson's next book on *The Making of the English Working Class* (1963) ends with the class having made itself by the early 1830s, twenty years before Dickens's delineation of the 'essential lines of truth', utilitarianism and political economy provide an antithesis to the main

---

[24] See postscript to Thompson, *William Morris: Romantic to Revolutionary*, revised edn (London, 1976), p. 769.
[25] For studies of what both Thompson and Williams taught during these years, see P. Searby and the editors on 'Edward Thompson as a Teacher: Yorkshire and Warwick' in J. Rule and R. Malcolmson, eds., *Protest and Survival: The Historical Experience* (London, 1993), pp. 1–23. On Williams see R. Fieldhouse, 'Oxford and Adult Education', in W. J. Morgan and P. Preston, eds., *Raymond Williams: Politics, Education, Letters* (Basingstoke, 1993); and F. Inglis, *Raymond Williams* (London, 1995), ch. 6. The contribution of Williams to adult education, and its contribution to his own work, is now dealt with in L. Goldman, *Dons and Workers: Oxford and Adult Education since 1850* (Oxford, 1995), pp. 286–98. [26] Thompson, *William Morris*, pp. 8–9.

thrust of that story as well. It is not surprising then that the spontaneous pleasures of the working class, instanced by the 'circus folk' in *Hard Times*, make a brief appearance, and that Gradgrind himself was judged to be 'most certainly out and about after 1815'.[27] As the insensitive spokesman 'for efficiency, cheap centralized government, *laissez faire*, and sound "political economy"', his entry on the scene predated the triumph of British capitalism after 1851. There was more than a hint, however, that Gradgrind might have been deprived of victory if things had turned out differently after the crucial period covered by Thompson's book. In its peroration he stressed the fact that the class whose fortunes he had traced 'suffered the experience of the Industrial Revolution as articulate, free-born Englishmen' whose consciousness had been forged, Burkean fashion, over several centuries. They had even achieved a temporary victory in the struggle 'between a capitalist and a socialist political economy' while 'Marx was still in his teens'. Here the native heroes were men such as Thomas Hodgskin and others who articulated a truly working-class version of the science. As a result of the 'collective self-consciousness' formed during the industrial revolution, where they 'met Utilitarianism in their daily lives' – the ideology of their employers – they had 'fought, not the machine, but the exploitive and oppressive relationships intrinsic to industrial capitalism'. The characteristic independence of the artisan had gradually given way to a sense of 'community' and 'cooperation' adapted to the new conditions of production and capable of resisting the 'blind operation of the market-economy'.[28]

At the end of this tribute to the native working-class tradition, however, attention was drawn to that other theme in the book, 'the great Romantic criticism of Utilitarianism' which was 'running its parallel but altogether separate course'. The finale is worth recalling because it contains much that signals Thompson's own interest in the romantics and working-class consciousness – a theme that parallels Williams' *Culture and Society*. Since nobody could doubt that Thompson was active in the continuing historical processes he was recounting, the importance of straddling these two worlds was as important to him as it was to his historical protagonists.

After Blake no mind was at home in both cultures, nor had the genius to interpret the two traditions to each other. It was a muddled Mr Owen who offered to disclose the 'new moral world', while Wordsworth and Coleridge had withdrawn behind their own ramparts of disenchantment. Hence these years appear at times to display, not a revolutionary challenge, but a resistance movement, in which both the Romantics and the Radical craftsmen opposed the annunciation of

---

[27] *The Making of the English Working Class* [hereafter *MEWC*] (Harmondsworth, 1968), pp. 64, 376.   [28] *Ibid.*, p. 913.

Acquisitive Man. In the failure of the two traditions to come to a point of junction, something was lost. How much we cannot be sure, for we are among the losers.[29]

The references to the self-taught 'culture of the craftsman' which precede this ending, and the emphasis on a lost sense of community before work and life were set asunder by 'violent technological differentiation', echo Leavisian (Sturtian) values, with Blake and D. H. Lawrence continuing to act, as they did for Leavis, as sources of inspiration. Thompson confirmed these allegiances by supporting Leavis in his exchanges with Snow.[30] This could account too for the fact that, when faced with Williams' critique of Leavis's lament over urban industrialism (instead of the real enemy, capitalism) in *The Country and the City*, Thompson felt that Williams 'could have looked more scrupulously than he does at the values at stake in that central Leavisite text, George Sturt's *Wheelwright's Shop*'.[31] Moreover, Thompson's defence of these values, on this occasion and later, bears a distinct family resemblance to the one originally given by Leavis himself.[32] The 'disenchantment' of the Lake poets after the failures of the French Revolution reminds the reader of Thompson's interest in Wordsworth and Coleridge, and of his frankness in hinting at the parallels with his own experience in breaking with the Communist Party.[33]

An interesting analysis of Thompson's narrative style by Renato Rosaldo has drawn attention to its Dickensian qualities, whereby the reader is moved 'more by the sentimental heroics of victimization than by the heroics of superhuman feats'. It is a form of melodrama that invites the reader 'to take sides in Manichaean battles between virtue and vice', with the consequence that they 'enter a field of combat where the middle ground has been eroded'.[34] Methodism is the best-known casualty of this

---

[29] *Ibid.*, p. 915.

[30] 'When Sir Charles Snow tells us that "with singular unanimity . . . the poor have walked off the land into the factories as fast as the factories could take them", we must reply, with Dr Leavis, that the "actual history" of the "full human problem [was] incomparably and poignantly more complex than that"', *ibid.*, p. 486.

[31] 'A Nice Place to Visit' a review of Williams' *The Country and the City* in *New York Review of Books*, 6 February 1975, reprinted in Thompson, *Persons and Polemics* (London, 1994), pp. 244–55.

[32] *Ibid.*, 'It may . . . be seen as a vast reserve of unrealized, or only partially achieved, possibilities – a past that gives us glimpses of other possibilities of human nature, other ways of behaving (even "organic" ones).'

[33] See *MEWC*, especially pp. 103–4, 109, 172, 180–1, 192–3, 243, 378–9. The reference to those 'exposed to similar experiences of revolutionary disenchantment in the past twenty-five years' (p. 109) is echoed more movingly in the distinction Thompson made between disenchantment and apostasy in 'Disenchantment or Default? A Lay Sermon', in C. C. O'Brien and W. D. Vanech, eds., *Power and Consciousness* (London, 1969), pp. 149–81.

[34] 'Celebrating Thompson's Heroes: Social Analysis in History and Anthropology' in H. J. Kaye and K. McClelland, eds., *E. P. Thompson: Critical Perspectives* (Cambridge, 1990), pp. 103–24.

approach, but the same can be said for that other pair of enemies, utilitarianism and political economy. On occasions the two targets are combined, as when dissenters are found to be addicted to 'the dogmas of free trade': hence the permeation of the movement 'by the values of enlightened self-interest which led on, in such a man as Francis Place, to the acceptance of a limited Utilitarian philosophy'.[35] As the organiser and annalist of the London Corresponding Society, Place has an important part in Thompson's story. His career becomes a moral tale about what happens when self-educated working men betray their class by allowing the 'self-respecting virtues' to lead them in a Malthusian and Benthamite direction, especially when compared with men of firmer resolve such as Hodgskin.[36] Having been given an early warning of the fatal defect in Place's character, the reader is prepared to be told that he was sitting for 'his own portrait as the White Man's Uncle Tom', with James Mill as his portraitist.[37] Although Place is credited with repeal of the Combination Acts, his motives are judged to be tainted by political economy.[38]

That there could be no middle ground on which any genuine leader of working-class opinion could stand in the struggle between capital and labour was an orthodox Marxian conclusion, though if Marx had been Thompson's actual source he might have had to consider why David Ricardo was exempted from the 'vulgar' category of defenders of capital. Thompson did accept, however, that Place, Ricardo's pupil, represented a 'new phenomenon' by virtue of his vain attempt to make utilitarianism the 'ideology of the working class'. Why vain? Because 'it is scarcely possible to think of middle-class Utilitarianism without thinking also of Malthus and of orthodox political economy', with the result that: 'If Utilitarianism was to enter working-class ideology it would make it captive to the employing class.'[39] Once more, then, we have returned to Leavis's Gradgrind with Marxian emphases.

V

The above sketch of how a nineteenth-century schism was given renewed relevance by some leading mid-twentieth-century partisans of the romantics is no more than that. It certainly does not pretend to be an adequate account of the intellectual biographies of those mainly responsible. Nevertheless, a good case could be made for the significance of the episode to the cultural and political history of Britain. That my three

---

[35] *MEWC*, p. 58.
[36] *Ibid.*, p. 63. For the contrast between Place and Hodgskin, see pp. 569, 818, 854–7.
[37] *Ibid.*, p. 170. Readers of the unrevised version, before 1968, would have had even less doubt: 'Trusty Nigger' appeared instead of 'Uncle Tom'.   [38] *Ibid.*, pp. 567–9.
[39] *Ibid.*, pp. 848–50.

authors generated large followings is reflected by the bio-bibliographical
industries begun since their deaths (Leavis in 1978, Williams in 1988, and
Thompson in 1993).[40] Singly and in combination, then, they provided a
potent means by which an interpretation of the industrial revolution, with
its inescapable mixture of myth and reality, has been appropriated and
diffused.

The story clearly has special resonances to historians of the British left
and those concerned with the cultural mission of English literature, but
the significance extends beyond these communities. Complementary
stories can and have been told about the industrial revolution as social
catastrophe. But for those who are not primarily concerned with the fate
of literary criticism or even with the social and economic history of
Britain, other questions can be posed. Does the story support and is it
supported by what we know about Victorian intellectual life? And how
should we, as denizens of the late twentieth century, come to grips with
the original schism between Romantics and Utilitarians? There can be no
easy routes through such treacherous because well-trodden territory. In
what follows I will chiefly seek to raise some questions future travellers
may need to bear in mind.

An obvious objection should be countered at the outset. None of the
figures with whom I have been concerned would have claimed that intellectual history was their main interest; they wrote as cultural and literary
critics, social historians, as political theorists and activists, or some combination of all these things. Nevertheless, each of them found it necessary
to advance or borrow ambitious versions of nineteenth-century intellectual history to support their case. Of my three authors, Thompson was
the one most acutely aware of, and frequently exasperated by, the criticisms of intellectual historians.[41] As Marilyn Butler has shrewdly

---

[40] See, for example, C. Baldick, *The Social Mission of English Criticism, 1848–1932* (Oxford,
1983) and *Criticism and Literary Theory, 1890 to the Present* (London, 1996); and Francis
Mulhern, *The Moment of 'Scrutiny'* (London, 1979). For broader appraisals see J. Rule
and R. Malcolmson, eds., *Protest and Survival; The Historical Experience* (New York,
1993); B. D. Palmer, *E. P. Thompson; Objections and Oppositions* (London, 1994); Harvey J.
Kaye, *The British Marxist Historians; An Introductory Analysis* (Cambridge, 1984); and *The
Education of Desire; Marxists and the Writing of History* (New York, 1992). See also A.
O'Connor, *Raymond Williams* (Oxford, 1989); G. McCann, *Theory and History; The
Political Thought of E. P. Thompson* (Aldershot, 1997); and N. Stevenson, *Culture, Ideology
and Socialism; Raymond Williams and E. P. Thompson* (Aldershot, 1995). To this can be
added J. McIlroy and S. Westwood, eds., *Border Country; Raymond Williams in Adult
Education* (Leicester, 1993).

[41] See especially the answers to A. W. Coats, Istvan Hont and Michael Ignatieff in 'Moral
Economy Reviewed' in *Customs in Common* (London, 1991), pp. 268–87. Williams'
Keywords (London, 1976) was subjected to close scrutiny by Quentin Skinner in 'The
Idea of a Cultural Lexicon', *Essays in Criticism*, 29 (1979), pp. 205–24, and his response
was simply to make a number of unannounced changes to later editions; see Inglis,
Raymond Williams, pp. 245–8.

observed, however, Thompson could be 'ultra-suspicious of tendencies which most tempt him'.[42] His criticisms of the 'disembodied' nature of the Williams version of The Tradition are essentially those of an intellectual historian, and he showed himself to be no mean exponent of stratospherically 'high' intellectual history when defending British empiricism later.[43] Thompson was also the one who most often found it necessary to engage with intellectual history for reasons partly connected with his interest in biography (Blake as well as Morris), but largely by virtue of the very nature of his enterprise, recapturing the consciousness of the past for the purposes of rescuing his chosen protagonists from 'the enormous condescension of posterity'.[44] The antagonists too were owed no less, though it was not Thompson's duty to undertake a task he believed had been only too well performed by others. By recognising the importance of 'struggle', the dialectical qualities of consciousness, however, he was committed to understanding the cross-currents within which and against which the forms of consciousness that interested him defined themselves. Indeed, as his work moved increasingly in an anthropological direction this commitment grew.[45] He certainly claimed that listening to the disparate voices of historical actors was an essential part of his own practice in recapturing consciousness.[46]

To describe the composite portrait of utilitarianism and political economy that emerges from the work of Leavis, Williams, and Thompson as tendentious is to overlook the warm-blooded normative intentions of their work. But an optic on the intellectual past that was serviceable for exercises in aerial bombing, 1940s' style, would hardly commend itself to those wielding scalpels, and not just for purposes of performing cosmetic surgery. Those seeking a more nuanced picture of the lines of force at work in Victorian thinking need something more appropriate to the task, a better ear, more tolerance, and less overt partisanship. Regard for complexity does not have to be associated with personal sympathies, still less does it mean endorsing the 'apologetics of a ruling class'.[47]

[42] M. Butler, 'E. P. Thompson and the Uses of History', *History Workshop Journal*, 39 (1995), p. 73.
[43] See, for example, Thompson, 'The Peculiarities of the English' in *The Poverty of Theory* (London, 1978), especially pp. 266–74.   [44] *MEWC*, p. 13.
[45] Notably in *Whigs and Hunters* (London, 1975) and *Customs in Common*.
[46] 'If he listens, then the material itself will begin to speak through him' and 'The historian may tend to be a bit too generous because a historian has to learn to attend and listen to very disparate groups of people and try and understand their value system and their consciousness', in H. Abelove *et al.*, eds., *Visions of History* (Manchester, 1976), pp. 14, 16.
[47] *Ibid.*, p. 8. Significantly, however, Thompson followed this crude charge with a warning against treating all history as ideology: it involved a 'precise discipline that entails distancing and objectifying – becoming aware of the questions one is asking', thereby preventing the intrusion of 'one's attitudes and values'.

VI

What little can be said by way of correction here is hardly going to be news to readers of this volume. We no longer believe that Leslie Stephen, Elie Halévy, and A. V. Dicey were right, according to their different lights, in attributing to philosophic radicalism such exclusive and persistent influence over Victorian legislation and public administration. As William Thomas has shown, in the process of rescuing the philosophic radicals from the 'ism' attached to the collectivity later, even during the brief period when they were attempting to act as a political force, they were disunited and largely ineffectual.[48] Bourgeois most of them may have been, but their cause would have benefited from being *more* attuned to the interests and beliefs of the new electorate after 1832. A stronger sense of the emerging class basis of English politics, outside the landowning classes, against whom much of their fire was concentrated, would have improved their prospects – as it did those of Cobden and Bright in the 1840s and beyond. Instead, they spoke a doctrinaire *philosophe* language of public good, priding themselves on standing above the crudities of class interest – a stance that separated them as much from the middle classes as it did from the working classes. *Pace* Leavis, then, far from opposing the sharing of the privileges obtained in 1832, their continuing efforts to destroy such privileges conflicted with the hopes and anxieties of a new electorate made fearful by Chartism. Robert Lowe provides an extreme example of the kind of utilitarian who opposed the extension of the suffrage. Perhaps that is why he complained most bitterly about the ingratitude of the middle classes towards his efforts on their behalf.[49] But one Lowe does not make a winter.

Gradgrind was certainly busy during the early decades of the century, arguing the case for 'good government', but he was rarely running the show.[50] Similarly with the single-issue politics of the day, those centring

[48] W. Thomas, *The Philosophic Radicals: Nine Studies in Theory and Practice, 1817–1841* (Oxford, 1979). For a more extended treatment of Halévy's misunderstandings of English politics see Thomas's 'L'utilitarisme et le libéralisme anglais au début du XIXième siècle', in M. Mulligan and R. Roth, eds., *Regards sur Bentham et l'utilitarisme; Recherches et rencontres* (Geneva, 1993), pp. 39–58.
[49] 'I was one of those – and they were very few indeed – who lifted their voices in favour of the middle class, not so much for their own sake as for the sake of the country . . . I never met with the slightest encouragement from those whose cause I was pleading.' See *Life and Letters of the Right Honorable Robert Lowe, Viscount Sherbrooke*, ed. A. P. Martin, 2 vols. (London, 1892), I, pp. 5–6.
[50] For a recent study of this see P. Harling, *The Waning of 'Old Corruption'; The Politics of Economical Reform in Britain, 1779–1846*, (London, 1996). See also P. Harling and P. Mandler, 'From "Fiscal-Military" State to Laissez-Faire State, 1760–1850', *Journal of British Studies*, 32 (1993), pp. 44–70.

on legal and penal reform, education, the Poor Law, public health, the
Factory Acts, and the creation of a meritocratic civil service, where back-
room tactics proved more influential, the philosophic radicals often
played second fiddle to others – to Whigs (Scottish and English), to
Tories, and especially to those with evangelical and dissenting affiliations
that were distinctly at odds with the atheistic materialism of Bentham and
his immediate disciples. Thompson's treatment of the religious dimension of nineteenth-century social thought concentrated more on its moral
declension than its positive influence on public dispositions. Leavis and
Williams paid it little attention, as the latter recognised when he confessed to 'tone-deafness' on the subject.[51]

Nor is it self-evident that Benthamism was indifferent to human interests. The efforts of Chadwick, Southwood Smith, and James Kay-
Shuttleworth as Factory and Poor Law Commissioners were not entirely
nugatory. It is also conceivable that they were fired by compassion and a
genuine concern for injustice. It seems unreasonable to deny that imaginative sympathy *as well as* righteous rationality played a part in the public
objects to which, after all, they (not us) devoted most of their lives.[52] This
may be more difficult to credit in the case of Bentham, whose normal procedures were undoubtedly rationalist, and whose plans for paupers and
prisoners provide opportunities to reveal our superior humanity.
Nevertheless, precisely the same kind of rationalism resulted in highlighting forms of exclusion and oppression – for example, of women, homo-
sexuals, and Jews – that often lay beyond the more conventional public
sympathies of Victorians.[53] Dickens' private verdict on Gradgrind now
seems nearer the truth than that passed by admirers of his novel.

The equation of Benthamism with laissez-faire individualism owes much
to Dicey's *Law and Public Opinion in England during the Nineteenth Century*
(1905), whose standards for admission to this club were notoriously lax, part
of his own polemical attempt to stem the tide of late nineteenth-century col-
lectivism.[54] During the period he assigned to Benthamite hegemony,
1825–70, everyone became a common-sense utilitarian without knowing it.
The well-documented and influential example of Gladstone now provides
the best test-case here. Though clearly more inclined towards Coleridge
than Bentham for confessional reasons, Gladstone's credentials as the
spokesman for free trade, sound finance, and laissez-faire are impeccable.

---

[51] Williams, *Politics and Letters*, p. 130.
[52] On 'The Utilitarian Conscience' see the contribution of D. Roberts to P. Marsh, ed., *The Conscience of the Victorian State* (Syracuse, N.Y., 1979), pp. 39–72.
[53] See L. Campos-Boralevi, *Bentham and the Oppressed* (Berlin, 1984).
[54] On the background to Dicey's work see S. Collini, *Liberalism and Sociology* (Cambridge, 1979), pp. 13–42.

But Colin Matthew has also taught us to appreciate that the Gladstonian idea of state, though minimal in its economic role, contained some powerful *étatist* features. It aimed to be strong and autonomous in relation to major interest groupings, where preservation of autonomy entailed reliance on municipal and voluntary agencies in a manner that was at least as 'corporatist' as the mercantile state Gladstone did so much to dismantle.[55]

Although Halévy's superior scholarship could be used to counter Dicey's emphasis on laissez-faire by showing the *dirigiste* aims of Benthamism, Halévy confirmed the prejudices of its opponents in another way. He absorbed political economy so thoroughly into utilitarianism, making Smith an honorary Benthamite *avant la lettre*, that Leavis can be forgiven for mistaking the ancestry. Halévy also succeeded in assimilating all political economists, radical, Whig, and Tory, into the Benthamite camp. He accepted Bentham's claim that he had indirectly sired Ricardo's economics, ignoring the fact that Ricardo and James Mill had severe doubts as to Bentham's orthodoxy as a political economist.[56] Moreover, as Boyd Hilton has shown, there was a large army of Christian or evangelical political economists whose thinking was more closely attuned to that of many Tory and some Whig politicians than the ungodly abstractions of Ricardo.[57]

By being treated as a composite set of doctrines, little scope existed for recognising any development in its separate elements, where development could entail decline as well as refinement. The versions of utilitarianism that emerged from the pens of Mill and Henry Sidgwick belong to the latter category, but Mill's efforts to refine Ricardian theory came to an end when he acknowledged some fundamental defects in the logic of the wage-fund doctrine in the 1860s, leaving a ruin that required the attentions of a new generation of economists before it could become habitable once more. In the oft-quoted phrase of Walter Bagehot, speaking in 1876, political economy lay 'dead in the public mind'.[58] During the next three decades, its orthodox supporters were engaged in furious methodological and political debate with their historicist critics. When political economy

---

[55] See H. C. G. Matthew, *Gladstone, 1809–74* (Oxford, 1986); and *Gladstone, 1875–98* (Oxford, 1995).

[56] See T. W. Hutchison, 'Bentham as an Economist', *Economic Journal*, 66 (1953), pp. 288–306; D. Lieberman, 'Political Economy and Jeremy Bentham', unpublished paper, dated 1982; R. D. C. Black, 'Bentham and the Political Economists of the Nineteenth Century', *Bentham Newsletter*, 12 (1988), pp. 24–36.

[57] See B. Hilton, *Corn, Cash, Commerce; The Economic Policies of the Tory Governments, 1815–1830* (Oxford, 1977); and *The Age of Atonement; The Influence of Evangelicalism on Social and Economic Thought, 1785–1865* (Oxford, 1988).

[58] *Economic Studies*, in *The Collected Works of Walter Bagehot*, ed. N. St John Stevas, 15 vols. (London, 1965–86), XI, p. 224.

regained confidence under its new banner, economics, in the early decades of the twentieth century, it had acquired a different agenda. Leavis's 'technologico-Benthamite' category was too all-encompassing to take account of such refinements, but as the residual category for all that was despised one might have expected Williams and Thompson, as overt political animals, to pay more attention to these shifts of focus, if only to show how devilishly cunning the enemy could be.

VII

For the period during which the schism between Utilitarians and Romantics was a central issue everyone agrees that Mill was still the crucial figure, whether or not they regard his bridge-building efforts as successful. Leavis was hardly being over-generous when he stated that Mill was no unqualified Benthamite. What Mill's mature version of utilitarianism lost in philistinism it may have gained in priggishness, but the result can hardly be described as 'complacent selfishness'. As Stefan Collini has shown, the moral requirements of duty and altruism could be strenuous in the extreme.[59]

Mill's reformulation of Ricardian political economy led to the espousal of many ideas that would have seemed distinctly peculiar to his mentors, not least in the explicit attention given to the claims and future of the labouring classes. Neither Leavis nor Williams seems to have made any effort to comprehend the *Principles of Political Economy*. For if Dickens really had this work in mind when indicting Coketown, he might have joined Williams in being disappointed to find how little Mill has to say on the subject of industrialisation and urbanisation. An underlying assumption in *Hard Times* that relations between capital and labour ought to be regulated by benevolence and mutual understanding appears in popular versions of political economy, but not in Mill's examination of cooperative forms of socialism. These were commended precisely as a means of overcoming the *essentially* conflictual relations between capital and labour.[60] Speaking as someone capable of appreciating the technological wonders of his day, Dickens might have been dispirited also by Mill's statement that 'it is questionable if all the mechanical inventions yet made have lightened the day's toil of any human being'.[61] One wonders too how Dickens would have reacted to other well-known pronouncements in that book: against paternalistic attempts to guide the labouring classes, and in

---

[59] See especially, S. Collini, 'The Culture of Altruism', in his *Public Moralists; Political Thought and Intellectual Life in Britain, 1850–1930* (Cambridge, 1991), pp. 60–90.
[60] *Principles of Political Economy* in *The Collected Works of John Stuart Mill*, ed. J. M. Robson, 33 vols. (Toronto, 1963–91), II, book IV, ch. 7.   [61] *Ibid.*, p. 756.

favour of measures that would 'pull down all large fortunes in two generations'.[62]

Many of Mill's contemporaries were bemused by his speculations about a world in which economic growth would no longer exhaust the energies of humankind for reasons connected with the quality of life and what was much later labelled as ecological catastrophe.[63] As public moralist Mill regarded it as his duty to explore new potentialities for human nature that were beyond present horizons. His record as seer may have been no better than most practitioners of this trade, but he devoted more effort to diagnosing future possibilities than to golden pasts and cannot be accused of wearing rose-coloured spectacles when looking at Britain's industrial society in the late 1840s and beyond. In one of his rare references to Mill, Thompson spoke of him as being 'revolted in disgust against the ethic of capitalism', but betrayed his normal expectations by prefacing it with a fatal 'even'.[64]

While a history of Victorian political economy and utilitarianism without Mill resembles a princeless *Hamlet*, Rosencrantz and Guildenstern also played their parts. Just as there were some Gradgrind schools, so there were popular exponents of political economy such as the Misses Marcet and Martineau, and unregenerate dogmatists like Lowe.[65] Equally, there were some 'cast-iron theories' purporting to explain the unalterable character of the laws of supply and demand, the harsh realities of wage determination, the harmful effects of restricting adult hours of work, and the benefits of machinery. Such theories were frequently employed to silence socialistic and 'sentimental' voices during the period when novel urban forms of industrialisation were receiving most attention from a middle-class public. We may wince at W. R. Greg's review of *Mary Barton*, his patronising lecture to Mrs Gaskell on the social economics of the 1842 depression. But what he has to say about the level of wages paid in Manchester, and the need and capacity for manufacturers with large fixed capitals to keep their businesses going longer during depression, still makes economic sense. What is less often noticed is Greg's related lecture to Mill on the non-viability of cooperative enterprises, where Sturt's later experience in

---

[62] Mill's description of the likely result of his proposals concerning taxation of rents and bequests, as reported to his friend, Alexander Bain; see Bain's *John Stuart Mill* (London, 1882), p. 89.
[63] Mill, *Principles*, book V, ch. 6. It seems symptomatic that Williams' article on 'Socialism and Ecology' mentions the romantic figures in the anti-capitalist tradition, but overlooks Mill entirely; see R. Gable, ed., *Resources of Hope* (London, 1989), pp. 210–26.
[64] Thompson, *William Morris*, p. 243.
[65] On the schools see R. Gilmour, 'The Gradgrind School: Political Economy in the Classroom', *Victorian Studies*, 11 (1967), pp. 207–24.

finding that his workers rejected his 'Ruskinian absurdities' could be cited in Greg's support.[66]

It is hardly surprising that when employers defended laying off men during slack periods, or made attempts to cut wages or quicken the pace of work in response to competition, they appealed to the one science that purported to explain the need for so doing. Mill was sympathetic to trade union activities before and after his recantation of the wage-fund doctrine, which meant that trade unionists, like employers, were not averse to claiming that legitimacy had been conferred on their activities by the science of political economy.[67]

On one occasion at least, Thompson recognised that Tom Paine and Adam Smith provided a joint revelation to his artisans, but his understanding of and sympathy with later versions of political economy was severely limited.[68] More generally, his response to arguments advanced by historians of economic thought was to draw a distinction between their focus on 'intention' and his own concern with 'ideological interest' and 'historical consequences'.[69] This had the polemical advantage of requiring the critic to show that the industrial revolution and the new Poor Law did not have the material consequences attributed to them by Thompson and his chosen protagonists. Only the most dogged apologist for capitalism would deny that the industrial revolution had a disastrous effect on some groups of workers and possibly on a large section of the working classes at some time during their lives. But we are not obliged to reach a definitive conclusion on the 'standard-of-living' controversy before deciding whether the opinions of contemporary commentators have been registered without distortion. To expect this would be like making it a requirement of Thompson that he should give an economic analysis of the causes and remedies for a depression before registering the claims of the victims, and without recourse to the question-begging assumption that in Jerusalem such things would not happen.

Nor is it surprising that some leaders of the working classes were impressed by the self-respecting virtues. The native English forms of radicalism, socialism, and working-class political economy were as diverse as the versions associated with Owen, Chartism, Hodgskin, and Place suggest. When dealing with a phenomenon that had no precedent and might have a different future we should expect some versions of working-class political economy to appeal to well-established political diagnoses of

[66] See Greg's review in the *Edinburgh Review*, 89 (1849), pp. 402–35.
[67] See E. Biagini, 'British Trade Unions and Popular Political Economy, 1860–1880, *Historical Journal*, 30 (1987), pp. 811–40.   [68] *MEWC*, p. 105.
[69] *Customs in Common*, pp. 202n and 270–1. In another formulation, he also spoke of being more interested in the 'sociology' of ideas than their 'identity'; see *MEWC*, p. 857n.

corruption and injustice; and to recall acceptable precedents by looking backwards, with or without nostalgia, to an earlier memory of greater autonomy and stability in working conditions. By paying attention to the plurality of languages to be found among the Chartists, for example, Gareth Stedman Jones was able to make sense of the theory of unequal exchange that underpinned much of their thinking, while at the same time showing why the Charter looked to a political solution to the social and economic problems being diagnosed.[70] A muddled Owen and a treacherous Place have certainly obtained more sympathetic hearings from others than they received from Thompson.[71] It is also unfortunate for Thompson's contrast between Place and Hodgskin that the latter's career should have ended as a supporter of the Corn Law League and as an assistant editor of *The Economist*. Hodgskin's theological commitments to a natural order made him a better member of Boyd Hilton's cast than Thompson's: he was a radical-Liberal rather than a Socialist, Ricardian, Smithian, or Lockean.[72]

VIII

Finally, there is my second question: how should we now regard the original schism between Romantics and Utilitarians? While it may have been crudely posed and artificially widened, nothing said so far supports the conclusion that it can be easily resolved. That a schism came into existence, that there was indeed a 'steam-whistle party', of which Dickens may or may not have been a fully paid-up member, cannot be denied. A portrait taken from the other side would contain some sharp characterisations of the romantic opposition, suggesting that an actual battle was taking place. Mill strove to achieve an open mind, but could not conceal his belief that on political economy Coleridge wrote like an 'arrant driveller'.[73] Macaulay, the scourge of utilitarian theories of government, ridiculed Southey's pessimism and ignorance of political economy. He also dismissed *Hard Times* as 'sullen socialism', a remark that gains rather than loses point by noting that he had applied much the same description to Wordsworth's *Prelude* in 1850.[74] Ruskin's articles attacking political

---

[70] G. Stedman Jones, 'Rethinking Chartism' in his *Languages of Class; Studies in English Working Class History, 1832–1982* (Cambridge, 1983), pp. 90–178.
[71] On Owen see, for example, G. Claeys, *Machinery, Money and the Millennium; From Moral Economy to Socialism* (Cambridge, 1987); and on Place see D. Miles, *Francis Place, 1771–1854; The Life of a Remarkable Radical* (Brighton, 1988).
[72] See D. Stack, *Nature and Artifice; The Life and Thought of Thomas Hodgskin*, (London, 1998).   [73] Mill, 'Coleridge' in *Collected Works*, X, p. 155.
[74] See *The Life and Letters of Lord Macaulay* ed. George Otto Trevelyan (London, 1901), p. 614. The remark about *The Prelude* was that it was 'to the last degree Jacobinical, indeed Socialist'. *Ibid.*, p. 541.

economy were discontinued after the public had registered dislike of their tone, and Bagehot's review of *Unto This Last* carried a title that hardly suggests a desire to cultivate the middle ground: 'Aesthetic Twaddle versus Economic Science'.[75]

There have, indeed, been those who have maintained that there can be no middle ground in any dispute between Romantics and Utilitarians. Resting, as they think it does, on a category mistake, they maintain that there can be no mediation between the two positions. It was on such grounds, for example, that Thomas De Quincey dismissed the criticisms of political economy made by the Lake poets.[76] Others have claimed that there could be no accommodation between a cultural stance that seeks an enduring holistic position on values and a social scientific perspective in which empiricism dictates that what may be true of some aspects of social life today may be false tomorrow.[77] Some aspects of the nineteenth-century dispute can be clarified by distinguishing between explanations for what existed and justifications for what might exist. Poetry and economic calculation may not belong on the same spectrum, but there has to be some means of mediating between what poets and economists said when they were talking about the same actual social conditions. However inadequate we may find Mill's attempts to bridge the gap, the effort was worth making. And if we are to confront the intellectual history we have rather than the one we think we ought to have had, we cannot follow Williams in complaining about Mill's tendency to talk about 'civilisation' when what we think he ought to have been talking about was 'industrial society'.[78]

Much the same can be said of Thompson, whose attentiveness to the languages of his protagonists did not extend to all participants in the conversation. As Rosaldo has said of Thompson from an anthropologist's standpoint, 'the historian's notions have been conflated with those of his subjects'.[79] Thompson often wanted the novelist's freedom to achieve an ending that was incompatible with his professed aims as historian–anthropologist, where this entails recognition that there are no endings,

---

[75] See Bagehot, *Collected Works*, IX, pp. 315–29.
[76] Since political economy was self-consciously limited to questions involving the 'production and circulation of wealth', it had nothing to do with ethical questions concerning 'estimates of social grandeur'. See *Recollections of the Lake Poets*, Penguin edn (Harmondsworth, 1970), pp. 244–5.
[77] This was Noel Annan's reason for regarding as mistaken the attempts of Basil Willey, Leavis, Williams, and Dorothea Krook to treat Mill as someone who 'tried and failed to spiritualise utilitarianism'. See 'John Stuart Mill' in J. B. Schneewind, ed., *Mill; A Collection of Critical Essays* (New York, 1968), pp. 22–45.
[78] See Williams, *Culture and Society*, p. 67. Annan, writing from the opposite point of view, makes much the same criticism of Mill.
[79] In Kaye and McClelland, eds., *E. P. Thompson*, p. 114.

merely persisting but not unalterable practices. Similarly with Dickens, with whom Thompson has been compared as narrator: as readers we can ask whether Dickens's sociological grasp exceeded his psychological reach, whether it is preferable to retain the holistic power of his darker social symbols by overlooking the bourgeois sentimentality of his happy endings.[80] Intellectual historians, however, in common with anthropologists, do not enjoy this freedom to ignore the teller of the tale.

Leavis was incensed by a response to his interpretation of *Hard Times* that suggested it simply amounted to saying that 'all work and no play makes Jack a dull boy'.[81] It seems worth asking whether another reductive commonplace can be applied to the schism depicted by my trio: man does not live by bread alone. Expressed thus, it is hard to think of anyone on either side of the schism who thought differently, though their priorities as between bread and other sources of life might differ. Even those heartless men of 'facts and calculation', those statisticians Dickens caricatured, were aware that percentages told you nothing about the human tragedy that lay behind them. A cheap laugh at their expense could easily become a sign of seeking cheap grace. The high moral ground is appropriated by accusing your opponents of something they would not have denied.

Living in the kind of society we have enjoyed or suffered for at least the past two hundred years or so, there is a persistent need to be reminded that market values are not the sole arbiter. It was also possible to go one step further by arguing that the market systematically perverted values for the kind of reasons suggested by Ruskin's contrast between 'wealth' and 'illth' – a contrast not unknown to Adam Smith that was given substance by Mill and later by a generation or two of welfare economists writing in the 1890s and beyond. The great strength of the British romantic moralists, whether on the left or right of the political spectrum, has lain in such reminders, particularly when delivered at historic moments when the market was either failing or threatening to carry all before it. But it also seems to be another characteristic of the same moralists that they extend their protest to include all those who have studied how everyone's bread has been earned. If there is a moral to the story told here, it lies in the persistent unwillingness of the moral tradition to be defiled by the pitch associated with such vulgar consequentialist calculations, while suggesting that they know the answers anyway. Unwillingness to comprehend the

---

[80] An argument employed, for example, by J. M. Brown in *Dickens: Novelist in the Market-Place* (Totowa, 1981), pp. 11–13, 26, 41–4, 74.
[81] John Holloway's comment in his essay on *Hard Times* in J. Gross and G. Pearson, eds., *Dickens and the Twentieth Century* (London, 1962), p. 166. For Leavis's response see F. R. and Q. D. Leavis, *Dickens the Novelist* (London, 1970), pp. 208–12.

workings of markets, it has been argued, has been a persistent weakness of the British socialist tradition.[82] Those on the left who assumed that Marx provided the correct analyses occupied a more defensible position. When Thompson criticised *Culture and Society* for its failure to call upon the insights of a historian, anthropologist, or sociologist of note, it was inconceivable that he could have added an economist to this list – apart, that is, from Marx. He confessed to his own 'weakness in economic theory', but could rely on the understanding of his allies on the Marxist left.[83] Once this faith had weakened, however, not much was left apart from a conventional rejection of the coarse apologetics of the economics Gradgrind was taken to represent. Economic man now had to be exiled for the economism to be found in the versions of Marxism that had been rejected, as well as for his supposed capitalist ancestry. It would be an interesting exercise in virtual history to ask what would have happened if Thompson had been willing to extend to economics the kind of understanding he showed in his later work towards anthropology and the rule of law.[84] Moral protest may serve the purposes of allowing a Jerusalem to be conceived, but it does not enable the failures of existing societies to be analysed or the foundations for new ones to be constructed.

[82] See, for example, N. Thompson, *The Market and its Critics: Socialist Political Economy in Nineteenth-Century Britain* (London, 1988).

[83] Thompson, 'The Politics of Theory', p. 404.

[84] That this need not be an entirely frivolous counterfactual can be seen in one of Thompson's answers to the Anderson–Nairn thesis, where he pointed out 'the distinctive contribution of English ideology in the late eighteenth century was neither traditionalism nor empiricism, but a naturalistic political economy most notably with Adam Smith'; see *Poverty of Theory*, p. 254.

Contributors

Stefan Collini is Reader in Intellectual History and English Literature in the Faculty of English and a Fellow of Clare Hall, Cambridge. His most recent books are *Matthew Arnold: A Critical Portrait* (1994) and *English Pasts: Essays in History and Culture* (1999). He is currently working on the question of intellectuals in twentieth-century Britain.

E. J. Hundert is Professor of History at the University of British Columbia. He has written on various aspects of the history of political thought and the European Enlightenment, including *The Enlightenment's 'Fable': Bernard Mandeville and the Discovery of Society* (1994), and is working on a study of role distance and Enlightenment social understanding from the Jansenists to Hegel.

Dario Castiglione is Senior Lecturer in Political Theory at the University of Exeter. His main research interests are in the history of political thought of the early-modern period and in constitutional theory. He is currently working on a book on Hume's political philosophy and a joint volume on political constitutionalism.

Nicholas Phillipson is Reader in History at Edinburgh University. His recent publications include *Hume* (1989), *Political Discourse in Early Modern Britain* (1993) (co-edited with Quentin Skinner), and essays on David Hume, William Robertson, and Sir Henry Raeburn. He is writing an intellectual biography of Adam Smith.

Richard F. Teichgraeber III is Director of the Murphy Institute of Political Economy and Professor of History at Tulane University. He is the author of '*Free Trade' and Moral Philosophy: Rethinking the Sources of Adam Smith's Wealth of Nations* (1986) and *Sublime Thoughts/Penny Wisdom: Situating Emerson and Thoreau in the American Market* (1995). He is also co-editor (with Thomas Haskell) of *The Culture of the Market: Historical Essays* (1993).

David Lieberman is a Professor in the Jurisprudence and Social Policy Programme of the School of Law (Boalt Hall), University of California, Berkeley. He is the author of *The Province of Legislation Determined: Legal Theory in Eighteenth-Century Britain* (1989).

Richard Whatmore is Lecturer in Intellectual History at the University of Sussex. He is the author of several essays on the political economy of the French Revolution, and *Republicanism and the French Revolution: An Intellectual History of Jean Baptiste Day's Political Economy* (2000).

Marilyn Butler is the author of books on the Romantic period of English literature, including *Maria Edgeworth: A Literary Biography* (1972), and a general editor of *The Novels and Selected Works of Maria Edgeworth*, 12 vols. (1999–2000).

Norman Vance is Professor of English and Director of the Humanities Graduate Research Centre at the University of Sussex. His books include *The Victorians and Ancient Rome* (1997) and *Irish Literature, a Social History* (2nd edn, 1999).

Jane Garnett is Fellow and Tutor in Modern History at Wadham College, Oxford. She has published on Victorian religious and intellectual history, and is currently working on the cultural history of religious images in Italy.

Sheldon Rothblatt is Professor Emeritus of History at the University of California, Berkeley, and STINT Visiting Professor of History at the Royal Institute of Technology, Stockholm, Sweden. Publications include *The Revolution of the Dons, Cambridge and Society in Victorian England* (1968, reprinted 1981); and *The Modern University and its Discontents, The Fate of Newman's Legacies in Britain and America* (1997). He continues to work on comparative university history.

Donald Winch is Professor of the History of Economics at the University of Sussex, where he has taught for the past thirty-seven years. His earlier work was largely concerned with the relationship between economics and policy during the classical and Keynesian periods. Since then his books have included *Adam Smith's Politics* (1978); *That Noble Science of Politics* (with Stefan Collini and John Burrow) (1983); *Malthus* (1987); and, most recently, *Riches and Poverty: An Intellectual History of Political Economy in Britain, 1750–1834* (1996).

Acknowledgements

Several individuals and institutions have given valuable help and support to this project. Foremost among these is Rosa Weeks who remained cheerful and resourceful through the challenges presented by contributors and power cuts alike, and who gave up weekends so that a diverse range of not always impeccable electronic missives might be transformed into publisher-ready disks. We are also grateful to Martin van Gelderen who, wearing his several administrative hats, gave practical and tactical assistance. At Cambridge University Press, Richard Fisher was, by turns, encouraging, constructive, and tolerant during the long process separating the initial gleam in the eye from the finished books. We are grateful to the British Academy and the University of Sussex Centre for Literary and Intellectual History for grants to support the colloquium held at Sussex in September 1998. And we are, above all, grateful to the contributors and, especially, our two honorands: not only have all friendships emerged unscathed, if severely tested at times, but also much enjoyment has been had along the way.

Index

(We are grateful to Dr Alicia Corrêa for assistance in compiling this index.)

Abbadie, Jacques, 33 n.4
Abercromby, General Sir Ralph, 169, 171
Aberdeen, University of, 226
Achill Mission, 186
Acland, Henry, 158 n.1
Act of Union, 52, 236
Addison, Joseph, in *The Spectator*, on public society as theatre, 39; on polite actions in a commercial society, 40; on polite conduct of the public persona, 42
Alexander, Francesca, 213
    Roadside Songs of Tuscany, 213–14
Alexander, William, Bishop of Derry, 187
America, 140; absence of social hierarchies in, 154–5; as a union of small states, 143; commerce of, 141; ethnography of, 31
American Revolution, 85, 97, 99 n.28, 107, 137, 155; impact of on British intellectual life, 141
Analytical Review, 165
Anderson, James, influence of on R. L. Edgeworth, 161
Anglican Church, 184; grammar school monopolies of, 228
Anglicanism, 27, 185, 192, 193, 241
Anne, Queen, 130, 178
Apolline, 212
apostasy, 233, 253 n.33
Aristophanes, 170
Aristotle, 118, 193, 207; analogy of hive and human society, 211
Armagh, Archbishop of, 191
Arnoldians, 241
Arthur, Archibald, 79 n.18
Athens, 207, 212, 213, 215
Atkinson, Mabel, 205, 221, 222, 223
Atlantis, 169
Augustinianism, 32, 33 n.5, 46; on morals, 35; on virtue, 72

Austen, Jane, 182, 193; on Edgeworth, 159
    Northanger Abbey, 180
    Persuasion, 180
Austin, John, on legal positivism, 108
Australia, ethnography of, 31

Bacon, Francis, 159, 193; on education, 162
Bagehot, Walter, 259; review of *Unto This Last*, 264
Baird, George, 77
Barrow, John, 176
Bastille, fall of, 144
Bathurst, Lord, 168
Baudeau, Nicolas, 149
Baxter, Richard, 179
Bayle, Pierre, on civil conduct, 32, 33
Beattie, James, 170
Beccaria, Cesare, *An Essay on Crime and Punishments*, 122
Bell, Andrew, 177
Bentham, Jeremy, 93 n.15, 174, 246, 247, 251, 254, 258; on law and politics, 107; on jurisprudence, 108; democratic theory of, 108; moral theory of, 108; on social conduct in jurisprudence, 108, 109; debt to Smith's *Wealth of Nations*, 108, 109, 115, 117, 118; 'economic' presuppositions of human nature, 108; radical political programme of, 108; utilitarianism of, 110, 112, 121, 125; relationship between art of political economy and legislative science, 24, 110, 112–13, 114, 115–16, 117; on public opinion, *see his Constitutional Code*; contributions to political economy, 110; science *versus* art in political economy of, 111, 112; on Adam Smith, 111, 112, 115, 117; science *versus* art in legislative theory of, (*cf. The Rationale of Reward*), 111; on civil law and civil code and the

establishment of security, 113–15, 116; relationship between legislative principles and psychological properties, 114; on security and the accumulation of wealth, 116; commitment to tradition of political economy, 117–18; on Scottish Enlightenment, 117 n.41; concept and treatment of human nature, 24, 118–24; on the importance of self-interest in human conduct, 120; explanation of human behaviour as a personal interest, 121; real *versus* perceived interests, 121; on the legislator as judge of an individual's self-interests, 122; requiring stability of social conduct, 122; treatment of proportionality in punishment, 122–3; use of trade metaphors in his treatment of human behaviour, 123, 124; ambiguities in treatment of human behaviour, 123; wealth as the most important of self-interests, 124; economic *versus* social conduct, 24, 124; programme for representative government, 124, *and see* his *Constitutional Code*; his legislative science and constitutional law, 24, 125; on expense and operations of government, 131–2; on national debt, 131; utilisation of Parliamentary publications, 132; constitutional programme of, 133–4; on literacy, 134; on French Revolution, 146 n.44; on Maria Edgeworth, 158, 175; on Tripoli, 127, 133
A Fragment on Government, 124
An Introduction to the Principles of Morals and Legislation, 123, 124
'Complete Code of Laws', 113
Constitutional Code: 108; his plan for democratic government in, 125; on moral aptitude, 126; on the Public Opinion Tribunal, 126–9, 133; (common law jury of), 127; (newspaper press of), 127; on freedom of the press, 128; importance of organisation and circulation of public opinion, 24–5, 128; on administrative accountability, 128; public opinion expressed in juridical terms, 129; coordination and dissemination of public opinion, 129; relationship with other writings of Bentham, 132 n.103; organisation and publication of political information, 132–4; on literacy, 134

Defence of a Maximum, 115
Defence of Usury, 110, 117–18
Deontology, 120, 123
First Principles Preparatory to Constitutional Code, 120 n.59
Fragment on Government, 127
Indications Respecting Lord Eldon, 132
Institute of Political Economy, 111, 115, 116
Manual of Political Economy, 111, 115
Official Aptitude Maximized; Expense Minimized, 132
Plan of Parliamentary Reform, 133
'Principles of the Civil Code', 113
Securities Against Misrule, 126 n.79
The Rationale of Reward, 112
Theory of Legislation: see Dumont
Benthamites, 246, 248, 259, 260; Technologico-Benthamites, 248
Berlin, Isaiah, 5; on two concepts of liberty, 48–9, 53; on political liberty and self-development, 50; on modern or negative liberty, 50
Bibliothèque britannique, 174
Birmingham, University of, 231
Bitzius, Albert (*alias* Jeremias Gotthelf), 213, 214
Ulric the Farm Servant, 213, 214
Blackmore, R.D., *Prince Arthur*, 169
Blackstone, William, *Commentaries on the Laws of England*, 118
Blair, Hugh, 170
Blake, William, 243, 248, 252, 253, 256
Blything Hundred, 199
Bodin, Jean, use of term *république*, 150
Bolingbroke, Lord, 188, 189, 190
book production, 98–9, 100–2; increase of, 130–1; *and see* publishing
Boswell, James, on the moral context of the theatre, 40–1
On the Profession of a Player, 41
Brants, Victor, 208
Brissot, Jacques-Pierre, 137; on republicanism, 152; against social hierarchies, 155; influence of on Paine, 156
British Critic, 165
Brougham, Lord, 182 n.4, 185, 232; on Bentham, 125
Buccleuch, Duke of, 100 n.29
Bulcamp, 190, 199
Burckhardt, Jacob, 21
Burgh, James, on mixed government, 142
Burke, Edmund, 16, 17, 143, 147, 150, 169, 250; against scepticism, 190; on social hierarchies, 154; on Adam Smith, 111; on economical reform, 132; on Paine,

Burke, Edmund (cont.)
  157; on the French Revolution, 146; on
  the Rights of Man, 107; refutation of
  by Paine, 137
  Reflections on the Revolution in France,
    139, 189
  Vindication of Natural Society, by a Late
    Noble Writer, 188–9
Burke, Peter, 9
Burns, Robert, 170
Burrow, John, vii, viii; as an intellectual
  historian, 5, 7, 8, 9, 12, 15–17, 19; on
  Gibbon, 10, 13; on Ruskin, 156, 157
  Evolution and Society: A Study in Victorian
    Social Theory, 5–6
  A Liberal Descent: Victorian Historians and
    the English Past, 9, 16–17
  That Noble Science of Politics: A Study in
    Nineteenth-Century Intellectual History
    (in collaboration), 9–10
  Whigs and Liberals: Continuity and Change
    in English Political Thought, 10
Bushe, Charles Kendal, on the Edgeworths,
  162
Butler, James, Duke of Ormond, 178
Byron, Lord, 180

Calvinism, 165, 174
Cambridge, University of, access measured
  by social class, 226; age of entry, 229;
  Caput of, 234; coaching at, 28;
  competition for recognition, 227;
  political teaching at, 242; student
  complaints at, 230; tripos system as
  market probe, 227
Cambridge Intelligencer, 95 n.18
Capet, Louis, on republicanism, 152
capitalism, 135, 252; in eighteenth-century
  England, 246
Carleton, William
  Parra Sastha, or the History of Paddy Go-
    Easy and His Wife Nancy, 197
  Traits and Stories of the Irish Peasantry, 197
Carlyle, Thomas, 220, 243, 244, 247, 248,
  250
Carr, John, Stranger in Ireland, 177 n.44
Castleisland, 179
Catholicism, 27, 144, 188, 193, 214, 215; in
  Ireland, 161, 169, 171, 177, 185, 190,
  196
Cercle Sociale, 137
Chadwick, Edwin, 183, 258
Chambers Cyclopaedia, 158, 177;
  'Intellectual Education', assessment of
  Maria Edgeworth's writings in, 158,
  177

Charles II, 169, 178
Chartism, 257, 262, 263
Christian Observer, 177
Christian Social Union, 220
La Chronique du mois, 155
Cicero, 77
Clare, Lord, 169
Clavière, Etienne, 137; on republicanism,
  152; against social hierarchies, 155;
  influence of on Paine, 156
Coleman, George, Polly Honneycomb, 41
Coleridge, S. T., 224, 247, 248, 252, 253,
  258, 263
Collingwood, W. G., translator of
  Oeconomicus, 208
Combination Act, 254
Committee for the Abolition of the Slave
  Trade, 130
Communist Party, 251, 253
Condillac, Etienne, Essai sur l'origine des
  connoissances humaines, on his theory of
  language, 23, 75, 77; on genera, 75; on
  the origin of abstraction, 75–6; on the
  principles of grammar and the
  development of the human mind, 23, 77
Condorcet, Marquis de, 25, 137, 168; on
  education, 163, 165; influence of on
  Paine, 152–3, 156
  Esquisse d'un tableau historique des progrès
    de l'esprit humain, 156
  Sketch for a Historical Picture of the
    Progress of the Human Mind, 94 n.16
  Vie de Turgot, use of term république in,
    151, 152
conservatism, 185
Constant, Benjamin, 48 n.4, 174; on the
  two concepts of liberty, 49; on political
  liberty, 49–50; on political liberty and
  self-development, 50; on modern
  liberty, 50; on indifference and civic
  privacy, 67
Contemporary Review, 219
Cooper, Anthony Ashley, third Earl of
  Shaftesbury, Characteristics of Men,
  Manners, Opinions, Times, 45 n.44
Copleston, Edward, Bishop of Llandaff,
  184
Corn Law League, 263
Corneille, Pierre, 76
Craig, John, on Millar, 57
Critical Review, 165
Croker, John Wilson, 177 n.44; attack on
  religious views of Maria Edgeworth,
  180
Crotobulus, 209
Cyrus, king of Persia, 209

Dante, 213
Darwin, Charles, 5, 6, 90, 159, 182
Davenant, Charles, on the greatness of a
 state, 140
Davis, Thomas, 196
De Quincey, Thomas, 264
Dee, John, 179
Delphi, 212
Demetrian, 212
Dennis, John, on the theatre and public
 actions, 37, 39
Descartes, René, *The Passions of the Soul*,
 37, 38
Devas, Charles, 222
Dicey, A.V., 115, 119; on Bentham, 107,
 109; on philosophic radicalism, 257
Dickens, Charles, 242, 243, 244, 245, 246,
 248, 249, 258, 260, 263, 265; treatment
 of Mr Gradgrind, 244
 Bleak House, 249 n.19
 Hard Times, 28, 243, 244, 245, 246, 248,
 251, 252, 260, 263, 265
Dickinson, H. H., Revd, 183 n.7, 191
Diderot, Denis, influence of on Paine, 156
 Vie de Senèque, on social hierarchies,
 154–5
Digby, John, 36–7
Dissenters, 142, 144, 185
Donaldson, James, 219; on women in
 ancient Greece, 219
Drury Lane, theatre, 40 n.25, 41; *and see*
 theatre
Du Bois, on polite actions in a commercial
 society, 40
Du Bos, abbé, *Critical Reflections on Poetry
 and Painting*, on passions in theatre,
 38–9
Du Châtelet, Achille, on republicanism,
 152
Du Marsais, C., *Traité des tropes*, 78 n.17
Dublin, 171, 186, 195; patriot parliament of,
 161
Dublin Protestant Operative Association,
 186
Dumont, Etienne, 174, 175; on Maria
 Edgeworth, 158
 Traités de législation civile et pénale
 (translated into English as Bentham's
 Theory of Legislation), 108
Durham, University of, 240

Ecclesiastical Titles Bill, 193
ecclesiology, 107
Eclectic Review, 177
Economic Journal, 220
Economic Review, 220

Economist, The, 263
Edgeworth, Charlotte, 174
Edgeworth, Frances, first wife of Richard
 Lovell Edgeworth, 174
Edgeworth, Henry, 167
Edgeworth, Lovell, 167
Edgeworth, Maria, 182; as a populariser of
 the late (Scottish) Enlightenment, 158;
 assessment of by nineteenth-century
 writers, 158, 174, 175, 177; assessment
 of by modern Irish historians, 166–7;
 teaching methods of, 25, 26, 158; links
 with and impact on of Scottish
 Enlightenment, 158, 160, 166, 168, *and
 see Edinburgh Review*; intellectual range
 of, 159; general themes and topics used
 by, 159–60; influenced by Smith, 160,
 163, 170; influenced by Bentham, 160;
 against the teaching of religion, 165–6,
 167; on the 'science of man', 167; as
 presenting the first fictional portrait of
 a national group (the Irish), 25, 167;
 influenced by Dugald Stewart, 167–8;
 intellectual and cultural background of
 writings of, 168, 172–3, 179–80, *and see
 individual works of*; educational
 methods of, 26, 161–2, 164, 173, 174;
 friendship with Pictet, 173–4; visit to
 Paris, 174; influenced by continental
 intellectuals, 174; on English
 institutions, 174; connections with and
 support from the *Edinburgh Review*,
 25–6, 175, 176–7; confrontation over
 her works between the *Edinburgh
 Review* and the *Quarterly Review*,
 176–7; attacks against over issue of
 irreligion, 176–7, 180; relationship with
 her father, 178, 180
 Belinda, 159
 Castle Rackrent, 158, 168
 Harrington, intellectual and cultural
 background of, 178
 Harry and Lucy Concluded, 180
 Helen, 159, 180
 Leonora, 159, 160, 174, 176; cultural and
 intellectual background of, 175–6;
 reviews of, 175
 Manoeuvring, 174
 Ormond, 158, 172; assessment of by
 contemporaries, 172; as philosophical
 tales, 172; style of, 172; cultural history
 of Ireland brought out in, 172;
 intellectual and cultural background
 of, 178–9; character of Richard Lovell
 Edgeworth in, 178; interpretation of,
 178–9

Edgeworth, Maria (*cont.*)
  The Parent's Assistant, 164 n.15
  Patronage, 158 n.1, 159, 160, 174; on
    English institutions, 174–5; assessment
    of, 174–5; review of, 175
  Popular Tales, review of, 175
  Practical Education, 158; syllabus of, 165;
    absence of religious teaching in, 165;
    assessment of by contemporaries,
    165–6
  Ennui, 163, 172; assessment of by
    contemporaries, 172, 176; as
    philosophical tales, 172; style of, 172;
    cultural history of Ireland brought out
    in, 172; plot of, 172; political and
    historical background of, 173; theme of
    land reform in, 173; intellectual and
    cultural background of, 176; review of,
    175
  The Absentee, 163, 172, 175, 177;
    assessment of by contemporaries, 172,
    180; as philosophical tales, 172; style
    of, 172; cultural history of Ireland
    brought out in, 172
  Manoeuvring, 160
  Emilie de Coulanges, 160
  Vivian, 160, 174
  Whim for Whim, 168
Edgeworth, Maria, and Richard Lovell
  Edgeworth, *Essay on Irish Bulls*, 178;
    structure of, 168–9; intellectual and
    cultural background of, 163, 169;
    sources cited in, 170–1; influenced by
    French Enlightenment, 171;
    influenced by Dugald Stewart and the
    Scottish Enlightenment, 171;
    progressive Irish politics expressed in,
    171; attitude towards Englishness in,
    168, 171–2; French interest in, 174;
    review of, 175
Edgeworth, Richard Lovell, reformed
  estate of Edgeworthstown in Ireland,
  160; and Scottish Enlightenment, 161;
  educational and social improvements
  on his Irish estate, 160–1, 162;
  emphasis on the individual, 161, 164;
  influence of on Maria Edgeworth, 161;
  educational methods of, 161–2, 164,
  177; importance of conversation for,
  162, 163; influenced by Smith and
  Condorcet on education, 164; his
  invention of the telegraph, 167;
  influenced by Dugald Stewart, 167–8;
  friendship with Pictet, 173–4; visit to
  Paris, 174; influenced by continental
  intellectuals, 174; participation in the

Irish Board of Education, 177; attack
  on religious position of, 180
  Memoirs, 180; attack on by Croker, 180
  Professional Education, 166–7; review of,
    175
Edgeworthstown, Irish estate of the
  Edgeworths, 160–2, 168; *and see*
  Edgeworth, Richard Lovell
Edinburgh, 71, 76, 95, 167, 168
Edinburgh Review, 167, 168, 171, 175;
  connections with Maria Edgeworth,
  175–6; position taken in support of
  Maria Edgeworth, 176–7;
  confrontation with *Quarterly Review*
  over Maria Edgeworth, 176–7, 180
Egypt, 171
English Revolution (1688), 143, 144;
  reactions towards in eighteenth-
  century Britain, 143–5
Englishwoman's Journal, 222
Epictetan: *see* Stoicism
Epicureanism, 72
Epicurus, 36
Erasmus, 159
Esprit, Jacques, 33 n.4
Evangelicalism, 107, 166, 184, 186, 188
Examiner, 175
Eyre, Governor, 244

Factory Acts, 258
Federalist, The, 151
Fénelon, 145, 178
Ferguson, Adam, his concept of history,
  70–1; liberty in modern societies,
  23; on government intervention, 68;
  on primitive liberty, 55; on public
  debt, 67; on social actions in
  commercial society, 45; on
  subordination of liberty, 58; on the
  judicial system, 64
An Essay on the History of Civil Society, on
  liberty as security and regularity, 57; on
  indifference, 67; on participation in
  public affairs on an international level,
  67–8
Principles of Moral and Political Science, on
  liberty as security and regularity, 57; on
  the resiliency of English liberty, 63
Ferguson, Samuel, on Whateson, 187 n.18
Fielding, Henry, *Tom Jones*, 41; on social
  pressures of society, 41–2
Figgis, J. N., *Gerson to Grotius*, 5
Firth, Julia, 213
Fletcher, Andrew, on family servitude, 56
  n.36; on separation of power, 64 n.77
Florence, 178, 179, 213

Flower, Benjamin, 95 n.18
Fontenelle, B. de, 167 n.27
 Pluralité des mondes, 45 n.44
Forbes, Duncan, 5
Foucault, Michel, 3
Fox, Charles James, on republicanism,
 145–6
Fox, William, on French Revolution, 145
France, commerce of, 141; government of
 compared with England, 143; *and see*
 French Enlightenment
Franklin, Benjamin, 137, 145, 155
Freeman, E. A., 9; *Norman Conquest*, 16, 17
French Enlightenment, influence of on the
 Edgeworths, 171
French Revolution, 24, 85, 93, 94, 97, 102,
 141, 143, 153, 158, 160, 169; intellectual
 reactions towards in Britain, 144–6

Garnier, Germain, criticisms of Smith's
 Wealth of Nations, 101 n.30
Garrick, David, 40 n.25, 41
 Essay on Acting, 38
Gassendi, Pierre, 179
Gay, John, *The Beggar's Opera*, 35–6
Geistesgeschichte, 2
Geneva, 174
Gentleman's Magazine, 165
George I, 178
German empire, 212
Gibbon, Edward, 194, 225
 Decline and Fall of the Roman Empire, 100
Gifford, William, against Maria
 Edgeworth, 176–7
Girondins, 145, 155
Gladstone, W. E., 258–9
Glasgow, 71, 72, 73, 76, 77, 95, 100 n.29
Godwin, William, 97 n.23
Goldsmith, Oliver, 100
Gotthelf, Jeremias, *see* Bitzius, Albert
Graham, Mrs, 163 n.11
Gray, John, his criticisms of Smith's *Wealth
 of Nations*, 101 n.30
Gray, Simon, 161 n.4
Great Reform Act, 107
Greece, ancient, 26; civilisation of, 206;
 restrictions on citizen women, 207;
 economic philosophy of, 206, 207;
 ethnography of, 31
Greg, W. R., 261, 262; review of *Mary
 Barton*, 261
Gregg, Tresham, Revd, *Protestant
 Ascendancy Vindicated*, 186
Grenville, Lord, 145
Grotius, Hugo, 179
Grub Street, 98, 100

Guardian of Education, 165
Halesworth (Suffolk), 190, 199
Halévy, Elie, on Bentham, 109; on
 economic psychology, 119; on
 philosophic radicalism, 257
Hamilton, Anthony, 171
Harrington, James, 159
 Oceana, 169, 178
Harringtonians, land reforms of, 162; neo-,
 135, 140
Hartley, David, 159
 Observations on Man, 161
Harvard University, 232
Harvey, William, 37
Hawkins, Edward, Provost of Oriel, 181 n.1,
 182 n.3, 195, 198
Hebrews, 206
hedonism, 119
Hegel, G. W. F., 2, 89
Herbert, Lord Edward of Cherbury, 179–80
 De Veritate, 179
Herbert, William, Sir, 179
Herodotus, 170
Hesperides, 169
Hoadly, Benjamin, 145
Hobbes, Thomas, on moral philosophy, 72;
 on law and liberty, 53, 54; Hobbesian
 ideology, 22
Hodgskin, Thomas, 252, 254, 262
Holland, 171; commerce of, 141
Hollis, Thomas, 142
Horace, 171, 212
House of Commons Sessional Papers, 132
household, concepts of on political
 economy and social relationships, 26;
 treatment of by economists, 205;
 management of, 205; paradise as a
 model for, 209
Howick, Lord, 200
Huet, François, 215
Huguenots, 32, 33 n.4
humanism, civic, 67
Humboldt, Wilhelm von, *The Limits of State
 Action*, 6
Hume, David, 157, 159, 160; attack on by
 Whately, 182, 188; his theory of human
 nature, 71, 73; his theory of utility, 83
 n.29; on commercial sociability, 45; on
 immoral actions in commercial society,
 46; on concepts of liberty, 52; on
 doubt, 188, 189; on early origins of
 liberty, 56; on Ferguson, 67; on
 government, 129, 139; on human
 behaviour, 119; on law and liberty, 53;
 on liberty in modern society, 23; on
 moral sentiments, 42–3; on

Hume, David (*cont.*)
    Mandeville, 43; on reasoning of the
    passions, 43–4; analogies with the
    theatre, 43; on opinion, 60; on political
    representation, 68; on power of the
    nobility, 60; on public debt, 67; on
    republics, 135; on subordination of
    liberty, 58; on the monarchy, 57; on the
    popularity of the London theatres, 38;
    on the preservation of liberty, 74; on
    the resiliency of English liberty, 63; on
    the role of custom and association of
    ideas, 23
    *Enquiry Concerning Human
        Understanding*, 188
    Essays, on conversation, 162
    Treatise on Human Nature, knowledge of
    by Adam Smith, 73–4; his theory of
    human nature and capacity for virtue
    in, 74; importance of speech and
    language in, 74; lack of a developed
    theory of language in, 74–5
Hutcheson, Francis, on liberty and natural
    law, 54, 57; against the Hobbesian view
    of law, 54; on sociability and natural
    law, 55; his theory of human nature
    and the capacity for virtue, 23, 72–3,
    74

Idealists, philosophical, 241
Ideengeschichte, 2
India, 206
Industrial Revolution, 109
industrialisation, 88, 245, 248, 260; effects
    on working classes, 262
Ingram, J. K., 217, 218
    History of Political Economy, 219
intellectual history, 8; justification and
    explanation of, 1–2, 10; development
    of, 3–4; as developed at the University
    of Sussex, 4; and *passim*
Ireland, as home of the Edgeworths,
    160–1; *and see* Edgeworth, Maria and
    Richard Lovell; debate over education
    in, 177; landlordism in, 178;
    educational reforms of, 185–6, 200,
    and see Whately, Richard; on poor
    relief, 200–2, problems confronted in
    the nineteenth century, 25, 26, 181,
    182
Ireland, William, *Vortigern*, 169
Irish civil war (1688), 169
Irish Famine, 26, 193, 194, 202, 201
Irish Rebellion (1798), 168, 169, 171
Irish Volunteer movement, 160–1
Ischomanchus, 209, 214, 216, 223

Jacobinism, 95, 96, 150; anti-, 189
Jansenism, 32
Jefferson, Thomas, 156 n.83
Jeffrey, Francis, 168; his reviews of Maria
    Edgeworth's writings, 158, 175, 176
Jerusalem, 243, 244, 247
Jews, in Parliament, 182, 194; Jewish
    emancipation, 240
Johnson, Joseph, on Paine, 146
Johnson, Samuel, 98, 100, 225; on the
    moral context of the theatre, 40
Joyce, Jeremiah, abridgement of Smith's
    Wealth of Nations, 94
jurisprudence, 49
Justamond, J. O., translations of Raynal's
    Histoire, 155
Kames, Henry Home, Lord, 162 n.8, 170;
    his stadial theory of history, 70, 71;
    influence of on Richard Lovell
    Edgeworth, 161
Kant, Immanuel, 159, 168, 176, 179;
    analogy between public actions and
    theatre, 46–7
Kay-Shuttleworth, James, 258
Keble College (Oxford), 239
Kent, Nathaniel, *Hints for a Gentleman of
    Property*, 162 n.8
Keynesian economics, 8, 18
King's College (London), 240
Kingsley, Charles, *Yeast*, 186
Kitson Clark, G., 5
Kotzebue, A. F. F., 176

La Rochefoucauld, 32, 73, 144, 159
Laclos, Choderlos de, *Liaisons dangereuses*,
    159
Lake Poets, 264; their criticism of political
    economy, 264; *see also* Coleridge,
    Wordsworth
Lamy, Bernard, *Rhetorique ou l'art de parler*,
    77
Lancaster, Joseph, 177
Lansdowne, Marquis of [William Petty,
    Lord Shelburne], as sympathiser of the
    French Revolution, 93–4
Lanthenas, French translations of Paine's
    works, 139 n.12
Laveleye, Emile de, 214, 215
Law, William, on the moral context of the
    theatre, 40
Le Marchant, Sir Denis, 182 n.4
Le Play, school of, 208
Le Républicain, 137
Leavis, F. R., 28, 245, 246, 249, 251, 253,
    254, 255, 260; analysis of *Hard Times*,
    246, 265; analysis of *The Wheelwright's*

Shop, 246–7; on Marxism, 247 n.15; on
J. S. Mill, 247, 248; 'technologico-
Benthamite' category of, 260; on
religious dimensions of society, 258;
portrait of utilitarianism, 256; ideology
of, 253
Nor Shall my Sword, 248
Leavisites, 241
Leibnitz, G. W., 167 n.27
Leland, John, 179
liberalism, 94, 95 n.18, 96, 97, 135;
economic, 225; political, 225
liberty, ancient, 57, 58, 60; and
republicanism, 53, 54; as security and
regularity, 56–7; development of within
legal system of commercial society,
22–3, 53, 54; regularity of, 54; in a
political context, 49; individual, 50;
modern, 60, 65; natural, 55; negative
versus positive, 48; systems of, 51;
primitive, 55
Licensing Act (1695), 130
Linton, Eliza Lynn, 219, on domestic life,
219
literacy, 98–9, 134
Locke, John, 169; on education, 162; on the
origin of abstraction, 75
Two Treatises on Government, 145
London, 27, 95 n.18, 130, 131, 140, 171, 213;
theatres of, 37, 38, 40, 47; University
of, 230, 232, 235, 241
London Corresponding Society, 95 n.18,
254
London Exchange, 40
London School of Economics, 241–242
Longford (county in Ireland), 160, 168,
178
Louis XIV, 143
Louis XVI, 144; execution of, 93
Louvain, Catholic economic thinkers at,
208
Lucian, 169, 170
Luddism, 248
Lunar Society of Birmingham, 161
Luxembourg, 137, 156

Macaulay, Catherine, on mixed
governments, 142, 145; on republics,
135
Macaulay, T. B., 9, 16, 119, 263
Machiavelli, Niccolò, 140, 159
Mackintosh, James, *Vindicae Gallicae*, on
republicanism in France and Britain,
143–4; on French Revolution, 143–4,
145; on English Revolution (1688),
143–4, 145

Magee, Archbishop, 186
Maine, Sir Henry, 6, 9; on Bentham,
109
Maitland, F. W., 9
Malthus, T. R., 18, 184, 251, 254
Essay on Population, 87, 101; first edition
of (June 1798), 85; 'population
principle' of, 88; comparison with
Smith's *Wealth of Nations*, 97 n.23, 102;
on Smith's *Wealth of Nations*, 96;
reception of, 97 n.23
Malthusian ideology, 187, 201
Manchester, 261
Mandeville, Bernard, 82, 194, 197; *Fable of
the Bees*, on the theory of the passions
in commercial actions, 22, 32, 33–4,
39–40, 43, 46; on outward displays of
wealth, 34; on social actions, 34–5;
mock-Augustinian stance of, 35;
theatrical analogies of, 35–6; on motive
and actions in a commercial context,
26, 35; as an Epicurean radical, 36; on
social actions of the theatre, 40, 42; on
social pressures of commercial society,
42, 46; rise of hypocrisy, 42; ideological
accomplishment of, 43; on the
'sensible knave', 46; moral philosophy
of, 72; cynicism of, 73; on a theory of
language, 75
Thesaurus Dramaticus, 38
Mansfield College, 231
Marischal College, Aberdeen, 226
Marivaux, P. C. de, 73
market, and British Universities, 224;
connection with suppliers, 239;
definition of, 225; educational,
volatility in, 231; factors of in
unreformed college system, 227;
conflict with state, 27
Marmontel, J. F., 159, 172
Marshall, Alfred, *Principles of Economics*,
220
Martineau, Harriet, 207; *Household
Education*, 207
Marx, Karl, 250, 252, 254, 266; on
nineteenth-century capitalism, 86; on
Bentham, 109, 118
Marxism, 247 n.15, 249, 250, 266
Mauss, Marcel, on the self in commercial
society, 31, 32
Maynooth Grant, 185 n.12
McCulloch, J. R., 1828 edition of Smith's
Wealth of Nations, 87, 91, 92, 103 n.34
Meade, James, 6
mercantilism, 92
militarism, 178

Mill, James, 254, 258; on British India, 108; on the polemics of Philosophical Radicalism, 108; on freedom of the press, 128; on representative government, 108
  Essay on Government, 119
  Selected Economic Writings, 6
Mill, John Stuart, 216, 244, 260, 261, 263, 264; essays of, 247; on representative government, 108; revisions of Bentham, 108
  Principles of Political Economy, 216
  Some Unsettled Questions of Political Economy, 217
  The Subjection of Women, 218
Millar, John, on economic dependence, 65–6; on indifference, 67; on liberty as security and regularity, 23, 57; on subordination of liberty, 58; on feudal law, 59; his stadial theory of history, 70, 71
Milton, John, 145
Mirabeau, Victor Riqueti de, *L'Ami des hommes*, 149
Molière, J. B., 159, 171
monarchy, 25, 135, 136, 146, 147, 150, 152, 153
Monmouthshire, 179
monopolies, 225–6
Montesquieu, C. L. de S., Baron de, 145; on feudal laws, 59; on law and liberty, 22, 53; on political representation, 68; on the security of liberty in political and civil perspectives, 61–2; on moderate governments as a safeguard for political liberty, 62; his stadial theory of history, 71; on republicanism, 143; on the Irish, 170
  De l'esprit des lois, on primitive liberty, 55
Monthly Review, 165
Moore, John, Major-General, 169, 171
Moralistes, 73
Moran, Michael, 8
More, Hannah, 166
More, Thomas, *Utopia*, 169
Morellet, André, 137, 174
Morris, William, 248, 256
Munster, 179
Murray, John, 180
Musgrave, Richard, 171; *Memoirs of the Different Rebellions in Ireland*, 169

Napoleon, 67, 163 n.11, 174, 192
National Assembly, 140; in France, 145
nationality, discussion of by the Edgeworths, 170

natural law, 135
natural theology, 184
Necker, Jacques, 176
Necker, Mme, 176
Nemours, Dupont de, 156
New Left, 249, 250
New Poor Law, 26
Newman, John Henry, 192; on political economy, 197
Newton, Isaac, 246
Nicole, Pierre, on the self in commercial society, 32, 33
Norton, Charles Eliot, 208

Oakeshott, Michael, lectures of, 6
Occam, William of, 170
Ogilvie, William, 162 n.8; influence of on Richard Lovell Edgeworth, 161
O'Halloran, Sylvester, 169
Oriel College (Oxford), 181
Ormond(e), Duke of, 178
Ossory, Bishop of, 186
Oswald, James, of Dunnikier, 73
Owen, Robert, 262, 263
Oxford, 27, 72, 73, 186
Oxford, University of, access measured by social class, 226; age of entry, 229; competition for recognition, 227; Hebdomadal Council of, 234; honours system as market probe, 227; philosophical idealists at, 241; student complaints at, 230

Paine, Thomas, 262; legacy of for modern political thought, 135; opposition to mixed governments, 136, 138, 147, 148; distinctive republicanism of, 25, 136, 138, 140, 141, 146, 156–7; his concept of a modern republic, 149–53; influenced by French political thought, 25, 136, 138, 140, 148–9, 152–3, 154–6; links with France, 136–7; political sympathies for France, 156; influenced by British political thought, 156; on commerce, 138, 140, 143, 146; his political testament, 139, *and see* his *Common Sense*; alteration of views of, 139–41; against monarchy, 139, 153; against social hierarchy, 139, 140, 153–4; influenced by Richard Price, 146–7, 156; influenced by Adam Smith's *Wealth of Nations*, 94, 111, 147–8, 156; on the American Revolution, 148; on the French Revolution, 148, 150, 153; on the creation of a national convention, 150; use of term 'republican', 150–2; on national unity, 152, 156; assessment of by Sieyès, 152, 154; influenced by Condorcet, 152–3; religious beliefs of, 156; assessment of by Burke, 157; on English radicalism, 129

Age of Reason, 156

Agrarian Justice, 156

Common Sense, 99 n.28, 137, 138, 139, 140, 148, 155

The Crisis, 138, 139

Letter to the abbé Raynal, 137, 155

Prospects on the Rubicon, 139 n.14

The Rights of Man, 94 n.16, 136–8, 139, 140, 141, 146, 148, 150; central message of, 153; popularity of, 99

Paley, William, 176, 182, 184, 193; *Principles of Moral and Political Philosophy*, 131

Palgrave, R. H. I., *Dictionary of Political Economy*, 220

Pappé, Helmut, 8

Paris, 137, 149, 168, 174, 175, 179

Parkes, Bessie Rayner, 222, 223

Pascal, Blaise, 159

passions, in a commercial society, 39; portrayal of in theatre, 38–9

patriotism, 25

Périn, Charles, 208

Peterloo, 189

Petty, William, Lord of Shelburne, Marquis of Lansdowne: *see* Lansdowne

Phidias, 213

Philosophical Radicalism, 108, 109, 125, 128, 224

physiocracy, 25, 149, 151, 156; anti-, 137

Pictet, M. A., 165; on the Edgeworths, 162, 173–4

Pitt, William, 93, 145

Place, Francis, 262, 263; organiser of London Corresponding Society, 254

Plato, 170, 193, 207, 221

The Republic, 215

Platonism, neo-, 150, 179

Playfair, William, 166

Plowden, Francis, *History of Ireland*, 173, 176

Plumb, J. H., 5

political economy, 214, 254, 259, 260, 262, 263–4; and gender, 218; and laws, 61; and problems posed to by Mandeville, 46, *and see* Mandeville's *Fable*; and social relationships, 26–7; Christian, 107; comparison with culture of ancient Greece, 26; foundation of as a distinct tradition, 24, 91, 103;

liberalism in, 24; moral dimension of, 26; operations of, 28; Ricardian, 260; science of, 110, 217; working class, 262

politics, and literary publications, 130; circulation of parliamentary proceedings in the press, 131–2

Pocock, J. G. A., 14

Poor Law (1834), 183, 184, 199–200, 246, 258, 262; Old Poor Law, 201; New Poor Law, 201

Popper, Sir Karl, 6

press, increase in publications for, 130–1, 167; liberty of, 130–1

Price, Richard, 93 n.15; attack against by Ferguson, 57; influence of on Paine, 146, 156; on the American Revolution, 147; on French and English Revolutions, 145; on mixed government, 142, 144, 148; on republics, 135

Priestley, Joseph, on republics, 135

Lectures on History and General Policy, on Smith's *Wealth of Nations*, 93 n.15, 94 abridged edition (1775) of Hartley's *Observations on Man*, 159, 161

Protestantism, 46, 166, 179, 197, 214; in Ireland, 169, 171, 177, 185, 186, 191, 196

Pryme, George, lectures of on political economy at Cambridge, 91

publishing, increase during eighteenth century, 24, 130–1; regulation of, 130

Quarterly Review, position taken against Maria Edgeworth, 176–7; confrontation with *Edinburgh Review* over Maria Edgeworth, 176–7, 180; intellectual and political stance of, 180

Quesnay, François, *Despotisme de la Chine*, opposition to mixed government, 149

Racine, Jean, 73

Radicalism, 107, 119, 142, 145–6, 148, 154, 262; philosophic, 257, 258

Raynal, abbé, *Histoire philosophique des deux Indes*, 154

Reform Act (1832), 246

Reid, Thomas, 79 n.18, 179

Républicain, 152, 155

republicanism, 22, 23, 25, 67, 135, 143, 144, 161; and liberty, 53, 54, 57, 58, 60 n.59; concept of in France, 145, 150–2; definition of as used by radicals, 141–3; *and see* Mackintosh, Paine

Ricardo, David, 87, 88 n.5, 251, 254, 258
Principles, 109
Richardson, William, 73, 79 n.18
Rivière, Mercier de la, opposition to mixed
    government, 149
Robertson, William, his stadial theory of
    history, 70, 71, 84
Robespierre, Maximilien, 150, 165
Romanticism, 28, 244, 247, 248, 252, 255,
    260, 263, 264; criticism of
    Utilitarianism, 252
Rome, 212, 213; civilisation of, 206; empire
    of, 213
Rose, George, on administrative reform,
    132
Rousseau, J. J., 145, 159, 178, 190; on
    republicanism, 143; on the origins of
    language, 77 n.13
Discours sur l'Inégalité, 189
Royal Irish Academy, 167
Ruskin, John, 219, 220, 221, 243, 244, 247,
    248, 263–4, 265; on the household, 26,
    222, 210; on kingship and queenship,
    211; on Maria Edgeworth, 158; on
    status of Xenophon, 208, 212, 223; on
    the Greek division of the living soul,
    212
Bibliotheca Pastorum, 208, 213
Cornhill Magazine essays in, 215, 216
Fors Clavigera, 247
Sesame and Lilies, 208, 211
The Political Economy of Art, 208, 215
Ulric the Farm Servant, preface to, 213,
    214
Unto This Last, 208, 211, 217, 218,
    243

Saturday Review, 218; anti-feminism of,
    218; on political economy, 219
scepticism, 72, 74
Schlegel, A. W., 174
Scotland, educational market of, 27;
    intellectual and academic
    achievements of, 232; national identity
    of, 236; *and see under* universities
Scott, Sir Walter, *Waverley*, 176
Scottish Enlightenment, on concepts of
    liberty, 25, 48–9, 51–3; 'scientific'
    perspective of modern liberty, 22, 52;
    on two distinct 'systems', 53;
    development of liberty within legal
    system of commercial society, 53, 54–5;
    on sociability, 55; on liberty as security
    and regularity, 57–8, 61, 65; restoration
    of liberty, 59; on the positive (and
    possible negative) effects of

commercial society on personal
    liberty, 66–7; on political
    representation for security of liberty,
    68–9; condemnation of in 1790s, 95;
    and Bentham, 117 n.41; impact of on
    Maria Edgeworth, 158, 160, 166;
    position taken against religion, 164;
    and see Edinburgh, Glasgow
self, concepts of, 48; definition of in
    commercial society, 22, 31, 45–6, 47;
    forces that shape conceptions of, 31–2;
    emergence of within theological
    context, 32–3; on the reasoning of the
    passions, 43
Selwyn College (Cambridge), 239
Senior, Nassau, 183, 184, 185; *Letter to Lord
    Howick*, 200, 201
Shakespeare, William, 193
    As You Like It, 36; on the self, 36
Shelley, P. B., 180
Sidgwick, Henry, 259
Siedentop, Larry, 8
Sieyès, abbé, on republicanism of Paine and
    Condorcet, 152, 154; on social
    hierarchies, 154
Sismondi, J. C. L. S. de, 174; on Aristotle,
    219; on republicanism, 178; on
    Xenophon's *Oeconomicus*, 219, 220
Skinner, Quentin, 14
Smith, Adam, 6, 12, 17, 52, 135, 159, 172,
    205, 216, 246, 251, 262, 265; on
    economic dependence, 65–6; on
    Ferguson, 67; on subordination of
    liberty, 58; on restoration of liberty
    through feudalism, 59; assessment of
    Bentham's *Defence of Usury*, 110;
    assessment of contributions to
    political economy by Donald Winch,
    110–11; disciples of, 109; his
    understanding of historical
    development, 23; confrontation with
    Hutcheson, 23; confrontation with
    Hume, 23; on society and language,
    23; influence on by Condillac, 23;
    moral theory of, 23; legacy of, 111; on
    a concept of the self in commercial
    society, 22, 43–4, 45–6; on social
    conduct, 44; on commercial
    sociability, 45; on development of the
    child, 25; on his science of man, 70; his
    stadial theory of history, 70, 71; on
    sociability, 72, 74, 80; influences of,
    72; his theory of human nature and the
    capacity for virtue, 72–3; intellectual
    life of in Oxford, 73; knowledge of
    Hume's *Treatise*, 73–4; his post-

Humean theory of language, 74–8; his indebtedness to Condillac's theory of language, 75–6, 77, 78; his theory of language, 76–7; his theory of grammar, 77–9; on *genera*, 77; on improvement generated from contact with other societies and other languages, 78–9; development of the theory in his *Lectures on Rhetoric and Belles-Lettres*, 79; use of language in polished societies, 79; importance of propriety in his theory of rhetoric, 79–80; on moral education in terms of natural history, 80; Epictetan Stoicism of, 83, 84; on Hume's theory of utility, 83 n.29; legacy of, 84; on mixed government, 148; on monopolies, 225; on republicanism, 143; regarded as an intellectual giant, 23–4, 93; regarded as a sympathiser of the French Revolution, 93, 94; high cultural status of, 100
Inquiry, 109
Lectures on Jurisprudence, 23, 83; on handling resentments, 83; against the pressures of commercial society, 83; on the early origins of government and civil liberty, 55–6; on the historical contingencies for securing liberty, 64
The Theory of Moral Sentiments, on immoral actions in commercial society, 46; his stadial theory of history in, 71; on the systematic theory of propriety, 80; on mutual sympathy, 81; on the 'impartial spectator', 81–2; on investing language with new meanings, 82–3; against the pressures of comercial society, 83; on frailty of judgement as a failure of language, 83–4; on conversation, 162; on family respect, 163; on education, 162, 163–5; assessment of, 166
The Wealth of Nations, 23, 24; as founder of political economy, 110; on security and the abundance of wealth, 116; on stability and justice, 116; emphasis on the individual in, 161; on political representation, 68; first edition of (March 1776), 85; audience of, 86; legacy of, 85–6; as foundation of liberal capitalism, 86, 88; as foundation of political economy, 86; interpretation of by revisionist scholarship, 86–7, 88; on lack of continuity in his theory of political economy, 87–8; seen in context of Malthus's *Essay* as set forth

by Himmelfarb, 88–9; his attempts to give moral context to Britain's commercial society, 88; intentions of in writing *Wealth of Nations*, 90; organisation and structure of, 90; self-styled disciples of, 91; 1828 edition of by McCulloch, 91, (*and see* McCulloch); acceptance of as founder of political economy, 91, 92, 93, 103; concept of tradition of political economy as expressed in, 91, 92; achievement of, 92; reception of, 92; radical interpretations of, 94–5; cultural background of, 98–102; (increase in book production), 98–9, 100–2; (changes in the extent and style of reading), 98–9; (fleeting reputation of writers), 99; (transition to a print culture), 99–100; publishing and reception history of, 89–90, 100–2, 103; comparison with Malthus's *Essay*, 102; canonisation of, 103–4; influence of on Bentham, 108, 109, 115; influence of on Paine, 147–8, 156; on natural liberty, 148
Smith, Sydney, 182; reviews of Maria Edgeworth's writings, 175
Smith, Thomas Southwood, 258
Sneyd, Honora, second wife of Richard Lovell Edgeworth, 161, 178 n.45
Snow, C. P., 253; as apologist for Gradgrind values, 248
socialism, 262
Société des amis des noirs, 155
Société Gallo-Américain, 155
society, commercial, 22, 32; and actions, in the London Exchange, 40; and 'stadial' theory of evolution, 23; division between political economy and social relations in, 28; role of modern liberty in, 22; effect of on conceptions of the self, 32; pressures of on moral actions, 46; self-misrepresentation of, 42; positive (and possible negative) effects of on personal liberty, 66–7; restoration of liberty in, 49; two concepts of liberty in, 49; importance of material conditions in for patriotism, 25; social conduct in, 109
Socrates, 209, 210, 213, 215
Solomon, 78
Sparta, 212
Spencer, Herbert, 6
Spenser, Edmund, 178
St Alban Hall (Oxford), 181

Staël, Germaine de, 159, 174; *Corinne*, 174;
    Delphine, 175; *De L'Allemagne*, 174
state, intervention of in British universities,
    27, 224, 231, 234, 242; and public
    involvement, 237; as buyer of
    university services, 242; as regulator of
    academic standards, 231; confessional,
    237; differentiation from church, 239;
    Georgian confessional, 224;
    instruments of, 225; unity of, 240
Steele, Richard, 40
Stephen, H. J., on Maria Edgeworth, 176
Stephen, Leslie, 115
    English Thought in the Eighteenth Century,
    107
Stewart, Dugald, 25, 108; as lecturer on
    political economics, 95; on Smith's
    Wealth of Nations, 73, 76–7, 96, 111;
    impact of on the Edgeworths, 167, 169;
    on 'conjectual history', 70; on Scottish
    cultural identity, 171; on political
    liberty, 61
    *Elements of the Philosophy of the Human
    Mind*, 167
Stewart, William, 177
Stoicism, 80, 83; Epictetan, 83, 84; neo-, 72,
    73; on virtue, 72
Strahan, William, publisher of Smith's
    Wealth of Nations, 100, 101
Stubbs, William, 9
Sturt, George (Bourne), 246–7, 250, 261;
    The Wheelwright's Shop, 246, 250, 253
Suard, J.F., 174
Sumner, John Bird, Archbishop of
    Canterbury, 184, 189
    *A Treatise on the Records of the Creation, and
    on the Moral Attributes of the Creator*, 184
'Sussex School', vii, 4, 12–13; publications
    associated with, 13–14; aim and
    characteristics of, 14–15; *and see* John
    Burrow, Donald Winch
Sussex, University of, 4, 7–8, 12–13
Swift, Jonathan, on the Edgeworths' *Essay
    on Irish Bulls*, 168–9, 172
Swing Riots, in Suffolk, 182, 190
Switzerland, 214

Tacitus, as a historian, 70, 71
Tatham, Edward, his criticisms of Smith's
    Wealth of Nations, 101 n.30
theatre, analogy of with public actions, 47;
    and the audience, 40; as a model for
    the expression of public actions, 41, 43;
    moral context of, 40–1; use of as a
    perspective for moral actions in public
    society, 35–8, 39; popularity of, 38

Theophilanthropy, 156
Thompson, E. P., 28, 250, 255, 256, 260,
    262, 263, 264; criticism of *Culture and
    Society*, 266; resignation from
    Communist Party, 251; review of
    Williams's works, 250; on religious
    dimensions of society, 258; portrait of
    utilitarianism, 256; references to Mill,
    261
    The Making of the English Working Class,
    251; narrative style of, 253
    William Morris, 251
Toland, John, 159
    Christianity not Mysterious, 190
Tooke, John Horne, 144
Toryism, 107, 132, 258, 259
Toulouse, Bishop of, 137
Townsend, Charles, 100 n.29
Toynbee, Arnold, 18; on economists and
    human beings, 28
Tractarianism, 183, 186; anti-, 195
trade unions, 195
Trench, Archbishop, on Whatley, 189
Trimmer, Mrs, 165
Trinity College (Dublin), 195
Tripoli, 127, 133
Tucker, Josiah, Dean of Gloucester, 93, 143
    n.29
Turgot, A. R. J., 145, 151

Unionism, 192–3
Unitarianism, 95 n.18
universities, English, 226; nature of in
    twentieth century, 27; North
    American, 232; Scottish: 226, 232;
    access to, 233; apostasy at, 233; as
    monopolies of, 225–6; civic, 321;
    curriculum in, 232; definition of, 230;
    degrees of, 233; influence of on English
    universities, 240; market relations of,
    234; relationship to state, 234; religious
    allegiances of, 240; student sub-
    culture in, 228; financing from the
    Scottish Crown, 234
Utilitarianism, 28, 107, 109, 110, 119, 125,
    244, 245, 246, 247, 248, 251, 252, 254,
    255, 258, 259, 260, 263, 264; ancestry
    of, 246; anti-, 243; Benthamic, 121;
    role of in Victorian civilisation, 245;
    Romantic critique of, 251

Valbourg Misson, Henri de, *Mémoires et
    observations faites par un voyage en
    Angleterre*, 40 n.23
Venice, 213
Viner, Jacob, 6

Virgil, 213
Voltaire, 40 n.22, 159, 160, 171, 176; on
  republicanism, 143
voluntarism, 22

Walpole, Horace, 130, 179; on Paine, 154;
  on Thomas Whately, 192
  *Historic Doubts on the Life and Reign of
  King Richard III*, 192
Washington, George, 139 n.14
Wedderburn, Alexander, translator of
  Oeconomicus, 208
Westminster Review, 207
Whately, Richard, 181; career of, 181,
  182–3; achievements of, 181–3; reform
  campaigns of, 182; liberal ideology of,
  182; on politics, 183–4; his ideology on
  political economy, 184, 193–4, 197; on
  Paley, Jane Austen, Maria Edgeworth,
  and Darwin, 182; attack on religious
  position of Maria Edgeworth, 180;
  centrality of his Anglican theology,
  183, 185, 194, 195; against over-reliance
  on tradition, 198; on Whig
  administration, 183; on state funding
  for religions, 185; achievements and
  experiences in the Irish church while
  archbishop, 185, 190–1, 202; leading
  position as archbishop, 191–2;
  distinctive manner of as archbishop,
  186–7, 202; criticism of by
  contemporaries, 187–8, 193, 202; on
  educational reforms in Ireland and
  Suffolk, 188, 191, 193, 194–8;
  refutation of Hume, 182, 188, *and see
  Historic Doubts*; his relationship to
  eighteenth-century rationalism, 188–9;
  influenced by Burke, 188–9; influenced
  by Malthus, 189, 201; interrelatedness
  of his religious and political thought,
  26, 190; his experiences in his Suffolk
  parish, 190–1, 199–200, 202; against
  tithes, 190–1; on human nature as the
  root of social problems, 192; his
  response to the Ecclesiastical Titles
  Bill, 193; his concept of ministers in
  Christianity, 195; on an Ordination
  College in Dublin, 195; on the
  importance of industry, as applied to
  prison sentences and church revenues,
  199; against the Poor Law for England
  and Ireland, 26, 184, 188, 199–202;
  charitable acts of, 202
Easy Lessons on Money Matters, 195, 197
*The Errors of Romanism traced to their
  Origin in Human Nature*, 192

*Historic Doubts Relative to Napoleon
  Buonaparte*, 188, 189–90
*Letter to the Directors of the House of
  Industry at Bulcamp, against making any
  allowance to unemployed labourers*, 200
Letters on the Church, by an Episcopalian,
  185 n.12
*The Use and Abuse of Party Feeling in
  Matters of Religion* (Bampton
  Lectures), 184–5; ecclesiastical outlook
  for both England and Ireland
  expressed in, 185
Whately, Thomas, *Observations on Modern
  Gardening*, 181, 192
Whiggism, 9, 10, 11, 23, 52, 63, 84, 107, 119,
  132, 135, 142, 183, 225, 258, 259
Wilberforce, Samuel, Bishop, 198
Wilkins, John, 167 n.27
William III, king, 144
Williams, David, 145
Williams, Helen-Maria, 145, 175
Williams, Raymond, 28, 248, 249, 250, 255,
  260; on utilitarianism, 256
Culture and Society, 248, 249, 252, 266
The Country and the City, 249, 253
The Long Revolution, 249
Winch, Donald, vii, viii; as an intellectual
  historian, 5, 6, 7, 8–9, 12, 15, 17, 18, 19;
  on Robert Malthus, 11, 13
*Adam Smith's Politics: An Essay in
  Historiographic Revision*, 8–9
Classical Political Economy and Colonies,
  6–7
Economics and Policy: A Historical Study, 8
*Riches and Poverty: An Intellectual History
  of Political Economy in Britain,
  1750–1834*, 11–12, 17
*That Noble Science of Politics: A Study in
  Nineteenth-Century Intellectual History*
  (in collaboration), 9–10
Wollstonecraft, Mary, 159; *Maria or the
  Wrongs of Woman*, 175
Woodard schools, 236
Wordsworth, William, 252, 253
The Prelude, 263
Wyvill, Christopher, on Paine, 143

Xenophon, 207, 208, 210, 211, 212, 213,
  214, 215, 221; his analogy of the hive
  and human society, 211; his ideal of the
  household, 26, 219; moral lessons of,
  212; on education, 210, 213; Ruskin's
  analysis of, 208–10; translation of, 207,
  208
Memorabilia, 207, 214, 215, 216, 218
Oeconomicus, 207, 208, 215